# Post-Revolutionary Europe, 1815–1856

## EUROPEAN STUDIES SERIES

General Editors: Colin Jones, Joe Bergin, John Breuilly and Patricia Clavin

This established and highly respected series focuses on major topics, both national and international, across European history since the Renaissance, while also considering Europe's interaction with the wider world. It reflects the changing face of historical research by incorporating studies in social and cultural history, especially those which develop comparative perspectives. Individual volumes are both challenging and scholarly, and provide high-quality syntheses based on original research. At around 90–100,000 worlds, each volume aims to render its subject accessible while serving as a starting-point for an in-depth exploration of the themes with which it deals. Titles in the series are ideal for upper-level undergraduates and graduate students, and will also be relevant for more experienced scholars in particular fields.

### Published

| | |
|---|---|
| Robert Aldrich | *Greater France: A Short History of French Overseas Expansion* |
| Nigel Aston | *Religion and Revolution in France, 1780–1804* |
| Yves-Marie Bercé | *The Birth of Absolutism: A History of France, 1598–1661* |
| Christopher F. Black | *Church, Religion and Society in Early Modern Italy* |
| Susan K. Foley | *Women in France since 1789* |
| Janine Garrisson | *A History of Sixteenth-Century France, 1483–1589* |
| Gregory Hanlon | *Early Modern Italy, 1550–1800* |
| Michael Hughes | *Early Modern Germany, 1477–1806* |
| Matthew Jefferies | *Imperial Culture in Germany, 1871–1918* |
| Dieter Langewiesche | *Liberalism in Germany* |
| Martyn Lyons | *Napoleon Bonaparte and the Legacy of the French Revolution* |
| Martyn Lyons | *Post-Revolutionary Europe, 1815–1856* |
| Richard MacKenney | *Renaissances: The Cultures of Italy, c.1300–c.1600* |
| Hugh McLeod | *The Secularisation of Western Europe, 1848–1914* |
| Robin Okey | *The Habsburg Monarchy, c.1765–1918* |
| Pamela M. Pilbeam | *Republicanism in Nineteenth-Century France, 1814–1871* |
| Helen Rawlings | *Church, Religion and Society in Early Modern Spain* |
| Tom Scott | *Society and Economy in Germany, 1300–1600* |
| Wolfram Siemann | *The German Revolution of 1848–49* |
| Richard Vinen | *France, 1934–1970* |

# Post-Revolutionary Europe, 1815–1856

MARTYN LYONS

First published 2006 by
PALGRAVE MACMILLAN
Houndmills, Basingstoke, Hampshire RG21 6XS and
175 Fifth Avenue, New York, N.Y. 10010
Companies and representatives throughout the world

PALGRAVE MACMILLAN is the global academic imprint of the Palgrave Macmillan division of St. Martin's Press, LLC and of Palgrave Macmillan Ltd. Macmillan® is a registered trademark in the United States, United Kingdom and other countries. Palgrave is a registered trademark in the European Union and other countries.

ISBN-13: 978–0–333–94805–7 hardback
ISBN 10: 0–333–94805–X        hardback
ISBN-13: 978–0–333–94806–4 paperback
ISBN 10: 0–333–94806–8        paperback

This book is printed on paper suitable for recycling and made from fully managed and sustained forest sources.

A catalogue record for this book is available from the British Library.

A catalog record for this book is available from the Library of Congress.

10   9   8   7   6   5   4   3   2   1
15   14   13   12   11   10   09   08   07   06

Printed in China

# Contents

# Illustrations

# Maps and Tables

## Maps

## Tables

# Abbreviations

| | |
|---|---|
| AmHistRev | *American Historical Review* |
| CUP | Cambridge University Press |
| EHQ | *European History Quarterly* |
| HUP | Harvard University Press |
| JMH | *Journal of Modern History* |
| MSH | Editions de la Maison des Sciences de l'Homme |
| OUP | Oxford University Press |
| PUF | Presses Universitaires de France |
| PUP | Princeton University Press |
| UCP | University of California Press |
| UP | University Press |
| YUP | Yale University Press |

# Acknowledgements

The author and publishers are grateful for permission to reproduce copyright material for the following:

Alinari Archives for an image entitled *Napoli. Vita delle strade. Venditore di lumache.*

Berg Publishers for a map from *Napoleon's Legacy: Problems of Government in Restoration Europe*, by David Laven and Lucy Riall.

Bibliothèque Nationale de France for images entitled 'Le Règne de Vingt Ans', 'L'Ordre règne à Varsovie' by Grandville, 'Les Poires' and 'Moeurs Conjugales no 6' both by Daumier.

Bridgeman Art Library for Horace Vernet's *King Louis-Philippe of France and his sons leaving the Château of Versailles on horseback, 1846.*

Cambridge University Press for a map from *The European Revolutions 1848–1851* by Jonathan Sperber (1984).

Imperial War Museum and Royal Archives, Windsor, for a photo entitled 'Thomas Walker and Joseph Conolly, Crimean War Wounded' by Howlett & Cundall.

Musée des Beaux-Arts, Bordeaux, for Eugène Delacroix's *La Grèce sur les ruines de Missolonghi* (1826) (© Musée des Beaux-Arts de Bordeaux/photographer Lysiane Gauthier).

Museo Centrale del Risorgimento, Rome, for an engraving entitled *Barricate di Palermo* (photographer Carmelo Catania).

Museo del Risorgimento, Milan, for an image entitled *Arresto di carbonari Lombardi.*

Réunion des Musées nationaux (Louvre Museum) for Ernest Meissonier's *La Barricade, rue de la Mortellerie, juin 1848*, also known as *Souvenir de guerre civile* (1849); and Eugène Delacroix's *Le 28 juillet 1830: la liberté guidant le people* (1830).

Rheinisches Bildarchiv, Stadt Köln, for Karl Begas, *The Begas Family* (1821).

Random House for a map from *Eastern Europe, 1740–1980: From Feudalism to Communism*, by Robin Okey, published by Hutchinson (1982).

Harry Ransom Humanities Research Centre for a photo entitled 'La Cantinière' by Roger Fenton (1855).

University Press of New England for a map from *Why the Crimean War? A Cautionary Tale*, by Norman Rich (1985).

Every effort has been made to contact all the copyright holders, but if any have been inadvertently overlooked the publishers will be pleased to make the necessary arrangement at the first opportunity.

# Introduction: Rethinking Post-Revolutionary Europe

It is time to rethink the history of Europe in the half-century following the defeat of Napoleon. Historians are in the process of renewing interpretations of this period, traditionally characterized as one of 'Restoration' and 'Reaction'. Recent research in many different areas has contributed to this rejuvenation. Revisionists argue, for example, that the reactionaries were not as blindly repressive as was once assumed. They stress continuities with the past, as many achievements of the revolutionary and Napoleonic era were preserved and consolidated by post-1815 rulers. Meanwhile historians of memory turn their attention to ways in which, especially in France, the Revolution and Empire were celebrated, effaced or exploited by subsequent generations. Cultural historians offer interesting examinations of the ways that monarchies represented and re-imagined themselves in the wake of revolutionary conflicts which shattered the mystique of kingship. New perspectives on the 1848 Revolutions have also re-evaluated their significance for the history of participatory democracy in Europe. In addition, issues like the abolition of slavery are given a new emphasis by historians who today are increasingly aware of Europe's imperialist connections with the Third World. This book draws on new approaches like these to re-examine Europe between Waterloo and the Crimean War. It discusses this period not in the rather negative light of 'restoration and reaction', but as a post-revolutionary age in search of a stable post-revolutionary settlement.

Many general surveys reiterate tired clichés and fail to register new historiographical interests. One account dominated by traditional viewpoints is that of Jacques Droz, *Europe between Revolutions, 1815–1848*, whose title unfortunately implied that all the exciting things happened *outside* the period.[1] Even a much more recent work by Jardin and Tudesq on France in the period failed to break the pattern.[2] Three perspectives have dominated traditional histories. First, the period has been characterized by a search for 'legitimacy' after the revolutionary and Napoleonic upheavals. 'Legitimacy', however, was usually envisaged within the narrow parameters of traditional diplomatic history. Today this question is raised more broadly, in the context of re-establishing or reinventing political culture under the returning monarchies. Secondly, the years 1815–48 have also been labelled as an age of revolutions, full of high hopes and ambitions, glorious in their failures, and looking forward to the emergence of triumphant nationalisms. This is the interpretation of the 'springtime of the peoples', which has been guilty of exaggerating the appeal of nationalists. Georges Weill's book described it in terms of a national awakening, as though the forces of nationalism were merely dormant, just waiting to be woken up.[3] Later works, in contrast, emphasise the 'constructed' or 'invented' aspects of national identities. A third traditional approach has been to dismiss radical movements as the inglorious regurgitations of the revolutionary legacy. Karl Marx's judgement on Napoleon III's seizure of power in 1851 was that history was condemned to repeat itself as farce, but Marx and Engels's commentaries were equally scathing about revolution-aries who failed to live up to expectations. Left-wing theorists were dismissed unhistorically as inadequate 'utopian' socialists, who had not provided the mature and 'scientific' theoretical analysis of economy and society which Marx claimed to supply.

This book considers the period after 1815 as a post-revolutionary age. Jonathan Sperber, who has greatly contributed to renovating the history of this period, pointed in this direction when he wrote that 'the model created by the French Revolution existed as an agenda, a program for potential change'.[4] The impact of 1789 was not confined to France itself. All Europe had been continuously at war as an indirect result of it between 1793 and 1815, except for the short truce of Amiens in 1802. The Napoleonic Empire had taken the ideals of the Revolution and French institutional models to Spain, Italy, Germany, Poland and other parts of conquered Europe. On the collapse of the Empire, France in particular, and Europe in general, faced the problem of moving beyond the experience of the Revolution and Napoleon, to find a new basis for stability.

The task of the restored monarchies was to generate a social and politi-cal stability which took account not only of conservative interests, but also of the political concepts put forward by the revolutionary and French impe-rial regimes. Questions of religious tolerance and Jewish emancipation, of representative or at least constitutional government, notions of economic freedom and civic equality were now permanently on the agenda. Democratic issues such as the freedom of the press and the nature of voting rights had to be redefined. This was to be an important and constructive period in the development of new forms of democracy.

Needless to say, many post-revolutionary regimes were not up to the task. Protagonists of the Old Regime were still influential; in France, ultra-royalists and *émigrés* returned to positions of authority in pursuit of revenge against those they still called 'Jacobins'. Yet even reactionary rulers perceived the need to accept and imitate some aspects of the revolutionary past, as far as they helped to strengthen the apparatus of the state. Whether regimes acknowledged or repudiated the past (they usually did a certain degree of both), their problems can be conceptualized as those of societies struggling with conflicting forces at work in a post-revolutionary world. The first chapters of this book, therefore, are concerned with the question of how Europe came to terms with its revolutionary past. How were the Revolution and Empire to be remembered or forgotten? What lessons were to be learned by democrats and administrators?

*Post-Revolutionary Europe* has been stimulated in part by parallels which spring to mind between 1815 and 1989–91. The fall of French hegemony suggests contrasts and comparisons with the collapse of the Soviet Empire in Europe. In both instances, the map of Europe had to be redrawn. A new structure of international relations had to be developed to deal with a completely new configuration. The collapse of the Napoleonic Empire in 1815 and the collapse of the Soviet Union both left a world dominated by a single global super-power: Great Britain in the first case, the United States in the second. Parallels therefore suggest themselves on the international scene; but they are striking, too, at the level of individual European societies. In 1989, Poland's first democratic Prime Minister Tadeusz Mazowiecki declared his intention to 'draw a bold line through the past'. Perhaps the restored French monarchy had similar intentions, but was such a rupture ever possible for either regime? Europe after 1815, as in the 1990s, was grappling with questions of 'transition politics'. But transition to what? After 1815, just as after 1991, there was a turn towards religion, a new interest in nationalism, a need to construct or resurrect a public sphere, and a problem of what to do with disbanded armies. In later chapters of this book, I take up two of these themes in particular. First, I consider the nature of nationalism in post-revolutionary Europe. In Eastern Europe, the revolutions of 1989 have revived interest in the so-called 'springtime of the peoples' in 1848. My tendency, however, is to play down its importance. Early nineteenth-century nationalism was a fragile ideology without a mass following. National identities were in the process of being manufactured by a small number of committed intellectuals.

Second, I address the theme of the reconstruction of a public sphere and of a civil society in a context where political debate was severely restricted. When the narrative of this book reaches beyond the 1830 Revolution, therefore, it shifts gear. I consider the rise of public opinion in Western and Central Europe in the 1830s and 1840s. New forms of protest and new forums for discussion appeared in this period, and the development of the newspaper press was an essential ingredient of the process. Important themes in this section are the growth of popular politics and its contribution to Europe's apprenticeship in democracy. A group of chapters then focus on aspects of social history before a substantial chapter on the 1848 Revolutions attempts to draw together several themes previously addressed. The unprecedented levels of popular participation in political life in 1848 now seem crucial to historians in any assessment of the revolutionary events of that year.

Authors rash enough to write general histories of Europe in any period are almost inevitably criticized for their geographical coverage. In my own treatment, France has a special place, because it was there that the problems of post-revolutionary transition outlined above emerged most clearly. This book, however, discusses all the major European powers (Britain, France, Prussia, Austria, Russia). I have incorporated Britain into the European story at important junctures. Although I have not tried to provide any systematic political history of Britain, to omit it altogether would be as foolish and irrational as trying to survey Europe since 1945 without mentioning the United States of America. In addition, I have paid attention to some of the lesser powers and smaller countries of Europe. For example, I have drawn consistently on material from Italy. I have paid attention where appropriate to Spain and Portugal, Belgium and Switzerland, Greece and Poland. I have personally consulted material in five languages (English, French, Italian, and to a lesser extent Spanish and Portuguese), and I have taken advantage of expert assistance in consulting sources in German. As for Russia and Eastern Europe, I have approached their history via sources published in English or French.

I am grateful for research and editorial assistance from Zora Simic, Harry Blatterer and Briony Neilson. I am also grateful for all I have learned from colleagues in the interdisciplinary programme in European Studies at the University of New South Wales, with whom I have shared lecturing duties in undergraduate courses on 'The New Europe'. In this collegial group, the insights of John Milfull, Dirk Moses, Martin Krygier and Stephen Fortescue have helped me to rethink the nature of sudden historical transitions. This project was supported by a three-year Large Grant from the Australian Research Council. Most notably, this allowed me to spend time during 2002 researching in libraries in Paris and Milan, without which the book could never have been produced. I appreciate the efforts of my friend Vittorio Scotti Douglas to introduce me to the battlefield of Marengo and the Museo del Risorgimento in Milan. I am grateful to Nick Doumanis for reading a draft of Chapter 5, and to John Breuilly for his constructive criticisms of the whole book. Lucy Taksa brought some important references to my attention. I dedicate this book to Lucy, for all we shared.

*Sydney, 2004*

# 1 Endings and Beginnings: Europe in 1815

## 1814–1815: the end of Napoleonic hegemony in Europe

The defeat of Napoleon in 1814 brought peace to a war-weary continent. For more than 20 years, the European powers had been almost continuously at war with revolutionary and Napoleonic France. To be sure, they had not always opposed France with a united front – far from it, since for many years their own ancient quarrels had overshadowed the French menace. Meanwhile, Bonaparte's diplomacy had offered powerful inducements to remain neutral, first to Prussia and then to Russia. Since 1813, however, an invincible coalition had gathered around France's two most persistent opponents: the Austrian Empire, ruled by the Habsburgs and guided by the architect of the coalition, Prince Clemens von Metternich, and Britain, led by its reserved and depressive Prime Minister Viscount Castlereagh. The victorious Allies dismantled the French Empire, restored the Bourbon King Louis XVIII to the French throne, and packed Napoleon off to the island of Elba, near the coast of Tuscany.

The peace of 1814 was short-lived. Napoleon escaped from Elba, landed on the south coast of France, and gathered his forces for another attempt at power. As Louis XVIII hurriedly repacked his luggage and fled to the safety of Brussels, Napoleon promised France a liberal constitution. In the Hundred Days, as this brief period was to be known, he tried to distance himself from his dictatorial past, in order to rally all anti-monarchical forces to his cause. Only with Napoleon's final defeat near the Belgian village of Waterloo in 1815, at the hands of the Prussians aided by the British, could Europe look forward to a definitive peace.

The year 1815 did not simply mark the end of a long cycle of general European warfare. It was a turning-point in two other senses. First, 1815 represented the end of the long Napoleonic hegemony which had redesigned the map of Europe, and imposed French rule on Italy, Germany, Switzerland, Belgium, the Netherlands, Poland, the Croatian coast and (temporarily) Spain. European strategists now had to organize the continent along new lines in the aftermath of the French imperial collapse. This chapter will examine how they went about this task, how they treated the defeated power which had dominated Europe for so long, and what priorities guided them.

Second, the ultimate defeat of Napoleon and his exile to St Helena in the Atlantic constitute an ideological turning-point. Conservatism was now triumphant after two decades of the social, religious and judicial reforms which followed the French Revolution. French conquests had brought in their wake an attack on the privileges of the aristocracy, an attack on the seigneurial system, the nationalization and sale of Church property, the introduction of the Napoleonic law codes and the new French system of secondary education. These changes offered a more egalitarian, secular and rationally administered alternative to the hierarchical structures of Old Regime Europe. French reforms could not be uniformly applied in every territory of the Empire. The French had to make compromises with local elites in order to secure their collaboration. In some parts of Europe, like Spain, French rule did not endure long enough for reforms to take root. But in those areas which had a long and continuous experience of French rule, the impact of the French Revolution was very tangible. In the areas closest to France, which Michael Broers has called 'the inner Empire',[1] especially in Belgium, the Rhineland and northern Italy, the revolutionary and Napoleonic era had a lasting influence.

The aftermath of 1815 therefore had three important characteristics: the disappearance of Napoleon inaugurated a long period of peace; it forced territorial and strategic adjustments in the wake of the collapse of the French Empire; and it comforted conservatives by neutralizing the threat of revolutionary change. Europe now had to face up to the realities and problems of its post-revolutionary condition.

## Problems of post-revolutionary transition

How was the legacy of the revolutionary and Napoleonic past to be assimilated or rendered harmless? How were the memories of those revolutionary years to be either nurtured or suppressed? These questions remained fundamental after 1815, both for the conservatives who came to power, and for their enemies. Later chapters will discuss some of the different responses they gave. Here it is appropriate to introduce some general themes.

The conservative monarchies of the Restoration period (1815–1830) had an ambiguous relationship with the revolutionary and Napoleonic past. Those who had been deposed by Napoleonic conquests needed to reclaim their legitimate right to rule, and to refashion the royal aura of sacrality which the execution of Louis XVI had terrifyingly shattered. This could only be done by condemning the French Revolution and its awful progeny – Bonaparte, the usurper of thrones. On the other hand, the Napoleonic machinery of state presented the Restoration regimes with unprecedented sources of power, based on a centralized administration, more efficient policing and tax collection, as well as a system of conscription whose wartime value had been fully demonstrated. In Turin and Rome, therefore, the new regimes retained Napoleon's enviable and efficient police force, the *gendarmerie*, renaming it the *carabinieri*. The French Bourbons, and others like them, had no wish to surrender such advantages inherited from the Napoleonic years. For them there was no question of 'turning the clock back' to the kind of political struggles which had embroiled the French monarchy before 1789. Instead, in the areas which had experienced French imperial rule, rulers found themselves at the head of a state apparatus which was now potentially more rational and effective than any Old Regime bureaucracy had dreamed of. The fall of the French Empire therefore produced governments whose rhetoric condemned the Revolution and all its works, but who in practice maintained a pragmatic view of what should be preserved from the changes of the recent past. Even in reactionary Spain, King Fernando would not reverse the sales of Church property conducted under French rule. Marco Meriggi called this the 'hidden legacy' of Bonapartism.[2] Many historians still find the vocabulary of 'Restoration and Reaction' useful to describe this period, yet what emerged was not a replica of the past, but something different, which incorporated many features of the French reforms.[3] Rather than a simple restoration of the dynastic Old Regime, this was a distinctive period of post-revolutionary change.

Naturally there were many all over Europe for whom the watchword was not reconciliation, but revenge on the revolutionary iconoclasts and Bonapartist sympathizers who had overthrown traditional institutions and attacked long-established beliefs. The French 'ultra-royalists' are an example of such a group apparently bent on widespread administrative purges, and demanding compensation for their sufferings in exile. The past, however, could not be so easily erased. The reactionaries themselves had no intention of forgetting it. They regularly observed the sinister anniversary of the execution of Louis XVI on 21 January 1793 – an anniversary which for them stood as a permanent warning of the disasters to which revolution could lead.

On the other side of the political fence, republicans all over Europe drew inspiration from the immediate revolutionary past. The surviving actors of the French revolutionary drama personally incarnated the continuity of the historical memory of radical egalitarianism. Ex-revolutionaries in exile in

Brussels and Switzerland, and ageing veterans of the French National Convention of 1792–3 were a living link with the past, and helped to keep alive what Alan Spitzer called 'the underground republic' in these conservative years after 1815.[4] Napoleon's belated adoption of constitutional liberalism in the Hundred Days provided a platform on which both liberals and Bonapartists could briefly unite.

Only later in the nineteenth century did the revolutionary tradition come under more intense scrutiny, as some socialists began to find it confining, suspecting that constant reference to the great example of 1789 was a symptom of the immaturity of the radical Left. But there was no doubting the importance of the revolutionary and Napoleonic decades. As Karl Marx commented in relation to the 1848 Revolution in France, 'the dead traditions of all past generations weigh like a nightmare on the spirit of the living'.[5]

The years of revolution and Bonapartist rule in Europe had been catastrophic for established regimes. How were these years and their impact to be confronted, forgotten, or used by the left as a platform for further radical change? We might envisage Europe's problem after 1815 as the problem of managing a post-revolutionary transition. There are perhaps instructive parallels to be drawn with other twentieth-century regimes which emerged after decisive historical ruptures. The issues and problems facing Europe after Napoleon may be compared with issues of change and continuity in Spain after Franco or Germany after Hitler. The fate of the Soviet Union and its European Empire after the fall of communism offers an even more interesting basis for reflection.

The fall of Soviet hegemony in East Central Europe ushered in a period in which post-communist societies searched for new political forms and the foundations of a new kind of civil society. Similarly, with the collapse of the Napoleonic Empire in 1815, the expansion of the newspaper press led to the revival or the creation of a public sphere in which politics could be debated, after years of strict censorship and control. Just as in Europe after 1815, there were voices seeking to wipe out entirely the memory of an odious Soviet regime. There were those clamouring for the restitution of confiscated property, like the French ultra-royalists after 1814, and residents of the former German Democratic Republic in the 1990s. Just as after 1815, there were other voices ready to accommodate some aspects of the past, and others still, especially amongst the older generation, who were increasingly nostalgic for some of the certainties of life in the former Soviet Union. Both 1815 and 1991 were endings and beginnings, intending to break decisively with the past but unable to dismiss it entirely.

Like the Napoleonic Empire, Soviet hegemony had imposed subordination to the economic needs of the dominant power, and after collapse both in 1815 and 1991 this economic subservience to imperial interests was over. A large part of the continent was again opened up to competition and to the economic powers of the age. In the 1990s, the potential beneficiaries seemed to be the United States and the European Union. In 1815, British manufactures were once more able to exploit continental markets which had been partially closed to them under Napoleon's Continental Blockade. Great Britain's new industrial strength and naval supremacy gave her a global influence which no other power could yet challenge.

The example of the end of the Soviet Union points to another problem of transitional politics: the survival of elites with material interests and power bases firmly embedded in the previous regime. The former Soviet *nomenklatura* (the administrative elite of high-ranking privileged functionaries) did not simply dissolve into thin air, but sometimes remained in positions of regional authority from which they could resist change. Similarly, former Bonapartist administrators everywhere after 1815 remained a source of anxiety for the 'restored' regimes. The former soldiers of Napoleon's Grande Armée posed another problem: when a great Empire collapses, what happens to its armies? Demobilization was a major political problem, both for the post-communist east and for post-Napoleonic Europe. Significantly, former officers of Napoleon's army were often implicated in revolutionary conspiracies and in nationalist movements after 1815.

To talk in terms of the post-revolutionary politics of transition begs an obvious question: it is fairly clear what the societies of 1815 and 1989–91 put behind them, but it is far less clear where they were heading. Transition, then, but transition to what? The political struggles and Revolutions of 1815–48 were all contests between rival versions of the ideal destination of this transitional process. Would that end-point be an ordered, peaceful and authoritarian Europe, as Prince Metternich desired, deferential to its monarchies and to organized religion? Or was Europe heading, as the liberals wished, towards some limited form of representative and constitutional government, in which private property would be sacred, and monarchies would be subject to the rule of law? What were the consequences in all this of the apprenticeship in popular democracy which the French above all had experienced during the French Revolution? Would that experience of popular sovereignty be developed and deepened in the following decades? For as the dominant classes were to discover, liberty and equality, like the wheel, could not be un-invented.

## 'Redemptive' and 'integrationist' transitions

There are no doubt many different models of post-revolutionary transition, but following Dirk Moses, we might categorize new regimes as either 'redemptive' or 'integrationist' in the positions they adopt towards a traumatic past. A 'redemptive' transition is one in which the dominant policy is to erase and to expiate the sins of the past. A redemptive transition aims at a spiritual rebirth and a social transformation. The new regime seeks to distance itself clearly and symbolically from the one it has replaced in order to establish its moral credentials. To some extent the French revolutionary regimes of the 1790s fit this model, as they attempted to transcend the perceived evils of what after 1789 they started to call the 'Ancien Régime'. The de-Nazification process in postwar Germany and the purges of Bonapartist personnel in Europe after 1815 also resemble a redemptive transition. The French clericals and ultra-royalists aimed to cleanse society of its subversive elements and to redeem a sinful and violent past. Redemptive change in this case was compromised by the tainted birth of the restored Bourbon monarchy, which was established by foreign powers in the wake of a French national defeat.

An 'integrationist' transition, on the other hand, is more pragmatic and willing to compromise with the previous regime and its followers. Integrationist regimes accommodate 'yesterday's men', hoping to achieve a smooth handover of power. Sometimes the expertise and experience of those who have served a compromised regime are commodities too valuable for an incoming administration to discard. In Germany after 1918, the persistence of old imperial elites in positions of power is one example of this, although this continuity with the imperial Reich is usually seen as a source of weakness rather than strength in the new Weimar Republic. To a certain extent, such an integrationist policy might miss some opportunities for a radical renewal of the national polity. Similarly, some perpetrators of the Nazi genocide were notoriously integrated into the German Federal Republic in the late 1940s and 1950s. In the Spanish model of transition, too, in the interests of social cohesion there were no trials of human rights abuses committed under the Franco dictatorship.

Europe after 1815 offers examples of both redemptive and integrationist transitions, and sometimes characteristics of both appear side by side. Neither set of protagonists was completely able to impose their particular vision on the course of events. Some regimes of our period were determined to repress any move to resurrect the spirit of revolution, and this was Metternich's aim above all. In contrast, other regimes (like the July Monarchy of Louis-Philippe) came to power as integrationist regimes. By

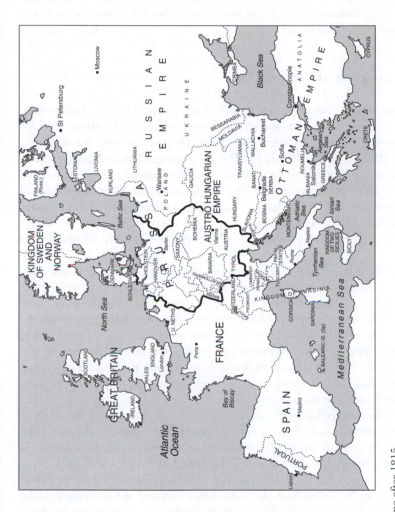

*Map 1.1* Europe after 1815

*Source:* Gordon Craig, *Europe since 1815*, New York (Holt, Rinehart & Winston), 3rd edn, 1971.

organizing the return of Napoleon's ashes from St Helena, Louis-Philippe's Prime Minister Adolphe Thiers tried to incorporate the Napoleonic legend, and at the same time to circumscribe its disruptive potential. The Revolutions of 1848 were to show, however, that both redemptive and inte-grationist regimes were vulnerable to the powerful forces of historical memory, when harnessed for a revolutionary cause or for the personal dictatorship of Napoleon III.

## The Congress of Vienna, 1815

The diplomatic elite of Europe gathered at Vienna in search of an equilib-rium between the national interests they each represented, and the need for European security as a whole. The leading protagonists were the 'big four': Great Britain, Austria, Russia and Prussia, although France, Spain, Sweden and Portugal would also be signatories of the final treaty. Metternich, as Austrian foreign minister since 1809, had most at stake, since Napoleon had destroyed the role of the Habsburg Empire as a leading force in Germany and Italy, and threatened to reduce it to the status of a Balkan power. He set out to re-establish Austria's dominant position in both Germany and Italy.

Metternich, like the other European statesmen, had a lingering eigh-teenth-century notion of the balance of power, whereby territorial gains made by one major power had to be 'compensated' by corresponding terri-torial gains by the others. This theory still influenced the way in which the Great Powers managed their own competing claims in East Central Europe. The 'balance of power', however, was always a flexible and dispensable concept. Thanks to British naval supremacy, it could only apply on the European continent itself. No-one contemplated trying to 'balance' Britain's awesome sea power.

Britain emerged in a very strong position, holding most of the overseas possessions which had been seized during the Napoleonic wars. She retained Gibraltar and Malta and exercised a protectorate over Corfu. In the West Indies, Britain acquired Tobago and St Lucia. The Cape Colony was also now a British possession. The creation of the new enlarged king-dom of the Netherlands made sure that the mouths of the Rhine and the Scheldt were in friendly hands. Similarly, when Norway passed from Danish control to Swedish rule, this ensured that no single power could dominate the vital entrance to the Baltic Sea, which satisfied another requirement of British maritime commerce.

Apart from the traditional, but very loosely interpreted idea of the balance of power, there were new forces operating in the field of European international relations. Ideological issues were important, as Metternich developed ways of suppressing liberal and national revolts wherever they might occur. European diplomacy had also to reckon with the new ideas of Tsar Alexander I, who believed international relations could be reconstructed on a moral and Christian basis. Alexander imagined himself as a victorious Messiah, emerging from the fires of Moscow to bring peace to Europe. The Tsar had experienced a religious conversion during the trauma of the French invasion. He immersed himself in the Bible and visited the English Quakers, whose pacifism corresponded with his own Christian vision of the world.[6] Metternich found it easy to ridicule such fantasies, but less easy to dismiss the presence of Russian troops in the heart of Europe. A Russian army now occupied Paris itself, signalling to the rest of Europe that Tsarist power could not be ignored. The Vienna Congress needed to settle the longstanding conflicts between Prussia, Austria and Russia in Eastern Europe, and it needed to find a framework for international co-operation and security in the future. Balance-of-power theory would prove a feeble instrument for achieving such grand ambitions. First of all, the diplomats had to solve Europe's 'French problem'.

## Europe's 'French problem'

The European powers sought guarantees for their own security. They needed protection against French aggression, fearing that any future revolutionary regime in France would launch another war of liberation against the conservative monarchies, as the French Revolution had done in 1792–3. At the same time as restraining France, Europe needed to rehabilitate her. The welcome presence of France's veteran diplomat Talleyrand at Vienna testified to this desire to reintegrate France as quickly as possible into the so-called 'Concert of Europe'. Nothing in the treatment of France at Vienna, therefore, prefigured the treatment of Germany in the Treaty of Versailles a century later. There was no war-guilt clause, no enforced disarmament, and a relatively light burden of reparations was imposed. At Vienna, the victors were magnanimous. France's frontiers were pegged back to their limits in 1790. She suffered an army of occupation and was forced to pay the allies an 'indemnity' – we might call this 'reparations' – of 700 million francs. Within three years, however, the occupying forces departed, and by 1820 the indemnity was paid.

The Treaty of Vienna established a ring of reinforced 'buffer states' which would stand between French expansionism and the rest of Europe.

On France's northern frontier, Belgium (formerly part of the Napoleonic Empire) and the Netherlands were united in a single kingdom, ruled by the Dutch House of Orange. This artificial unification of French and Flemish speakers, and of Catholics and Calvinists, endured only until 1830.

On France's eastern frontier, the Rhineland now became a part of Prussia, with enormous consequences for the future. The absorption of the Rhineland was both an asset and a problem for Prussia. The Rhineland cities had an advanced economy, French-influenced social and legal institutions, and a substantial Catholic population. They also had strong traditions of municipal independence, all of which made the culture of the Rhineland quite different from that of Prussia's Protestant agrarian elite. The Köln banker Schaaffhausen shrugged his shoulders in 1815 and lamented: 'Well! We have married into a poor family here.'[7] The Prussian annexation of the Rhineland also made it inevitable that any future French aggression would instantly bring France into direct conflict with north Germany's leading military power.

Switzerland, or to be more accurate the federated Swiss cantons, formed another link in the protective chain of states encircling France. In 1815, the general principle of Swiss neutrality was first advanced and accepted by all the powers. It has been a 'given' of international relations ever since. Finally, Vittorio Emanuele of Savoy returned to Turin from his refuge in Sardinia to reassume the throne of Piedmont, his small Alpine kingdom in northwestern Italy, which had been absorbed into the Napoleonic Empire. He profited from some territorial reinforcement, as his kingdom was now to include the old Ligurian Republic, based on the important commercial port of Genoa. The Piedmontese now had a Mediterranean outlet.

These arrangements were inherently fragile in at least two respects. First, the union of Belgium and the Netherlands would not endure. Second, the system depended on the compliance of the Piedmontese monarchy with Great Power strategy. As the Austrians were later to discover, this compliance would be reluctant at the best of times, and Piedmontese policy could as easily take an anti-Austrian as an anti-French turn.

More generally, however, the notion of the ring of states encircling France was predicated on a false assumption and accompanied by an impossible contradiction. The assumption that France was Europe's most likely disturber of the peace turned out to be alarmist. France after Napoleon did not have an expansionist agenda in Europe. In 1830 and 1848, the revolutionary regimes which came to power in Paris carefully reassured the European powers of their peaceful objectives. Europe, however, remained fearful of French intentions. In 1815, the diplomats fell into the habit, common to their species, of trying to prevent the last war, rather than forestalling the next one. The impossible contradiction of neutralizing France was exposed in 1823. Then Metternich, far from wanting to restrain France's military action, actually invited armed French intervention in order to crush the liberal movement in Spain.

## Italy, Germany and Central Europe

The reorganization of Italy and Germany incorporated much of Napoleon's rationalization of the political map, but it put Austria firmly in control. Austrian domination in the Italian peninsula was based on her direct rule of Venetia and Lombardy. The port city of Trieste and the Dalmatian coastline were also annexed by the Habsburg Empire. Habsburg princes or their acolytes returned to power in the Duchies of Tuscany, Modena and Parma, which was handed to Napoleon's second wife, Marie-Louise of Austria. Pius VII returned to govern the Papal States, which included Umbria, the Marches and the Romagna (the papal enclave of Avignon had been definitively lost to France in the Revolution). Within the Papal States, the Austrians maintained military bases at Ferrara, Piacenza and Comacchio in the 'Legations', the Papal provinces of the Romagna, so named because they were delegated to cardinals to administer. The Neapolitan Bourbons ruled the sprawling Kingdom of Naples and Sicily in alliance with Austria. All these rulers depended on Vienna to protect them from threats of revolution.

Austria assumed a similar controlling position within the new German Confederation, which comprised 34 states, including Prussia, and four free cities. The member states renounced war with each other, and agreed to establish a German Federal Diet, or council. The Diet, however, was not an elected representative assembly, but a body made up of delegates appointed by the governments of the various German states. Luxembourg was included, represented by the King of the Netherlands, while Holstein was represented by the King of Denmark. The final power structure of the Confederation was the outcome of considerable wrangling between Prussia, Austria and other German states. Eleven major states each had a single vote, and the smaller states were to share their votes in units of six. Austria presided over the Confederation, and many small German states looked to Vienna for protection against Prussian expansion, as well as against domestic upheavals. This, then, was a body of German princes held together by its opposition to German nationalism. Metternich was soon to enlist the German rulers in his crusade against liberalism and nationalism.

In post-revolutionary Germany, however, the enduring legacy of

1. Duchy of Parma          3. Duchy of Massa and Carrara
2. Duchy of Modena         4. Duchy of Lucca

*Map 1.2*  The Italian States in 1815

*Source*:   David Laven and Lucy Riall, eds, *Napoleons Legacy: Problems of Government in Restoration Europe*, Oxford (Berg Publishers), 2000.

Napoleon was clearly apparent. The independent cities, bishoprics and micro-states which had dotted the map of Germany before the French conquests were not revived. The Napoleonic secularization of Germany was permanent. The main beneficiaries of this process, alongside Prussia itself, had been the middle-sized kingdoms of southern Germany. Under Napoleon's territorial reorganization, for example, the territory of Baden had grown by 750 per cent, and its population almost doubled.[8] Together with Württemberg and Bavaria, Baden therefore had strong material reasons to align itself with France. In Metternich's vision, however, such sovereign *Mittelstaaten* (middle states) were a useful barrier against the development of German nationalism. Chapter 3 will examine how Metternich was able to enlist the German Confederation in the counter-revolutionary cause.

The territorial settlement in Eastern Europe posed difficult problems, and threatened to resurrect ancient antagonisms between Prussia, Austria and Russia. Prussia wanted control of Saxony, while Russia demanded Poland, and these conflicts brought the powers to the brink of another war. The compromise solutions which emerged reflected Russia's impressive military strength. The Russians took control of Finland, and it was they too who essentially determined the fate of the Poles. The Napoleonic Duchy of Warsaw was now reduced to a smaller Polish state, known as 'Congress Poland', with a population of 3.3 million, which was effectively dependent on Tsarist Russia. Between 1815 and 1830, therefore, Poles found themselves dispersed among several different territories. About 850,000 lived under Prussian rule in Poznàn (Posen), and approximately 4 million lived under Austrian rule in Galicia, the poorest of all these Polish regions. Others were subordinated to Russia, in the Ukraine, Bielorussia or Lithuania, or inhabited Congress Poland itself, which had its own army and its own Polish schools.[9] Only in Cracow, which was declared an independent city, were Poles temporarily free of foreign rule.

Throughout the eighteenth century, French support had sustained Polish aspirations for independence from the Eastern powers. Deprived of this source of assistance, the fractious Polish gentry faced limited options. For the time being, Prince Czartoryski's policy of accommodation with the Russians seemed the only one possible. This strategy was vindicated by a bizarre turn of events, in which Tsar Alexander granted the Poles a limited constitution – something which would have been unthinkable in Russia itself. Although only the Tsar could initiate legislation, Poland had a Parliament, for which over 100,000 electors, mainly members of the gentry or *szlachta*, had voting rights. Paradoxically, the exiled Polish revolutionary Kosciusko wrote a letter of gratitude to Tsar Alexander, thanking him for 'protecting' Poland. Even before the death of Alexander I in 1825, the future of this relatively liberal arrangement was in doubt and, as discussed in Chapter 6, a Polish revolution was brewing, which would have fatal consequences for the existence of a Polish state.

Since Russia dominated Poland, Prussia looked for territorial 'compensation' elsewhere for this increase in Russian power. Prussian and Russian

greed for territory threatened to impede the progress of the Vienna negoti-
ations. In the past, the powers might have solved the problem simply by
partitioning Poland between them. This time, however, the Tsar insisted on
a nominally independent Polish state, which was a far more advantageous
solution from Russia's point of view. The situation was rescued by handing
most of Saxony (except for its capital Dresden), as well as the Rhineland
and the Napoleonic Kingdom of Westphalia, to Prussia. Austria, as we have
seen, annexed Lombardy and dominated the German Confederation.

## A framework for international co-operation

Designing a blueprint for European stability was one thing; making it work
in practice was another. At Chaumont in 1814, the allies had already
declared their plans for continuing postwar co-operation when they optimistically announced that their alliance would last for 20 years. In a series
of conferences after 1815, European leaders continued to meet in order to
regulate the security arrangements they had put in place, and to deal with
crises as they occurred. This so-called 'Congress System' simply consisted
of a series of summit meetings of the five major powers – France, Britain,
Austria, Russia and Prussia. It worked for as long as it did because all the
powers were in fundamental agreement about maintaining the international order which had been established at the end of the Napoleonic wars,
and because they found it useful to tackle problems within a collective
framework.

This consensus was underpinned by two treaties of alliance. The
Quadruple Alliance united Austria, Britain, Russia and Prussia. Tsar
Alexander's Holy Alliance of the three eastern Empires – one Catholic, one
Protestant and the other Orthodox – was another element of conservative
solidarity, but it also reflected Alexander's own Christian and ecumenical
objectives. Castlereagh dismissed the Holy Alliance as 'a piece of sublime
mysticism and nonsense' but, as far as Metternich was concerned, if
Christian humanitarianism united reactionary rulers against revolutionary
contagion, then he could use it to advantage. In any case, enclosing Russia
within a system of alliances seemed the best way to restrain her expansionist tendencies.

Rifts naturally occurred amongst the victorious allies of 1815, and the
system of congresses did not survive beyond 1823. It had marshalled its
forces to suppress revolutionary movements in Italy in 1821 and Spain in
1823. Tsar Alexander I and his Greek-born foreign minister Capodistria
saw these repressive projects in terms which prefigured the rhetoric of

George W. Bush. In 1820, the Tsar had faced a mutiny of the Semenovsky Guards in his own capital, and he now attributed all the revolutionary movements of the early 1820s to 'the empire of evil'. Paris was the sinister epicentre of subversion, propagated by 'the synagogues of Satan'.[10] The outbreak of the Greek War of Independence in 1822, however, introduced tensions of a new kind between the major powers, confronting Metternich and the British with the disturbing reality of Russian military power in the Mediterranean. As we shall see in a later chapter, Metternich's system of congresses could not survive this.

Castlereagh's untimely suicide in 1822 further altered the pattern of international relationships. Even before his death, Britain had been relatively unmoved by Metternich's attempts to organize armed intervention in Europe's revolutionary trouble spots. Britain's principal interests lay outside continental Europe, and were increasingly focused on protecting her global commercial connections. For Austria, on the other hand, the stakes were very different. The Habsburg Empire was a multi-ethnic dynastic state, which had been thoroughly bankrupted by the Napoleonic wars. At the heart of Europe, Austria felt uniquely vulnerable to revolutionary threats. Austria had had no English Channel to protect it from the Napoleonic onslaught at Wagram, Ulm and Austerlitz. Moreover, the very idea of national independence threatened its cohesion; it would set Germans against Czechs, against Poles, against Italians and against Magyars, it would set Magyars against Slavs, and everyone against Jews. Nationalism was potentially a centrifugal force which could destroy the Habsburg

*Table 1.1*   The 'Congress System'

| | |
|---|---|
| 1814 | Treaty of Chaumont: the coalition against Napoleon pledged a 20-year alliance |
| 1815 | Quadruple Alliance: Austria, Britain, Prussia, Russia offered mutual support against French aggression, and agreed on regular conferences |
| 1815 | Holy Alliance: Russia, Prussia, Austria announced a new counter-revolutionary order based on Christian morality |
| 1818 | Aix-la-Chapelle (Aachen): Allies decided to withdraw troops from France, and renewed Quadruple Alliance |
| 1820 | Troppau (in Galicia): Austria, Russia and Prussia (but not Britain) supported principle of armed intervention to forestall revolutions |
| 1821 | Ljubljana (Laibach): Austrian intervention in Naples and Piedmont approved |
| 1822 | Verona: French intervention in support of Ferdinand VII of Spain approved |
| 1822 | Suicide of Castlereagh |
| 1825 | Death of Tsar Alexander I |

Empire. In this sense, Metternich's struggle against the spread of revolutionary ideologies was a struggle for the survival of the Austrian Empire itself. Although their priorities were very different, Castlereagh and Metternich had nevertheless co-operated closely, and Metternich was shaken by the British Prime Minister's violent demise. Castlereagh was, he said, my second self. In his place, the brilliant George Canning gave British world policy a more independent direction. For Metternich, Britain soon became 'gangrenous to the bones with the revolutionary spirit'.[11]

## An evaluation of the Congress of Vienna

The settlement of 1815 gave Europe a century of peace. This is not to deny that wars broke out, but the Crimean War, the wars of German and Italian unification, and the Balkan wars were all localized wars, and most of them were short. Between Waterloo and Sarajevo, Europe was spared a generalized conflict, and this makes the Treaty of Vienna one of history's outstanding diplomatic triumphs. Territorial changes proved necessary, like the creation of independent Belgium in 1830, but they did not spark off any widespread conflagration. The Vienna Settlement sought a lasting settlement in which hegemony would be shared, conflicts could be managed, and the rights of all states collectively recognized. As Paul Schroeder, the most incisive recent historian of the Vienna Congress, concluded: 'No other general peace settlement in European history comes anywhere close to this record.'[12]

It was a settlement drawn up by reactionaries keen to crush any revival of liberalism or Bonapartism in Europe. Yet under Metternich's influence they maintained a pragmatic view of the recent past. They were not vindictive towards the defeated power, and after all they wanted to strengthen the position of the Bourbon monarchy in France. When it suited them, they believed in the doctrine of the balance of power, and at other times they ignored it. They believed in principle in defending the legitimate rights of monarchs, but in practice many petty princes, swept away by the Napoleonic conquests, were not restored to their miniature thrones. In the interests of stability, the settlement of 1815 recognized and incorporated much of the Napoleonic legacy in Germany.

The European statesmen who negotiated the Vienna settlement are often accused of ignoring popular aspirations for self-determination. Indeed, they saw no need for democratic consultations. 'Peoples?', asked the Austrian Emperor Francis I, 'What does that mean? I know only subjects.'[13] The French people were not asked whether they wanted the

Bourbon monarchy back or not. When the Austrians took control of Lombardy, no-one thought to consult the disgruntled bourgeoisie of Milan. Nor did the Genoese have any say in the liquidation of their Republic, or in suddenly becoming subjects of Turin. The rights of nations did not come into consideration.

One reason for this was that in 1815 most nationalist movements were merely whispers in the wind. The Vienna statesmen were inclined to view conspiracies and uprisings as the inevitable aftershocks of the revolutionary earthquake, which would eventually die away. The idea of national self-determination was still the obsession of a handful of intellectuals without a mass following. We should not read the enormous power of nationalism in the twentieth century back too far into the early nineteenth. The idea that there had been a German 'War of Liberation' against the French oppressor in 1813 was largely a myth elaborated retrospectively for nationalist purposes. When, in Livorno in March 1814, the British Admiral Bentinck invited the Italians to rise up in defence of their liberties, his appeal fell on deaf ears. In Poland, the French military presence in the country had not aroused the gentry, although the *de facto* Russian protectorate produced a revolution in 1830. To say that the 1815 settlement ignored nationalism is therefore an anachronistic criticism, for nationalism had not yet emerged as a serious political force.

With hindsight, we might level another criticism at the Vienna statesmen, and one that they would perhaps have recognized on their own terms: they had not found an answer to the 'Eastern Question'. Europe's so-called 'Eastern Question' stemmed from the weakness and long-term decline of the Ottoman Empire. This posed a serious problem for the Great Powers: when the Ottoman Empire did eventually collapse, how would the spoils be divided? Russia's ambitions for a Mediterranean foothold dated back at least to Catherine II's so-called 'Greek project'. Containing Russian expansion in south Eastern Europe was thus a priority for all the other powers. Yet international antagonisms in this region were too thorny to disentangle, and the Treaty of Vienna largely left them conveniently alone. As a result, the Balkans soon became the source of serious threats to European peace, from the Greek struggle for independence to the Crimean War and beyond. Like many of their successors, the statesmen of Vienna found the problems of the Balkans and the eastern Mediterranean too baffling to resolve.

# 2 Re-Inventing the Monarchy: France, 1814–1830

## Continuity and rupture

The rulers of Western and Central Europe had experienced a long odyssey of emigration, displacement or exile. The French revolutionary and Napoleonic armies had pushed them aside to create sister republics, which were later transformed into Bonapartist monarchies or simply absorbed directly into imperial France. The Pope himself had been virtually imprisoned by Napoleon in Savona in 1806. After 1815, the rulers returned to a post-revolutionary world in which the mystique of monarchy had suffered fatal damage. They had once claimed to rule by divine right and with the sanction of the Church. The French Revolution, however, had proclaimed the sovereignty of the people, nationalized Church property and dismantled the rituals, the symbolism and the ideological apparatus of the Old Regime monarchy. Louis XVI, divinely ordained and the patriarch of his people, had been tried, guillotined and his all-too-human severed head displayed before the Parisian crowd. He was no longer the Bourbon king, but merely Citizen Capet, and a traitor into the bargain. In post-revolutionary Europe, the prerogatives of monarchs could never again be asserted with the confidence of previous times. The Revolution had shown that even rulers could be tried for treason and that the justice of the people was implacable. At her own trial, Queen Marie Antoinette had been accused of incest with her own children. Nothing was sacred any more. After the French Revolution and the Napoleonic Empire, no regime could take itself for granted. European monarchs needed to fashion new ways to legitimate their authority.

The returning monarchs all faced, to a greater or lesser degree, a crisis of post-revolutionary legitimacy. The Spanish king had fled, Vittorio Emanuele of Piedmont had left for the safety of Sardinia, while the Portuguese court had decamped under British protection to Rio de Janeiro in 1808, and liked it so much they were very reluctant to return. After 1815 the work of re-inventing their monarchies had to begin. In the latter case, the transformation was indeed remarkable, as exile to Brazil transformed the moribund Portuguese regime into a regenerated monarchy within a multi-racial slave society. King João VI declared Brazilian independence and found a place for his uprooted dynasty in a new 'tropical Versailles'.[1] Dynastic credibility was also a problem in Germany, where about half the population had new rulers after 1815. Some royal houses promoted their claims in a neo-Gothic architectural style which resonated with the medieval origins of kingship. In 1842, Frederick William IV of Prussia presided over the completion after centuries of work of Köln's medieval cathedral. It was in France, however, where the Bourbons returned as passengers of the allied armies, that the need to re-invent the monarchy was most acute. This chapter will consider how the governments of Louis XVIII (1814–24) and his brother Charles X (1824–30) went about re-imagining the role of monarchy in French society.

Louis XVIII and Charles X were both brothers of the executed Louis XVI. They had been amongst the first wave of political *émigrés* to flee the French Revolution, departing immediately after the fall of the Bastille on 14 July 1789. The 25 years they had spent in exile were poor preparation for the enormous task of reconciling the Old Regime with the social and political realities of post-revolutionary France. Louis XVIII's search for legitimacy was weakened from the start by his dependence on the armies of the Allies. His new subjects could not fail to contrast this dependence with the military power France had enjoyed under Napoleon. Contemporary cartoonists characterized Louis XVIII as a corpulent pig, in contrast to Napoleon's predatory eagle.[2]

Louis XVIII, Charles X and their followers were 'legitimists' – in other words they believed in the Bourbon dynasty's legitimate and hereditary right to rule, regardless of the French Revolution and the Napoleonic Empire. Yet like many new regimes established after a significant historical rupture, the Bourbon monarchy faced a classic legitimacy dilemma. It needed to distance the monarchy from the revolutionary and Napoleonic regimes which had preceded it; but at the same time it needed to incorporate some of the personnel who had been implicated in the 'crimes' of the recent past. This dilemma of rejection or incorporation created tensions between the desire to repudiate France's recent history, and the need to absorb some aspects of it.

Inevitably, there were compromisers who accommodated themselves to any change of regime. Among the best known survivors of France's rapid changes of regime was Talleyrand, the Old Regime aristocrat who, as a revolutionary bishop, had proposed the nationalization of church property in 1790. Talleyrand subsequently served the Republic and then Napoleon, before facilitating the Bourbon Restoration. All in all, he served five different regimes and took 14 oaths of allegiance. He was a notorious turncoat, although his latest biographer asks posterity to deal more generously with Talleyrand's own claim that he consistently worked for peace and France's rightful place in Europe.[3]

Louis XVIII had to use the resources of this experienced political elite. He also wanted to demonstrate continuity, not with the immediate past but with his own dynastic predecessors. Hence he took the name of Louis XVIII to show that in spite of Louis XVI's execution, the legitimate line of Bourbon kings had never been broken. All the same, when he made his solemn entry into Paris on 3 May 1814, he had to devise a route to the Tuileries palace which did not compromise his legitimism. He avoided both the Arc de Triomphe, which commemorated the victories of the hated Napoleon, and the Place Royale (now Place de la Concorde), where his unfortunate brother Louis XVI had been guillotined.[4] Cartoonists represented Louis satirically as an unlikely Ulysses returning to Ithaca, racked with gout, greedy for taxes, and quite unsure when his reign had actually begun (see Plate 1).

## The impact of the Hundred Days

The task of reconciliation with the revolutionary and Napoleonic past was made more difficult by Napoleon's return in the Hundred Days. Once again, there were sudden reversals of loyalty, as some born-again monarchists of 1814 deserted Louis for the resurgent Emperor. Benjamin Constant, the dilatory novelist and unconvincing spokesman for parliamentary liberalism, was one of these self-seeking survivors. He had called Napoleon worse than Genghis Khan, and then unscrupulously helped him draft a new constitution as soon as he returned from Elba.

When Louis XVIII and his supporters returned for a second time in 1815, they were not in the mood for leniency. Die-hard royalists were out for revenge. The Napoleonic Marshal Ney was shot for treason: an exemplary act which demonstrated the desire to erase and redeem the past discussed in Chapter 1. There had been important defections to the Emperor in the army, and so the Bourbons now carried out a military purge, and retired many junior officers on half-pay. These demi-soldes remained Bonapartist sympathizers for years to come. In 1816, the monarchy exiled the surviving regicides of the National Convention of 1793 who had gone over to Napoleon in the Hundred Days. Altogether, 74 per cent of surviving regicides were forced to leave France, many of them fleeing to Brussels.[5] Orders were given to destroy all Napoleonic flags, eagles,

LE REGNE DE VINGT ANS

CE ROI PAR SA HAUTE SAGESSE | IL PASSAIT TROIS HEURES A LA MESSE

SUT METTRE LE TEMS A PROFIT | SEPT A TABLE ET QUATORZE AU LIT

*Plate 1*   'The Twenty-Year Reign' of King Louis XVIII. This cartoon plays on
Louis's greed and his insistence that the Bourbons had never ceased to be
France's legitimate monarchs. The caption below the cartoon reads: The
King in his great wisdom knew how to use his time well. He would spend
3 hours at Mass, 7 at the table and 14 in bed

*Source*:   Bibliothèque Nationale de France.

emblems and busts of the Emperor. Schools and public buildings were emptied of the signs and statues, liberty trees and red caps, which recalled the revolutionary or Napoleonic regimes.

From a royalist perspective, returning from Elba was the most irresponsible act of Napoleon's career. It was reckless and selfish, and severely damaged the chances of a smooth transition of power. Royalist forces themselves, however, also contributed to instability. We should not exaggerate Louis XVIII's capacity to compromise. This capacity, as we shall see, was limited by his inability to rein in the wild hunting dogs of royalist extremism.

In spite of the spirit of revenge against Bonapartism which prevailed in 1815–16, the new Bourbon regime preserved important elements of the Napoleonic state. Napoleon's Concordat with the Catholic Church remained in force during the nineteenth century. Napoleon's law codes and secondary schools remained the basis of France's legal and educational systems. Religious freedom was maintained, notwithstanding the growing clerical nature of the monarchical regime. The jury system, the legion of honour, and the framework of the Revolution's tax system were all preserved. The Napoleonic system had created modern institutions which vastly strengthened the state and which no subsequent regime wished to reverse. Napoleon's prefectoral system, above all, offered the machinery the Bourbons needed to dominate their new parliamentary regime and win elections. Prefects removed liberal opponents from the electoral rolls, and added royalists to them, either real ones or dead ones or those who did not necessarily pay enough tax to qualify for the vote. While Marshal Ney was the victim of a 'redemptive' transition after the Hundred Days, the survival of Napoleonic institutions indicated the deeper reality of an 'integrationist' approach.

### The White Terror and ultra-royalism

A peaceful transition between Empire and monarchy was ruined not only by the return of Napoleon from Elba, but also by demands for retribution from the ultra-royalists, and by popular violence. In the so-called 'White Terror' of 1814–16, popular royalist gangs exacted vengeance on revolutionary and Napoleonic administrators and supporters. As Provence was 'liberated' from Bonapartist control in 1815, the murder gangs summarily killed dozens of victims in Marseilles. The Napoleonic General Brune was assassinated and his corpse thrown into the river Rhône. Self-appointed executioners sought out those who had held public office under the Empire, had bought property of the Church or the *émigrés*, or who were Protestants, supposed Jacobins or sympathizers with the French Revolution. In the southwestern department of the Gard, where about one-third of the population was Calvinist, old scores were settled in a violent outbreak which continued the sectarian conflicts of the 1790s.[6] In Toulouse, General Ramel who had commanded the garrison during the Hundred Days was assassinated by royalist paramilitaries. Daniel Resnick estimated that the royalist murder gangs killed 200–300 in the south in these months.[7] One reason why this violence remained unchecked for so long was the inertia of the Duke of Angoulême's brief provisional government in the south during 1815. Based in Toulouse, Angoulême's government was supported by extreme royalist organizations and armed bands like the *verdets* in Toulouse. For a short time, his rule attracted elements of southern society who were sympathetic to regional autonomy and vague notions of southern independence. For the time being, political violence went unpunished.

Bourbon society and politics as a whole were characterized by the return to France of the *émigrés*, many of them aristocrats who entertained extreme royalist views but had little in common with the popular royalist movements responsible for the White Terror. These men had demonstrated their loyalty to the monarchy by leaving France during the Revolution, and they now expected to receive due reward for their devotion and self-sacrifice. They belonged by definition to an older generation, and their return to office installed a gerontocracy which blocked the rise of many young aspirants. One social climber was Julien Sorel, hero of Stendhal's novel *The Red and the Black*, and it was no coincidence that political opposition and romantic revolt were closely associated in this period with discontented youth. The return of the *émigrés* to positions of influence aggravated a generational conflict: under Napoleon men like Julien had enjoyed unprecedented opportunities for early advancement, especially in the army; after 1815, their paths were blocked by older royalists. The ultra-royalists opposed Louis XVIII's compromises, and insisted on positions of influence and special treatment. As a result, the Restoration period witnessed the return to power (for the last time) of an embittered provincial nobility, for whom exile had represented a refusal to accommodate the revolutionary and Napoleonic past.

In the Old Regime, the provincial nobility may have sought a career in the local judiciary or *Parlement*, but for the older generation of *émigrés*, these once-familiar institutions no longer existed. Most of them were too old for the army, the traditional aristocratic career path, and so they chose an administrative career in the prefectures and sub-prefectures. About 70 per cent of the prefects appointed in the Bourbon Restoration were nobles, and

20 per cent of these were ex-*émigrés*.[8] A record of loyalty to the dynasty was enough to secure promotion to such positions during the ultra-royalist ministries of Villèle and Polignac. The Restoration was the swansong of the French rural nobility: after the purge which followed the 1830 Revolution, only 5 per cent of the prefects kept their jobs.

In David Higgs's analysis, the ultra-royalists were 'social fossils' defending a vanished historical order.[9] They were nostalgic for a deferential world in which the authority of the landed nobility was undiminished, and the bonds of the local community firmly held together by *seigneur* and priest, fulfilling their social responsibilities to the poor. They looked back to the provincial assemblies of pre-revolutionary France, which they contrasted favourably with the excessively centralized bureaucracy of Napoleon. They regretted what they saw as the weakening of the patriarchal family with the introduction of divorce. They thought Catholic values had disastrously declined. Like many lost causes, Ultra-royalism was based on a rather idyllic view of the past. For instance, it romanticized the memory of the revolt of the Vendée in 1793, when the peasants of the west had risen against the Republic. In ultra-royalist mythology, Vendean peasants and nobles had stood side by side for God and the King. But this fantasy was becoming increasingly irrelevant.[10] There had been no repeat of the Vendean uprising in 1814, and the White Terror had no significant repercussions in the west. There was no Vendean royalist rising in support of the Bourbons in 1830, either. There was a fantastic element, too, in the ultra-royalists' visceral hostility to Jacobinism and the French Revolution, which in the view of many had been brought about by an evil conspiracy of intellectuals and freemasons. Ultra-royalists also resented Louis XVIII for his mistakes and compromises, especially the Charter of 1814 which installed a parliamentary regime. They often seemed more royalist than the king.

A good example of ultra-royalism at its most sensible was Count Joseph Villèle, prime minister from 1821 to 1828. Villèle was a noble landowner, who had sat tight on his estate at Mourvilles-Basses with its 13 farms (*métairies*) during the Revolution and Empire. He was elected mayor of Toulouse under the Duke of Angoulême in 1815. He represented the frugality and austere values of the provincial squire. Making his political career in Paris, he felt too poor in the big city to rent a personal carriage. His main political contribution was to transfer this financial caution into the national sphere, making economies, balancing the budget and re-establishing public credit. Villèle represented the local landowners who lived on their own estates and remained close to their provincial roots. He was a careful and unimaginative legitimist. In a Restoration society tired of war and financially exhausted, this perhaps was what was needed.[11]

## The crisis of legitimacy

In 1824 Louis XVIII died, and Charles X succeeded to the throne. In the context of the recent past, this banal event seemed remarkably significant. For the first time since 1774, the monarchical succession was smooth and uncontested. Louis XVI had died on the scaffold, and 'Louis XVII' had died in prison without ever ruling. But when Louis XVIII died a peaceful Christian death, on his throne, it seemed as though the Bourbons had achieved some level of normalization.[12] How then did the Bourbon monarchy reconstitute a legitimate claim to rule post-revolutionary France? It did so by accepting certain enduring consequences of the immediate past, and by trying to forget other aspects which undermined its traditional claims. At the same time, the Bourbons attempted to re-establish some of the sacred character of monarchy. They tried, in other words, to 'resacralize' the tarnished throne of France.

Five aspects of the crisis of monarchical legitimacy can be identified. First, the monarchy accepted that, unlike the Old Regime, it now presided over a parliamentary system, established in the Charter of 1814. The Charter guaranteed the Napoleonic law codes, and in principle enshrined civic equality, an independent judiciary and a free press. The Charter inaugurated a two-chamber parliament, with an upper house of peers appointed by the king. In this French version of the Westminster system, deputies to the lower house were chosen by indirect election for five years. The franchise was extremely limited, and conservative royalists sought to limit it even further to an elite of the wealthiest property-owners. Adult males over 30 could vote, if they paid 300 francs annually in direct taxes, and they formed an electorate numbering just 110 000 in a total population of about 29 million. In 1822, the 16 000 wealthiest citizens were awarded a double vote, and in 1823 the life of a parliament was extended to seven years. Such measures were designed to return and prolong a strongly royalist majority, which eventuated as planned in the 'blue horizon' chamber of 1816 (the *Chambre Introuvable*), and again in 1824 (the *Chambre Retrouvée*).

The relationship between king and parliament remained problematic. The king retained important powers, such as the right to dissolve parliament, to create peers, and to appoint the prime minister, who did not need to be a member of parliament let alone the leader of the majority. The monarchy had significantly insisted that the 1814 system was protected by a royal Charter, granted personally by the grace and favour of the monarch, rather than a Constitution, which the nation claimed by right. It was even more important for the future that Clause 14 of the Charter allowed the monarch to assume extraordinary powers in an emergency. Since the king himself defined what constituted an emergency, this provision was fraught with danger, and when Charles X decided to activate it to his advantage in 1830, a revolution overthrew him. The 1814 Charter was a very liberal document in European terms, and embattled constitutionalists both in France and elsewhere on the continent defended it as a worthwhile model of representative government under a monarchy.

Second, the monarchy accepted the irreversible sale of the *biens nationaux*, the property of the Church and the *émigrés* which had been auctioned in the French Revolution. This was an unwritten condition without which the return of Louis XVIII would not have been tolerated. The king accepted the property settlement of the Revolution in order not to alienate the royalist bourgeoisie. Many returning *émigrés*, however, demanded the restitution of their land, just as after 1989 many West Germans demanded restitution of property they had lost in the Soviet occupation zone between 1945 and 1949. In both cases, the debates about property restitution became debates on the legitimacy of former regimes – the German Democratic Republic and the governments of revolutionary France. In Bourbon France, these demands were met in token fashion. The *émigrés* had to be satisfied with the indemnity law passed by Villèle's government in 1825, which awarded them a billion francs paid in government bonds. This *milliard des émigrés* simply enabled many of them to repay some of the debts accumulated during their exile.

A third way to establish a legitimate claim to govern was the time-honoured method of military action. By 1818 the foreign army of occupation began to leave France. In 1823, the Bourbon army fought a successful war against liberal forces in Spain, where the Napoleonic army had spectacularly come to grief 15 years before. The loyalty of the army in this campaign suggested that the Bourbons' work of consolidation was having some effect.[13] Then, in 1829, France embarked on imperial conquest in North Africa (see Chapter 15). Although it was some time before the French secured complete control, the foundations of French Algeria were laid. None of this saved Charles X from the July Revolution of 1830.

The Bourbon monarchy, fourthly, preserved its authority by deliberately trying to persuade France to forget the past. Through censorship, the regime discouraged any public reference to the traumatic events of recent French history. Mentioning the guillotine, Robespierre or the seizure of power by Bonaparte was simply banned. The politics of forgetting (*la politique de l'oubli*) was even made explicit in the Charter, for Clause 11 ordered that

All investigations of opinions held and votes expressed before the restoration are forbidden. The same disregard (*oubli*) is demanded of both the courts and the citizens.

In a similar vein, post-Soviet Russia changed the names of cities and streets to eliminate references to Stalin and symbolically terminate the veneration of Lenin. After 1815, too, new symbols were adopted, like the white Bourbon flag which officially replaced the tricolour. But there were many ways of 'forgetting' the unforgettable. One mayor in the Dordogne did not bother to replace the tricolour flag, but simply cut away the red and blue panels, leaving a politically correct white flag.[14] Presumably the discarded sections could be resewn if this was one day required. The mayor of the Pyrenean town of Orthez did verbal somersaults to conform with orders *not* to recall the Revolution of 1789. He referred to erasing 'all the signs of the usurpation as well as all the emblems which bring to mind the calamitous times of despotism and anarchy'. He thus managed to condemn 25 years of history without actually mentioning the Revolution (the 'calamitous times') or Napoleon (the usurper) by name. The monarchy did not want to keep reminding its subjects about the fate of Louis XVI and Marie Antoinette. All physical traces of Marie-Antoinette's imprisonment in the Conciergerie prison before she went to the guillotine were destroyed, including even the walls of her cell. Plans for a monument to Louis XVI on the site of the guillotine were also dropped.

The Marseillaise was banned – it was, after all, the international anthem of revolutionaries, and Napoleon himself had never entirely trusted its democratic call to arms. Even mentioning the Marseillaise was illegal, and its 66-year old composer, Rouget de l'Isle, was pathetically imprisoned for debt in 1826.[15] Years later Balzac brilliantly summed up the politics of forgetting when he wrote *Colonel Chabert*, imagining a Napoleonic veteran, left for dead on the Russian campaign, who returned to France in 1816 to claim his wife and property. His wife had remarried and his property now belonged to another. Chabert could not reclaim his true identity or his Napoleonic past – he himself was a distant memory, and his unexpected resurrection was an embarrassment and an intrusion into a society that wished to forget.

The fifth significant aspect of the re-invention of the monarchy was 're-sacralization', that is to say, restoring some of the sacred character of the monarchy which had underpinned royal power under the Old Regime. A ritual cleansing of the past took place, as all revolutionary and Napoleonic emblems were replaced with crucifixes and the monarchical lily (*fleur de lys*), and masses were sung in thanks to God for the return of France's legitimate king. The Catholic Church enjoyed higher status under the Bourbon monarchy. In 1824 Cardinal Frayssinous was appointed head of a new ministry which combined both ecclesiastical affairs and education. The ecclesiastical budget was greatly expanded: government expenditure on the Church rose in the Restoration period from 12 to 33 million francs.[16] New religious orders appeared, and the seminaries started to fill up again with clerical recruits. In *The Red and the Black*, Julien Sorel kept a secret portrait of Napoleon and longed to be part of the glory associated with the military uniform (the red of the novel's title). While Julien despised the mediocrity of Restoration society, he knew that his advancement and personal ambitions could only be fulfilled by pursuing a clerical career, and donning priestly black. After 1815, the Church not the army was the route to fame and power for upwardly mobile young men.

Clerical influence extended to the control of parliamentary legislation. In 1816, for instance, divorce was abolished, and the legitimacy of marriages conducted in the revolutionary period by civil magistrates or constitutional priests was questioned. In 1825, a law of sacrilege was passed, which made thefts from churches and the profanation of the sacraments into secular crimes punishable by death. This law, however, was a monarchical gesture which marked the limit of clerical influence in politics, and it was never applied. All the same, it fuelled the myth of a Jesuitical conspiracy to manipulate the government.[17]

The Catholic Church organized a series of missions in the French provinces in an attempt to recover the ground lost in the revolutionary and Napoleonic decades. The rationale of the missions was to compensate for the shortage of priests. In 1815, the surviving clergy were old, poorly trained and inadequately prepared to mend the ravages of the revolutionary period. The missionaries of 1817–29, however, went further. They were drawn from among the zealots of various religious orders, and they promoted an energetic programme of reconversion. They encouraged attendance at mass, confession and penitence.

Missionaries organized theatrical book-burnings of the works of Voltaire, Rousseau and other writers of the eighteenth-century Enlightenment, whom the clericals blamed for all the evils of the French Revolution.[18] The book-burnings were inspired by an attempt to neutralize a powerful historical memory: the memory of the French Revolution. They were part of an intense effort of spiritual reconquest, aimed at reclaiming post-revolutionary France from atheism and unbelief. This effort resembled a cultural revolution, in that it instilled guilt, urged collective repentance and identified individual scapegoats. Above all, the missionaries warned against the dangers of pernicious literature. Sermons against *mauvais livres* were the immediate prelude to book-burnings, and the war against the Enlightenment was never so vigorous as in the years before 1830.

The missionaries attacked purchasers of *biens nationaux*. They asked for the 'restitution' of Church property lost, sold or purloined during the French Revolution. They preached fidelity to the king, but the message was reinforced by a reminder of the disasters which befell France following the abandonment of monarchist loyalties in 1793. The communal act of penitence was one of the key rituals of the mission. It was made to coincide as closely as possible with the anniversary of the death of Louis XVI on 21 January. In this way, the ceremony was manipulated to express collective repentance for the sins of the French Revolution.

In many ways, the Bourbon monarchy and the Catholic Church relied on each other for mutual support and justification. Indeed, conventional historians have often spoken of an alliance between 'throne and altar' governing Restoration France. In so doing, they echo the cry of contemporary liberals against the combined tyranny of monarchy and clericalism. This view is a simplistic one, for in their attitudes towards recent history, the monarchy and the Church did not see eye to eye. The monarchy, as we have seen, officially favoured the politics of forgetting, preferring not to debate the conflicts of the French Revolution for fear of resurrecting them. The Catholic missionaries, on the other hand, pursued the opposite policy. They referred constantly to the evils of the Revolution, the violation of Church property and the execution of Louis XVI. They wanted them remembered, and they wanted them punished.[19] Throne and altar thus found themselves on opposite sides when it came to dealing with the past. The king was more inclined to avoid conflict; but the Church was interested in collective guilt and repentance, not in healing the wounds. Catholic missionaries were the militants of a 'redemptive' solution to post-revolutionary problems.

They were fighting a rearguard action. In a longer perspective, the sacred nature of monarchy had been significantly eroded long before 1789 in a long-term trend towards the secularization of society and of all political authority. Many outbreaks of popular anticlericalism suggested the inexorable enfeeblement of religious authority. Such incidents frequently took the form of public demands for the performance in local theatres of Molière's play *Tartuffe*, his celebrated satire on the hypocrisy of the priesthood. *Tartuffe* became a literary weapon to attack the missionaries, the Catholic clergy and their alleged power over the government. Sheryl Kroen has chronicled 41 riots and incidents involving *Tartuffe* between 1825 and 1829, some of which developed into anticlerical street demonstrations lasting several days, as at Rouen in 1825, on the eve of Charles X's coronation.[20] Twenty-three

French departments experienced *Tartuffe* agitation, which implied the profundity of the regime's crisis of legitimacy.

Charles X's coronation in Rheims cathedral in 1825 presented the monarchy in its own theatre of power. Louis XVIII had never had a coronation, perhaps wisely, but Charles X felt the need for a ceremony which would wipe out the memory of Napoleon's imperial coronation, and reaffirm the legitimacy of the hereditary royal line. Charles X insisted on all the trappings of Old Regime pageantry. He succeeded in representing the monarchy as a medieval caricature of itself.

Rheims cathedral, scene of medieval coronations, had to be specially restored for the events. No expense was spared. Together with the lavish funeral of Louis XVIII, the coronation cost the enormous sum of 8 million francs.[21] A rood screen five metres high was specially constructed. Fashionable Gothic-style decorations were installed. The ceremony revived the legend of the Holy Ampulla (the holy balm allegedly carried from heaven by a dove for the baptism of Clovis, first king of the Franks, in 496). In a remarkable revival of the monarchy's obsolete claims to charismatic power, Charles administered the 'royal touch', to heal victims of scrofula, in Saint Marcoul hospital. But whereas 2400 had come to be touched by Louis XVI in 1775, only about 120 offered themselves for Charles X's touch in 1825 – an indication of the collapse of public faith in the monarch's claim to divine status.[22]

The years 1825 and 1826 were the high point of clerical reaction. These were the years of Villèle's ultra-royalist ministry, of Charles's coronation, of the law of sacrilege and the indemnity law in favour of the *émigrés*. After this point, the influence of the Church appeared to decline. Increasingly after 1827, Charles was depicted by the press as the Jesuit-King, the passive tool of power-hungry clerical machinations, even though after 1828 the Society of Jesus was forced to suspend educational work in France.[23] In the last years of the Bourbon Restoration, political conflicts and social tensions were further complicated by a deepening economic depression.

### An alternative style of monarchy

The popularity of Marie-Caroline, Duchesse de Berry, stood as a nagging criticism of the uncaring and distant nature of the Bourbon court.[24] As a royal couple, the duke and his Italian-born teenage duchess presented an image of royalty which was radically different from the stuffy traditions which then prevailed. They gave balls and parties. Marie-Caroline loved to dance. She rode the new Paris omnibus for a bet. She bathed in the sea at Dieppe. The couple was accessible, and could be seen walking in the Tuileries gardens. The duke publicly addressed Marie-Caroline with the informal 'tu', in complete violation of court protocol. This was a new and more open style of monarchy, which the Bourbon court did not ultimately accept. Marie-Caroline embodied the revolutionary proposition that royal women could aspire to more than just the mechanical production of male heirs.

When, in 1820, the duke was assassinated near the Opera by the Bonapartist Louvel, Marie-Caroline's behaviour was exemplary. Bloodstained and distraught, she cradled the dying duke. She wept buckets. She generously embraced his illegitimate daughters by his English mistress. She fainted on cue when he eventually died. She was the immaculate heroine of a real-life melodrama. Then she announced that she was pregnant and duly gave birth a few months later to the male heir for which the regime had been desperately waiting.

Marie-Caroline well knew that questions would be asked about this highly convenient posthumous birth. She was clear-headed in her extremity. In the hours immediately after the birth, she rounded up some National Guardsmen to witness in writing that the child was authentically hers. Four bemused strangers were ushered in to view the Duchess in all her nakedness, with the umbilical cord still attached to the baby. Some courtiers were furious. Not only had Marie-Caroline made an indecent exhibition of her royal nudity before complete (male) strangers, but the spectators of the royal vagina were a mere grocer, a pharmacist, a clerk and a wholesale merchant – hardly persons of honour and reputation. Marie-Caroline had pulled off a media coup, but the court was not impressed, and she never completely silenced those who found the arrival of a son at this point too convenient to be true.

It should be emphasized that Marie-Caroline was no democrat. She had ultra-royalist sympathies, and in 1832 she was involved in a royalist conspiracy and ended up in prison. Once again, she was found to be pregnant, this time by an unnamed father, and the news finished her reputation. She had nevertheless offered an alternative representation of monarchy – one in which royalty could show affection and have fun. It was a representation in which the monarchy mixed socially with the upper bourgeoisie and did not remain aloof from Parisian society. The image of monarchy she represented, however, was not the one envisioned by the Bourbon kings and their clerical supporters. Their closeted and hierarchical construction of the monarchy prevailed, and it was this version that was to be overthrown in the 1830 Revolution.

## Conclusion

The Bourbon regime was compelled to adapt to France's recent past of revolutionary upheaval and Napoleonic reform. It incorporated the essence of Napoleon's settlement with the Catholic Church, his educational and administrative reforms and his law codes. To call this regime a 'Restoration', then, is misleading, for there could never be a return to the pre-1789 system. The new monarchy of 1814, furthermore, was a parliamentary monarchy, based on a *de facto* Constitution, the Charter of 1814.

To some extent the Bourbons brought about their own downfall, through tactlessness and a lack of skill in dealing with their critics. The regime was attacked on both left and right for its compromises. For the ultra-royalists, many of whom had been political exiles for the last 20 years, there was not enough of a cathartic break with the previous regime. For the liberal opposition, the Charter was weak, the regime leaned too far towards its clerical supporters, and France was the pawn of the victorious Allies.

In 1829, Charles X appointed as prime minister his crony Polignac, a hard-line ultra-royalist who opposed the 1814 Charter and did not have a seat in parliament. The government immediately faced constitutional problems and an economic depression. Charles responded with a naked assertion of royal authority. He rejected the spirit of the Charter – an attitude fully in keeping with the reactionary policies of ultra-royalism. His Four Ordinances of 1830 sought to dissolve the hostile parliament, call new elections, restrict press freedom and impose further limits on voting rights. 'I should prefer to saw wood', Charles is reported to have said, 'than to be king under the conditions of the kings of England.'[25] In his rashness and refusal fully to accept the demands of a parliamentary system, he too bears some responsibility for the collapse of the regime.

The personal incompetence of the Bourbons, however, does not in itself explain all the difficulties of the Restoration. Their failure was partly a consequence of political factors they did not control, and only partly the result of their own obtuseness. The possibility of a smooth transition of power in 1814 was removed by Napoleon's return from Elba and the disruptive interlude of the Hundred Days. The White Terror which followed made it even more difficult to promote the cause of conciliation. Then the assassination of the Duke of Berry in 1820 produced another swing to the right.

In addition, there was a deeper failure of self-representation. Pierre Rosanvallon dubbed the Restoration 'the impossible monarchy', and at a fundamental level of political credibility, this verdict may with hindsight be convincing.[26] Ultimately, the Bourbon regime failed to come to terms with

France's recent past, and to fashion a role for the monarchy which would accommodate the lasting changes which had occurred during the Revolution, Consulate and Empire. Louis XVIII and his ministers tried to restrain both the moderate liberals and the unruly tendencies of the ultra-royalists. But the Bourbons did not succeed in reinventing themselves in their new post-revolutionary conditions. As Kroen concluded, the government made 'an impossible effort to return its population to a world where alternative ideologies did not exist'.[27] In other words, after 1793 the monarchy could no longer take itself for granted. The events of 1789–1815 had critically undermined the Bourbons' claim to be France's legitimate rulers. The governments of Louis XVIII and Charles X failed to resolve the crisis of legitimacy which plagued the early years of post-revolutionary Europe.

# 3 Conservatism and Political Repression, 1815–1830

## Metternich and conservatism

The Treaty of Vienna had reorganized the map of Europe, but the conservative powers still needed to put in place the mechanisms of control and political repression which they hoped would protect them from revolutionary upheavals. They used censorship, extensive police powers and the threat of their dank impregnable prisons. Almost everywhere, they called the influence of established religion to their aid. In Paris, a cardinal was entrusted with the Education Ministry. In Russia, the education portfolio was merged with the Ministry for Spiritual Affairs. In Spain the Inquisition and the Jesuits returned. In Piedmont, the state intervened to protect Catholic family values and marital fidelity.[1] All means of coercion, political and ideological, were applied to ensure quiescence. In his memoirs, the Piedmontese politician Massimo d'Azeglio identified the Restoration in Italy with a new kind of despotism, succinctly defined as 'Napoleon dressed as a Jesuit'.[2]

Meanwhile the worst subsistence crisis for decades brought widespread starvation and high mortality rates to Europe. The crisis of 1816–17 was the most terrible to affect the continent until the famines of 1846–7, and the resulting social tension exacerbated revolutionary threats, even in Great Britain. In the post-revolutionary years, the fear of another revolutionary outbreak dominated diplomacy and political thinking. As this chapter will show, the forces of European conservatism dealt successfully with attempted revolutions in Spain and Italy in 1820–1, and in Russia in 1825. Revolutionary forces were still too weak to offer a serious threat. They produced bungled coups and inglorious martyrs, but had little political impact.

The Austrian Chancellor Metternich was the leading figure in the organization of repression in continental Europe. Metternich was a Rhinelander by birth, dispossessed of his aristocratic title and property by the French conquest of Germany. In the service of Vienna, he had found a way to devote his considerable political and diplomatic talents to the conservative cause. He spent his life trying to contain two forces which he could not permanently control: the first was Napoleon, and the second the movement for constitutionalism and national autonomy which was to erupt and bury him in the 1848 revolutions.

Metternich defended the traditional ruling classes of Europe – the landed aristocracies – and pinned his faith on the conservative peasant masses to defeat the subversive intellectuals he despised. He hated his revolutionary opponents. The Neapolitans who rose up in 1820 were in his opinion 'a barbarous half-African people', and as for Greece, it was a 'vast sewer open to all revolutionaries'.[3] In his fantasy he sometimes imagined a secret revolutionary committee, based in Paris, acting as the nerve centre directing sedition all over Europe. Under Metternich, Austria's role was to supervise counter-insurgency operations in Germany and Italy. As Talleyrand put it, 'Austria is Europe's House of Lords: so long as it is not dissolved, it will keep the Commons in check.'[4]

Metternich's policy was one of active armed intervention to put down revolutionary outbreaks wherever they occurred. This would only work in weak states where Austria was already influential. For example, sending troops against insurrections in small Italian states was a practical possibility: invading France when revolution broke out in Paris in 1830 was not. It would have provoked a full-scale war against a great European power. Armed interventions inspired by Metternich were successful (from a conservative point of view), but he only intervened when he was certain of victory.

The policy had its limitations and its contradictions. The British were reluctant to sanction armed intervention to suppress revolution. When the British did eventually intervene, in Portugal in 1825, Palmerston supported the constitutional liberals against the Miguelists, who were among the most reactionary monarchists in Europe. In Castlereagh's thinking, the system of regular congresses set up after 1815 had a limited security role. He refused to regard the Quadruple Alliance as a war machine. 'The alliance', he said, 'was made against France. It was never intended as a union for the government of the world, or for the superintendence of the affairs of other states.'[5]

Metternich had a broader conception of the alliance; its principal aims were not just to contain French aggression, but also to restrain Russian power. When the threat of a Russian presence in Greece loomed in the 1820s, Metternich would rally the alliance to prevent Russian encroachment. Metternich, then, was no dogmatist. When Austrian interests demanded intervention against incipient revolutions, he pursued intervention; when Austrian interests dictated steps to minimize Russian influence in the Balkans, then he opposed intervention.

Metternich was a statesman on a European scale, but his domestic power base in Vienna was fragile. While he worked for the peace of Europe, the apparatus of government in the Habsburg Empire was never modernized. Austria had in fact been reduced to bankruptcy by the Napoleonic wars. It could not even afford to maintain its own army without sending one-third of it on leave at any one time. Metternich's active foreign policy, then, was ultimately beyond Austria's own resources. 'I may have governed Europe occasionally', reflected Metternich, 'but Austria never.'[6] He struggled to get the better of his political rival Kolowrat and, after 1835, he faced the extra difficulty of dealing with a mentally retarded ruler, the Emperor Ferdinand I.

Until 1848, Metternich worked to preserve the integrity of conservative Europe as far as was practical. He became enemy number one for liberal and nationalist conspirators all over Europe. In the long run nationalist forces would dominate, but for 30 years Metternich successfully kept them at bay. Even in moments of triumph, he developed a very clear-sighted sense of his own futility. 'I spend my time shoring up crumbling edifices', he lamented in 1822. In this instance the crumbling edifice in question was probably the dilapidated monarchy of Bourbon Naples. But the metaphor may describe his policies more generally. He knew that the Old Regime values on which aristocratic power was based were in decline, and he knew at the same time that his power to protect conservative interests was also waning. He confided in Churchillian terms to the Russian diplomat Nesselrode in 1830:

> My most intimate opinion is that the old Europe is at the beginning of its end. Having decided to die with it, I will do my duty, and this is not only my intention, but also the Emperor's. In any case, the new Europe is only at its beginning. Between the end and the beginning there will be chaos.[7]

It is now time to turn to Metternich's chaos, and to his attempts to impose order on it.

## Metternich's policy in Germany

Through the German Confederation, established in 1815, Metternich extended Austrian influence in Germany, and tried to secure the co-operation of other German states in improving security against subversive threats. The Confederation had only a very loose organizational structure, and its existence hardly impinged on the sovereignty of individual states. Nevertheless, it served Metternich's purpose. He prevented Prussia from dominating the fate of Germany, and he exploited revolutionary panics to persuade German rulers to adopt new forms of censorship and repression.

During the Napoleonic period, the smaller states had benefited enormously from the reorganization and secularization of Germany carried out by the French. The southern states of Baden, Bavaria and Württemberg had been enlarged and strengthened. Rather than challenge the gains of these German states, Metternich supported the sovereignty of their rulers, and defended them both against Prussian influence and revolutionaries. At the same time, he pushed them towards federal measures against liberal-constitutional movements.

Surprisingly, considering their anti-liberal stance, several German states had acquired a constitution after 1815. Bavaria and Baden introduced constitutions in 1818, and Württemberg followed in 1819. There was little, however, in these German constitutions which would alarm conservatives. They were granted by the grace and favour of the monarchs, who retained extensive powers. A corporate model prevailed, redolent of Old Regime social structures. In Bavaria, for example, one-quarter of the seats in the lower house was reserved for representatives of the nobility and the Churches. Lower-house elections were indirect, and voting rights were usually highly restricted by a property qualification. According to the constitution of Nassau, only 70 males in the principality were wealthy enough to qualify for the vote. In Bavaria, only 6 per cent of adult males could vote.[8] In spite of these limitations, however, parliamentary forums now existed in the 'third Germany' (outside Prussia and Austria) where political life could later develop.

In Prussia, on the other hand, any steps towards a constitutional monarchy were blocked by King Frederick William III with Metternich's full approval. The Prussian reform movement, led by Stein and Hardenberg after the catastrophic defeat at Jena in 1806, now came to a dead-end. It had introduced the abolition of serfdom with compensation for landlords, and established the *Landwehr*, the reserve army based on universal conscription, but these would be the limits of its achievement. With the dismissal of Humboldt in 1819, hopes for a constitution were dashed. All the same, Prussia, unlike its Russian neighbour, was a bureaucratic state which operated under the rule of law, defined in its general law code, the *Allgemeines Landrecht* (although Napoleonic codes were still the basis of the legal system in the Prussian Rhineland).

A nascent German nationalist movement appeared amongst university students in Jena, Heidelberg and other centres. The student leagues (*Burschenschaften*) will be discussed further in Chapter 5, but they sent shock-waves through the drawing-rooms of Germany when a Jena University theology student assassinated the elderly playwright Kotzebue in 1819. Metternich confided to Friedrich von Gentz his firm belief that the assassination was informed by the collective decision of a 'secret alliance'.[9] No such conspiracy existed except in Metternich's imagination, but he used the Kotzebue assassination as an excuse to put into place an extensive apparatus of censorship and police repression. In the Carlsbad Decrees of 1819, Metternich persuaded Prussia and the German states to co-operate in the censorship of published works and seditious university teaching. If one member of the Confederation was to ask for a book to be banned, all the member states would implement it. Austria banned the works of Rousseau, Goethe and Schiller, and the Austrian playwright Grillparzer declared that anyone, like himself, who kept working under such conditions was a hero.[10] If a university professor was dismissed in one city, the rest of the Confederation would refuse to employ him. This was not just a theoretical possibility: the brothers Grimm were both removed by the King of Hanover from their university positions at Göttingen. Police inspectors would henceforth be planted in lecture theatres, and governments had wide-ranging powers over university administration. The Investigation Law (*Untersuchungsgesetz*) set up a central office to uncover all 'revolutionary undertakings and demagogic connections'.[11] The fear of revolution in the wake of the Kotzebue murder drove Prussia and the other states into the arms of Metternich.

Five years later, the Carlsbad decrees were renewed by the Confederation. Metternich had paradoxically achieved a rare display of German unity in support of continued political repression. Historians have habitually searched this period for the origins and precursors of German national unity, finding them usually in the Prussian Customs Union (*Zollverein*) of the 1830s. The Carlsbad Decrees, however, might be seen as the fullest expression of pan-German co-operation in the post-revolutionary years.

## Metternich's policy in Italy

Austrian influence was predominant in post-revolutionary Italy, too. Habsburg garrisons reassured hesitant rulers who looked to Vienna for protection against a recurrence of revolutionary violence. Only the state of Piedmont, where the monarchy was equally afraid of revolution, aspired to an independent role. The efficiency, however, of Metternich-inspired repression must be questioned. The risings of 1820–1 in the south caught conservatives on the hop.

The provinces of Lombardy and Venetia were under direct Habsburg rule, and had no effective autonomy whatsoever. The administration was run by non-Italian officials, usually Tyroleans, and even the mayors (*podestà*) of large cities were appointed by Vienna. The Empire imposed customs barriers to protect Austrian commercial interests, and there was a strong local suspicion that the Habsburgs were milking their lucrative Italian provinces to reduce the Empire's enormous deficit, and there was some truth in this. Although the Austrian educational system was progressive by Italian standards, Austrian consumption taxes and the tobacco monopoly were resented, as was the poll-tax, inherited from Napoleon, until it was abolished by the revolutionaries of 1848. Venice, however, remained calm, which has prompted the historian David Laven to question the conventional assumption that Habsburg rule was tyrannical and oppressive.[12] According to Laven, Napoleon was perceived as an even greater tyrant, and as long as Venetians remembered French rule they accepted the lesser evil of the Habsburgs. The Austrian bureaucracy moved at a snail's pace, but provided the best administration in Italy.

Under Habsburg constraints Venice continued its long-term decline, but the economy of Lombardy maintained its momentum. An increasingly commercialized agricultural sector supplied a booming London silk market. Milan was already well-connected with the European economy by the St Gotthard pass and it was here above all that a threat to Austrian rule was to take shape. Milan, in contrast to Venice, had a more positive memory of Napoleon, who had made the city his Italian capital; the Milanese were thus more likely to regard the Habsburgs as their enemies.

In Piedmont-Sardinia, the Savoyard monarchy returned in 1815 and King Vittorio Emanuele reimposed the dead hand of religious conformity. Although Piedmont aspired to a degree of independence both from France and Austria, it was now one of the most reactionary of all Italian states. Vittorio Emanuele was an out-and-out absolutist who envisaged no constraints on his personal authority. To assist his favourite courtiers, the king thought nothing of personally ordering law cases to be reopened.[13] All important posts went to nobles who had followed the king into his Sardinian exile. The Jesuits were welcomed back in 1818, freemasonry was banned, and in the words of the historian Giorgio Candeloro, 'a heavy atmosphere of bigotry spread over the whole kingdom'.[14] A law against sacrilege was introduced. Jews had a 9 p.m. curfew and were excluded from public office.

On the other hand, there were important continuities with the Napoleonic regime. Although the king abolished all French legislation, he needed to retain the French tax system, the French conscription system, and a Piedmontese version of the French *gendarmerie*. The Napoleonic sale of Church property (the *beni nazionali*) was irreversible, and there was no vendetta against ex-supporters of the French. The booming port of Genoa was now part of Piedmont, which opened up new horizons – both Italian and international – for this otherwise backward-looking regime.

Tuscany retained the reputation for moderate and enlightened government which had originated in the reforms of the Habsburg Grand Duke Leopold in the 1780s. French rule had been accepted, and Napoleon's sale of Church property had resolved the government's debt problems. Savings banks developed, and the old landed money of the Florentine nobility now started to merge its investments with the 'new money' of the commercial bourgeoisie of Livorno.[15] Work was begun in the 1820s to drain and desalinate the Maremma marshes, which reduced the incidence of malaria. This was a major effort and a model of progressive administration. Tuscany still remained a Habsburg satellite. According to tradition, Grand Duke Ferdinand III was the Emperor's younger brother.

In the Papal States, the administration remained exclusively in clerical hands, and the Austrians maintained military bases in the Romagna. Here, and in the kingdom of Naples and Sicily, secret societies like the *Carbonari* proliferated, and they became the focus of many discontents, including the cause of Sicilian separatism. In Rome, Cardinal Consalvi introduced administrative reforms, in spite of extremist opposition from the reactionary *zelanti*. Consalvi had Metternich's support, which serves as a reminder that Austrian influence was not uniformly reactionary. In Tuscany, it supported enlightened reform, and in Lombardy-Venetia the Habsburgs reintegrated some Napoleonic personnel into the bureaucracy. Metternich realized that completely reactionary regimes would provoke revolutions, and this in turn would enable the French to regain some leverage in Italian affairs. In Italy, then, traditional Habsburg rivalry with the French was closely entangled with Vienna's counter-revolutionary strategies.

The small duchies of Parma, Piacenza and Modena stretched 'like a garter across the leg of Italy', in Metternich's own flirtatious phrase, but if trouble brewed in the Papal States, they would become the front-line of the counter-revolution. This is exactly what was to happen after the election of Pius IX in 1846.[16] Parma, with a population of about 30,000, was entrusted to Napoleon's wife Marie Louise, who was a Habsburg and a reliable ally of Austria, and her lover Count Neipperg. Their rule has a reputation for progress and enlightenment, but taxation was heavy, and it had to finance her miniature court and a useless army. Censorship was in complete Austrian control.[17]

In fact a censorship regime was imposed all over Italy, but this was nothing new – after all, Napoleon too had insisted on the pre-publication scrutiny of texts. In Lombardy, neither Napoleonic nor Austrian censorship was harsh enough to hinder the development of a flourishing publishing industry in Milan, which became the centre of the Italian book trade and perhaps the cultural capital of Italy.[18] The works of the eighteenth-century Enlightenment were banned in Lombardy-Venetia, including those of Rousseau, Diderot and Voltaire. Macchiavelli was on the Austrian black-list, as were the Italian poets Alfieri and Foscolo.[19] The system was regularly evaded, as proscribed literature could be smuggled in from Switzerland, and forbidden books were freely imported into Italy through the port of Livorno in Tuscany. At the same time, personal mail was intercepted, there were restrictions on travel and government spies and *agents provocateurs* infiltrated secret societies.

## The 'movements' of 1820–1821 in Italy, Spain and Portugal

Metternich's police kept Habsburg lands free of conspiracies; but he was constantly taken by surprise. In 1846, the election of a Pope apparently sympathetic to liberalism was catastrophic for Metternich's interests. In 1820–1, risings occurred in Naples, Piedmont and Spain which required a response.

The 'movements' (*moti*) of 1820 – as Italian historians call them – were the work of discontented army officers inspired by the democratic Spanish Constitution of 1812. Before its work was annulled by the return of King Fernando VII, the revolutionary Cortez (or parliament) of Cadiz had proclaimed universal male suffrage and a modern constitutional regime. This remained an important slogan and reference point for democratic movements (although whether the Neapolitan revolutionaries had actually read it is another matter). The rising of 1820 in Naples owed much to the secret society of the *Carbonari*, who unfurled their tricolour of blue, black and red and lit the beacons of revolution (literally) on the hilltops around Avellino. Army officers, always a potential revolutionary force in developing societies, together with the Neapolitan bourgeoisie, quickly triumphed and an elected parliament met in Naples, the first ever to do so. About a half of its membership had served in the administrations of the French revolutionary and Napoleonic period.[20]

The 'movement' of Naples was almost entirely bloodless; the rising in Palermo, capital of Sicily, however, was more violent, as the workers and guilds took temporary control of the city. Palermo wanted to be free of rule from Naples, but the new Neapolitan parliament was hostile to Sicilian separatism. While Neapolitans accordingly sent troops against the Sicilian revolution, Austrian troops put an end to the revolution in Naples itself and restored the monarchy to its full authority. The Bourbon regime, without the loyalty of its army, had yielded to the revolution immediately but, with the Austrian army behind it, it crushed the opposition easily. The *Carbonari* had never been able to mobilize the masses behind the cause of constitutionalism.

Count Santarosa's short-lived rebellion in Piedmont captured the citadel of Alessandria and proclaimed the Spanish Constitution of 1812. It was most notable for the surprise abdication of King Vittorio Emanuele in favour of Prince Carlo Alberto. He was soon replaced by the conservative Carlo Felice, who as the elder brother was the rightful heir to the throne. The young Carlo Alberto had met Santarosa personally and flirted for a time with the revolutionaries. His equivocal position made him for the time being *persona non grata* with the dynasty. The appearance of Austrian troops was sufficient to disperse the rebels. They went into exile, but did not necessarily abandon their struggle. Santarosa, for example, was to fight and die in 1825 in the war of Greek Independence.[21]

In Spain the return to the throne of Fernando VII encouraged the rejection of liberalism and strengthened the power of clericalism. The Inquisition was restored in 1814, and the Jesuits returned. Many army officers were retired on half-pay and their discontent was a factor in 1820. The monarchy, which could not afford to pay its army, even passed a law making soldiers' complaints illegal.[22] Moreover, the risings of 1820 in Spain occurred against a background of economic crisis. Spain had a huge trade deficit, and a backward agrarian system in which seigneurialism persisted. The enormous lands of the Church were an obstacle to the development of commercial agriculture. The domestic market was not well-integrated, and an antiquated fiscal system actually produced declining tax revenue for the monarchy. In these circumstances, the loss of the American colonies after 1814 was disastrous for the financial stability of the state.[23]

Since the Peninsular War against Napoleon, the military staked a claim to political power. Not surprisingly, the rebellion broke out amongst the army in Cadiz, as troops were waiting there to depart for another unpopular expedition to South America. The revolt took the peculiarly Spanish form of a *pronunciamento*, the issuing of a revolutionary manifesto by a group of army officers claiming to represent the popular will. A liberal constitutional experiment was then installed. Fernando VII was forced to accept the 1812 Constitution and summon a Cortes. The Great Powers hesitated: Metternich did not wish to fall into the same Spanish trap that had paralysed Napoleon when he had invaded in 1808. Nor did he wish to see a

Russian army moving into Spain, as the Tsar Alexander suggested it should. Instead, the army of Bourbon France played the policing role on this occasion, invading Spain in 1823 and restoring the absolute monarchy. The Church, which had so bitterly opposed the French in the Napoleonic era, now blessed their presence.

In 1833, however, a new phase of struggle began, in which Spanish liberals and constitutionalists defended the claims of King Fernando's daughter Isabella against the monarchist extremists who supported the claims of his brother, Don Carlos. These were the Carlists, described by the historian Raymond Carr as classic counter-revolutionaries. They refused to accept liberalism, freemasonry or any threat to their image of a united and traditionally Catholic Spain. Like the French ultra-royalists, they represented 'a revolution of frustration, a revolution of the inadaptables'.[24] They were strongest in Navarre and the solidly Catholic Basque provinces, but waged a losing battle against the constitutional monarchy and the British Navy. A new Constitution was introduced in 1837, but Spain had become peripheral to the strategies of the Great Powers and they could afford to ignore it.

In 1821, a liberal Constitution was also forced on the Portuguese monarchy, leading (as in Spain) to a period of warfare between monarchist reactionaries (Miguelists in Portugal) and constitutionalists backed by Britain. The Miguelist cause was supported by loyalist peasantry in the north. The constitutionalists, on the other hand, relied on sections of the intelligentsia and the commercial elite in Oporto, Portugal's second city. In 1820, the liberals aimed to end the British occupation and restore the empire. In their eyes, Britain had 'stolen' their prized Brazilian market for wine and textiles. They failed in both these aims.

King João VI died in 1826, and his son Dom Pedro decided to stay in Brazil, rashly leaving the defence of the crown and the Constitution to his 7-year-old daughter the Infanta Doña Maria. This was a recipe for civil war. Dom Miguel seized the throne in 1827 and tore up the Constitution. Only in 1835 was the situation stabilized and the Miguelist threat neutralized. Without British aid, liberals were too weak to establish themselves in Portugal.

The fragile condition of liberalism on the Iberian peninsula in 1820–1 showed the risks involved when an army tried to introduce a liberal-bourgeois constitution without a strong bourgeoisie to defend it. Furthermore, the revolutionaries in Spain and Italy lacked support from the lower classes who remained indifferent to their political programme. When the forces of the Spanish revolutionary Major Riego marched through Andalusia in 1820, no-one came to support them and nobody tried to stop them either.

Equally, when the French invaded Spain in 1823, there was no significant resistance. This divorce between the conspirators and the masses was a structural weakness for the revolutionary movements of this period.

When liberal regimes did come to power, as in Spain in 1820–3 and Naples in 1820–1, the limitations of their policies were clearly revealed. They inherited much from the authoritarian monarchies they briefly replaced. These new regimes were in no sense republican. Although Spanish liberalism was viscerally anticlerical, and the Church was a landowner on a massive scale, there was no serious attempt by revolutionaries in 1820 to introduce thoroughgoing agrarian reform. In both Naples and Spain, the liberal revolutionaries defended the integrity of the monarchical state. The Neapolitans did not accept Sicilian autonomy; nor would the Spanish liberals abandon Spain's vanishing American empire. For all their constitutional radicalism, they did not embark on radical social reform and they remained loyal to a tradition of the unitary state.

The 'movements' of 1820–1 had shown the power of the forces of repression marshalled by Metternich. The Austrian army stayed in Piedmont until 1823, and left Naples only in 1827. The trial and imprisonment of dozens of Italian revolutionaries severely weakened the liberal and nationalist cause. At the same time, the events in Italy also contained some encouraging messages for revolutionaries: they revealed an extraordinary level of political radicalism in the so-called 'backward' countries of the European periphery. The lasting inspiration of Napoleonic rule was partly responsible for this. It was significant that, without Austrian bayonets to back them up, regimes in Spain, Piedmont and Naples had crumbled easily. Clearly the absolutists could not rely on the loyalty of their own armies.

## Threats of revolution in Britain, 1817–1820

Historians have often treated Britain as a world apart from continental Europe in this period. In the immediate postwar period, British society was troubled by the early consequences of mechanization and suffered the same cyclical economic depression in which the rest of Europe floundered. Britain, too, faced high food prices and unemployment. The same antagonism between conspiracy and repression which characterized continental politics was echoed, with important variations, in Britain.

In 1816, public demonstrations in Spa Fields, east of London, reflected the discontent of artisans and craft workers in a time of acute misery, and they worried the authorities. In the following year, the Seditious Meetings Act banned meetings of more than 50 people held without magistrates' permission. In 1817, the right of *habeas corpus* was suspended, so that suspects could be imprisoned without being charged with a specific crime. Conspiracies were hatched in London pubs, but they were always likely to include a government informer or *agent provocateur*, like the spy Oliver who was part of many radical networks.

British radicalism, however, differed significantly from European movements. For one thing, it aimed at the reform of a corrupt and unrepresentative Parliament. One of its favoured weapons was the petition, sometimes signed by hundreds of thousands of supporters, in favour of an extension of voting rights which would secure working-class representation. British revolutionary threats were certainly exaggerated by the authorities. Peaceful petitioning was far more significant than lunatic conspiracies. A fundamental respect for Parliament and the power of the vote were to be foundations of the Chartist movement in the 1840s. British reformers may have been dubbed 'Jacobins', echoing the radicalism of the French Revolution, but their inspiration had largely English roots. They drew on a long tradition of radical Dissent reaching back to the English Revolution of the 1640s, and envisaged the recovery of democratic rights which were grounded in history, and which formed the Englishman's mythical 'lost birthright'.

British radicalism was essentially provincial. Whereas in France, Paris was the centre of power, and therefore the centre of attempts to overthrow it, British radicalism thrived far from the capital in places like Leicester, Nottingham, Yorkshire and Lancashire. Here there were concentrations of artisans, weavers and other textile or metal workers whose livelihood was threatened by mechanization and low wages. Jeremiah Brandreth, who led a small army of workers to march on Nottingham in 1817 (the 'Pentridge Rising'), was himself an unemployed stocking-maker. His motley band fled at the first sight of troops. The rather ridiculous Pentridge Rising indicates another difference between Britain and the continent: in Britain, radical working-class groups did exist in these agitated years, and were ready to act in the cause of reform without middle-class leaders.

These two aspects of British radicalism – the drive for parliamentary reform and its lower-class dimension – came together in the huge, but disastrous rally held at St Peter's Fields outside Manchester in 1819. A peaceful demonstration of over 60 000 was dispersed by force. At least 11 were killed, and hundreds more sabred or trampled by cavalry. This event, known satirically as the Peterloo massacre, was a horrific expression of class panic.[25] It was immediately followed by the Six Acts, the British government's equivalent of Metternich's Carlsbad Decrees. New legislation gave police and magistrates wider powers of search and arrest in cases of sedition or seditious libel. In addition, it banned political rallies and raised the stamp duty on periodicals in order to stifle the radical press. This drove a few men to desperate remedies. In 1820, Arthur Thistlewood organized the abortive Cato Street Conspiracy, which aimed to assassinate the entire cabinet.

These were isolated conspiracies. They often involved small working-class groups, which distinguished them from the top-hatted and well-educated rebels of continental Europe (see Plate 2). They tended to draw their support from domestic and skilled workers in depressed trades, notably the weavers, who were reacting to low wages and unemployment. The Peterloo massacre of 1819 was unique in Europe, because it indicated mass support for peaceful reform.

In the British context, the culture of repression was also different. Although Peterloo and the Six Acts have direct European parallels, there were some things a British government could not get away with. For one

*Plate 2*   The arrest of *Carbonari* in Lombardy. Note the rebels' elegant dress
*Source:*   Engraving in Museo del Risorgimento, Milan (*Arresto di carbonari Lombardi*).

thing, a radical press existed. The government could make the circulation of a paper like Wooler's *Black Dwarf* difficult and expensive, but it was nevertheless legal. Furthermore, in order to convict suspects of treason or seditious libel, the prosecution had to convince a jury, and London juries showed themselves very prone to acquit if they thought government tactics were too 'despotic'. This is a problem Metternich never had to face.

After 1820, prosperity began to return, and the tense agitation of the postwar years dissipated. The violent repression of Peterloo would not be repeated. When the radical programme gathered strength again in 1830–2, Parliament would respond with concessions.

## Revolution and repression in Russia

In 1815, Tsar Alexander I had preserved the continuity of a Polish state under Russian auspices (Congress Poland). Furthermore, he granted Poland a Constitution, something Russia itself did not enjoy. This seemed to vindicate the policy of collaboration with Russia defended by the aristocratic Polish nationalist Adam Czartoryski. Czartoryski took comfort in the existence of a Polish parliament (the 'Diet' or Sejm), an independent judiciary and a Polish army. Apparently some degree of Polish autonomy could be preserved within the Russian connection.[26]

Gradually, however, the truly repressive nature of Russian domination became apparent, for Tsarist Russia typified in an extreme form the authoritarian conservatism we have already encountered elsewhere in post-revolutionary Europe. The Sejm was only summoned four times before 1830, and in 1820 censorship was reintroduced, even though the Constitution guaranteed press freedom. Real power lay not with the Sejm, but with the army, commanded by Grand Duke Constantine, and the army's political role became crucial. In 1820, Alexander suppressed the Semenovsky mutiny and, as a result of this scare, sporadic political repression continued. The regiment was disbanded, Masonic lodges were banned in 1819, and in 1825, the Tsar ordered the end of all public debates in the Sejm. The last years of Alexander's reign were marked by a retreat from his earlier reforming impulses.

In 1825, on the death of Alexander I, the Decembrist revolt broke out in St Petersburg, and its suppression inaugurated a new phase of reaction under Tsar Nicholas I. The Decembrist revolt sprang once again from the elite guards regiments. Like the political struggles in Spain and Portugal, this Russian uprising took the form of a succession dispute, for the rebels supported the candidacy of Constantine, thinking, probably mistakenly, that he was responsive to their demands for representative government. Unknown to the rebels, Constantine had already abdicated his rights in favour of his brother Nicholas. As a rebellion in the name of the Tsar, therefore, the Decembrist revolt was doomed from the start – it had attached itself to the wrong Tsar. The rising proved hopelessly incompetent. The nominated leader, Prince Trubetskoi, had second thoughts and did not show up. The rebels killed the governor-general of St Petersburg, but then over 500 Decembrist suspects were arrested without difficulty.

This aspect of the Decembrist revolt recalls the traditional palace *coups* familiar to students of medieval Russian history. But Decembrism had a deeper meaning. It was a landmark in the history of Russian revolutionary movements, and its significance was to be recognized by Lenin as part of the prehistory of Bolshevism. The Decembrist manifesto demanded representative government and the end of autocracy, the end of censorship, religious toleration and the end of serfdom. Prince Trubetskoi's Manifesto for the 'Northern Society' of Decembrists specifically called for the 'abolition of property rights over persons', prefiguring a change in the legal status of the serf.[27] In the more ambitious 'Southern Society', Pavel Ivanovich Pestel advocated serf emancipation coupled with collective landownership by the village commune. This was the first time a revolutionary movement had so radically addressed this fundamental problem of Russian society.

Russia was overwhelmingly a peasant society – over 90 per cent of the population lived on the land. In the 1830s, the factory proletariat of the Empire numbered a mere half a million workers, less than one per cent of Russia's total population. By almost every criterion we may invoke, Russia was underdeveloped by Western standards. Levels of urbanization were very low. There was a very low per capita income. Perhaps two-thirds of the population was illiterate. The Tsars were complete autocrats – in other words, their personal will was supreme. Serfs were owned by their landowners like goods and chattels. They owed the lords labour service and complete obedience. Serfs could be beaten, locked up, or simply sold by their landlord. Technically, they could appeal to a local court against seigneurial injustices, but since these courts were run by other landlords, they were most unlikely to receive satisfaction. Serfs had little remedy against a cruel landlord except either to flee or to rise up in one of the ferocious outbreaks of bloody protest which punctuated the history of the Russian countryside. Decembrism helped to put the reform of serfdom on the agenda.

Decembrism, furthermore, revealed the influence of Western liberal thinking on Russian revolutionary movements. Certainly, Russia had its own distinctive problems which Western reformers did not always address.

Most Russian revolutionaries, however, had imbibed some of their political radicalism from contact with Western Europe. Many Decembrists were young officers who had seen service in the Napoleonic wars, and had been part of the army of occupation in Paris in 1814–15. Visiting a Western capital for the first time, they had seen at first hand the nature of Western European economic progress and constitutional thinking. This experience led many to make comparisons and to question the institutions of their own country. Their eyes had been opened, and they returned home with a new critical attitude towards Russian economic stagnation and political authoritarianism. Thus the intellectual development of the Decembrists connected them closely to the European post-revolutionary ferment. Pestel even envisaged a 'Jacobin' dictatorship in French revolutionary style, and thought it advisable to put the royal family to death.

The Decembrists illustrate the importance to the Russian revolutionary movement of the *intelligentsia* – significantly a Russian concept. The *intelligentsia* refers to the educated classes in general, most of whom in this period were aristocrats. But they remained socially isolated, and were chronically incapable of generating a widespread rebellion involving the masses. As Marc Raeff has argued, they had increasingly become strangers in their own country, educated abroad or by private foreign tutors, speaking French and dressing fashionably in English clothes, acquiring at least a veneer of Western culture.[28] They were frustrated Hamlets – misfits coming home to find something rotten in their own state. In Tolstoy's novel *War and Peace*, members of the Moscow nobility made the uncomfortable discovery in 1812 that they had more in common with the invading French officers than with lower-class Russians.[29] A few aristocrats developed a bad conscience about their position as serf-owners. They felt estranged from fellow Russians. They dabbled in revolution, but had no effective strategy for political action.

Out of 36 death sentences passed on the Decembrists, only five were actually carried out. 121 rebels were sentenced to hard labour, exile to Siberia or punitive military service.[30] The new Tsar Nicholas I drew simple conclusions from the Decembrist revolt: the nobility could never be trusted, and repression was needed. He was reputed to keep a list of the Decembrist nobility always on his desk, as a permanent reminder of their treachery.[31] He imposed a cultural quarantine on Russia, to prevent Western ideas from contaminating the minds of his subjects, and to prevent Russians from going abroad and catching the Western liberal disease. A Tsarist-style 'iron curtain' came down over Russia in the 1830s and 1840s. A new political police was established – the notorious Third Department. It spied on religious schismatics, foreigners, the army and on the *intelligentsia*. For Dubbelt, the xenophobic Director of the Third Department after 1839, foreigners were 'snakes whom Russia warms with her sunshine and as she does so they creep out and bite her'. It exchanged information regularly with Metternich. Yet in spite of its wide brief, the Third Department was not always as effective as its reputation implied. In 1836, it had a staff of only a little over 4000 to carry out its task of national surveillance over a vast Empire.[32] It proved unable to detect a conspiracy when it happened in St Petersburg right under its nose. When another plot emerged in 1849 (the Petrashevsky conspiracy) it was actually uncovered by the ordinary city police.

## Conclusion

Until the late 1820s, the Great Powers dealt successfully with uprisings and conspiracies of nationalists, constitutionalists and radicals. They had put in place a powerful apparatus of censorship, espionage and repression, backed up by the teachings of established religion. Metternich had made sure that no revolutionary outbreak occurred within the Habsburg Empire, and he successfully enlisted German and Italian rulers in the counter-revolutionary cause. In Britain and Russia, the only government response in this period was a repressive one.

To some extent, the conservative regimes exaggerated the danger to stability. Perhaps Metternich did so deliberately, in order to frighten German and Italian states into co-operating with his system of surveillance. How strong, then, *were* the revolutionary movements of these years? As yet, their ideological foundations in liberalism and nationalism failed to find mass support. Their strength lay, first, in groups of the educated classes, either aristocratic or middle-class, and second, in the postwar armies, where disgruntled junior officers aspired to a political role. Disaffected social elites and utopian romantics would not succeed without a secure base among urban workers. Only in Britain was the government faced with clumsy attempts to organize specifically working-class resistance. Not until 1830, and more explosively in 1848, did economic change provide revolutionary leaders with the armies of threatened artisans and journeymen they needed to topple regimes. As a consequence of this weakness, these movements depended for their success or failure on the foreign powers. Austria still determined the fate of Italy and Germany, and Russia that of Poland. France absorbed Spain into its sphere of influence in 1823, and Portugal remained part of Britain's informal Empire.

Chinks appeared, however, in the armour of political repression. The effort to control and anticipate subversion was not completely effective. In spite of literary censorship in Germany, publishing expanded and print became an important medium for the dissemination of the concept of national unity. The uprisings of 1820 took Metternich by surprise. The Tsarist regime had not infiltrated the Decembrist movement. Furthermore, the common international front against post-revolutionary conspiracies was not easy to maintain in the face of continuing Great Power antagonisms. As we shall see in Chapter 5, the unity of the conservative powers was to be severely tested in 1827. The powers then faced an uprising in Greece which proved much more complicated to resolve than the 'movements' of 1815-25. In the Greek War of Independence, rivalries between the Great Powers and the fear of Russian expansion eclipsed their hostility towards nationalist movements.

# 4 The Underground Republic: Opposition Movements, 1815–1848

## The four sergeants of La Rochelle

Jean-François Bories was a sergeant-major in the 45th Infantry Regiment posted from Paris to La Rochelle on the west coast of France. In February 1822, he and three young fellow sergeants tried to organize a mutiny in their garrison. Brandishing a banner proclaiming support for Napoleon II and a constitution, they hoped to link up with other military risings planned to break out in western France. Without effective support, they were soon arrested and guillotined. The 'four sergeants of La Rochelle' became instant romantic heroes, celebrated as legendary martyrs in the liberal cause. They even had a camembert cheese named after them.

The abysmal failure of the sergeants of La Rochelle illustrates some features of the conspiratorial movements of the immediate post-revolutionary era. Bories and his hapless colleagues had formed a cell of the *Carbonari*, or 'charcoal-burners', a clandestine revolutionary organization with many followers in France and even more in Italy. Like many other rebels of this period, they were soldiers, they were young and they were incompetent. The series of military plots in which the sergeants thought they were involved were all exposed before they had even begun. Such inept operations would have made a schoolboy cadet camp look like the execution of the Schlieffen Plan. Finally, in defending Napoleon and a constitution, the sergeants remind us that the causes of liberalism, Bonapartism and republicanism were sometimes hardly distinguishable in the Bourbon period.

This chapter considers the different sources and networks of opposition movements, such as republicanism, Bonapartism and, later on, socialism. These movements frequently overlapped. Revolutionary ideologies were vague and shapeless, so that French republicanism could at times embrace liberal monarchists and Bonapartists. The distinguishing features of the rebels, whatever their political hue, were bravery and incoherence. This chapter will also consider some of the techniques of revolution in this romantic phase, including the secret society and the street barricade. They

56

all belonged, however loosely, to what the historian Alan Spitzer called the 'underground republic'.[1]

## The frustrations of youth

To argue that young people experience frustration is to state the obvious. In the period after 1815, however, there were specific historical circumstances in Europe tending to produce a generational conflict. Young middle-class men in France, the Rhineland or northern Italy, educated in Napoleonic schools, who had started a career in the service of a glorious Empire, found their hopes prematurely dashed in 1815. The Revolution was over. Their parents had sold out and accepted the returning monarchies. They were now faced with new regimes which seemed mediocre and materialistic in comparison to the great Napoleonic epic in which they had shared. More to the point, their careers were shattered as army officers were retired and an older generation of ex-*émigrés* was given preferential treatment. They had a choice to make. Like Stendhal's Julien Sorel, they could put on a mask and conform to the demands of contemporary society, while secretly cherishing their memories of the Emperor. Or else, bored and idle, they might join a secret society or a revolutionary movement.

Like all theories of generational conflict, this one obscures other important social cleavages. The frustrated youth in question were specifically male, and they belonged to a distinct social group – the educated middle class.[2] They included students from elite educational institutions. In 1832, for instance, when the barricades went up again in Paris, the French government closed down the Ecole Polytechnique. Lenore O'Boyle has argued that the excessive number of university graduates in Western Europe constituted a social danger.[3] In Germany and France, professions like the law and the civil service were overcrowded, and there was intense competition for jobs. In France, all youthful resentments gathered in Paris, which was the focus of every ambitious careerist. Britain, however, managed to escape much of the risk caused by the educated unemployed and idle soldiers. Britain sent 6000 troops to fight with Bolivar in South America.[4] The colonies provided British society with another safety-valve which gave a refuge and a constructive role to the restless, the ambitious and the misfit. This was a reasonable description of many continental conspirators of the post-1815 era.

Students in Paris and Germany were an important element of the liberal opposition. In Paris, students in the Law and Medicine faculties were heavily involved in the July Revolution of 1830, even though many had already left town for the summer vacation. This was the period when the students of the Latin Quarter in Paris emerged as a distinct social group, character-ized by a strong sense of male solidarity, and a defiance of conventional social mores.[5] Unlike the rather anodyne Parisian bohemia of the later nineteenth century, the bohemia of the 1820s was highly politicized. In this it prefigured the student revolution of May 1968.

Youth was the theme of Giuseppe Mazzini's subversive organizations. In 1832 in exile in Marseilles, he established Young Italy, dedicated to propa-ganda in the cause of Italian unification along republican lines. He tried to organize a European-wide network, involving a Young Germany, a Young Spain and a Young Poland. The only one to get off the ground was Young Switzerland, which did produce its own journal.

In Germany, too, a political culture of youth developed, and it embraced not just undergraduates but also secondary school students.[6] Middle-class students, however, did not always share the same perspectives as young journeymen. Although youth became synonymous with rebellion, and was associated with new political, literary and artistic ideas, there was no united youth culture spanning class boundaries. 'Youth' effectively referred to educated urban males. By the end of the 1848 Revolutions this youth protest culture had evaporated in disillusionment. The young men of 1820 became the social establishment of 1850.

### *Carbonari* and secret societies

The *Carbonari* were not the only network of secret societies which emerged in Europe in the 1820s. There were many others, like the Guelphs, the Adelfi and others in northern Italy. The *Carbonari*, however, were the most widespread and for a time, the most threatening.

Their origins are obscure, but in their structure and elaborate initiation rites they resembled the ritualistic tendencies of Freemasonry. Initiation rites began with a symbolic journey, a test such as passing through fire, and then a series of solemn oaths of loyalty to the brotherhood.[7] Individual cells were formed of anything up to 40 men, who were supposed to have weapons at the ready. They were part of a strictly hierarchical organization with many different grades of initiate. Mazzini, for example, rose through six grades. The members of one cell did not necessarily know of the exis-tence of the others, nor did they know who the leaders of the organization were. This scheme was intended to preserve secrecy, but it also meant that groups like the four sergeants of La Rochelle were easily isolated. The emphasis on secrecy was in part a defence against repressive police regimes.

In France, for example, unauthorized meetings of over 20 people were illegal; and after 1834, unauthorized meetings of *any* size were illegal.

The numbers of *Carbonari* have been estimated at over 300,000 in Italy, mainly in the south, and 50,000 in France.[8] By no means all of them were revolutionaries, any more than all Freemasons were hostile to established religion. The *Carbonari* had no consistent political doctrine. Some were monarchists, some were very moderate liberals, and no doubt some were in it to make useful social contacts. But others were pledged to overthrow tyranny and the priesthood, and they were involved in the insurrections of 1820–1.

The *Carbonari* recruited a disproportionate number of soldiers, nourishing the resentments of the officer cadres of the Napoleonic armies. The army of the Napoleonic kingdom of Italy was demobilized after 1814 and replaced with Habsburg troops. In France, 80,000 former imperial soldiers had been pensioned off after 1814, including 15,000 officers reduced to half pay.[9] The *Carbonari* naturally targeted garrison units like the one at La Rochelle in 1822, where Bonapartist sympathies lingered. In 1824, 75 per cent of French officers were veterans of the Grande Armée. Just as the post-Soviet regime faced opposition within the former Red Army, so too the Bourbons had to cope with opposition from Napoleon's army.

A large proportion of *Carbonari* were from middle-class backgrounds (see Plate 2). They were a social elite with dangerous illusions about their own influence. In fact, they had no means of mobilizing support on a wide scale either in the cities or the countryside, and the *Carbonari* remained isolated from the masses. The failures of 1820–1 and attempted uprisings in 1833–4 in Italy suggested that Mazzinian hopes of igniting a general popular insurrection were misplaced or at least premature.

Many political figures had *Carbonarist* connections. Louis-Napoleon (the future Emperor Napoleon III) was a member in his youth, while the veteran revolutionary Lafayette finished his career with the *Carbonari*. Mazzini was another, French republican socialists Raspail and Cabet were others – a mixture of recruits which illustrates the incoherence of the 'underground republic'. They included the professional revolutionary Auguste Blanqui, a veteran of secret societies. Blanqui was permanently committed to the revolutionary overthrow of aristocracy, religion and the capitalist order. Decorated by the July Monarchy for his contribution to the 1830 Revolution, he immediately began to conspire to overthrow it. In 1834, he established the Société des Familles, but was arrested for the illegal possession of firearms. In 1837, he formed with Barbès the Société des Saisons on the old *Carbonarist* model, with a disciplined hierarchy of isolated cells. In 1839 he attempted an uprising in Paris and was sentenced to death. Louis-Philippe commuted the sentence to life imprisonment. Blanqui in fact spent 40 years of his 76-year-long life in one prison or another. He was *L'Enfermé*, the permanent prisoner, the personification of the clandestine revolutionary.

He has sometimes been seen as an inheritor of the conspiratorial tradition of revolution begun by Gracchus Babeuf in his Conspiracy of the Equals of 1796. This tradition was continued by the Tuscan revolutionary Buonarroti, who published his own history of the Babeuf plot in 1828.[10] Blanqui, however, rarely referred to Babeuf. Left-wing historians have nevertheless insisted that the notion of a professional, highly disciplined revolutionary *coup* descended in direct lineage from Babeuf via Blanqui to Lenin.[11] Right-wing historians, too, have seen the origins of twentieth-century dictatorships in this strand of French revolutionary thinking.[12] As we have seen, professionalism and discipline were sadly lacking in the revolutionary plots of the 1820s and 1830s. After nine years of prison, Blanqui once again emerged into daylight after the Revolution of February 1848. De Tocqueville was horrified by the sight of this dedicated but now emaciated public enemy: 'He seemed', he wrote, 'to have passed his life in a sewer and to have just left it.'[13] The 'underground republic' had risen disturbingly to the surface.

### Bonapartism in France

After the fall of the Berlin Wall in 1989, massive statues of Stalin were pulled down all over Eastern Europe, yet the ghost of the dictator lingered on. After the rupture of 1814, it became illegal to remember Napoleon in public, but like Stalin he remained an ever-present political force. Napoleon was responsible for the deaths of hundreds of thousands on the battlefield, but unlike Stalin in 1989, Napoleon was still alive, and might one day return (of course he *did* return from Elba). Furthermore, he represented a dynasty. His son, hailed by the four sergeants of La Rochelle as Napoleon II, was potentially a pretender, and after him there was his nephew, the future Emperor Napoleon III.

Bonapartism, rather than Blanqui or the *Carbonari* or the diffuse republican movement, was the biggest threat to the monarchical regimes of 1814–48. The revolutionary potential of Bonapartism had been evident in the Hundred Days in 1814, when Napoleon gathered support from former Jacobins and revolutionaries in the *fédéré* movement.[14] On his return from Elba, Napoleon issued a constitution, rallying liberal support, and presenting the last line of defence against the return of nobles, priests and a reactionary monarchy arriving in the wake of foreign invasion. By 1815, Bonapartism meant different things to different people. It offered constitutional rule to liberals, universal male franchise to those deprived of a vote under the July Monarchy, and an alternative to monarcho-clerical rule to republicans, while its unchallenged patriotic credentials appealed to all nationalists. Bonapartism provided the best single focus for the diverse strands of opposition.[15]

Bonapartism was a strong element in the *Carbonarist* movement, and it also had popular appeal. It was not merely a movement of the young – the Napoleonic veteran who became a common character in nineteenth-century fiction was usually a grumpy and embittered old recluse living in a time-warp. Napoleon inspired messianic expectations of a triumphant return. After 1815, sightings of the Emperor were reported in various parts of France. He was rumoured to be in the United States and about to return at the head of an American army, well-stocked with grain supplies.[16] Even after he died in 1821, rumours of his imminent return continued to spread, especially in times of dearth and high food prices.

The Napoleonic myth was disseminated to a wide popular audience. The songs of Béranger, full of Bonapartist nostalgia, had an enormous vogue at the time of the 1830 Revolution. Popular chapbook literature provided stories based on Napoleonic military exploits. Portraits of the Emperor circulated, while consumer articles like decorated tobacco-boxes, pipes, clocks, braces and embroidered handkerchiefs perpetuated his image. Bonapartism invited a nostalgic longing for a regime which was now dressed in democratic clothes, and which had provided jobs and cheap bread. The Napoleonic myth used all available media, even the Lord's Prayer, in the following anticlerical parody:

> Our Emperor which art in St Helena
> Hallowed be thy name
> Thy kingdom come
> Thy will be done
> Against all the ultras who take our pensions
> Deliver us from the accursed Bourbons, Amen.[17]

In eastern France, Pellerin produced a series of 59 cheap wood-cut engravings of Napoleon's career, which had a print run of 100 000 copies. For just one *sou*, customers in the countryside could buy prints and posters of Napoleon as a paternal benefactor to his people, a defender of emerging nations, and a just and egalitarian republican hero.[18] Pellerin's prints relied on the repetition of stock images, featuring Napoleon on horseback, at his coronation, standing defiantly on a rock at St Helena, enduring the ordeal of the retreat from Moscow or in fraternal and compassionate bivouac with his soldiers. He was portrayed not in full military regalia, but in the more 'republican' and egalitarian simple grey overcoat. It is a tribute to the power of this post-Napoleonic construction that this is still the pose most readily identified with Napoleon today.

Pellerin's prints corresponded to the image of the Emperor produced by Las Cases in his memoirs of St Helena. Las Cases's *Mémorial de Sainte-Hélène* was published in 1823, and went into six editions before 1831. He claimed it was based on personal conversations with Napoleon in exile. Las Cases created Napoleon as a frustrated democrat, who saved France from chaos, but was perpetually victimized by foreign powers, notably the English.

Hopes that the 1830 Revolution would usher in a Bonapartist regime proved illusory, just as hopes for a republic also failed. No political leader came forward to champion the Bonapartist cause. In 1832, the July Monarchy confirmed the permanent exile of all Bonapartes from French territory. The death of Napoleon II in 1832 deprived the movement of a dynastic focus, and so it became even harder to distinguish it from republicanism. Popular Bonapartism could not be ignored, however, and Louis-Napoleon, nephew of the great Napoleon, made sure of this. Two pro-Bonapartist conspiracies in Strasbourg (1836) and Boulogne (1840) were fiascos, but they advertised the existence of a pretender who had not given up the struggle. Louis-Napoleon used these years and his prison sentence to good advantage, publishing works that kept him in the public eye as a true heir of the Empire (*Des Idées napoléoniennes*, 1839) and a progressive social thinker (*L'Extinction du paupérisme*, 1844).

With Napoleon's son dead, the July Monarchy of Louis-Philippe tried to harness the myth for its own purposes. In 1840, Prime Minister Thiers, in need of a boost for his aggressively anti-British foreign policy, organized the return of Napoleon's ashes from St Helena. A decision had to be made about where the ashes were to have their final resting-place.[19] This problem highlighted the contested memory of Bonaparte. French kings had traditionally been interred in the cathedral crypt of St Denis, but to put Napoleon in this company would have angered royalists who always regarded him as a usurper. A republican Napoleon would have been at home on the Left Bank in the Panthéon alongside celebrated revolutionaries. This risked making him a focus for left-wing demonstrations. The regime solved the problem by building a special tomb at the Invalides, the home for war veterans, where Napoleon's military conquests above all would be emphasized. The July Monarchy hoped to incorporate the Napoleon myth by closely associating it with French conquests on the battlefield. In this way, perhaps his legacy could be depoliticized. The

Orleanist monarchy, however, could not monopolize the memory of Napoleon. Napoleon was the subject of a personality cult after his death, and this could be used by those who hoped to bring about political change.

## Republicanism in France

Whereas a nostalgic myth enveloped memories of Bonaparte, republicanism struggled to shake off its negative associations with Robespierre and the 'Reign of Terror' of 1793–4. This was hard to achieve as long as it relied heavily on veterans of revolutionary struggles, like the surviving members of the National Convention who had voted the death of Louis XVI. In harness with liberalism, however, republicanism rallied those who pushed for a wider franchise. In harness with Bonapartism, republicanism signified egalitarianism and patriotism.

Republicans were united only in their opposition to the Bourbons. After Charles X was overthrown in 1830, it was more difficult to identify what republicanism stood for in institutional terms. Would it sweep away the upper house in favour of a one-chamber parliament in the image of the National Convention of 1792? Would it introduce a strong executive as the Bonapartists demanded? How would a republican head of state be elected? Would a new republic reassure the bourgeoisie by avoiding the financial chaos and popular risings which had characterized its predecessor in the 1790s? The underground republic could only achieve success by remaining ambiguous about such issues.

After 1815, European republicanism had two influential models. One was the French Charter of 1814, under which the returning Bourbons accepted a parliamentary regime with a limited franchise. The other was the 1812 Constitution proclaimed by the Cortes of Cadiz, which became the model for liberalism in Spain and Southern Europe. This 'sacred codex' of 1812 was much more radical than the French Charter. It put forward a blueprint for a centralized and enlightened state, which would abolish seigneurial justice and weaken the traditional powers of Church, aristocracy and the regions. It was a radical assertion of popular sovereignty, to be embodied in an elected one-chamber assembly. Both these sources of liberal and republican inspiration were of course designed to be implemented under a monarchy. This contradiction became insuperable in 1830, when the Parisian opposition rose to defend the monarchical Charter against the claims of Charles X. France emerged after 1830 with Lafayette's uneasy compromise of a 'monarchy surrounded by republican institutions'.

The most important insurrections of the July Monarchy occurred in

France's second city, Lyon, in 1831 and 1834. Lyon was a 'proto-industrial' city dedicated to silk manufacture, where journeymen, master-weavers and merchants concentrated production using largely pre-industrial methods. Of Lyon's population of 200,000, one-quarter was involved in the silk industry and the city produced, within a few square kilometres, one-third of the value of all France's exports.[20] As yet, mechanization had made little headway – in 1830 only about one in four of Lyon's weaving looms incorporated the new apparatus designed by Jacquard. The Lyon silk-weavers formed a traditional tightly knit community of workers, in which masters and their journeymen identified a common hostility towards the merchants who were keen to push down prices. Masters and journeymen struggled to control the price of their labour. The merchants tried to undercut them by distributing work in outlying areas to less skilled and therefore cheaper hands. The master-weavers, about 8000 of them, rose in 1831 to demand fixed minimum pay rates. In 1834, they rose again to defend their co-operative organizations against state legislation to ban all workers' associations.

The government blamed these outbreaks on a widespread republican conspiracy centred on the Society for Human Rights. This was a hysterical over-reaction, but the Lyonnais situation does permit some conclusions about the conditions where the underground republic could prosper. It prospered amongst artisans – in other words amongst skilled craft workers who wanted to regulate their trade and who challenged the freedom of the entrepreneur to dictate terms and reduce wages in the name of economic necessity. Artisans formed a literate elite within the workforce as a whole. They had a self-conscious pride in their work and a tradition of organization and mutual help. They were relatively well-off: the Lyon weavers wore boots rather than clogs. They often worked as a family unit, so that in Lyon, the average home workshop possessed fewer than four looms, and half of the labour force was female.[21] They contributed to mutual aid societies, set up to collect funds for workers' burial expenses or to cover the costs of illness or injury. Employers everywhere were almost invariably suspicious of such workers' funds, which could on occasion support strike activity. In England and Wales, such legally registered societies had an estimated 1.5 million members in 1850, and there were probably many more unregistered members.[22] Mutual aid societies were part of an organizational structure which was highly gendered: cafés, newspapers and workers' associations were essentially male arenas of discussion and mobilization. Such associations sustained networks of artisan militancy, as did the workers' press, although both British and French governments tried to muzzle radical newspapers in the early 1830s.

Republican militancy could thrive where it responded to the skilled workers' sense of independence, and their desire to form associations to thwart rampant economic competition. It was far less successful in highly industrialized sectors where mechanization was more advanced, and craft workers did not find common ground with new factory employees.[23] In traditional areas of production, French artisans could imagine a republican state apparatus as one which would be neutral or sympathetic to their demands, rather than a state which would defend the interests of employers and limit workers' rights of association. Although the leading historian of the Lyon uprising of 1834 plays down workers' politicization, and dismisses the republican press as 'shoestring publications without an audience', we must not underestimate the importance of state action in influencing worker militancy.[24] As Bezucha himself explains, the silk workers of Lyon were reacting to proposed government legislation to ban all workers' associations. Faced with a hostile government, their defensive action could not help being 'political'. The repressive state of the July Monarchy thus helped to reinforce the underground republic. This was just as significant a cause of militancy as changes in the silk industry or the persuasive power of ideology.

Republicanism made ground in the French countryside, too, as the events of the 1848 Revolution would later reveal. In his classic study of southeastern France, Maurice Agulhon tried to explain the progress of rural republicanism in a region which as recently as 1814 appeared to support ultra-royalism.[25] Agulhon located the main growth of peasant radicalism in the 'urbanized villages' of the Midi, where peasant cultivators lived in small towns of fewer than 5000 inhabitants. Rising literacy and the spread of the French language (in place of Provençal) assisted the circulation of new ideas. In imitation of bourgeois literary clubs, local *chambrées* – evening meetings after work where (male) peasants socialized and had a drink – were important in the formation of radical networks. Agulhon emphasized the role of the local bourgeoisie as cultural intermediaries, spreading anti-clericalism by example and sometimes assisting villagers in their disputes with landlords. Skilled artisans and professional bourgeois acted in Agulhon's view as apostles who disseminated republican and socialist opinions in the countryside.

Not all historians accept this model of cultural diffusion via local bourgeois culture-brokers. Some like Peter McPhee regard such a 'trickling down' scenario as inherently elitist, casting the peasantry as passive receptacles for middle-class ideologies.[26] More stress should perhaps be placed on peasants' contacts with the national market economy, and the development of cash-cropping for commercial sale. McPhee and others have pointed out the radicalism of small peasant wine-growers, who sold in distant markets which gave them broad geographical and political horizons. Memories of the French Revolution, and the local presence of Republicans of the 1790s cannot be ignored, either.

Both Agulhon and McPhee would perhaps agree that peasant republicanism had a character of its own, and was expressed through traditional practices deeply embedded in rural culture. Village festivals and the carnival were easily transformed into vehicles of social protest. Burning a carnival effigy of the king or the prefect can hardly be classified as a modern form of protest, but it nevertheless signified the politicization of a section of the peasantry in the decades before the 1848 Revolution.

## The barricade

The street barricade was an essential technique of mid-nineteenth-century urban revolutions. Insurgents blocked their street with any materials they could lay their hands on, including cobblestones, barrels, scrap iron, doors, mattresses, church pews and confessionals, bales of straw, uprooted trees and overturned carriages. Barricades might stand between one and two metres high. Building them was a spontaneous collective effort in which both men and women of the neighbourhood worked together. With this protection, a rising could seal off the popular districts and for a while hold the forces of order at bay (see Plate 3). A tunnel would be made at one end to allow communication with other barricades. Control of the surrounding buildings enabled insurgents to hurl projectiles on to their assailants from a great height. Behind the barricade, premises would be taken over for making ammunition, nursing the wounded and feeding the insurgents. Such was the role of the café Musain at the barricade of the rue de la Chanvrerie in central Paris in 1832, imagined by Victor Hugo years later in his novel *Les Misérables*. They were neighbourhood centres, gathering-points where people of all classes met for the latest news. Although spontaneity and improvisation were the hallmarks of the barricade, professional expertise in barricade-building gradually developed. In 1848, the Milanese even invented a mobile barricade, rather like a fortified carnival float.[27] In the barricades of the Paris Commune of 1871, military engineers dug trenches and piled up sandbags.

Before and during 1848, the barricade was an improvised and defensive response to a crisis. Behind the barricade, a neighbourhood reclaimed urban space and defied troops to reduce it to obedience. Building a barricade became the instinctive reflex of the revolutionary city. Barricades went up in Paris in 1830, 1832, 1834, briefly in 1839, again in February and June

*Plate 3* Palermo barricades, 1860. Note the policeman's hat displayed defiantly on the first barricade

*Source*: Museo Centrale del Risorgimento, Rome (*Barricate di Palermo*).

1848, and in 1851. The phenomenon, however, was by no means confined to Paris. The barricade was effective in the narrow alleys of any pre-modern city, before urban modernization carved out the wide, straight boulevards familiar to Parisians after the 1850s. The historic centres of European cities were teeming labyrinths of tiny streets where heavy artillery was ineffective. In 1848, between 200 and 400 barricades sprang up in central Prague, and there were over 1600 in the old heart of Milan.[28]

Barricades were inevitably ephemeral, whether part of a successful uprising or not. But they had enormous symbolic value, representing popular defiance and sacrifice. Victor Hugo romanticized the barricade, populating it with generous workers, idealistic student martyrs and Gavroche, the carnivalesque street urchin. Ernest Meissonnier presented a more chilling scenario of littered corpses in the aftermath of defeat. His *Souvenir of Civil War* (1849) was painted after the insurrection of June 1848 in Paris had brought the threat of civil war dangerously close (see Plate 4). Meissonier himself was a captain of artillery in the National Guard at the time – he was there in person at the barricade in the rue de la Mortellerie, fighting with the forces of order against the rebels. He shows us cobblestones, workers' smocks, stains of blood, a mess of bodies in an empty street. There are no leaders, no flags, no heroic gestures, and even no weapons. According to Tim Clark, we see men 'like rubbish in the street, ready for the common grave'.[29] The noblest visual interpretation remains that of Delacroix in his allegorical tribute to the 1830 Revolution, *Liberty Leading the People* (see Plate 5). Delacroix imagined the insurgents at a moment of conquest, as they advanced defiantly over the debris to claim the future. Delacroix's version corresponds most closely to the spirit of the Spanish revolutionary motto: 'Barricades close off streets but open up horizons.'

## Utopian socialism and the 'social question'

The development of socialist thought in the 1830s and 1840s lent a new ingredient to the post-revolutionary ferment. Engels dubbed the social theorists of the romantic period 'utopian', in order to contrast their shortcomings with the 'scientific' approach to history and the economy which he and Karl Marx allegedly pioneered. Today, historians interpret the romantic socialists in a kinder light, especially since their views on women's emancipation made some of them prophets before their time. In some senses, though, Marx and Engels were right: theoreticians of ideal communities like Robert Owen or Etienne Cabet did not focus systematically on class conflict. Owen rather sought means to minimize it. They

*Plate 4*    Ernest Meissonnier, *Souvenir of Civil War*, 1849. In Meissonnier's unglam-
          orous vision of the barricade, bodies are strewn like rubbish in the street
*Source*:    Louvre, Paris.

*Plate 5*   Eugène Delacroix, *Liberty Leading the People*, 1830. Delacroix's allegory of
Revolution, inspired by 1830, was too subversive to remain on public view
after 1831

*Source*:   Louvre, Paris.

were largely anti-political and, unlike Blanqui, they did not think about
ways of seizing state power. Nor did they concentrate as Marx did on the
dynamics of industrial capitalism. Early socialism was a product of a largely
pre-industrial age – a doctrine for small masters and employers. Socialist
ideas inevitably sprang from an economic context still dominated by small-
scale artisan production.

Romantic socialism nevertheless wrestled with very real problems of a
post-revolutionary age which abounded in schemes to regenerate society on
the ruins of the old order. Cut-throat competition forced down wages and
piecework rates, threatening the livelihood of skilled artisans. Socialists
sought remedies for the evils of competition, and found them in co-operation or 'association' between workers and producers. 'Association' was one
of the buzz-words of the 1840s, a response to social problems which
inspired the co-operative organizations promoted by Proudhon. Proudhon

believed the state should provide credit to establish producers' co-opera-tives. Louis Blanc, too, in his influential *L'Organisation du Travail* (1839) wanted state intervention to provide and organize work for all in 'social workshops'.

The early socialists subscribed to a labour theory of value, in other words they believed that it was the worker's skill and labour which conferred value on a product. If middlemen and merchants did not pay the worker a living wage, then his labour, which was his only property, had been stolen. This is what Proudhon had in mind when he coined his notorious statement 'property is theft'. 'I dream', wrote Proudhon, 'of a society in which I would be guillotined as a conservative.'[30] In fact, Proudhon did not oppose private property in itself, and Marx denounced him as a petty-bourgeois.

The socialists were horrified by blatant social inequalities which discred-ited the progressive claims of political liberalism. To them, a social organi-zation professing to embody freedom, but which tolerated wide extremes of wealth and poverty in its midst, was clearly dysfunctional. The poor man, in Fourier's metaphor, was always waiting outside the restaurant door, passively breathing in the mere aroma of a liberty which he could never attain.[31] Socialists looked for solutions to what was becoming known in France as 'la question sociale', denoting the problems associated with social inequalities and antagonisms of all kinds. Utopian socialists were worried about the nature of work, which they wanted to make interesting, creative and rationally organized. They believed in promoting working-class educa-tion, and with a few exceptions they fervently wished to improve the situa-tion of women. For two leading theorists, namely Saint-Simon and Fourier, the two biggest problems of their time were capitalism and monogamous, patriarchal marriage.

The socialist critique of capitalist competition often had a religious foun-dation. New Testament morality inspired the Christian socialism of Buchez and the abbé Lamennais's immensely popular book *Paroles d'un Croyant* (1834). Christian principles were an inspiration for the kind of egalitarian fraternity which was fundamental to early socialist aspirations. God, Lamennais seemed to confirm, was on the side not of the establishment, but of social justice and compassion. Christianity could provide ammunition for attacking the 'iron laws' of liberal economics.

Socialist groups had deep religious tendencies of another kind. They formed sects and organized themselves into secular religions. The Saint-Simonian 'Church' had its own hierarchy, and followers wore distinctive uniforms. Their leader, Père Enfantin, was known as 'pope', and exerted emotional and sexual power over some female disciples.

In the strange world of early socialist cults, Charles Fourier (1772–1837) seems the most imaginative and eccentric of all. Fourier envisaged a paradise in which oranges would grow in Warsaw and the ocean would turn to pink lemonade. He prophesied that having achieved a state of true harmony, men and women would live to 144 and grow tails (cartoonists had a field day drawing dragon-like socialists). Even Fourier's masterly biographer found it difficult to decide whether Fourier was mad or joking.[32] In the absence of more evidence of Fourier's sense of humour, we must lean towards the former. But Fourier's lunacy was laced with sharp insights.

Fourier noted capitalism's periodic crises of over-production. He saw that market forces did not always meet human needs, but instead created unemployment and reduced respectable workers to begging for bread. He therefore drew up a design for the elimination of poverty and unhappiness. His fantasy world, or phalanstery, was an elaborately conceived community of between 1500 and 2000 members, in which communal living did not obliterate differences of wealth and status. The inhabitants of the Fourierist phalanstery were essentially shareholders dividing profits amongst themselves. By eliminating middlemen and bankers, Fourier hoped to counteract the failures of the market economy. Every member was guaranteed a minimum income, together with all basic comforts. Work would become attractive, not only because all shareholders had a material interest in it, but because it was rationally organized. Work would be done in groups, and the day would consist of a series of short, ever-changing tasks. The really disgusting jobs would be carried out by pre-adolescents who, according to Fourier, loved wallowing in dirt anyway.[33] Fourier was more interested here in avoiding the monotony of work than increasing productivity. Unlike Saint-Simon who wanted to promote industrial production, Fourier was afraid that industrialization would reduce workers to robots. His utopia was one in which work and pleasure were almost indistinguishable. The Owenite community of New Lanark was too spartan and monastic for Fourier. He wanted people to enjoy themselves. In his phalanstery, there would be periodical feasts and theatrical festivals, not to mention organized episodes of communal sexual intercourse.

Fourier's fundamental belief was that human happiness rested on the expression of passions, which society repressed but an ideal community would liberate in a way guaranteeing social harmony. He developed an absurd calculus of the passions and sensations, all tabulated and numbered. Social harmony would emerge from an absence of sexual constraint. Monogamous marriage was thus a barrier to social harmony. It was especially a barrier to the liberation of women, which Fourier saw as the key to all social progress.[34] Heterosexual marriage seemed a waste of female labour which could be liberated by communal child care. Fourier equated marriage with the enslavement of woman. These ideas inevitably shocked respectable married couples and exposed his doctrines to widespread ridicule. In his emphasis on releasing repressed passions, however, we might see Fourier as a precursor of Freud.

Socialism, as Pamela Pilbeam insists, was a pluralistic doctrine, in which many divergent currents had a few ideas in common.[35] When the Saint-Simonian group split in 1831, and a faction joined the ailing Fourierists, there was clearly enough overlap between them to make co-operation possible. Saint-Simon's ideal, however, was a society organized rationally by intellectuals and scientists. If intellectuals had guided the Old Regime monarchy, Saint-Simon argued, the French Revolution would never had occurred. It followed that Saint-Simon took more account of the active role of the state in organizing society than did many other socialists, including Fourier. His notions had an inherent appeal for engineers, scientists and bankers. There were, however, anti-democratic implications in Saint-Simon's stress on the role of the chemist and the engineer in progressive society. If the intellectuals hold the key to progress, then majority rule can get things wrong and democracy could become government by the ignorant. The French Revolution had guillotined the chemist Lavoisier, which was a case in point and illustrated for Saint-Simon the irrationality of violent revolution.

Etienne Cabet's utopian ideal of the Icarian community had a larger contemporary following than either Fourier or Saint-Simon, because he appealed more successfully to workers and artisans. Cabet was a non-revolutionary communist, who had been a *Carbonaro* and was elected to the Chamber of Deputies after 1830. He had spent five years in radical circles in England before returning to France in 1839. In *Voyage en Icarie* (1840), he designed an egalitarian community in which there would be no property and no money. Thus the evils of the market economy would be eliminated. Work in clean and well-lit factories would be as pleasant as possible. The community would be governed by a democratically elected representative body, but Cabet wanted to burn all harmful books and institute pre-publication censorship. This coercive policy seemed to contradict his notion that a police force would be unnecessary in Icaria, and Cabet's historian compares his authoritarian tendencies to those of Metternich.[36] The communist project would be achieved gradually, through the abolition of inheritance and the reversion of all deceased estates to the state. Cabet added the revolutionary suggestion in the French context that a progressive income tax should be introduced. Cabet was ambiguous about the rights of women. He was vague about recommending female suffrage, and he remained convinced that monogamous marriage was necessary for the happiness of both sexes.

Unlike other theorists, Cabet had a substantial audience in the 1840s. His *Voyage en Icarie* went into five editions between 1842 and 1848. His four-page newspaper *Le Populaire*, established as a weekly at first in 1833, had a wide circulation, reaching a print-run of 4500 in the pre-revolutionary year of 1847.[37] The journal would be shared and read aloud in cafés, so that its real 'readership' may have numbered tens of thousands more than this. Cabet had a large proportion of subscribers in provincial France, particularly in Lyon.

The romantic socialists were not revolutionaries. They responded to social problems by fashioning 'dream worlds', and trying to realize them, as Cabet did first in Texas then at Nauvoo, Illinois, and as the Fourierists did at Condé near Paris.[38] Such experiments were always under-capitalized and usually collapsed. Their wildest notions embarrassed their followers. Victor Considérant, who took over the mantle of Fourierism, tried to rescue the cause from the taint of sexual immorality and he reaffirmed Christian values, although these had been conspicuous by their absence from Fourier's own theories.

Except for Cabet, Louis Blanc and later Proudhon, the romantic socialist theorists had little impact on their own societies. As Fourier's biographer explains, his imaginings demonstrated 'a close connection between the sublime and the ridiculous'.[39] Yet they presented an early critique of liberal capitalist society in its post-revolutionary phase. They tried to alert contemporaries to the contradictions of liberal claims to represent progress. They helped to define 'la question sociale' and they insisted that it should be inserted into the political agenda. They refused to accept the liberal view that workplace relations were a matter for the private sphere and did not concern legislators. They realized that political liberalism excluded two categories of citizens whose 'capacity' to exercise political rights was denied by the system – namely workers and women. Their idealism was a response to this exclusion and to the ravages of uninhibited capitalist competition.

In considering several elements of opposition in the same chapter, we risk blurring the distinctions between them. As will be discussed further in Chapter 8, liberalism never challenged monarchical rule in the way that Bonapartists or republicans did. Liberals believed in constitutional rule and a property-owning franchise, but they had a limited view of democracy. Republicans wanted to go further and many were prepared to champion universal male suffrage. Bonapartism was a many faceted movement which could cut across all these opposition currents and lend its strength to any one of them. Only after 1830, when the common Bourbon enemy was defeated in France, did the differences between these various causes become truly apparent.

**Afterword**

In 1841, Karl Marx's doctoral thesis was accepted by the University of Jena. He became one of the editors of the *Rheinische Zeitung* (The Rhineland Gazette) in Köln and helped to double its circulation before it was closed down in 1843. Having married Jenny von Westphalen, he moved to Paris, where he first met his lifelong colleague and patron, Frederick Engels. Expelled from Paris, he moved to Brussels and in 1846 he and Engels established the Communist League. Following his *Theses on Feuerbach* and *The German Ideology*, he and Engels issued the first Communist Party Manifesto in 1848. Although its contemporary impact was minimal, and it rejected the forerunners discussed in this chapter as 'utopian', it announced the development of a new form of socialism, based on a systematic analysis of the history and political economy of nineteenth-century capitalism. For the first time, a socialist theorist pinned his hopes on the transformation of society by a class which as yet hardly existed in most of continental Europe – the industrial proletariat.

# 5   The Fragility of Nationalism

## The fragility of nationalism

When the grip of Soviet imperialism was relaxed in the 1990s, a great upsurge of Eastern European nationalisms was released like steam from a pressure cooker. Former communist politicians, whose positions suddenly lacked any legitimacy, played the nationalist card in order to bolster their authority. When the French Napoleonic Empire unravelled in 1814, however, nothing of this sort happened. The forces of nationalism which dominated European affairs from the 1890s onwards were as yet in their infancy. The power of nationalism, therefore, should not be read back into the past. Metternich and the diplomats of 1815 could rearrange the map of Europe and put new kings on new thrones without any popular consultation because they simply did not face any mass demands for self-determination. In the twentieth century, self-determination was to become a potential force for democracy and liberation, especially in struggles for colonial independence. It would also be used to justify intolerance, racial conflict and murderous wars. But all this lay in the future. Europe's national movements had not yet taken shape.

Miroslav Hroch put forward a typology of nationalism in three developmental phases: in the first, Phase A, the national idea is a matter for isolated scholars with little social influence; in the second, Phase B, they have moved to active political agitation; in the third, Phase C, nationalism becomes a mass movement, with a strong and extensive organization.[1] Most of the cases studied in this chapter were moving from the first to the second phase. In other words, early nineteenth-century nationalist movements were still at a very embryonic stage of development. Some of them didn't reach the final stage of maturity until the end of the nineteenth century, and a few never reached it at all.

Most of early nineteenth-century Europe lacked the infrastructure which unifies a modern nation state, such as an integrated national economy, universal taxation and voting systems, a universal system of state primary schools, general access to the mass media, and a universally recognized national language. The idea of the nation meant very little to ordinary people, whose horizons were limited to their immediate surroundings. The

76

majority lived out their entire lives within earshot of the church bells of their native village or town. Carlo Cattaneo wrote of raising at the same time 'the flag of the nation and the banners of its one hundred cities'; as an Italian nationalist, he was well aware of the powerful municipal traditions which handicapped the growth of national identities.[2]

In these circumstances, national identity was something to be constructed or 'invented'. There was nothing inherent or natural about belonging to a nation, although nationalists claimed their nation existed since time immemorial. Today, many scholars play down the 'essentialist' approach to national identity which saw it as an objective reality, and emphasize instead the 'imagined' nature of the national idea. E. J. Hobsbawm wrote of nationalisms inventing their own traditions. Benedict Anderson described the nation as an 'imagined community' – a phrase which has stuck, because it sums up well the subjective nature of national identity. Ernest Gellner has also argued that nations are not just 'there', and did not simply emerge naturally from a dormant state in the nineteenth century.[3] These modern analysts see national identity as something artificial, rather like an item of IKEA furniture, with the symbolic repertoire of flag, anthem, heroic ancestors and foundation myth awaiting assembly.[4] Anthony Smith, on the other hand, refuses to go to such extremes, stressing the potential longevity of a sense of ethnic community and the links between the modern and pre-modern *ethnos*.[5] All these views force us to examine the process through which European national identities were manufactured. In this process, important roles were played by religious affiliations, economic modernization, language and the medium of print.

In some cases, religion was clearly a core element around which a national identity could grow. Belgian Catholics, for example, fought a struggle for independence in 1830 against a Calvinist Dutch state. The Catholic Church was similarly identified with the nation in Ireland and Poland, where the local oppressors (British or Russian) represented a foreign religion. The Greek Orthodox Church was a similar focus for national identity in the struggle against the Ottoman Empire. In Catholic Italy, on the other hand, the situation was different. After 1848, it was clear that the presence of the Papacy on the Italian peninsula was a complicating factor rather than a reinforcement for the cause of national unity. Both French republicanism and Italian nationalism developed distinctly anticlerical characteristics.

The growth of modern nationalism occurred at a particular historical moment (the French Revolution and the nineteenth century), and Gellner and others explain this by suggesting a link between nationalism and the development of industrial societies. The modern industrial state, it is argued, needed a literate, mobile and culturally homogeneous population, and national unity would provide these conditions for economic growth. A national market, subject to a standard commercial legal code, with a common currency and the abolition of internal customs walls, would facilitate the capitalist process. Like all overarching theories of nationalism, this one is open to question. It may fit industrializing areas like Belgium or Germany, but it is harder to relate it to more backward economies like Greece. The link between nationalism and industrialization is difficult to defend in many countries in the light of the political reticence of the commercial bourgeoisie, and the tendency of nationalist ideologies to focus on age-old rural values (rather than bourgeois-capitalist ones). In Lithuania and elsewhere in Eastern Europe, for example, national consciousness was constructed around an idealized version of peasant culture. Here the urban entrepreneurs were of German or Jewish origin and were an obstacle for protagonists of national unity.[6]

For nineteenth-century nationalists, language was an important criterion in determining who belonged to which 'imagined community'. The German philosopher Herder (1744–1803) had conceptualized the Volk as a nation bound together by a common culture expressed through language. Herder saw the Volk as an organic and egalitarian community in opposition to the rule of hereditary dynasties or serf-owning aristocracies. In his influential thinking, language rather than race was the defining feature of any nation and its culture.[7] Herder was no racist, and his 'theory of cultural respect' condemned claims of national superiority or domination.[8] Many early nineteenth-century nationalists built on his views. Unlike most commentators today, they saw the nation as something pre-existing and God-given, rather than as an artificial construction.

In spite of this emphasis on language, linguistic identifiers were not the exclusive basis for nationality, as Brian Vick has argued in the German case.[9] Liberal German nationalists were quite prepared to grant citizenship rights to Poles, Czechs, Danes and even Jews if they would accept the use of German as the language of public discourse. A process of Germanization of all minorities was regarded as inevitable to create a homogeneous national society, but those of non-German birth or language could participate. The often-heard view that the German conception of nationality excluded those who did not qualify by language and descent does not take account of the more open conceptions which were expressed in the Vormärz (pre-1848) period.

Where a national language did not exist in a standardized written form, nationalists set out to create one. In Slovakia, for example, intellectuals and philologists fashioned a literary language from several spoken dialects, and a standardized form of Ukrainian was also devised in the nineteenth century. In the Ukraine the dialect of Kiev was elevated into the national language, while in Slovenia the dialect of Ljubljana prevailed.[10] In Italy, too, finding a national language meant choosing one of several regional languages. The Tuscan version, the language of Dante and Petrarch, was to become the official version of Italian, even though only a tiny fraction of the Italian population actually used it when Italy was unified. Once the intellectual elite had established the national language, grammars and dictionaries were needed to explain it and help people to spell it correctly. Thus in 1819, the first Ukrainian grammar appeared. In 1848, a new Norwegian grammar was published, and similar scholarly work supported the development of Slovene and Serbo-Croat in this period.

Eventually, the purity of the national language had to be defended, and foreign borrowings which 'contaminated' it had to be purged. According to the Bulgarian Karavelov: 'Every nation should take pride in its language . . . and purify it of foreign garbage – namely, Turkish, Greek, Russian and Church Slavonic words.'[11] What he disparaged as 'foreign garbage' had to be either eliminated or domesticated. Hungarian philologists tried to 'magyarize' vocabulary imported from German or Latin which was indispensable. In 1832 and 1845, the Hungarian Academy of Sciences issued spelling and grammar rules for the new national language.

The role of the intelligentsia was crucial in this phase of developing national consciousness. Linguists, academics and other members of the educated elite were in the forefront of promoting the national idea and the national language. In Finland, for example, patriots worked through the Finnish Literary Society and the same was true for other Baltic nationalisms.[12] Scholars and officials, however, did not necessarily have any appeal for the rest of the population. Norwegians declared that the peasantry was the essence of the nation, but when the National Assembly (Storting) met in 1814, it did not include a single one of them.[13] Middle-class nationalists rarely had anything to offer the rural masses.

Nationalists assumed with dubious logic that people who spoke the same language should belong to a single nation state. This assertion seemed to depend on a further assumption that every nation had or should have a single language. These propositions ignored some vital realities. The fact that North Americans and British spoke the same language did not persuade anybody that they should be a single state, and the same could eventually be said for the relationship between Spain and the newly-independent South American republics. Besides, many nation states were multilingual, like Switzerland or Spain, whose languages included Basque, Catalan, Castilian and Galician. In many parts of Europe, furthermore, there existed a bilingual bourgeoisie, adept both in the official national language and in local idioms which often had more practical use. The Russian and Habsburg Empires were dominated by polyglot elites, speaking German and Czech, German and Hungarian or Russian and Polish. They defied the nationalist precept that every language should have its state and every state its language.

The role of print was sometimes significant in the development of a national consciousness. It enabled people to actually read the standard version of their own vernacular language, sometimes for the first time. In Schleswig, Danish patriotism was kept alive through Danish high schools and popular rural libraries which disseminated literature in Danish.[14] Perhaps in the long run the rise of print accelerated the decline of Latin and rise of vernacular languages. Nevertheless, Anderson's much-quoted emphasis on 'print nationalism' has been taken too much for granted. Print culture did not produce modern nationalism: a causal relationship seems impossible to sustain given the 400-year time lag between the invention of printing and the appearance of nineteenth-century nationalist movements! Furthermore, there is a missing link in the postulated chain between print and nationalism – namely the reader. Any speculation about the impact of printed literature must proceed via a study of literacy, reception and the readers' responses. So far it has rarely done so. In addition, nationalism often spread through oral rather than printed channels, in spoken verse and song. Scandinavia again provides good examples. Swedish romantic nationalism was disseminated in songs, which were published in print form but intended to be performed aloud. In Norway, scholars collected folk songs. In Denmark, the priest and poet Nikolaj Grundtvig translated the early medieval sagas and epic poems which he considered to be lost treasures of 'Danishness'. But his work was disseminated largely through oral media: sermons, psalms and the 1500 songs he composed to be sung by his Lutheran followers.[15]

The nationalist movements mentioned briefly so far were all movements that eventually 'won' – in other words they represent nationalist causes which later passed through all Hroch's developmental stages to achieve the creation of an independent nation state. But not all nationalist movements did achieve this desired goal. In the middle of the nineteenth century, nationalist movements emerged in opposition to existing nation states. These movements usually represented regional or minority cultures, like the movements for the Breton and Provençal languages in France. In Spain in the 1840s, romantic intellectuals tried to rehabilitate regional languages like Galician and Catalan in a literary form, encouraging interest in folklore and regional history-writing. Such regional movements, however, had characteristics very similar to those of other movements already outlined, especially in their concentration on linguistic revival led by small literary elites. A regional culture, therefore, could have all the characteristics of a nation, except for the scale, but some regional identities were antagonistic towards the centralizing state. The region, too, was an 'imagined community'.[16]

The appeal of regionalism faded in the second half of the century. It seemed obsolete and archaic in the face of economic modernization and state centralization. The triumph of the nation state involved the marginalization of minority cultures like Welsh or Breton. Successful nations were usually formed through the domination of one self-defined ethnic group over several others. The age of nationalism therefore was not one in which nations naturally 'emerged' from slumber and came to maturity: rather it was an age where nationalisms aggressively competed against each other in a conflict whose outcomes were far from given. In some situations, to be sure, state power ensured the victory of one particular ethnic group: thus Tsarism endorsed a policy of Russianization throughout the Empire, at the expense of Baltic, Polish and Ukrainian cultures among others. For these reasons, many nationalisms failed to 'emerge' into statehood.

## Imagined communities in the Habsburg Empire

The Habsburg Empire was a patchwork of different ethnic groups, languages and religions which defied the logic of the nineteenth-century nation state. It was a dynastic and supranational state, in which national and linguistic communities sometimes co-operated and often competed against each other. It was here that the national idea appeared most disruptive of German and Hungarian domination of Empire.

In East Central Europe, there was the same intense search for a national literary heritage and usable symbolic reference-points that we have noted in Scandinavia and other parts of Europe. A handful of intellectuals followed the precedents set in Germany by the Grimm brothers, Jacob and Wilhelm. They pioneered the collection of German legends, myths and folktales, thus outlining a model project for national enthusiasts elsewhere. The search for a literary lineage sometimes went to extraordinary extremes: ancient manuscripts would be conveniently 'discovered' in old barns or monasteries, providing allegedly authentic bases for the resurrection of medieval national glories. In one of a series of Czech forgeries, Josef Linda announced in 1816 the 'discovery' of a thirteenth-century Czech ballad, the 'Lay of Visegrad'.[17] Then in 1817 the young Bohemian poet Vaclav Hanka published a collection of epic poems and songs, based on manuscripts supposedly dating from the thirteenth century which he claimed to have found hidden in a church organ. These literary hoaxes helped to prove that the Czech language had a distinguished and ancient literary ancestry.[18] National groups needed the legitimation of a shared and long-established culture. Norwegians found this in the Viking sagas, while some French writers now claimed they were descended from the inhabitants of Gaul. The Romanians chose as their historic ancestors the Dacians, conquered by the Romans in the second century. This enabled them to assert a distinct identity as descendants of Latin culture in the midst of an ocean of Slavdom. Romanian linguists adopted a Latin alphabet and new words of Latin or French origin. They were perhaps unique in Eastern Europe in that they did not refer primarily to Slavic peasant roots.

Linguistic politics were particularly fraught in East Central Europe. So many language groups coexisted that Latin was still a useful lingua franca. It was used in the Hungarian Diet and the Croation *sobor* up to the 1848 Revolutions. In 1825, the Hungarian reformer Count Szechenyi became the first member to speak to the Hungarian Diet in Magyar instead of Latin. Yet Szechenyi represented the cosmopolitan elite of the Empire: he wrote his personal diary in German, French and English.[19]

Minority leaders, however, promoted their own cultural autonomy. The historian František Palacky defended the Czech language and rejected absorption into German national culture. He saw the Habsburg Empire as a form of protection against this. 'If the Austrian Empire did not already exist', he said, 'we would have to hurry to invent it not merely in the interests of Europe but of humanity.'[20] Palacky was a dissident Moravian and thus paradoxically belonged to a minority among Czechs. He had a varied cultural background, however, because his Protestant education in Hungary and Slovakia had brought him into contact with Magyars, Serbs and Slovaks.[21] His *History of the Czech Nation* was first published (in German) in 1836–45, and in it Palacky saw the Hussite Protestant Reformation as the formative period of Czech identity. Like many others of both Slav and German origin, he envisaged a future 'clash of civilizations' between Germans and Slavs.

The Slovak Jan Kollar demanded more dictionaries and grammars, more university chairs in Slav studies and the elimination of foreign borrowings from Slav languages. Kollar conceived of a common Slav culture and a single Slav language to counteract German domination. For such leaders, more was at stake in defending a national language than cultural identity. It mattered greatly which language – German or Czech, German or Magyar – was taught in schools, because this would also determine which language was demanded of applicants for posts in government service. The struggle for language was also a struggle for access to jobs. Explicitly or implicitly, these Czech and Slovak intellectuals were Austro-Slavs. They had a sense of the unity of Slav culture, and the need to protect it against German or Hungarian hegemony. They looked to Austria as a potential ally. There were 4 million Czechs and 1.7 million Slovaks in the Empire. In the early nineteenth century, both nationalist movements belonged to the Phase A of Hroch's typology, in which a small group of scholars work in isolation. The Czechs, who were more urbanized, more industrialized and more literate, were eventually far more successful in developing a nationalist movement with a popular basis.[22] The upheavals of 1848 showed that businessmen and artisans were now involved, as well as students, professionals and intellectuals.

The aim of linguistic unity was always hard to realize. Social elites needed plenty of convincing that they ought to be speaking the same language as their uncouth peasants. The task was particularly difficult where not only different dialects but also different alphabets coexisted, as they did in Albania where Arabic, Latin and Cyrillic scripts were used. The formation of Serbo-Croat illustrates the complexity of the issue in the process of national identity formation. One early manifestation of South Slav nationalism was 'Illyrism', which developed in Croatia in the 1830s as a reaction to Hungarian cultural imperialism. The name recalled both Roman and Napoleonic imperial antecedents. Within the ex-territories of Napoleonic Illyria, however, the Slovenes staged their own separate national revival. This left the Croatians in need of help from their Slav neighbours to resist 'magyarisation'. In Zagreb (then known as Agram), capital of Croatia, the problem of creating a national language for southern Slavs was posed: which, of several peasant dialects, could become their national tongue?

The development of a Serbo-Croat language became possible when some Croatian leaders joined with Serbs to select the *shtokavsky* dialect, which was used by Serbs, Montenegrins and some Croatians, rather than the *kajkavski* dialect which was common in Zagreb itself. The unity of southern Slavs, however, was only partial. Croatians emphasized their attachment to Catholicism which distinguished them from the Orthodox Serbs, and insisted on maintaining their own Latin alphabet, while the Serbs used a Cyrillic script. In 1850, an agreement signed by five Croatian writers, two Serbian philologists and a Slovenian professor of grammar formally established Serbo-Croat as a single language with two alphabets.[23] The fact that this agreement was signed in Vienna is not surprising, given the political context of the Habsburg Empire. Vienna encouraged such minority movements in order to undermine and balance the power of the Magyar elite. Croatian nationalism could find more breathing space under the Habsburgs than it was likely to enjoy in a Hungarian nation state.

## Italy – Mazzinianism

The banner of Italian nationalism was held aloft throughout the 1830s by Giuseppe Mazzini, an untiring writer, agitator and journalist-in-exile. For Mazzini, the nation was sacred. Every nation according to his vision had a God-given mission to fulfil, and harmony could be achieved when Germans, Italians, Poles and others had at last achieved their national destinies. Mazzinian organizations like Young Italy, Young Switzerland, and Young Poland were founded to propagate the idea of democratic nationhood (see Chapter 4). Harmony between sovereign nations proved to be an impossible dream, but it has found new favour recently among defenders of the European Union.

For Mazzini, there was nothing artificial about nations. He conceived of the nation as an organic and democratic entity. Like all nationalists, he attacked communism, regarding class conflict as harmful and divisive of the true national community. Above all, he was a republican, which brought his followers into conflict with existing Italian monarchies, particularly in Piedmont, where many Mazzinians were imprisoned for subversive activities. Mazzini hoped for a genuine insurrection of the people which would overthrow existing regimes, expel the Austrian oppressor and create a united Italy. Once again, he was dreaming: the peasant masses could make little sense of his prophetic ravings and a mass uprising never occurred. Nevertheless, Mazzini entertained messianic hopes of Italian nationhood. After the Rome of the Caesars, he proclaimed, and the Rome of the Popes, the Third Rome would follow, the Rome of the People.

Young Italy, according to Mack Smith's provocative suggestion, should be regarded as Italy's first ever political party, with a programme, membership, subscriptions, a news network and a journal which would be smuggled back to Italy.[24] It had all these things, but some of its activities were far from parliamentary. Mazzini himself was a born conspirator. While based in Switzerland in 1833, he was involved in attempts to provoke a military uprising over the border in Piedmont. His disciples were executed and Mazzini himself was condemned to death *in absentia*. Mazzini appears to have been surprisingly untroubled by this squandering of idealistic lives. He had a wide network of correspondents, but his mail was intercepted and read by Metternich, the Papal police and also the Neapolitan government.

It is no wonder that further attempts to organize a *coup* in Piedmont collapsed and brought even more culprits to the scaffold.

## Germany – the *Burschenschaften*

German nationalists had to contend with many obstacles to their romantic aspirations for unity. They confronted the political fragmentation of Germany: even after 1815, the German Confederation still had 39 different governments. They also faced the rivalry between Prussia and Austria for influence over the smaller states, and the power of Metternich's repressive apparatus. Germany was culturally divided between the mainly Protestant north and mainly Catholic south, and there was an economic division between the east, which was largely agricultural, and the west which was more urban and industrialized. All these factors militated against cohesion, and in the history of the German national state the post-revolutionary decades sometimes appear as a period of inertia. German historians call this the Vormärz, the 'Pre-March', indicating a hiatus before the revolutionary outbreak of 1848. This is an unnecessarily negative view of post-revolutionary Germany, in which the much-maligned German Confederation provided the framework for peaceful development. The formation of the Prussian-led Customs Union (*Zollverein*) in the 1830s is sometimes seen as a stepping-stone on the road to unification, but this view requires considerable qualification (see below).

The flag-bearers of romantic nationalism in the post-revolutionary era were university students, united in the *Burschenschaften* (student leagues). Nationalist students at universities like Jena and Heidelberg drew their inspiration from the armed struggle to expel the French in 1813, known as the 'War of German Liberation', and they adopted the red, black and gold colours of that movement which would eventually become the national colours of Germany. In October 1817, they organized a festival at Wartburg castle where they presented their critique of the political situation. They called for freedom of speech, and declared their objective was a federal German state which would somehow incorporate existing dynasties like the Hohenzollerns. The Wartburg Festival commemorated a double anniversary. It marked exactly 300 years since Martin Luther worked at Wartburg to translate the Bible into German. This was also the fourth anniversary of the defeat of Napoleon at Leipzig, which threw his armies out of German territory. The Protestant and anti-French affiliations of the *Burschenschaften* were clear. Books including Napoleon's Civil Code were burned, a French corset was ceremonially consigned to the flames, and

Hessian, Prussian and Austrian military regalia were destroyed. The symbolism of liberation was more impressive than the numbers who supported it: fewer than 500 took part in the festival.

The Wartburg programme was moderately liberal. A more radical wing of the *Burschenschaften*, who called themselves 'the Blacks', advocated a central German Reichstag and the overthrow of existing German governments. Their intensely Christian patriotism was coloured by overtly antisemitic rhetoric.[25] This radical version of nationalism was responsible for the murder in 1819 of the prolific playwright Kotzebue, by Karl Sand, a theology student from Jena University. Kotzebue had worked as a Russian agent in the Napoleonic period, and was identified as a traitor. Nationalists hated Kotzebue, however, for moral and aesthetic reasons as much as from political motives. His sentimental dramas of seduction and adultery offended the serious and vigorous spirit of the radical *Burschenschaftler*, to whom Kotzebue seemed effeminate and un-German. Nationalist and deeply religious students like Sand did not forgive Kotzebue his cosmopolitan attitude. It disgusted them that he had spent his life's work composing nothing but weepy melodramas for a mainly female audience. Instead they demanded literature that upheld Christian, national and masculine values. Kotzebue, in turn, found these young critics unbearably arrogant and self-righteous.[26] His murder was exploited by Metternich as a pretext for the introduction of the Carlsbad decrees and the banning of the *Burschenschaften*.

Alumni networks kept the spirit of the *Burschenschaften* alive during the 1820s, even though the original organization was illegal. In 1832, the Bunsen brothers established the Vaterlandsverein (Union of the Fatherland), and in 1833 they plotted an uprising against the German Confederation at Frankfurt. After this ended in fiasco, the conspirators dispersed abroad (Gustav Bunsen died fighting in Texas in 1836). This was the last major *Burschenchaft* action, although individual members surfaced again in the 1848 Revolutions.[27] Only in 1848 did political agitation suggest that the German nationalist cause was moving towards Hroch's Phase C, with the potential to become an organized mass movement.

## Germany – the *Zollverein*

Historians traditionally regarded the German *Zollverein*, or Customs Union, formally established in 1834, as the forerunner of German political unity. It was formed, however, not for nationalist reasons, but rather to serve specifically Prussian fiscal and commercial interests. The *Zollverein* did help to enlarge the German market, but it did not have much impact on industrialisation. Its tangled political history suggests that it divided Germany as much as it united it.

There was patently an urgent need for some consolidation of tariff barriers in post-Napoleonic Germany. Before the *Zollverein*, there were 1800 different customs tolls in Germany as a whole, including 57 in Prussia east of the Elbe.[28] The end of the Napoleonic wars brought a severe economic crisis, and an influx of British manufactured goods. Austrian tariffs discriminated against Silesian cloth, while German manufacturers found access to French and Dutch markets more difficult than before. The development of a customs union was in part a reaction to this adverse situation.

Most importantly, Prussia was now a country divided in two between her eastern and Rhineland territories (see Map 5.1). Her interests lay in uniting the smaller states, like Hesse-Darmstadt and Hesse-Cassel which lay between east and west Prussia, into a common trading zone. Furthermore, some tiny sovereign territories like the Anhalt duchies were almost completely surrounded by eastern Prussia. At its origin, the *Zollverein* was designed to ensure the cheap transit of goods from one part of Prussian territory to another. The intervening states, or *Enklaven*, were integrated by a Prussian combination of 'coercion and generosity'.[29] The threat of higher duties on their goods and the prize of financial concessions worked to achieve Prussia's aims, which were an integrated Prussian market and greater tariff income.

The Prussian tariff laws of 1818 were a compromise between free trade and protectionism. Internal Prussian customs barriers were abolished. Import taxes were set at zero for raw materials, and at 10 per cent for other agricultural goods. There were higher tariffs on luxury goods and colonial imports like coffee. Further progress, however, could only take place within the framework of tension between the two German powers, Prussia and Austria, and the desire of smaller rulers to preserve as much independent sovereignty as possible. Several different customs unions came briefly into being in the 1820s, including a South German Union and a Middle German Union, supported by Metternich. But the Prussian economy dominated, and drew smaller states into its orbit. Security factors like the fear of French aggression also persuaded German states to seek Prussian protection. The new German *Zollverein* of 1834 embraced a population of 23 millions. It soon included Hesse-Darmstadt, Hesse-Cassel, Saxony, the Thuringian states like Saxe-Coburg-Gotha, together with Bavaria and Württemberg. By 1836, the stragglers – Frankfurt, Baden and Nassau – also became members. Expansion proceeded through a series of bilateral contracts between Prussia and the new member state, so that the defence of Prussian interests remained paramount. In 1841, Brunswick and

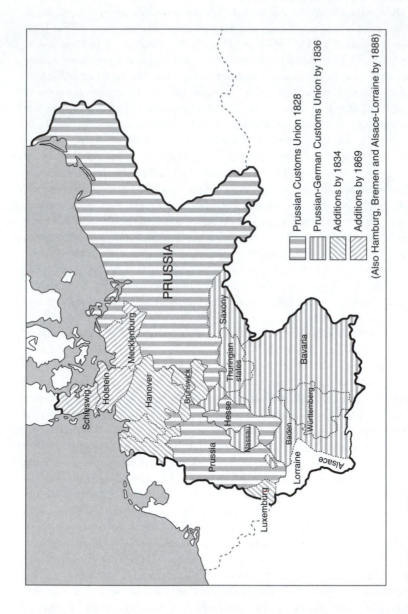

*Map 5.1*  The German *Zollverein*

*Plate 6*   'Felling the Forest'. This anonymous cartoon of 1834 depicts the destruction of customs posts to form the German *Zollverein*

*Source*:   Archiv für Kunst und Geschichte, London. Reproduced in: Martin Kitchen, *The
Cambridge Illustrated History of Germany*, London (CUP), 1996, p. 165.

Luxembourg joined and the *Zollverein* decided to renew itself for a further
seven years. In 1854, Hanover entered the customs union (see Plate 6).

Productivity and commercial exchanges expanded. Between 1837 and
1855, the value of imports for the member states rose by 4.6 per cent annually, and the value of their exports by 4.5 per cent.[30] By this time, however,
the European boom of the 1850s had begun, and the growing railway
network was contributing to German economic expansion. It is therefore
impossible to isolate the role of the *Zollverein* from these other factors in the
prosperity of the middle decades of the century. Robert Lee argues that the
*Zollverein* did little to mitigate regional differences within the German economy, both between east and west, and north and south.[31] The agrarian
north sought outlets for its grain. The industrializing Rhineland and Silesia
favoured protection against British competition. The smaller states and the
south were a mixture of agriculture and small-scale artisan production. The
interests of these sectors did not always coincide, and the continuing debate
over the merits of free trade versus protectionism reflected these tensions.

The *Zollverein* was never complete. It excluded Austria, and the northern maritime cities looked to Britain and the Baltic: Hamburg and Bremen did not join until the 1880s. Even within the *Zollverein*, states retained separate currencies and systems of weights and measures. Although a process of 'widening' occurred, it was not accompanied by any parallel process of 'deepening'. Economic integration did not become more profound, and there were no federal institutions or legal systems to make it so, since until 1867 decisions taken at *Zollverein* congresses had to be unanimous. According to A. J. P. Taylor's provocative assessment, the existence of the *Zollverein* actually made German political unification *less* necessary.[32] Certainly the *Zollverein* did not bring about German political unification. Many of its members, for example, did not support Prussia in its war against Austria in 1866. Rather than a step towards unity, the *Zollverein* was an expression of Prussian hegemony, which made smaller German states suspicious as they surrendered a portion of their independence. It was perhaps significant for the future that it defined a German economic space which excluded Austria. Austria, the traditional protector of smaller German states, remained largely unreformed after its triumphs in 1848–9, and was increasingly distracted by events in Italy and the Balkans. The Habsburg Empire had been bankrupted by its effort in the Napoleonic wars, and it was paying 30 per cent of its income as interest on its worsening debts.[33] This inevitably limited its options.

## The War of Greek Independence, 1821–1829

The nineteenth century was the formative period of the European nation state, and the unification of Italy (1861) and Germany (1870) are the most prominent examples. Long before this, however, nation states had already emerged both in Belgium (discussed in Chapter 6) and in Greece. The disparate and conflicting forces involved in the Greek struggle illustrate the precarious nature of national aspirations and their ultimate dependence on foreign assistance. The Greek state was established in the long shadow of its powerful patrons, and its creation can only be understood in the context of prevailing European power relations.

Greek and Balkan nationalists liked to portray Ottoman rule as a brutal and oppressive tyranny. In practice, the ramshackle Ottoman Empire was an extraordinarily decentralized and pluralist federation. About 9 million lived in the European part of the Empire, divided into religious and fiscal units called *millets* which enjoyed considerable independence. Greeks held privileged positions. The Orthodox Patriarch, who was always Greek, was

*Map 5.2*   Greece and the Ottoman Empire in Europe in the War of Independence

based in Constantinople (present-day Istanbul). The rulers or *hospodars* of the Danubian Principalities of Moldavia and Wallachia (present-day Romania) were Greeks, and the admiral of the Ottoman fleet was also Greek. Well-educated Greeks provided the Empire with a bureaucratic elite, known as the Phanariots because they inhabited the Phanar, the lighthouse district of Constantinople. Greeks, therefore, were agents as much as they were victims of Ottoman imperialism.

This well-to-do Greek elite did not have much in common with the other heterogeneous forces available to the nationalist movement. These included the merchant communities of the Danube, Odessa and the Mediterranean, and the sailors of the islands. The movement owed its intellectual leadership to educated and Westernised Greeks in the diaspora. Hroch identified such educated groups as significant elements in the early phases of nationalist movements. Diaspora Greeks however, inhabited a different world from the impoverished and illiterate peasants of the interior, who felt oppressed by their Moslem landowners. Peasants gave their allegiance more readily to guerrilla captains (the *klephts*) like Theodore Kolokotrones. Nationalists later idealized such chieftains, portraying them as folk heroes like Robin Hood or Ned Kelly. These local warlords, however, who enjoyed quasi-feudal authority, were a poor basis for national cohesion. Most of them were Albanian speakers, although they adopted a Hellenic identity. They acted independently. In fact when the Greek authorities later tried to disarm Kolokotrones, he would simply resort to kidnapping the government.[34] The Greeks therefore were very divided. Some intellectuals promoted 'Hellenism', a term which identified Greek nationalism with the pre-Christian past. This was naturally opposed by the Greek Orthodox Church. Orthodox Christianity itself was not completely homogeneous – it was found in Greek, Romanian and Albanian versions. Northern Greeks did not easily co-operate with Peloponnesians (Greeks from the southern peninsula), and islanders despised both. What could unite such divergent elements? – only their common language, opposition to the Turks and desire for their land, and the pervasive influence of the Orthodox Church, which saw the national struggle as a war for Christianity against Islam.

Many Greek patriots pinned their hopes erroneously on Russia. Tsar Alexander's Christian principles were well-advertised, and many Greeks had found employment in the Tsarist army and civil administration. Alexander's Foreign Secretary was John Capodistria, an Italian-speaking aristocrat who was a Greek expatriate from Corfu. The Tsar, however, had no burning interest in the Orthodox Church, and was reluctant on principle to sanction any rebellion, Greek or otherwise. The Greek conspiratorial organization *Philike Etaireia* (Society of Friends) nevertheless gave its recruits the impression that Russian co-operation was almost guaranteed.[35] The organization, founded in Odessa in 1814, used this deceit to enlist artisans, merchants and military personnel in the Danubian Principalities and parts of the Peloponnese. It tried to instil in all of them the idea of a sovereign Greek state. One of its leaders was Major-General Ypsilantes, an aide-de-camp to the Tsar. Ypsilantes approached Capodistria for support for the Greek cause, but was rebuffed. Undeterred, he launched a revolt in

Romania in 1821, which was immediately followed by indiscriminate slaughter and looting of Greek property. The War of Greek Independence had inadvertently begun. It was started in Romania by a freelancing Russian officer.

Ypsilantes was captured in Austrian territory, but the Greek uprising fared better in the islands and the Peloponnese. In 1821, a National Assembly convened at Epidauros and issued a liberal constitution. But the war degenerated into a series of ghastly atrocities. In 1821, the Moslem population of Tripolitsa on the Greek mainland was massacred. On Easter Sunday, the Patriarch was publicly lynched in Constantinople in retaliation. In 1822, Turks massacred 3000 wealthy Greek inhabitants of the island of Chios, although they had played no part in the war. In the Peloponnese, the Greek captains could not co-operate and the Turks were too incompetent to crush them. In 1824, the Turkish Sultan enlisted his vassal, Mehmet Ali Pasha of Egypt and his son Ibrahim, who landed a fresh army in the Peloponnese. At this point, the Greeks appealed for assistance, and their struggle would have been lost if it had not been internationalized.

Meanwhile a widespread and remarkable Philhellenic movement had developed to aid the Greek cause in Western Europe. The Greeks were seen, with considerable romantic exaggeration, as the descendants of the classical Greeks who had given Europe its tradition of liberal democracy. The glories of classical Athens, it was argued, were on the verge of revival, after centuries of Byzantine darkness and Ottoman oppression. Money was donated to the London Greek Committee and enormous public sympathy developed in France, Germany and Britain in favour of Greece and hostile to the barbaric Turks.[36] This was the context for Delacroix's painting *Greece on the Ruins of Missolonghi*, exhibited in 1826, just two years after his *Massacre at Chios* (see Plate 7). An allegorical female figure of Greece sinks to her knees in a pleading attitude, while behind her are seen an Egyptian leader and the crumbling ruin of a Byzantine church. This was great romantic art and a superlative fundraising effort which played on the liberal conscience. Greece mobilized European intellectual opinion more effectively than any other international cause before the Spanish Civil War in 1936-7.

Nostalgic solidarity with Greece was personified by the English poet Byron, who died a martyr at Missolonghi in 1824. Byron had memorably written:

> The mountains look on Marathon –
> And Marathon looks on the sea;
> And musing there an hour alone,
> I dream'd that Greece might still be free.

*Plate 7*   Eugène Delacroix, *Greece on the Ruins of Missolonghi*, 1826. Delacroix's painting helped to mobilize Western support for the cause of Greek independence

*Source*:   Musée des Beaux-Arts, Bordeaux (photo Lysiane Gauthier).

Byron did not die fighting; he unfortunately succumbed to disease. His sacrifice inspired the cause and probably enhanced the poet's posthumous romantic aura. Like the engaged intellectuals and trade unionists who volunteered for Spain in the 1930s, however, supporters of Greece had only the remotest comprehension of local realities. The Philhellenes expected classical Athenians and Byronic heroes: they found ignorance, disease and brigand leaders accustomed to unlimited looting. Their idealism should not be belittled, but it diminished their capacity to influence the outcome of the struggle.

In 1821, Austria had intervened in Italy to disperse revolutions; in 1823, French intervention had crushed a revolt in Spain. This pattern was not repeated in Greece, because Metternich's major consideration was the danger of Russian expansion into the Balkans. The last thing either he or the British wanted was some form of Russian protectorate over Greece, which would give their rival direct access to the Mediterranean. Metternich and Castlereagh succeeded in restraining Tsar Alexander, even though in 1822 Capodistria advised the Tsar to intervene.[37] Alexander agreed not to act unilaterally, but in 1825 he died and the new Tsar Nicholas threatened to be less compliant. The best way to limit Russian expansion was to act in concert with her. This was the conclusion drawn by the British, who in the Treaty of London (1827) agreed with Russia to impose a joint peace on Turkey. France also became a signatory. This represented a notable reversal of the normal functioning of the international system since 1815, and it had been motivated by anxiety about Russian expansionism. Greece thus survived as a nation for two main reasons, neither of which was within her control. First, Greece existed because of the mutual suspicion between the European powers. Neither of them would allow another to interfere alone. Second, Greece survived because the European powers all needed to postulate the existence of the Greek nation in order to justify any such intervention in Greek–Ottoman affairs.

The British sent a navy to Greece under Admiral Codrington to join the Russians. The French, not wanting the British to steal a march on them, followed suit. Off Navarino in 1827, the Allies annihilated the Turkish-Egyptian fleet. It is not at all clear to historians who initiated this bombardment or why it was necessary. The consequences, at any rate, were decisive. The Turks were defeated, and before long a French expedition arrived to clear the Peloponnese of Egyptian troops. In 1829 the Treaty of Adrianople forced the Turks out of Serbia and the Danubian Principalities, and declared Greece an autonomous state, under the tutelage of the European powers. The war was over, but her troubles had only just begun.

The European powers were ungenerous to the new state; in 1830, they limited Greek territory to the area south of Lamia (it was extended to the Arta–Volos line after 1832). Neither Crete nor Samos was yet incorporated into Greece, and Athens was in Turkish hands. Over the next century, frustrated nationalists would claim more territory in pursuit of the *Megali Idea* – the idea of Greater Greece. In 1827, the National Assembly had elected Capodistria President for a seven-year term. He faced a country ruined by war and plague, and he failed the impossible task of reconciling the warring factions of the independence struggle. He was hated both as a Russian protégé and as an Ionian.[38] His authoritarian methods antagonized Phanariots, liberals and *klephts* alike. In 1831 Capodistria was assassinated in the capital Nauplion and civil war erupted. In 1832, the Allies made Prince Otto of Bavaria King of Greece. Russia had not been as rapacious as Metternich and the powers had feared. She extended her influence over the Danube delta and the Black Sea coast, but she was not yet willing to contemplate the disappearance of the Ottoman Empire in Europe.

Three-quarters of the Greeks were still under Ottoman rule, but now they no longer enjoyed their privileged position of the pre-independence era. Central authority had broken down, and the Peloponnese was devastated. A Greek population of about 750,000 now lived under an absolute monarchy with a teenage Catholic king, who thus became the nominal head of the Greek Orthodox Church. The new kingdom had been created not by Greeks, but by the European powers eager to limit Russian hegemony. Such were the contradictions of early nineteenth-century nationalism.

## Conclusion

The nationalist movements of this period (1815–48) tended to be movements led by liberals against monarchies and empires. Their hopes for nationhood or autonomy were founded on democratic principles and, as in the case of Mazzini, could have a revolutionary dimension. The great revolutionary outbreak of 1848 was to allow brief expression to many nationalist aspirations. Conservatism, however, triumphed. The threat of nationalism was not yet strong enough to break the hold of Europe's old Empires. After 1848, the traditional social and political elites of Europe adapted to calls for national sovereignty. Later in the century, even Europe's monarchies saw a need to re-invent themselves as symbols of national identity.

Certainly, by 1848, national identity mattered to large numbers of educated people, in Germany, Lombardy, Bohemia and Hungary. Among the subject peoples of East Central Europe, however, nationalist movements had not yet developed beyond Phase B defined by Hroch. Nationalists among them were few and their ideas had limited resonance. Like their counterparts in Western Europe, they conceived of the national community in exclusively masculine terms. Only males could be patriots and full citizens.

Nationalism in the early nineteenth century was the affair of historians, linguists, students and bureaucrats. They often had allies amongst the clergy and the teaching profession. Occasionally, they enlisted support from merchants and artisans. In general, however, nationalism had a fragile social base amongst the militant intelligentsia. In Hroch's outline, their movements were passing from Phase A to Phase B – in which a small number of nationalist intellectuals began to engage in political action, but could not form a coherent organization with any popular support. In 1847, the Tuscan newspaper *L'Alba* (The Dawn) recalled that in the 1830s, the idea of the nation existed only 'in the minds of a few, [as] a sectarian utopia, an aspiration of the free'.[39]

# 6   The Revolutions of 1830

## Introduction

The dates 1789 – 1830 – 1848 represent a trio of revolutionary years, but the middle voice is often the most neglected, drowned by the great upheavals which preceded and followed it. When the veteran revolutionist Lafayette lent his support to the July Revolution in Paris, it may have seemed as though the Revolution of 1789 was repeating itself, only this time on a smaller scale. Looking back from today's vantage-point, it may also seem as though this was no more than a dress rehearsal for the greater conflagration of 1848. Nevertheless, as Clive Church has argued, 1830 is worth considering in its own right, not simply as an echo of 1789 or as a distant overture for 1848.[1] Certainly, some movements of that troubled year ended in outright failure while others had only qualified success. But 1830 had a character of its own: or perhaps we should say characters in the plural, because the revolutionary outbreaks which occurred all over Europe had distinct domestic problems to resolve. They were neither a prelude nor an aftermath, but rather responses to unresolved tensions in the post-revolutionary settlement of 1815.

From food riots to festering civil war, the 'Revolutions of 1830' covered a variety of disturbances in France, Switzerland, the Netherlands, the Papal States, Poland, Portugal, Spain, Norway and Germany. In Britain, too, the social and political crisis took a particular form. In spite of inevitable local differences, some common features can be picked out. In general terms, two sets of issues predominated. First, constitutional liberalism and the question of parliamentary representation were at stake in France, Britain and Switzerland. Second, national autonomy was high on the agenda in Belgium, Italy and Poland. The '1830 Revolution' actually spanned an extended period which was not confined to 1830 itself. Instability endured until at least 1833, producing not a single wave of revolutions, but what Church calls '50 months' of crisis.[2] The post-revolutionary settlement of 1815 was now subjected to a prolonged period of shocks and spasms.

Political conflicts were fought out everywhere against a background of economic and social unrest. Europe had not fully recovered from the economic depression of 1827, and the resumption of population growth after the Napoleonic wars pushed rents higher and wages lower. Artisans were increasingly threatened by mechanization and the deregulation of employment, in crafts which could no longer exclude cheaper products made by less skilled labour. These economic changes had repercussions in 1848, too, but they were already evident in 1830 in Western Europe. Peasant protest and artisan agitation were essential ingredients of the disturbance, especially in France and Britain.

### France: the July Revolution

In the July Revolution in Paris, the restored Bourbon dynasty lost its struggle for legitimacy. Some reasons for this were given in Chapter 2, but we must emphasize here the reactionary attitudes of Charles X and his Prime Minister Polignac in the political crisis of 1829–30. Polignac was an ultra-royalist who had never accepted the constitutional arrangements of 1814. He was appointed Prime Minister in 1829 as a royal candidate, although he was not an elected member of parliament. The Charter of 1814 had never been very precise about the crucial relationship between the king and the legislature, but Polignac's extreme interpretation of the royal prerogative was to destroy the Charter and it cost Charles his throne. Faced with a hostile chamber, the king retaliated by issuing Four Ordinances, which provoked a revolution. He announced the dissolution of parliament and new elections, ordered restrictions on press freedom and decreed new limits on voting rights and a new Chamber of Deputies much reduced in size. Within a month, the Bourbon dynasty would disappear for good.

The problems of the Charter were at the root of the political crisis of July 1830. Clause 14 allowed the monarch to invoke emergency powers but left him the judge of when this might be necessary. In activating Clause 14, therefore, Charles X was acting strictly within his constitutional rights. But in so doing, he was stifling the chance of peaceful development towards a genuine constitutional parliamentary monarchy, and he aroused liberal rage. His attempts to limit press freedom were challenged by the liberal newspapers, especially *Le National* and *Le Temps*, which became epicentres of the revolt. The failure of the Bourbons to fashion a convincing role for the monarchy in post-revolutionary France was demonstrated when significant numbers of troops went over to the rebels. About 2000 were killed in fierce fighting at the barricades; Charles abdicated and fled to England.[3]

The liberals, fighting for a free press, an elected National Guard, representative government and a wider franchise, made common cause with discontented artisans who were suffering in a period of economic depression.

Poor harvests in 1828 and 1829 pushed up the price of bread, at a time when wage rates were falling in the Paris building trade and in the provincial textile industry. By June 1829, one-quarter of the capital's population applied for poor relief in the form of bread rations.[4] In 1830, printing workers attacked and destroyed the mechanical presses at the Royal Printing Works (Imprimerie Royale): both they and political journalists like Adolphe Thiers of *Le National* joined forces against the Bourbons. This alliance between the worker's blouse and the bourgeois frock-coat, to use Ed Newman's sartorial expression, was temporary and contradictory.[5] It was cemented for a moment by the power of Parisian anticlericalism. Both Parisian workers and bourgeois resented the wealth and the politics of the Catholic Church, especially since it had allied itself so closely with the defeated monarchy. This hostility erupted in 1830 in the ransacking and looting of the archbishop's palace. Ultimately, however, the political aims of blouse and frock-coat would not necessarily coincide. In 1830, workers paradoxically fought to defend a constitutional Charter which had never given them the vote, and although they accepted the Orleanist monarchy, they only did so in the absence of a clear republican or bonapartist alternative. Their alliance with the bourgeoisie was therefore problematic, and the 1848 Revolution eventually produced a brutal confrontation between moderate liberals and the Parisian lower classes.

The unity of bourgeois and worker in the democratic cause was idealized by Delacroix in his painting 'Liberty Leading the People', completed in 1831 (see Plate 5). The centre of Delacroix's painting is an allegorical Marianne, symbol of liberty and of the republic which of course did not materialize in 1830. Each protagonist at the barricade represents a social group: on the left, a bare-chested worker with a cutlass, behind him a student from the elite Polytechnic School with uniform and cocked hat, the young bourgeois with a top hat slightly the worse for wear, and a street urchin with pistols. Before them lies the dead body of a National Guardsman. In Delacroix's vision of revolution, all social classes are united in a victorious struggle. In reality, the bulk of the fighting was done by artisans and skilled workers, the carpenters and shoemakers and printers of Paris, more than half of them under 35 years old.[6]

Who was to replace the Bourbons? The liberal leadership were reluctant to establish a republic, fearing social revolution at home, and the hostility of foreign powers in Europe. Lafayette appeared at the Hotel de Ville (City Hall) to endorse a new monarchy, this time under Louis-Philippe, descendant of the Orleanist branch of the ruling family. He was the son of Philippe-Egalité, Duke of Orleans, who had sat with the Jacobins in the National Convention of 1792. His own democratic and patriotic credentials rested on the fact that he had fought for revolutionary France at Valmy in 1792, and had refused allegiance to the exiled king, the future Louis XVIII. Louis-Philippe had spent the Napoleonic Empire quietly in Twickenham, and returned to France definitively in 1817. He had two essential qualifications for the throne in the eyes of the conservative revolutionaries of 1830: he was related to the Bourbons and yet he was not one of them. This ambiguity suited the Orleanists, who wished to eliminate Charles X without causing a dramatic upheaval. Louis-Philippe seemed to represent both continuity and a rupture at the same time. As in 1814, it was irrelevant whether ordinary people wanted him on the throne or not.

The political leadership of what now became known as the July Monarchy played down the insurrectionary origins of the new regime. For Prime Minister Casimir Périer, there had been no revolution, simply a change of government. The Orleanist view was that the July Revolution had been very regrettable, and provoked solely by the stupidity of the Bourbons. Louis-Philippe graciously bought Delacroix's famous painting, and then removed it from public view. It was not to be exhibited again until the Revolution of February 1848, and even then its appearance was very brief, such was its power to recall the spirit of revolution. The victorious liberals of the July Monarchy did not wish to be reminded that their supremacy derived from a popular uprising. They felt uneasy about the idea of a union between the middle class and the workers. Seeking order and stability, they did not identify with Delacroix's combative image of Marianne. But artisans and republicans, many of whom had died at the barricades in 1830, felt cheated. The 1830 Revolution was a defeat for republicans, and the socialist leader Louis Blanc accused the bourgeoisie of stealing their revolution.

Karl Marx thought the Orleanists represented a new breed of middle-class financiers, but he was reacting superficially to the conspicuous presence of bankers like Laffitte and Casimir Périer in the revolutionary leadership.[7] Lawyers, public servants and landowners still dominated the ranks of the ruling class, which was becoming an amalgam of aristocrats and the bourgeoisie. It would take a much more drastic reduction of the property qualification to allow a substantial influx of businessmen into the Chamber of Deputies. For Adolphe Thiers, 1830 resembled England's Revolution of 1688, signifying a change of dynasty without violence or upheaval, with a constitution guaranteed by Louis-Philippe, France's equivalent of William of Orange.[8] Such historical references came thick and fast in a revolutionary leadership full of distinguished historians like Thiers, Mignet and Guizot.

There was some truth, then, in Casimir Périer's insistence on business as usual after 1830. The new Chamber of Deputies was filled with a mixture of landowners, professional men and public officeholders, much as before the 1830 Revolution.[9] In spite of the Orleanists' emphasis on continuity, however, some things had certainly changed. Voting rights were slightly extended, although their basis remained a property qualification. An electorate of about 166 000 was created and the number of voters would rise to a quarter of a million by 1848. This was about one-quarter of the number of men who had the vote in Britain after the 1832 Reform Bill. The tricolour replaced the white flag of the Bourbons. The hereditary peerage was abolished, but the upper chamber remained in existence as a house of life peers. The National Guard, a militia much valued by the urban middle class, was reformed and its officers were to be elected.

The most significant consequence of all was a thoroughgoing purge of administrative personnel. Seventy-five peers appointed by Charles X were expelled from parliament. The magistracy, the army and the public service were purged of Bourbon appointees, almost all the largest cities had new mayors, and only three out of 86 prefects remained in office. The main beneficiaries of this massive turnover were former servants of Napoleon's Empire, ex-imperial prefects and army officers who made a silent return to power after 15 years in the wilderness.[10] The importance of the 1830 Revolution lay in the demise of the provincial aristocracy, who had come to office in 1815 but now disappeared as a political force. In their place, 1830 produced a Bonapartist reprise. The popular songs of Béranger, the troubadour of the anti-Bourbon opposition, were at the height of their popularity. Béranger's songs celebrated poverty, wine and anti-English sentiment and they were often infused with a strong dose of Bonapartist nostalgia. Béranger's songs were the number one bestsellers of the years 1826–30 – another indication of the Bonapartist revival of 1830.[11]

The events of 1830 had revealed a level of popular distress both in town and countryside which the Revolution did not alleviate. The Revolution was not solely a Parisian phenomenon. It was accompanied by bread riots in the provinces, attacks on bakeries and winegrowers' protests in Burgundy and Alsace.[12] The Lyon silk workers rose in revolt in 1831 and 1834, as discussed in Chapter 4. Peasants protested against the Forest Code of 1827 and the guards who enforced it. In the Ariège department in the Pyrenees, peasants blackened their faces and dressed in hoods and loose shirts resembling women's clothes to drive out the forest guards, in the so-called 'Ladies War' (*La Guerre des Demoiselles*).[13] They were acting in defence of their ancient communal rights to graze sheep and goats in the forest, to cut wood and gather fuel. The revolt of the Ariège peasants took on aspects of carnival disguise, but it was a serious protest to reclaim the forest which had been taken over by state regulation and private concessionaries in the iron industry who used timber for their charcoal forges. These were traditional forms of protest by groups reacting in defence of custom against the incursions of state-backed capitalism.

## Britain: the crisis of parliamentary reform, 1831–1832

Eighty years ago the French historian Elie Halévy published his history of nineteenth-century England and boldly entitled his chapter on the parliamentary reform of 1832 'The July Revolution in England'.[14] It is still unusual especially among British historians to integrate British and continental events in this way, Eric Hobsbawm being the notable exception. Yet tricolours were unfurled in England, and radical leaders crossed the channel to meet Lafayette. Although the Tories were hardly the counterpart of France's ultra-royalists, and the British situation was in many ways unique, there were convergences and parallels with events in France, not the least of which was the timing of the crisis. In Britain, barricades and bloodshed were not necessary to pass the Reform Act of 1832, but there was something approaching a revolutionary crisis in 1831 and it concluded with the end of Britain's parliamentary 'Old Regime'.

There was widespread acceptance that parliament needed reforming, since glaring anomalies had developed which even the most ardent defenders of the system had difficulty in justifying. There were too many 'rotten' or 'pocket' boroughs, returning members of parliament elected by perhaps only a handful of eligible voters. In such tiny seats, a landed proprietor could virtually appoint his own MP in his own private constituency. In contrast, the new industrial centres of the north were under-represented. The struggles both to redistribute seats and to extend the franchise aimed to weaken the aristocratic landed interest in favour of the urban and manufacturing middle class. At the same time, there was some conservative sympathy for reform, as many Tories felt that the Whigs had exploited the corrupt system to push through what they regarded as objectionable measures such as Catholic emancipation.

Although the need for moderate change was widely recognized, there was no mass movement for parliamentary reform. The cause received a major boost when the Prime Minister, the Duke of Wellington, rashly declared that his government would not contemplate any reform measure. Wellington had presided in 1828–9 over the removal of disabilities preventing both Protestant Nonconformists and Roman Catholics from holding office. These liberal changes had divided the Tory party, whose traditional role had always been to defend the Church of England. Wellington perhaps felt the need to demonstrate his fidelity to the Tory cause by opposing reform. As with Polignac's Four Ordinances, his surprising intransigence succeeded in galvanizing liberals and radicals. Wellington had unwittingly brought reformers together, and his mistake was to topple his government and the old system.

The 1831 election was fought virtually on a single issue – parliamentary reform – and it brought the Whigs into office after decades in opposition. Lord John Russell's Bill sought to satisfy the middle-class demand for change without seriously endangering the supremacy of the great landowners. The Whigs themselves were led by representatives of England's great landowning families, like Grey and Russell, but as long as they accepted some measure of reform they, rather than the Tories, appealed to factory owners and Dissenters. Championing moderate reform could serve several purposes for the Whigs – it might satisfy their middle-class clientele and bring them to power. It might also prevent something far worse, inoculating Britain against the continent's revolutionary contagion. As Lord Grey unequivocally put it: 'The principle of my Reform is to prevent the necessity for Revolution.'[15]

The 1832 Act introduced a uniform franchise for all males who occupied, either as owners or tenants, houses worth 10 pounds a year or more in rent and who paid their own rates (local taxes). This gave the vote to many shopkeepers and the urban lower middle classes. The Act abolished 168 parliamentary constituencies outright, including many rotten boroughs, and 98 new seats were established, mainly in industrial areas. The redistribution of seats operated in favour of the manufacturing centres, and at the expense of mainly southern landed interests. London, too, was better represented in the new system. The electorate would thus be increased from about half a million to about 800,000 voters.[16] Some pocket boroughs still remained, and in Asa Briggs's calculation, ten southern counties with one-quarter of the population still returned one-third of the members of the House of Commons.[17] Few observers, however, had expected Grey to go even this far.

The election result of 1831 fully endorsed parliamentary reform, but the rejection of the Bill by the House of Lords created a crisis in the country. Riots erupted in Derby and Nottingham. In Bristol, crowds burned down the Town Hall and the bishop's palace. Twelve were killed and four executed. In the South Wales iron-mining town of Merthyr Tydfil, which was a stronghold of radical Dissent, an armed insurrection was put down by troops, who shot dead two dozen insurgents.[18] Radical associations like Attwood's Birmingham Political Union agitated for reform in support of the Whigs. The Political Unions threatened a tax strike, and a co-ordinated withdrawal of private deposits from the Bank of England. Meanwhile working-class organizations like the National Union of the Working Classes met weekly in Blackfriars in London to demand more fundamental reforms, including universal male suffrage, the secret ballot and annual parliaments. The conflict was only resolved by the threat to create enough new peers to pass the Bill. Wellington was no Polignac, and he conceded defeat in the Lords. In 1834, the Tory leader Robert Peel accepted the 1832 Reform Act as a permanent settlement.

Grey's strategy was a success; the conservative landed interest emerged strengthened. As long as there was no secret ballot, and no limit on election expenses, wealthy landowners and employers could still wield electoral influence over tenants and dependents by means of intimidation, a generous distribution of alcoholic beverages and pork-barrelling. Like the French parliament after 1830, the reformed House of Commons looked remarkably like its predecessor, populated by country gentlemen and aristocrats, together with a handful of radicals and followers of Bentham.

Like the Orleanists in France, the Whigs enlarged the franchise but eliminated any radical alternative. The situation in Britain was in some ways very different. In Britain, the last thing the reformers wanted was to overthrow King William IV. Unlike their French counterparts, they had to take into account increasingly articulate middle-class demands from the manufacturers of Birmingham and Yorkshire, and the cotton-masters of the northwest. In both countries, dissatisfied radicals turned to other solutions – republicanism and socialism in France, Trade Unionism and the Chartist movement in Britain – which revived the unmet demands of 1831–2, like the secret ballot.

Above all, moderate political reform in both countries occurred in a similar context of unrest. In the English southern counties, peasants and radical craftsmen carried out an extensive rebellion whose distinctive tactics were arson of farm property and machine-breaking. These were known as the 'Captain Swing' riots, described by their historians as the greatest machine-breaking episode in English history.[19] Falling wheat prices, the enclosure (or privatization) of common land and the concentration of landholdings all contributed to reducing agricultural labourers to landless rural proletarians. Through village craftsmen and the radical press, they were aware of revolutionary movements in Paris and elsewhere. Although they had no revolutionary programme, they struggled against low wages, against the introduction of cheap Irish labour, and against the new threshing machines. Their revolt was entirely bloodless. Almost 2000 Swing rioters were tried, of whom 19 were executed, 644 imprisoned, and 505 sentenced to transportation to Australia.[20] It took another 40 years before their descendants organized their own agricultural Trade Union.

### Germany and Switzerland: the 'regeneration' of the cantons

In Germany, a variety of disturbances occurred, but most of them were ephemeral. Perhaps the most significant was the revolt in Brunswick, which forced the duke to flee. Here, and in Saxony and the Electorate of Hesse, constitutions were introduced for the first time. Agitation developed in the Rhineland in the wake of the bad harvest of 1831. In the Palatinate, between 20,000 and 30,000 attended the Hambach festival in 1832 to celebrate liberal aspirations and the goal of German unity. Metternich, however, used this just as he had exploited the Kotzebue assassination in 1819 – to reactivate counter-revolutionary forces. The conservative powers rallied once more against revolution in the agreement they signed at Münchengrätz in 1833. But in Switzerland it was a different story.

Switzerland after 1815 was not a unitary state, but a loose federation of individual cantons. These now included Geneva, previously a separate republic. Some cantons were predominantly Protestant and others Catholic, some rural and mountainous and others centred around a thriving commercial city like Basle or Zurich. A variety of languages and dialects were spoken by the cantons' population of about 2 million. The federation of Swiss cantons was the ultimate in decentralization. A Federal Diet existed, but it had very limited powers and the cantons enjoyed equal voting rights regardless of their size. The federal executive rotated regularly between Bern, Zurich and Lucerne, and it has been said that the entire Swiss national government could usually be found on the road, travelling in a single coach.[21] Switzerland was an archipelago of micro-democracies, in which the village or the alpine valley was the true centre of sovereignty. In 1828, the Pope even allowed the cantons to elect their own bishops.

In Switzerland, aspirations for a more liberal and democratic state always came up against traditional localism, and the events of 1830 were no exception. The liberals who gathered in Lausanne around the Société Vaudoise d'Utilité Publique argued for free trade and the abolition of customs duties between cantons. They promoted individual self-help and criticized lavish ecclesiastical charities. They demanded a national government with a federal court, a single currency and a national postal service. For Swiss liberals, a stronger central government was desirable, in order to break down the authority of the powerful merchant oligarchies which had become entrenched in the urban cantons. In some cases, the urban elite completely dominated its surrounding canton. The city of Zurich, for example, had less than 6 per cent of the population of its canton, but accounted for two-thirds of its elected representatives.[22] Not only did the liberals push for national unity, but they also wanted a wider franchise at the local level. Thus the balance of power between the centre and the canton was entwined with the issue of political representation, which as we have seen was also central for British and French liberals in 1830–2. As the Protestant evangelical revival gathered force, religious conflicts would further embitter political debate in Switzerland.

The liberal movement of 1830 temporarily united intellectuals, peasants and craftsmen, and it succeeded in imposing more democratic constitutions in a dozen cantons by 1831. Peasants marched into Fribourg and Lausanne demanding reform and a better balanced representation. As a result of this cantonal 'regeneration', the hold of the patrician elite in urban centres was loosened. In the Vaud canton, about 15 per cent of the population had qualified for the vote in 1814; the 1831 Constitution enfranchised about 20 per cent of cantonal residents.[23] In Bern the oligarchs surrendered their monopoly of power, and in Basle, the canton was split in two, so that the ruling oligarchy remained in power but over a much reduced territory. The democratic alliance, however, was fragile, and religious divisions would grow sharper before the war of the Sonderbund in 1847. Moreover, 1830 may have succeeded in reforming the cantons, but it achieved nothing at national level. On the question of centralization, there was still an impasse. As with the other movements of 1830 already considered, the Swiss regeneration was incomplete.

### Southern Europe: liberalism and clericalism

In Spain, Portugal and the Papal States, the liberals of the early 1830s opposed virulent forms of clerical despotism. Without a strong bourgeoisie to support them, their struggle was doomed to failure unless foreign assistance materialized. In Portugal, Dom Pedro, Emperor of Brazil, had entrusted the Regency to his brother Dom Miguel, who authorized a severe clerical reaction until British intervention forced him to surrender in 1834. In Spain, the Carlists conducted a similar crusade to preserve Catholic Spain from liberals and anticlericals. The government of the Papal States, entirely in the hands of the upper clergy, was notoriously arbitrary and corrupt. Political prisoners were held without trial and the economy was moribund. Unfortunately attempts to reform this situation were repressed by Austrian troops.

In 1831, there were uprisings in the duchies of Parma and Modena, and much of the Romagna rebelled against Papal government. A rebellion in Bologna proclaimed the provisional government of the 'United Italian Provinces'. The *Marseillaise* was sung and officers of the army of the old Napoleonic kingdom of Italy emerged from the woodwork. The attempt to lead an army to Rome, however, collapsed in the Umbrian hills. While the rebel force surrendered at Spoleto, the Austrians put down the revolt in the Romagna behind its back. Once again, it was clear that liberals and ex-Bonapartists had little popular support. They could only hope for success with foreign aid, but the French government was unwilling to frighten the European powers (as it had done in 1793) by launching into a new war of liberation. The risings of 1831 in Italy were total failures, and they demonstrated once and for all the bankruptcy of *Carbonarist* conspiracies.[24]

## The Netherlands: Belgian independence

At the end of the Napoleonic wars, Belgium had been incorporated into the kingdom of the Netherlands. The Belgians had little choice but to acquiesce in this experiment, dubbed by one historian as the 'Great Netherlands Hypothesis'.[25] The European powers would not tolerate a merger with France, and Belgians had no desire to become part of the Austrian Empire again as they had been under the Old Regime. The Belgians themselves were by no means a homogeneous group. In Flanders, the Flemish-speaking population was massively Catholic; in the French-speaking areas in and around Brussels, and in the south of Belgium, the middle classes were more anticlerical, and opposed the ultramontanism (i.e. pro-Papal loyalties) of the Belgian Church. Neither of these groups, however, was happy under the Dutch Calvinist monarchy.

The administration of the kingdom was dominated by Dutch personnel, and presided over by the Dutch King William who was an out-and-out absolutist. Flemish was recognized as the official language, although its use was not compulsory. The Dutch expanded primary education, but it was primarily conducted in the Dutch/Flemish language and seemed to threaten the survival of both Catholic and French-speaking culture in Belgium. The religious issue was particularly fraught: in 1827, King William negotiated a Concordat with the Pope but, faced with Protestant opposition, he never implemented it. The Belgian coal industry developed rapidly, but mainly in French areas, while Flemish textile production remained vulnerable to growing British competition. The Revolution of 1830 challenged and eventually overthrew the unitary state. It was a rebellion against the Dutch bureaucracy, against the trend towards linguistic unification, against the erosion of the position of the Catholic Church, and against monarchical arrogance. The commercial and manufacturing elites of Antwerp and Ghent began to envisage the creation of a state more in tune with their cultural and economic needs.[26]

As elsewhere, the economic downturn allowed liberal and separatist forces to mobilize discontented workers against the Dutch monarchy. In 1830, an insurrection broke out in Brussels, accompanied by machine-breaking in Liège, and spread to southern Belgium. Catholics and middle-class anticlericals formed an unlikely marriage of convenience against Dutch rule, but they were fearful of popular violence. They wanted to establish a liberal monarchy, which would recognize the French language and give the Catholic Church control over education. The Revolution in Brussels declared independence, but fighting continued in Antwerp, where the Dutch navy bombarded the city.

The European powers now took control. They were prepared to recognize the new state. but they firmly vetoed Belgian attempts to elect a French king. Just as after the break-up of the Soviet Union the powers aimed to contain Russian foreign ambitions within an international framework, so too after 1815 they limited the revival of French influence. Metternich accepted the liberation of Belgium, and because the Russian army was absorbed in Poland, there was little the conservative powers could do to prevent it. In 1831, King William renewed his attempts to defeat the independence struggle, but he met opposition from both France and Britain. Thanks to some skilful crisis management by the English foreign minister Palmerston, the Allies found a peaceful solution. The union of the new state with France was prevented and, as in the Greek case, a handy German prince was found to occupy the new throne. He was Leopold of Saxe-Coburg-Gotha, beloved uncle of Queen Victoria, and he was paradoxically a Lutheran reigning over Catholics. The Allies had allowed Belgium to become an independent state for the first time in its history. By 1846, the new kingdom had 2.4 million Flemish speakers and 1.8 million French speakers. They were governed in French by a German-speaking king.[27] These contradictions were only possible in a situation where nationalist forces were relatively weak.

## Poland: the 'November Rising' of 1830

Romantic nationalism inspired the Polish Revolution of 1830, known in Polish historiography as the 'November Rising'. Here national leadership

*Plate 8*    Grandville and Forest, 'Peace reigns in Poland', 1831. French cartoonists
comment sardonically on the Russian repression of the 1830 Revolution in
Poland

*Source*:   J. J. Grandville and E. Forest, 'L'Ordre règne à Varsovie', Aubert, 1831, engraving
in Bibliothèque Nationale de France.

was in the hands not of the urban middle classes, as in Western Europe, but of the Polish aristocracy (*szlachta*) of landowners and army officers. The rising was sparked off by infantry cadets who were about to be sent off to fight the Belgian Revolution.[28] A poor harvest and high food prices enabled them to call initially on wide support. In 1830 a coalition of aristocrats, romantic intellectuals, patriotic students and discontented Warsaw artisans declared the Russian Tsar deposed, and elected Prince Adam Czartoryski president of a new Polish government.

Czartoryski was a very reluctant rebel. His career was built on the premise that concessions could be extracted from the Russians, and that Polish–Russian coexistence was possible. The 1830 Revolution showed this position was untenable, as Nicholas I was in no mood to compromise. The Tsar's violent reaction to this suicidal insurrection turned his ally Czartoryski into a militant Polish nationalist. Although an uprising followed in Lithuania, the Polish Revolution eventually capitulated to the Russian army at Grochow near Warsaw in 1831. The rural masses remained indifferent to the revolt of the *szlachta*. Polish noble landowners refused to alleviate the subjection of their peasants, or to make it easier for them to buy their own land. The social limitations of the nationalist revolt were thus clearly exposed. Near Cracow, peasants declared: 'We will march against the Muscovite but first we will cut down the *szlachta* because they are the cause of our misery.'[29]

At Grochow, Russian casualties numbered almost 10,000.[30] This was the largest land battle fought in Europe between Waterloo and the Crimean War.[31] With no foreign aid, and unwilling to mobilize the peasantry, the Poles were crushed and the consequences of their adventurism were disastrous. Between 5000 and 10,000 of them went into exile, Czartoryski among them, adding an international ingredient to subsequent revolutionary movements in Western Europe. Nicholas confiscated the estates of the rebels, sentenced 250 of them to death and deported thousands to Siberia. He abolished the rebellious Polish Diet and what remained of Poland's separate army. Two hundred monasteries were closed. Poland fell completely under Tsarist rule (see Plate 8).

## Conclusion

The risings of 1830 had mixed results. In Italy and Poland they ended in utter failure. In Britain, France and Switzerland they initiated constitutional reforms and a moderate widening of the electorate. In Belgium they produced a new nation state. The conservative powers had managed to limit the damage. Unlike the precedent of 1793, there was no French military aggression, and revolts in Belgium, Italy and Poland were concluded or suppressed without foreign aid. At the Convention of Münchengratz in 1833, Prussia, Austria and Russia confirmed their mutual co-operation against revolutionary tendencies. The settlement of 1815 was in this sense renewed. The independence of Belgium had forced the Metternich system to adapt, but a general war had been averted. The post-revolutionary settlement was 'bent not broken' in 1830.[32]

The liberals and nationalists of 1830 had formed uneasy alliances with artisans and workers. This had been made possible by adverse economic conditions, poor harvests, high rents and depressed wages. The coalition of the 'Blouse and Frock-Coat', however, disguised conflicts of interest between the middle-class left-wing leaders and popular democrats. In France and Britain, the democratic movement had not been appeased by the change of ruling dynasty or the passing of the parliamentary Reform Act of 1832. Unrest would continue after 1833, as the Chartist movement, the Lyon silk workers' revolt of 1834, and several Mazzinian conspiracies in Italy indicated. Post-revolutionary stability still remained elusive.

# 7  The Rise of Public Opinion

## The revival of a public sphere

At the end of the eighteenth century, public opinion had become an important factor in the politics of Western Europe for the first time. The growth of the newspaper press in Britain, and the outpouring of pamphlet literature in pre-revolutionary Paris created a new space in which politics could be debated and government policies scrutinized. The political philosopher Jürgen Habermas identified this period as an important one in the formation of a 'public sphere', an arena where political discussion could take place independently of the control of the state or the monarch.[1] Under the Napoleonic Empire, however, debate was stifled and there was little room for contestation. Essential requirements for the working of a democratic society were absent. In 1811, the number of newspapers was severely limited, and pre-publication censorship was enforced for the press, books and the theatre. After 1815, the development of a public sphere revived in France, and elsewhere in Europe too, in spite of government controls. New forms of political action developed in the post-revolutionary era, and by the 1840s, new kinds of political mobilization appeared. Some, like the Anti-Corn Law League in Britain, had specifically middle-class objectives, while other movements like Chartism embraced broad and amorphous working-class support.

In 1989, after the fall of Soviet Communism, there was a similar need to make civil society grow and function. Instead of following the directives of an authoritarian system, individuals had to be encouraged to take initiative and responsibility in a new democratic framework. The conditions for democracy included the existence of a free press and independent communications media, free elections with a choice of political parties, free Trade Unions and religious groups, and so on. Europe after 1830 experienced similar social and political changes. In considering the period 1830–48, therefore, our focus must now shift away from the memory of Napoleon and the French Revolution and towards these new political developments. This chapter focuses accordingly on a revival of the public sphere in Europe in the 1830s and 1840s. The growth of a broad culture of opposition was a significant precondition of the 1848 Revolutions.

## The 'conspiracy in broad daylight'

The public sphere outlined by Habermas in the second half of the eighteenth century was limited to a small educated elite, whether of aristocratic or middle-class origin. In addition, the public sphere was gendered, in the sense that only educated men participated in public debate. It was furthermore geographically restricted to Western Europe, and especially the highly developed urban societies of London and Paris. In Metternich's Europe, Britain and France still stood out as states with functioning elected parliaments. From the 1830s on, however, restrictions on political debate were being eroded. The reading public was growing, as cheaper literature increasingly found an audience amongst the urban lower middle classes. A provincial public developed outside capital cities, and the periodical press also expanded in Germany and Italy, often imitating British or French models. There were growing signs that women also wished to contribute to political life. The movement for the abolition of slavery, for example, launched in the 1820s, was a humanitarian cause capable of mobilizing unprecedented female support for legislative change.

In 1846, the Piedmontese aristocrat Massimo d'Azeglio published an eloquent defence of democratic society and the strength of the public sphere. In his book *On Recent Events in the Romagna*, D'Azeglio declared that two great new principles dominated the world: the first was the rule of law, together with the acceptance of a legal structure underpinning political authority; the second was the power of public opinion. On one hand, D'Azeglio condemned the political repression which he encountered in the Papal States, and on the other he denounced abortive conspiracies on the Mazzinian model. The future lay, he wrote, in open propaganda and the long-term mobilization of public opinion. The age of secret uprisings was over, and what was now required, in D'Azeglio's phrase, was 'a conspiracy in broad daylight', with its name clearly inscribed on the forehead of every member. Public opinion was not yet as powerful in his own country as D'Azeglio wished: the Piedmontese censors refused to publish his book, and it first appeared in Florence after anti-Mazzinian passages had been removed. The complete text had to be produced out of the range of Italian censors in Switzerland.[2] In spite of these very significant problems, D'Azeglio's book indicated a turning-point in the development of democratic politics.

The conspiracy in broad daylight could not put down roots without the expansion of the newspaper press. Mechanization made it possible for daily papers to envisage large-scale circulation with corresponding economies. Before the invention of the all-metal Stanhope press in 1800, a traditional wooden hand-press could produce only about 3000 sheets per day. The development of a cylindrical, steam-driven press soon allowed the London *Times* to print at the unheard-of rate of up to 5000 copies per hour. The mechanical Koenig press promised an end to hard labour, and did away with the need to ink every folio. By the 1820s, large circulation dailies were able to print on both sides of paper at once, and by 1850, the Applegarth press was capable of producing 10,000 copies per hour. Until this period, the essential conditions of publication had hardly changed since Johannes Gutenberg invented the printing process in the fifteenth century. The industrialization of production in the early nineteenth century, however, marked a watershed: in political terms, the Old Regime had ended in 1789, but the typographical Old Regime expired in the 1830s.

In Britain, all periodicals which carried news, cost less than sixpence, and appeared more often than monthly were subject to a stamp tax. This burden severely limited the circulation of the radical press, as it was designed to do. Workers who could not afford to buy a daily newspaper had to improvise, by clubbing together for a collective subscription, or by buying week-old papers which were reduced in price. Cobbett's immensely popular *Political Register* attempted to evade the law by omitting the news, but Cobbett was threatened with arrest, and fled to the United States in 1817. Wooler's *Black Dwarf* achieved a circulation of 12,000 per week in 1819, but the stamp tax forced its price up to sixpence.[3] Radicals mounted a concerted war on the stamp duty in the 1830s. The 'war of the unstamped press' was led by Henry Hetherington, whose weekly *Poor Man's Guardian* defied the law and sold for a penny. The tax was reduced to a penny per sheet in 1836, but it was not repealed altogether until 1855.

In France, the total circulation of the Parisian press had reached 50,000 copies by the 1830 Revolution. The role of the editorial offices of *Le National* in the July Revolution was already mentioned in Chapter 6. Expansion continued, even though French editors were obliged to pay a security deposit, a postal tax and a stamp duty on newspapers. The newspaper was just beginning in this period to develop the distinctive characteristics which differentiated it from the book: regular and more frequent editions, and a large format which allowed the inclusion of different articles on the same page. French editors still relied heavily on subscription sales, rather than on income from direct sales of individual issues.

The mass-circulation daily only became possible in France after the press revolution brought about in 1836 by the imaginative entrepreneur Girardin, manager of *La Presse*. Girardin set his subscription price at half the level of his competitors, relying on a wider circulation and increased advertising income. The duel he fought with the journalist Armand Carrel in

1836, in which Carrel was killed, did nothing to harm the publicity campaign for his new project. Girardin's successful recipe combined several key ingredients: cheapness, a large format, a serialized novel and the avoidance of any controversial political views. Before long, other journals like *Le Constitutionnel* had introduced a serialized novel (*roman-feuilleton*) to boost sales, and *La Presse* had been overtaken by rival editors quick on the uptake. Nevertheless, Girardin had shown the way, like many other brash self-made press barons who followed. In 1846, the aggregate print-run of all Parisian newspapers had risen to over 180,000 copies.[4]

This was the age of monthly or bi-monthly journals, which published substantial articles on political and literary developments. Britain set the example with the *Edinburgh Review* and the *Quarterly Review*, and in France the *Revue des Deux Mondes* followed in 1831, opening its pages to romantic writers like De Vigny and De Musset, and recruiting 2000 subscribers by 1843.[5] History, foreign news, music and art criticism all became important features of such quality journals.[6] In Italy, the banner of moderate liberalism was carried briefly by the Milan journal *Il Conciliatore* (The Conciliator) until it was banned in 1819. Its successor *Antologia*, published in Florence and edited by the Swiss wine merchant Vieusseux, took up progressive causes like Greek independence, savings banks and religious toleration.[7] Such journals had both international and provincial readerships, and they expressed the intellectual concerns of the liberal bourgeoisie all over Europe.

The early years of the July Monarchy were the golden age of political caricature. Using the new technique of lithography, Charles Philipon collected a talented stable of graphic artists, including Honoré Daumier, in the editorial offices of his two illustrated papers, the weekly *La Caricature* and the daily *Le Charivari*. *La Caricature*, which was the more political of the two, conducted a systematic character assassination of King Louis-Philippe, portraying him as a greedy manipulator. Daumier and Philipon drew Louis-Philippe in the shape of a pear (see Plate 9). This was a stroke of artistic genius – a censor could hardly object to a drawing of a simple pear, but educated readers understood the joke. Thousands of graffiti pears appeared in Paris streets – a sign of the new power of visual satire. In French, 'le poire' became slang for a mug or a dimwit, which lent extra force to this insulting image of the monarch. Other targets were the 'ventrus' (potbellies), bloated and complacent members of parliament whose loyalty had been bought by the King, and Robert Macaire, a fictional rogue and sleazy con-man who was identified with Louis-Philippe. Although the circulation of these journals did not exceed 1400 copies, they were read in reading-rooms all over the capital, posted on walls and exhibited in shop windows.[8]

# LES POIRES,

Faites à la cour d'assises de Paris par le directeur de la CARICATURE.

## Vendues pour payer les 6,000 fr. d'amende du journal le *Charivari*.

(CHEZ AUBERT, GALERIE VÉRO-DODAT.)

Si, pour reconnaître le monarque dans une caricature, vous n'attendez pas qu'il soit désigné autrement que par la ressemblance, vous tomberez dans l'absurde. Voyez ces croquis informes, auxquels j'aurais peut-être dû borner ma défense :

Ce croquis ressemble à Louis-Philippe, vous condamnerez donc ?

Alors il faudra condamner celui-ci, qui ressemble au premier.

Puis condamner cet autre, qui ressemble au second.

Et enfin, si vous êtes conséquens, vous ne sauriez absoudre cette poire, qui ressemble aux croquis précédens.

Ainsi, pour une poire, pour une brioche, et pour toutes les têtes grotesques dans lesquelles le hasard ou la malice aura placé cette triste ressemblance, vous pourrez infliger à l'auteur cinq ans de prison et cinq mille francs d'amende !!
Avouez, Messieurs, que c'est là une singulière liberté de la presse !!

*Plate 9*　Honoré Daumier, 'Pears', 1835. Daumier's version of King Louis-Philippe as a pear was sold to pay for a fine imposed on the magazine *Le Charivari*

*Source*:　H. Daumier after C. Philipon, 'Les Poires', *Le Charivari*, 16 April 1835, engraving in Bibliothèque Nationale de France.

Both Philipon and Daumier faced short prison sentences from time to time, which gave their activities more publicity without deterring them one bit. Although the July Monarchy had declared the freedom of the press, a worried government banned political caricature in 1835, and *La Caricature* was forced to fold.

The rate of book production increased rapidly. In Britain, between 2000 and 3000 titles were published annually in the 1840s, surging to over 5000 titles annually in the 1850s. Not only did more titles appear, but the size of print-runs increased as well. At the beginning of the nineteenth century, the average print-run for a novel was 1000 or 1500 copies only. The first edition of Stendhal's *The Red and the Black* appeared in 1831 in only 750 copies. A second edition followed, but it too only had a run of 750 copies. By the 1840s, however, some bestselling authors like Victor Hugo appeared in editions of 5000. The French publisher Charpentier pioneered a revolution in the 1830s, by producing novels in small in-18° (octodecimo) format, rather than the customary larger and multi-volume in-octavo format, which had been designed for sale to circulating libraries. Charpentier made the text more compact, and reduced novels to one instead of three volumes, thereby reducing the price and expanding the clientele of purchasers. This was an important breakthrough in the expansion of a mass-reading public for cheap fiction.

History-writing itself became a forum for political commentary. When Adolphe Thiers wrote his *Histoire de la Révolution française*, he expressed an implicit criticism of the Bourbon regime, arguing that the Revolution and the National Convention of 1793 were necessary outcomes of political circumstances. By 1845, 80 000 complete multi-volume sets had been sold.[9] Under the July Monarchy, Thiers then embarked on his *Histoire du Consulat et de l'Empire*, which by 1862 had absorbed 20 volumes. As a celebration of French military triumphs, it marked Thiers out as a popular nationalist politician.

## Forms of political action

The expansion of the press and the industrialization of literary production provided new means of communication through which public opinion could come into being and speak to itself. Other media for political expression and action also gave substance to the formation of a 'public sphere'.

In France, the political banquet was popular in the years leading up to the 1848 Revolution. In gastronomic terms, 'banquet' was often a misnomer for what was essentially a political fund-raising rally with a very simple sit-down meal accompanied by cheap wine. One or two invited speakers would harangue the diners and the meal would culminate in some well-chosen and occasionally subversive toasts. The banquet was a very static rally, however, and normally had a restricted audience who subscribed in advance.

Funeral processions were much rowdier forms of political protest, in spite of the respect owed to the dead. In 1825, the funeral of General Fay, who had fought at Jemappes in 1792 and at Waterloo, and who was a noted republican deputy, attracted a crowd of at least 40 000 (some reports claimed 100 000).[10] Slogans would be chanted, and students struggled with the police for the right to carry the coffin for part of the way to Père Lachaise cemetery. Carrying the coffin on foot was against police regulations, but to do so was a way of expressing solidarity with the dead hero. In 1832, the funeral of General Lamarque, at a tense time of economic crisis and the cholera epidemic, sparked off two days' street-fighting in Paris. Lamarque was the son of a deputy in the Constituent Assembly of 1791. He was a noted Bonapartist and a liberal. Occasions like this gave the opposition a voice and a reason to mobilise public support.

Political discussion continued behind closed doors, in middle-class literary clubs, and in lower-class *chambrées*, gatherings in drinking-shops in the small communities of Provence, which Maurice Agulhon identified as distinctive forums for political discussion and radicalisation.[11] In Russia, where political life as it was known in Western Europe hardly existed, Masonic lodges were (male) arenas for discussion of social and political issues. In fact they were made illegal in Russia for this reason in 1822. In Vienna, the Legal Reading Club became a focus for political discussion in the mid-1840s. In Hungary Kossuth edited the *Pesti Hirlap*, which boasted 5000 subscribers and campaigned for parliamentary representation and the abolition of serf labour obligations.[12] In 1847, the Austrian author Andrian-Werburg thought 'we are now where France was in 1788': he was probably referring to the incompetence of the Habsburg monarchy, but he might just as well have been talking about the growth of an opposition of educated intellectuals and liberal-minded aristocrats in both countries.[13]

Learned societies and academies developed agendas for social and political change all over Europe. In Italy, members of the landowning and professional elite discussed various projects of modernization in scientific and agricultural societies. In many ways they resembled the model of French provincial academies in the eighteenth century. Since they operated under the auspices of governments (as in Naples) and collected statistical information for government ministries, they were hardly subversive. Nevertheless, they developed a modernizing discourse on tax reform, share-cropping, the merits of protectionism against free trade and new agricultural techniques. In the south of Italy, the learned academies represented virtually the only forum for intellectual debate.[14] They were exclusively male and they excluded the lower classes, but they were part of an educated public opinion which was beginning to emerge on a national scale. The first Italian national scientific congress was held in Pisa in 1839 and the second in Lucca in 1843 (its Tuscan origin illustrates the duchy's reputation for enlightened paternalism). Further meetings followed in Milan and Naples. A national intelligentsia had found a way to exist.

To find more direct and popular expressions of D'Azeglio's 'conspiracy in broad daylight', we must turn to revolutionary songs, like those of Béranger in France, sold at street-corners and extremely popular in the 1830s for their nostalgic Bonapartism. When theatre audiences struck up the revolutionary hymn of *La Marseillaise*, they were making a democratic political statement defying decorum and the authorities. Patriotic cheers at Verdi operas like *Nabucco* or *The Battle of Legnano*, or anti-Austrian graffiti in Milan were further signs of middle-class or more popular political participation. Forms of political expression could often be quite traditional. An unpopular official might be subject to a charivari, in which he would be publicly lampooned and forced to listen to a satirical 'serenade' outside his window. The burning of carnival effigies with contemporary targets also demonstrated that there could be a folkloric context for political expression. Philipon's *Le Charivari* and the English journal *Punch* both drew on and politicized these carnival traditions. Traditionally offenders had been mocked in obscene songs, now they were satirized by popular journalism.

## The gendering of the public sphere

The public world of business and politics was conceived as masculine territory, while women's talents were best suited to the domestic arena. Women who insisted on contributing to political debate were thus transgressing conventional gender expectations, and were criticized as unnatural and unfeminine. Certain public roles, such as the hostess of a literary salon, were acceptable and commanded respect. The emergence of the female intellectual in the 1840s, however, remained controversial.

Germaine de Staël had established a precedent as writer, literary critic and lover of the insipid novelist Benjamin Constant in the Napoleonic era, but most female authors were careful to identify themselves by their respectable married name (Madame de Genlis, Madame Cottin, etc.).

George Sand, *née* Aurore Dupin, broke this pattern, to incarnate a new and challenging model of the female intellectual.

George Sand's works in various genres fill 50 volumes. She wrote 70 novels, the most enduring of which are the 'rustic' novels (*romans champêtres*) like *François le Champi*. Her challenge to accepted gender expectations lay not so much in the novels she published, but in the life that she led. It was new and rare for a woman to live as a professional writer, and this intrusion into a male domain was revolutionary enough. Sand however, made her own life into a manifesto for female emancipation. She occasionally dressed as a man. Her informal lifestyle, and her well-publicized relationships with De Musset and Chopin made her into the archetypal feminist bluestocking: she was an active writer and intellectual who challenged the conventions of bourgeois marriage. She was vilified and condemned by conservatives and Catholics, earning an important place in the nightmares of the nineteenth-century patriarchal bourgeoisie. She had socialist sympathies, took promising worker-poets under her wing, and had an intimate relationship with one of them. Her notoriety was complete when Daumier devoted entire series of humorous cartoons in *Le Charivari* to the bluestocking, and to the effect George Sand was having on the tranquillity of married life. In *Moeurs Conjugales* (Married Life), 1839, for example, a harassed husband complains that his wife is too busy reading George Sand to mend his torn trousers. Divorce, he says, should be re-introduced and such authors suppressed (see Plate 10). Sand had become a household (or anti-household) name.

In the literary salon, a woman could shine, and debate issues with intellectuals without causing the havoc created by George Sand. The French salons of the eighteenth-century Enlightenment have been much studied, but the institution had a new role in the post-revolutionary history of literary romanticism. The salon was a gathering of writers and intellectuals at the home of a respected hostess, where new works were read before publication and leading intellectuals discussed contemporary issues in an informal atmosphere. The salon occupied a space somewhere in-between the public and the private in which women could for a time conduct an intellectual dialogue on an equal footing with writers and philosophers. In the relaxed and civilized ambiance of the salon, the norms of social hierarchy and gender expectations were briefly suspended. In Germany, middle-class Jewish women, like Rahel Varnhagen in Berlin, used their roles as *salonnières* to merge with cultivated bourgeois society.[15] Varnhagen's guests included the author Heinrich Heine, the philosopher Humboldt, the historian von Ranke and the Austrian playwright Grillparzer.[16] A glittering array of (male) talent revolved around her. The salon hostess, it has been said, was

*Plate 10*   Honoré Daumier, 'Married Life', 1831. In this humorous cartoon by
Daumier, an irate husband blames George Sand for his wife's failure to
mend his pantaloons – 'They should bring back divorce', he says, 'or else
ban authors like that!'

*Source*:   H. Daumier, in *Le Charivari*, 30 April 1839, series *Moeurs Conjugales no. 6*, photo from
Bibliothèque Nationale de France.

valued for her conversation and 'erotic radiance' (*erotische Aufstrahlung*). She also helped to legitimize the role of female intellectuals in the public arena.

## Public opinion mobilized in Germany

Public opinion could now be effectively mobilized. In Germany, as we have seen, political life was restricted after 1815, but political agitation developed in the 1840s in the southwestern states, the free cities, the Rhineland and Saxony. Festivals like the Leipzig Schillerfest of 1841 were used as political rallying-points, and religious disputes exacerbated political conflict. Ludwig I of Bavaria ignited controversy by demanding that his Protestant subjects should kneel as the annual Corpus Christi procession passed by. The Prussian monarchy's attempts to consolidate Lutheran and Calvinist organizations into a single state Church were opposed by traditional Lutherans. The Protestant *Lichtfreunde* (Friends of Light) movement aimed primarily at religious reform but was also aligned with political radicalism. The idea of mixed marriage (i.e. between a Catholic and a Protestant) animated politics for years in Baden and Bavaria, as Dagmar Herzog has demonstrated.[17] In 1837, the Archbishop of Köln was arrested in Prussia for opposing the law that children of mixed marriages should be educated in the faith of the father (but he was reinstated). In 1845, the Catholic Archbishop of Baden took a public stand against mixed marriages *per se*. Meanwhile the *Deutschkatholischer* (German Catholic) movement criticized the Catholic hierarchy, attacked priestly celibacy and pressed for a more humane approach towards marriage. The forces of liberalism and conservative Catholicism grew increasingly polarized in Germany.

The historian Wolfram Siemann, focusing on the origins of the 1848 Revolutions in Germany, has charted the growth of political associations and the development of participatory politics during the Vormärz era. In his brilliant account, political life survived censorship and restrictions, and it thrived in local reading clubs, choral societies (*Gesangvereine*) and gymnastic associations (*Turnvereine*). These were not exclusively middle-class groups. Economic change produced a crisis of modernization, in which threatened artisans and journeymen rallied to defend their interests in democratic clubs like the 'fatherland associations' (*Vaterlandsvereine*) which had 10 000 members in Saxony, and the General German Workers' Fraternity with its 15 000 members.[18] In the Rhine-Main region, gymnastic clubs attracted journeymen, but master craftsmen tended to join the choirs, while the Frankfurt Monday Circle (*Montagskränzchen*) tried to make them all collaborate in the cause of reform.[19] On the eve of 1848 in Germany, petitions for a free press flooded into the Baden parliament, and newspapers proliferated in all major cities. As Siemann argues, when the Frankfurt Parliament was being prepared, political organization and political parties did not simply spring from nowhere. Germany had already acquired a political education well before 1848, and a democratic movement did not have to organize itself from scratch.

Political life was especially active in the Rhineland. In 1832, 30 000 were estimated to have attended the Hambach festival and some of the crowd got close enough to the speakers to hear some radical oratory. The leaders were arrested, but in 1833 a local Rhenish jury acquitted them.[20] Coffee-houses and left-wing gymnastic clubs denounced Metternich's repression, and the democrats mobilized successfully during the 1846 municipal elections in Köln. In such campaigns, bourgeois liberals did not always heed the grievances of craftsmen and journeymen, and this problem would resurface later during the 1848 Revolution, but all of them participated in Germany's 'apprenticeship in democracy' during the 1840s.

### Public opinion mobilized in Britain and France

Public opinion was coming into being, and it coalesced around a number of causes. As discussed in Chapter 5, the philhellenic movement recruited support, gathered donations and sent volunteers to Greece to join the independence struggle. Daniel O'Connell's Catholic Association, founded in 1824, had campaigned successfully for Catholic Emancipation in Britain, which was enacted by parliament in 1829. The Association had claimed a six-figure membership, which was an astonishing feat of organization.[21]

The Anti-Corn Law League was similarly effective in bringing about the repeal of the Corn Laws in 1846, thus removing the barriers to the free importation of grain, and weakening the position of the landed, protectionist interests. It was a weapon in the struggle for middle-class power against those whom northern British manufacturers regarded as effete aristocrats. They argued their own class interests: cheaper imported grain would reduce the price of food, which would dampen wage demands and allow them to produce more competitive goods for export. The Anti-Corn Law League had the advantage of focusing on the removal of a single piece of legislation: it was an early lobby group rather than a mass movement.

The movement for the abolition of slavery in both Britain and France was more diffuse, but the British movement succeeded in sustaining momentum over three generations. The slave trade had been abolished in the British colonies in 1807, but the movement subsequently re-gathered to combat slavery itself, and the worldwide slave traffic. An additional target was the 'apprenticeship system' – a transitional phase introduced between slavery and complete emancipation.

The British abolitionists had mixed social origins, but the movement rested on an alliance between Evangelical Protestants, radical Dissenters and especially Quakers. For these groups, the abolition of slavery often figured in a bundle of causes which included free trade, prison reform and temperance (i.e. the campaign to limit or abstain from alcohol consumption). Economic arguments for the greater productivity of free labour added another layer to the scriptural foundation of the movement, inspired by the New Testament command to 'love thy neighbour'.

The movement launched an enormous propaganda campaign. The Anti-Slavery Society alone published nearly 3 million copies of tracts between 1823 and 1831.[22] It issued a monthly newsletter, which was becoming the norm for such organizations. There were antislavery medals, antislavery bags and antislavery china. Sympathizers were urged to boycott produce grown by slave labour – a tactic with startlingly modern echoes. This strategy was particularly promoted by women, and West Indian sugar was the main target.[23]

The involvement of women in the movement was remarkable. In 1825, Lucy Townsend underlined their contribution by forming a separate Ladies' Society for the Relief of Negro Slaves. Some campaigners, including William Wilberforce, were uncomfortable about the level of female participation and preferred to limit women agitators to an auxiliary role. At the World Anti-Slavery Convention in 1840, women were confined to the visitors' gallery.[24] The movement nevertheless relied on many local organizations in which perhaps 10,000 middle-class women were active. They adopted the technique of house-to-house canvassing, and drew up antislavery petitions which amassed several hundred thousand signatures.

The Anti-Slavery Society was formed in 1823, and slavery was officially abolished in British colonies from 1834. In 1837, the Birmingham-based Central Negro Emancipation Committee was established to combat the apprentice system, which was abolished by colonial legislatures in 1838. The abolitionist movement now assumed an international role. In 1839, the British and Foreign Anti-Slavery Society came into being, and the World Anti-Slavery Convention met in London in 1840. The push against the international traffic in slaves was an expression of British world power. As the world's only super-power, Britain enjoyed naval hegemony, and could threaten to impose the right of search on foreign vessels which did not subscribe to her liberal values. As the greatest financial power in the world, Britain was acquiring an increasingly global vision.

In France, however, hostility to British power handicapped the antislavery movement. France had abolished slavery in 1794, but Napoleon had reestablished it in 1802. There were perhaps a quarter of a million slaves in the plantations of France's Caribbean and Indian Ocean colonies, and they were not emancipated until the 1848 Revolution. French abolitionism battled against mercantile interests which sought to postpone abolition for as long as possible, and against anglophobic sentiment which made co-operation with Britain problematic. The French movement lacked the Protestant inspiration which was so important in Britain, although Protestant support, led by Constant and Guizot, was conspicuous in the Société de la Morale Chrétienne which gave birth to an abolitionist committee in 1822.[25]

The French antislavery movement was far more focused on parliament than was the British movement. It was led by eminent individuals like the Duc de Broglie and other members of the July Monarchy's political elite. It also had the support of black activists like Cyrille Bissette, a merchant from Martinique who in 1834 inaugurated the first French periodical run by blacks, *La Revue des Colonies*.[26] Although a petition campaign managed to gather 8000 working-class signatures in 1844, the French movement could not mobilize public opinion on the same scale as its British counterpart.[27] It was led by the Orleanist liberals, but the radicals of 1848 who overthrew them, led by Victor Schoelcher, were responsible for ending slavery.

## Conclusion

The broadening horizon of the political arena is a feature of the decades before 1848 which is often overlooked. It gives this period a distinctively progressive character that is obscured by the traditional label of 'Restoration Europe' from which it must be freed. Petitions, demonstrations, boycotts, public lectures, the widespread distribution of propaganda tracts and the use of the newspaper press were new instruments with which a public opinion could be created and mobilized.

It is no coincidence that this chapter has concentrated on Britain and France, together with urban centres in Germany and Italy. It was in the highly developed and literate societies of Western Europe that the public sphere could exist and grow, in spite of restrictions on freedom of speech which existed even in these countries. In Central and Eastern Europe, dominated by Metternich's system and Tsarist Russia, there was far less opportunity for the development of political life. Even so, the 1848 Revolutions in Germany revealed that a profound process of politicization had been taking place in spite of these limited opportunities. 'Public opinion' was still a Western and an urban phenomenon, but it was no longer either exclusively bourgeois or exclusively male. Women, usually of the middle class, were actively intruding into public life, and the mobilization of workers on a mass scale for peaceful reformist purposes was now possible. This was illustrated by the Chartist movement of the 1840s, to be discussed in the next chapter.

# 8 The 'Juste Milieu' and Gathering Unrest, 1830–1848

### Introduction: threats to the 'happy medium'

In 1835, a powerful home-made bomb (the *machine infernale*) was detonated on the Boulevard du Temple in Paris. Eighteen people were killed in the blast, but the target, King Louis-Philippe, escaped with a graze to the head. This was one of eight assassination attempts on the king. Like the Bourbons before him, Louis-Philippe had failed to establish the legitimacy needed to secure the Orleanist dynasty. The July Monarchy had been spawned by the 1830 Revolution, and while the regime played down its insurrectionary origins, it reigned through a period of turmoil. It survived popular risings in Lyon and Paris in the 1830s, an attempted legitimist *coup* in 1832, and a Bonapartist rising in 1836 (see Chapter 4). In the midst of unrest, the ruling classes sought the peace and equilibrium of the *juste milieu* – the 'happy medium' between order and freedom. Their assumptions about politics and society will be outlined in this chapter. The French monarchy was not alone in its social conservatism and desire for tranquillity. Other versions of the *juste milieu*, embodying moderation, gradual reform and modernization were to be found in Britain under Sir Robert Peel, in Spain under Queen Isabella and, at a slightly later date, in Piedmont under Count Cavour.

In the 1840s, called the 'Hungry Forties' mainly because of the subsistence crisis of 1846–7, stability was elusive and it sometimes seemed as though the rulers of post-revolutionary Europe were dancing on a volcano. In Britain, the Chartist movement reached a climax in 1842 and mustered a final rally in 1848. In 1846, Galician peasants rose up to slaughter their Polish landlords. In Italy, the political ground rules which had been laid down in 1815 were thrown into complete confusion by an unthinkable development – the election of the so-called liberal Pope Pius IX (Pio Nono). This event, more than the assassination attempts on the French king or the fluctuations of the Chartist movement, was the prelude to the Revolutions of 1848.

## The July Monarchy and the search for legitimacy

The cartoonists discussed in Chapter 7 ridiculed Louis-Philippe as a flaccid, pear-shaped criminal (see Plate 9).[1] Louis-Philippe's personal appearances in a National Guardsman's uniform, or in dark suits with a rolled umbrella represented monarchy in the image of its unpretentious bourgeois supporters. But he easily became a joke in the eyes of a public still attracted by forceful military leadership. Louis-Philippe attempted to harness the continuing appeal of Napoleon Bonaparte for his own purposes. In 1833, Napoleon's statue was placed on top of the Vendôme column in Paris. The Versailles palace was renovated and its galleries furnished with large-scale paintings of Napoleon's military exploits. In 1837, he opened the Arc de Triomphe, the hideous Parisian monument to French victories, and in 1840, Napoleon's remains were shipped back from St Helena.

Louis-Philippe, however, did not resolve the contradictions of history and memory. His credentials rested on the fact that his father Philippe-Egalité had sat in the National Convention in 1792 and voted for the death of Louis XVI, and yet the July Monarchy did not wish to advertise its own revolutionary (and hence illegitimate) birth in 1830. Louis-Philippe tried to graft the Napoleonic legend on to his Orleanist pedigree, but it had a persistent life of its own. In recognizing and incorporating the military glory of the Napoleonic era, Louis-Philippe could not make Bonapartism's subversive popular appeal go away. Horace Vernet's 1847 painting of the king and his sons illustrates official attempts to legitimize the Orleanist dynasty (see Plate 11).[2] In this equestrian scene, the King poses on a white horse as if at the head of a military parade. The group rides out from the palace of Versailles, which Louis-Philippe did much to redecorate, and in the background is the equestrian statue of Louis XIV, suggesting a direct line of descent from the great Sun-King. Of the five sons depicted, one was in fact dead, after a fall from a carriage four years previously, but the painting wanted to assert the dynamism and fertility of the dynasty, and its ability to produce male heirs. We go back a long way, the painting seemed to argue, and we have a solid future to look forward to. None of this worked. A year later the dynasty was overthrown.

## The *juste milieu*

In France, the Orleanist majority sought a *juste milieu* which would defeat the die-hard legitimism of the Bourbons and silence Bonapartist rabble-rousing.

*Plate 11*    Horace Vernet, *King Louis-Philippe of France and his sons leaving the Château of Versailles on horseback,* 1847. Vernet showed the king parading with his sons outside the Château of Versailles, in a visual expression of confidence in the Orleanist dynasty and its ability to produce heirs

*Source*:    Bridgeman Art Library.

The Orleanists had prevented France from becoming a republic in 1830, although later in life, leaders like Thiers came to accept republicanism, albeit of a very conservative kind. Many disparate groups joined the search for a moderate, middle-of-the-road path, including Napoleonic nobility like Marshal Soult, liberal aristocrats like de Broglie, intellectuals like Guizot and middle-class opportunists like Thiers.

Guizot, who dominated French politics from 1840–8, was a typical exponent of *juste-milieu* liberalism. Guizot was a serious-minded Protestant, the son of a bourgeois from Nîmes who had been guillotined in 1794, so he had no love for radicalism. He was a Sorbonne history professor and later became ambassador to England. As Education Minister in 1833, he was responsible for landmark legislation which laid down the blueprint for the development of primary schools in every French village. In social terms, Guizot was a conservative; his governments of the 1840s introduced no important social legislation. Problems of poverty were considered to be matters requiring individual solutions, not government remedies. The only exception to this was state intervention in 1841 to regulate child labour in factories – a rare and ultimately ineffective breach in the principle of *laissez-faire*. Liberals did not recognize the existence of *la question sociale*, a phrase designating a range of social problems connected to poverty and unemployment.

Guizot was a parliamentary operator who realized the necessity of organizing a majority in the Chamber of Deputies which would support government projects. Since a large number of deputies were government officials (40 per cent of them in 1846) parliament could be manipulated.[3] Political parties, however, were not allowed to develop. For Guizot, the only legitimate party was a pro-government party.[4] Guizot consistently resisted the extension of the franchise. The July Monarchy limited political rights to substantial male taxpayers, which satisfied the liberal notion that political rights were the preserve of those with the 'capacity' to exercise them. For *juste-milieu* liberals, the property qualification guaranteed that voters and candidates had an interest in maintaining order, and there was also a presumption that the leisured and educated classes could see more clearly than anyone else where public interests lay.

This oligarchical regime was supported in the country by local landowners, businessmen, lawyers and government officials. These were the local *notables* on whom the July Monarchy relied. As great landlords or factory-owners, their power had provincial roots, and they generally had a paternalistic view towards their social inferiors. The liberals of this period believed in some form of constitutional and representative government according to rational principles. They were elitists rather than democrats, who assumed that the vote should be given only to the educated classes (like themselves) and those with property and therefore a stake in the country (like themselves). Although the liberal middle classes were in principle in favour of parliaments, in practice they desired strong government to maintain law and order and protect property from the violence and envy of the 'vile multitude'. They lived in an age of revolutions and they were afraid of the masses. They believed in the *juste milieu*, avoiding the extremes of personal monarchy on one hand and majority rule on the other.

### Italy – the modernization of Piedmont

The liberalism of the *juste milieu* was not unique to France. Different versions of it could be found in other European states both before and after the 1848 Revolutions. In Piedmont, King Carlo Alberto's 1848 Constitution set up a parliamentary regime which looked very much like the limited representative system of the July Monarchy. Carlo Alberto encouraged progressive reforms while at the same time suppressing radical movements and secret societies. He produced new law codes based on Napoleonic models, developed the port of Genoa and gradually dismantled protective tariffs. Carlo Alberto's liberalism, however, was superficial. He was viscerally anti-Austrian, but this did not make him a democratic ruler. On the contrary, he was a devoutly Catholic absolutist who supported legitimism in France and Carlism in Spain.[5] He did temporarily relax royal censorship in 1832 to allow the publication of Sylvio Pellico's *My Prisons*, after Pellico's release from imprisonment in the dreaded Austrian fortress of the Spielberg. But this book echoed Carlo Alberto's deepest convictions: it was both profoundly Christian and implicitly anti-Austrian.

A better example of Piedmontese liberalism in the mould of Guizot was provided by Cavour, who became Minister of Agriculture in 1850, and served as Prime Minister from 1852 until 1859. The most significant period of Cavour's career came *after* 1848, which makes him the odd man out here, but as an exponent of the *juste milieu* he had much in common with Peel and Guizot. Cavour attempted to integrate Piedmont into the rational and moderately progressive world of Western European liberalism. He personally looked to London and Parisian models of political economy. He read Bentham, he listened to Peel and Guizot making speeches in parliament, he spoke and wrote in French. Napoleon's sister Pauline Bonaparte had been his godmother. Cavour never travelled as far south as Rome or Naples: his aim was to attach Piedmont to the most advanced forces in Europe rather than bury it in Italian provincialism. Perhaps this is why he acquiesced in Piedmont's participation in the Crimean War alongside Britain and France in 1856, although Mack Smith has argued that this was an initiative of King Vittorio Emanuele rather than of Cavour himself.[6]

Cavour dominated the Turin parliament and cynically negotiated whatever alliances were necessary to maintain a working majority. He formed an alliance (*connubio*) with the centre-left which ensured that his government encountered no effective opposition. The *connubio* established a tradition of mergers and coalitions which delayed the appearance of clear political parties in Italy. This was the foundation of Cavour's *juste-milieu* policy: his majority grouping of the centre isolated both clericals and radicals.

Cavour's notion of the *juste milieu* was if anything more forward-looking than that of Guizot. Cavour encouraged banking, railway building and agricultural improvements. Banks, railways, shipping lines and postal services were all part of the technical infrastructure which the liberal state aimed to provide (with the assistance of private capital) in order to simulate economic progress.[7] He reduced tariffs on a wide range of consumer goods. For Cavour, free trade was essential to social progress, and he signed commercial treaties with Britain, Belgium, Switzerland and the German Zollverein. He improved irrigation canals in the Vercelli region, where he happened to own rice-fields. The abolition of entails and primogeniture allowed the redistribution of aristocratic estates. For Cavour, progress was a secular goal, and he needed to neutralize the clerical party. In 1850, he had supported the Siccardi Laws (named after the Justice Minister) which introduced a bundle of secularizing measures. Ecclesiastical courts were abolished, the number of religious holidays was reduced, and moribund convents and monasteries were sold. Cavour also spoke in favour of introducing civil marriage, but this was thwarted by the king who personally detested him. These policies enormously improved Piedmont's image in Protestant Britain, but made the Catholic Church a permanent enemy of liberalism. They also made Piedmont the leading state in Italy. When Cavour's great antagonist Garibaldi sailed home from South America in 1854, he recognized that 'Today the whole of Italy looks to Piedmont as the sailor looks to the north wind (*tramontana*).'[8]

## Liberal Spain

Spain is sometimes regarded as a backwater in this period, on the margins of mainstream European developments. Currents of liberal thought, however, flowed here too, and the oligarchical elite that emerged triumphant from the Carlist Wars (1833–40) had similar preoccupations to those of the dominant classes in France and Piedmont. Liberal society developed as long as great landowners and manufacturers saw reason to collaborate against the endemic threat of rebellion.

Liberal forces were divided between *moderados* and *progresistas*, but both accepted the 1837 Constitution, which installed a two-chamber parliament. A narrow property-based franchise was created, so that the electorate numbered about 5 per cent of the population.[9] Under *progresista* leadership, the legislative programme of the 1830s struck decisive blows at Spain's feudal structure. Guilds were abolished in 1834, as were seigneurial jurisdictions and the ecclesiastical tithe. The Mesta, the powerful and exclusive corporation of sheep graziers, was abolished in 1836. In the 1840s, which were dominated by the *moderados* under General Narváez, these liberal advances were consolidated in a more conservative framework. Narváez reduced the size of the electorate still further, and gave the crown greater power to nominate members of the upper house. A new national police force, the Guardia Civil, was established. The textile industry developed in Catalonia, and railway building made a tentative beginning. Under Queen Isabella, liberal power relied on a narrow basis of local landowning notables, while the court and ruling oligarchy became notorious for corruption.

Relations between liberalism and the Church were particularly vexed. For liberals, the Church's immense landed wealth was an obstacle to the growth of industry and of agricultural entrepreneurialism. It also seemed to offer a way out of government debt. The Inquisition was abolished (again), and in 1835–7, Mendizábal's government decreed the suppression of almost all male religious orders, nationalized monastic property and started to sell it by auction. These sales had close parallels in Portugal, where the government hoped the income would defray the massive debt incurred during the Miguelist wars. Liberal landowners in Spain and Portugal were happy to buy lucrative church assets, but they had no desire to unleash the violent forces of popular anticlericalism, which if provoked would burn down convents and murder priests. In 1851 the Spanish *moderados* reached a compromise with the Church. Previous nationalizations of ecclesiastical property were made permanent, and the state agreed to pay the salaries of the secular clergy. A universal land tax was introduced under General Narváez's government. In 1854, a popular uprising broke out in Barcelona, and street-fighting erupted in Madrid. This reminded liberals of all political hues that they needed the monarchy and the army to protect them from the poor and volatile urban working class.

The conservative regimes of Queen Isabella and her successors were subject to regular incursions into politics by the military. The ranks of the top-heavy officer corps had been swollen by the Carlist War, and no government was strong enough to reduce the enormous military budget. Civil society thus remained fragile, and the liberal programme of the 1840s was only successful because a large group of generals identified with it.

Attempts to build a liberal nation state in the Isabelline period ran up against traditional obstacles. Power, as in France and Piedmont, lay in the hands of an oligarchy with little popular appeal. Poverty and high rates of illiteracy hindered the growth of liberal society. Liberals attempted to modernize Spain's institutions in the midst of extremes of squalor and despair which had fuelled popular support for the Carlist cause. The strength of non-Castilian languages and the nationalisms of Spain's peripheral provinces (Catalonia, the Basque provinces, Galicia) also weakened the project of national integration. In 1854 a revolution brought the *progresistas* back to power, and it was clear that political stability had not been achieved.

## Britain – Peel and Chartism

Sir Robert Peel, the greatest British statesman of this period, had a reputation for cold efficiency. He was driven by an extraordinarily demanding work ethic, dedicating himself and his government of 1841–6 to a series of unglamorous, but important administrative reforms. He was a Tory (i.e. conservative) reformer who, with his intellectual heir Gladstone at the Board of Trade, led Britain away from protectionism and towards free trade. The tragedy of Peel's career was that in his greatest reform, the Repeal of the Corn Laws in 1846, he was unable to take all of his own Conservative Party with him. For Peel, however, the public interest was a higher imperative than party advantage.

Peel's administration exhibited the same kind of moderate reforming impulse evident in similar European governments. Legislation on the railways created the infrastructure within which private enterprise could develop the transport network. The Bank Charter Act of 1844 regulated the issue of banknotes and made the Bank of England the supreme issuing source. Measures were taken to mitigate some of the worst consequences of industrialization. In 1842, a Mines Act banned employment underground of women and of boys under 10. The Factory Act of 1844 limited working hours for women and children. These laws clearly acknowledged the need for state intervention, and as such they dented the doctrines of *laissez-faire* liberalism.

Peel was more flexible than his contemporaries Guizot or Cavour. In 1834, his Tamworth Manifesto had recognized the 1832 Reform Bill, enacted by his political opponents the Whigs, as 'final and irrevocable'. In 1835, he also accepted a sweeping Whig municipal reform, which weakened closed corporations and opened up new borough councils to election by all ratepayers. In 1846, a series of tariff reductions on many goods culminated in the Repeal of the Corn Laws, and the end of a sliding-scale system which allowed imports of grain as domestic prices rose. Repeal recognized the influence of the manufacturing and commercial middle classes, and promised cheaper bread for consumers. Agricultural interests were now deprived of protection. They saw Peel as a traitor to the conservative cause, and the opportunistic Disraeli called Peel 'a burglar of other's intellect'.

Corn Law repeal, however, was an important sign of the shifting power balance in industrial society.

Both Peel and the governments which preceded him had to deal with the threat of Chartism. Chartism was a broadly based movement for parliamentary reform, which aimed at solving Britain's 'social question' by increasing genuine working-class representation in the House of Commons. Massive petitions were presented to parliament in 1839, 1842 and 1848. The Six Points of the Charter demanded the vote for workers and the secret ballot which would free voters from intimidation by employers and landlords. The Charter also demanded the payment of members of parliament, which would make it possible for workers to stand for election without complete loss of income. At the same time, the Charter wanted to make parliament more accountable to the electorate by making annual elections mandatory (see Table 8.1). Although women played a role in the early years of the movement, Chartism was far more concerned with votes for working men than with votes for women.

The Charter was produced by the London Working Men's Association and approved by a range of workers' groups in 1838, but its origins lay deeper in the past. Chartism grew out of popular disillusionment with the Parliamentary Reform Bill of 1832, and resentment against the 1834 Poor Law, which had forced the poor into workhouses and abolished the provision of outdoor relief from parish funds. The repression of early trade unionism also nourished the Chartist cause. In 1834, a reformed parliament ordered the deportation to Australia of six Dorset labourers (known to posterity as the 'Tolpuddle Martyrs') for trying to form a union and administering illegal oaths. This persuaded many that nothing less than the reconstitution of parliament itself would eliminate the oppressive class bias of politics and the law. E. P. Thompson argued that Chartism was the next step on the way to the 'Making of the English Working Class', but he insisted that it was informed by a long tradition of radicalism going back to the English Civil War, and that it incorporated an old folk culture.[10] Gareth Stedman Jones also emphasized continuities with earlier forms of radicalism, which

*Table 8.1*  The 'six points' of the charter

| |
|---|
| The secret ballot |
| Universal male suffrage |
| Annual parliaments |
| Electoral constituencies of roughly equal population |
| The abolition of property qualifications for Members of Parliament |
| The payment of Members of Parliament |

suggested that Chartism was not so much a response to the industrial revolution, but rather the expression of long-standing democratic currents in working-class culture.[11] The Chartist movement thus had complex origins.

In the style of the Charter itself, 'six points' can be noted about the nature of Chartism. First, Chartism was a genuine mass movement. Feargus O'Connor's radical newspaper, the *Northern Star*, printed 42 000 copies per week on average in mid-1839, and it was read aloud to untold numbers of listeners.[12] Early Chartist rallies in Manchester and Yorkshire attracted crowds of a quarter of a million, and the Chartist petition of 1842 was reputedly signed by 3.3 millions (admittedly, not all of the signatures were genuine).[13] As a result, and second, it inspired great fear. Chartism was perceived by elites as a grave social menace and a threat to property. It provoked into action all the repressive apparatus of the state. Several hundred Chartist leaders were arrested in 1838–40 and many were transported to Australia. In 1848, crowds marched through Glasgow demanding 'Bread or Revolution' and five rioters were shot. Queen Victoria left London for the safety of the Isle of Wight. The forces of order made a huge effort to contain the danger. In 1848, 85,000 special constables were recruited in London to police the Chartist demonstration.[14]

Third, Chartism was a political movement. Unlike trade unions which aimed at economic reforms, and unlike utopian socialists who put their faith in independent co-operatives and egalitarian communities, Chartism wanted to reform political institutions at the highest level. It aimed at the political emancipation of the working classes. It follows, and this is a fourth point, that Chartism was essentially a movement of the working classes, although it was not exclusively so. 'Working classes' are mentioned here, rather than a singular 'working class', because Chartism drew support from many different groups. Its social composition was mixed and contradictory. Some were factory workers, including the miners and cotton-spinners who were involved in the attempt to call a General Strike in 1842. The so-called Plug Plot was a plan to remove boiler plugs, thus paralysing cotton mills and coal-pit engines. Chartist supporters also included members of declining trades like the Lancashire handloom weavers. In the workshops of Birmingham, small businessmen might be Chartists. In the later stages of the Chartist struggle, the movement also mobilized skilled artisans who formed the backbone of London Chartism. Chartism was a disparate movement, which drew support from diverse local initiatives in South Wales, Scotland, the North, West and Midlands of England and tried to mould them into a national force. Chartism recruited skilled self-improving artisans, industrial workers and impoverished outworkers who were the victims of industrialization.

Fifth, Chartism was not only socially broad-based, but it was also politically eclectic. The historian R. K. Webb called Chartism nothing more than a 'miscellaneous cluster' of different protests, questioning whether it ever was a single coherent movement.[15] Irish nationalists, currency reformers, supporters of the ten-hour day, agitators for Poor Law reform, temperance reformers and many others found a home under the wide umbrella of the Charter. They were divided about objectives and also about tactics: how should Chartists respond to parliamentary rejection of the petition and the inevitable government repression? Middle-class Chartists favoured the use of 'moral force', but impoverished weavers were more sympathetic to 'physical force' Chartism.

Sixth, Chartism failed. The last march from Kennington Common in 1848 was a disappointing surrender. The movement had never been united, either socially, geographically or ideologically. Its multiple identities made it the antithesis of the Anti-Corn Law lobby, discussed in Chapter 7, which campaigned on a single issue with tunnel vision and unrelenting concentration. The reforms of the 1840s reduced the urgency of the Chartist programme. Peel had repealed the Corn Laws, which did lead to cheaper bread, and parliament passed a Factory Act in 1847, which implied that the House of Commons was less oppressive than had been feared. Above all, the prosperity of the 1850s killed the Chartist movement.

Although many historians emphasize its tendencies towards disintegration, Chartism remained a significant attempt to form a broad movement for political change. It attempted to reconcile different interests, social groups and local organizations in a national campaign. Strikes and demonstrations frightened the wealthy, and it was not until Chartism was defeated that they were ready to respond more readily to working-class grievances. In spite of its failure, Chartism was a milestone in the development of the democratic movement and of independent working-class action in Britain.

## Pio Nono

In Catholic Europe, the liberalism of the 1840s came into conflict with the Church. After 1815, Catholicism had attempted to make up ground lost in the revolutionary and Napoleonic years by orchestrating a religious recovery and a 'resacralization' of society. In Spain, the Inquisition had been re-established. In France, the number of ordinations to the priesthood doubled under the Bourbon Restoration.[16] New religious orders were established: Marcellin Champagnat formed the Marist brothers and Frédéric Ozanam founded the Society of St Vincent de Paul in 1833. Catholic missions inspired fear of God's retribution and used the cholera epidemics as illustrations of his wrath against revolutionaries and socialists.

Bourgeois anticlericals reacted against Pope Gregory XVI's official condemnation of liberalism in 1832, and suspected the Jesuit order of conspiring to undermine liberal forces. There was a current of liberal Catholicism, however, which sought to end the divorce between Catholicism and political liberalism, and to make Catholicism the ally of popular causes. After 1830, the *abbé* Lamennais in France led this break with Bourbon legitimism, defending the freedom of the press and expressing sympathy for struggling movements in Belgium and Ireland. Lamennais, however, remained completely obedient to the Pope, and when Pope Gregory condemned his ideas in 1832, Lamennais accepted the verdict of authority. Then, in 1834, he broke with the Church completely by publishing *Paroles d'un Croyant* (Words of a Believer), which was a bestseller. Pope Gregory called Lamennais to Rome and forced him to recant.

In Italy, the Piedmontese priest Vincenzo Gioberti also thought that Catholic influence would best be restored if the Church could be reconciled to modern ideas like liberalism and nationalism. In his influential book *The Moral and Civil Primacy of the Italians*, published in Brussels in 1843, Gioberti linked a Catholic revival with an Italian Risorgimento under Papal supervision. As a loyal ultramontane, he faced the same dilemma as Lamennais: how could progressive Catholic ideology succeed under oppressive and reactionary Papal rule?

In 1846, Pope Gregory died and it seemed as though the dilemmas of liberal Catholics were suddenly resolved. Cardinal Mastai-Ferretti, bishop of Imola, was elected Pope Pius IX. 'Pio Nono' was hailed as the 'liberal Pope'. Today it is difficult to comprehend the upsurge of hopeful enthusiasm inspired by this event, which swept through not just Rome but all of Italy. Pius IX actually did little to deserve his epithet. He issued an amnesty for political prisoners, which was interpreted as a desire to depart from the bigoted and tyrannical practices of his predecessor. So perhaps it was, but it did not in itself imply a substantial political change. He created a Consulta, a State Council in which for the first time laymen would take their place alongside the cardinals. The Consulta, however, was a strictly consultative body and did not seriously dilute the reality of clerical rule. He relaxed censorship and lifted some discriminatory rules against Jews. Popular support reached boiling point when he challenged the Austrian occupation of Ferrara, and secured the withdrawal of their troops. The infectious adulation for Pio Nono can only be explained by the context of his election, which occurred in the midst of an economic recession, and by the previous work of liberal Catholicism which had won over many clergy.

The barometer suddenly rose for nationalist aspirations, too, because Gioberti's neo-Guelph programme for a federated Italian state led by the Papacy seemed a real possibility.

A liberal Pope, according to Metternich, was a contradiction in terms. Once again Metternich, reviled as Europe's arch-conservative, was correct. Pius IX, perhaps a little intoxicated by the cheering crowds and his easily won popularity, was bound to disappoint both liberals and nationalists. The pursuit of either of these causes in Italy could not proceed without a confrontation with Austria. Yet the Pope could not be expected to join a war against Europe's greatest Catholic power. Pius IX was first a world spiritual leader, and only incidentally the temporal ruler of a small Italian state. His first loyalty was to the Catholic Church rather than to any individual European country. As for his liberalism, it was superficial. When the revolutionaries of 1848 demanded that he introduce a Constitution, he did so only under duress, and as soon as he managed to flee Rome, he renounced it. The events of 1848 were soon to show that the Papal solution to the question of Italian unity was bankrupt. The excessive hopes invested in Pius IX in 1846 were to be dashed on the impossible contradiction of a head of a global Church who was asked to perform as a liberal Italian nationalist.

## Conclusion

European liberals in the mid-nineteenth century, like Guizot, Peel and Cavour, had grown up during the French Revolution or its Napoleonic sequel. They had come to maturity in a post-revolutionary world dominated by absolute monarchies resting on clerical support. They turned away from both of these experiences to find a *juste milieu*, which would protect order and property from violent revolution and preserve individual liberties from oppressive reactionary governments. They took the middle ground, supporting the use of force against radicals, whether they were Mazzinian republicans, French socialists, trade unionists or Chartist rebels. At the same time they defended constitutionalism and parliamentary power against undue interference from the crown.

The liberalism of the *juste milieu* does not seem very 'liberal' by today's standards. Liberals defended an oligarchical style of government, in which only a relatively narrow elite of wealthy property-owners enjoyed political rights. They nevertheless tried to adapt and modernize post-revolutionary society according to rational principles. In continental Europe, they were identified with anticlericalism, perceiving the Catholic Church and its enormous landed wealth as barriers to economic progress and productivity. Not only this, but the traditional intolerance of the Church seemed opposed to their conception of individual freedom.

Liberal doctrines were often extremely harsh towards the lower classes. Liberalism implied no state intervention in social affairs, for instance to alleviate poverty or unemployment. Such hardships were seen as the inevitable result of market forces and working-class improvidence. Only gradually, in the regulation of child and female labour, did the state begin to soften the edges of *laissez-faire* doctrines. Liberals, however, were not united on the issue of free trade. Britain, as the leading industrial power, was a consistent supporter of free trade. So too, were the agrarian sectors of the European economy which wanted to sell in the large British market. These included the French wine industry, and Italian silk, olive and rice producers. Textile manufacturers, however, were less enthusiastic about free trade, because they feared competition from British products. In spite of these differences, liberals looked to a strong state, which would build the banking and transport infrastructure which allowed capitalist enterprise to flourish.

During the 1840s, liberals faced growing popular unrest as well as the breakdown of censorship controls put in place during the immediate post-revolutionary years. In many parts of Europe, of course, educated liberals themselves were actively engaged in promoting freedom of expression. Government control of public debate was increasingly ineffective. This was partly because the huge expansion in the reading public and in book and newspaper production swamped the limited apparatus which was supposed to control it. The number of book titles published in the German states, for example, almost doubled between 1830 and 1846.[17] Authors and editors used age-old methods of evading the censor. They changed the title of a banned journal or they bribed the censor, who was himself probably another underpaid writer trying to make a living. They published controversial works in a country where this was permissible and then smuggled them in to Austria or Italy, where it wasn't. The collapsing structure of repression was a common feature of the prelude to revolution in Europe in 1848, 1789 and again in 1989.

# 9    The Jews: The Dilemmas of Emancipation

## Introduction: the Mortara Affair, 1858

The Mortara family ran a grocery store in the small Jewish community of the city of Bologna, then part of the Papal States. Their son, Edgardo, was only 6 years old when, one summer evening in June 1858, Papal troops came to their house to remove him from his distraught parents. The Inquisition had been informed that Edgardo had been secretly baptized in his infancy by a former Catholic servant of the family, a young girl aged 14 at the time. Having been baptized as a Christian, however informally, Edgardo could not be brought up in a Jewish family. He was to be re-educated in a Catholic seminary under the protective eyes of his new foster-parent, His Holiness Pope Pius IX. The Mortaras, desperate to recover their son, mobilized Jewish support in Italy and internationally. Even Sir Moses Montefiore travelled to Rome, as President of the Board of Deputies of British Jews and a roving ambassador for Jewish causes, but the Pope declined to see him. All protests were in vain. Pius IX obstinately refused to compromise. Edgardo had become one of the 'stolen children' of the era of so-called Jewish emancipation.[1]

That process of emancipation, whose origins are indelibly associated with the French Revolution, is one theme of this chapter. Liberals saw Jewish liberation as part of a common struggle for the emancipation of humanity, embracing the freedom of black slaves, oppressed Greeks and all other struggling peoples. The story of Edgardo Mortara, however, illustrates that the great liberal cause of Jewish emancipation faced many obstacles, even in Western Europe. Emancipation was not a continuous, linear process. It proceeded by fits and starts, and it sometimes went into reverse. After 1815, for example, in some parts of Italy and Germany, there was a 're-ghettoization' of Jews after the defeat of the French.

The emancipation process must also be considered from a Jewish perspective. It provided unprecedented social and economic opportunities for Jews, but at the same time it posed unprecedented problems. Cultural integration was an attractive option for many, but it was achieved at a cost, namely the loss of their separate identity as Jews. Traditionalists rejected integration altogether, and saw freedom as the 'poisoned gift' of European

142

liberalism, designed to draw Jews away from their cultural roots. The responses of Western European Jews to these new dilemmas will be examined.

Historians have often located the birth of modern antisemitism in the second half of the nineteenth century. In this period, the growing forces of nationalism, combined with new theories about race and racial inequality, created new forms of racist xenophobia. The Jews, like other races, became identified by inherent biological and psychological characteristics which a religious conversion could no longer eradicate. But the motives for the abduction of Edgardo Mortara had little to do with such racial conceptions. The problem for the Inquisition was not Edgardo's race but his religion, and this is why he was redeemable. Historians of modernity too often underestimate the virulence and persistence of this archaic, religion-based Jew-hatred. For Catholics and other Christians, the Jews were always the people of the deicide. They were condemned as depraved, bigoted and unwilling to be a part of normal society, but above all they were seen as the killers of Christ.

Edgardo Mortara had to be rescued from them. By the Pope's standards his abduction and rehabilitation were successful. As a teenager Edgardo renounced his parents, and was then ordained as a priest. He lived an exemplary Catholic life until his death in 1940. The unification of Italy in 1860 had brought the activities of the Papal Inquisition to an end. The Mortara family, supported by money from the Rothschild family, had long since decamped to the more favourable climate of Turin. The scandal which had galvanized liberal Europe in 1858 had by then been long forgotten. It reminded Catholics too much of embarrassing survivals of medieval intolerance; it reminded Jews uncomfortably of the ease with which many of them had abandoned their cultural and religious roots.

## Before emancipation

The Jews formed the most significant religious minority in European society. Their story is closely linked to some of the most important historical developments of the century. The rise of modern nationalism made Jews its victims; at the same time they were important agents in the growth of modern capitalism; and Jews were major beneficiaries in the formation of liberal societies. In 1815, however, Jews in many parts of Europe were still subject to legal restrictions inherited from medieval times.

In many European cities, the Jews were still confined to ghettos. After curfew hour, the gates of the ghetto would be locked, and no Christian could enter nor could any Jew leave without special permission. In addition, Jews had to remain confined in the daytime on Christian religious festivals. Conditions of life in many ghettos were squalid as a result of overcrowding and poor sanitation. In Old Regime Frankfurt, Jews were banned from coffee-houses and public parks, and they were permitted to visit the markets only at fixed times. Like Jews in many cities, they needed a passport to leave town. Jews' mobility was restricted, and from time to time they might be expelled from Christian society, as the Jews were expelled from Spain in 1492 and from Portugal soon afterwards (as a consequence the Iberian peninsula is not considered in this chapter). Jews were subject to special taxes. They had few or no civil rights. They were not permitted to own land, or to belong to a guild. They were excluded from positions in government service, from the professions and from military service. They were thus neither peasants nor burghers: they were a people apart, with no place in the social order. The ghetto gates encouraged a feeling of separateness within Jewish communities themselves.[2] A Jewish community under the Old Regime enjoyed a certain degree of autonomy, with its own rabbinical court, its administrative council (*kahal*), links to a rabbinical seminary (*yeshivah*) and its own language, which in Eastern and Central Europe was predominantly Yiddish, a Jewish dialect of German.

The vast majority of European Jews, contrary to a growing myth, were desperately poor. Before emancipation and right through the nineteenth century, most Jews eked out a living as peddlars, small dealers or sellers of second-hand clothes. Others were cattle or horse-dealers, and in this role a few were sometimes able to make substantial profits out of supplying the European armies in time of war. In Eastern Europe Jews might be innkeepers, distillers of alcohol or rent-collectors. The traditional Christian prejudice against usury (lending money at excessive rates of interest) had given Jews an opening as money-lenders. In some parts of rural Europe, before the age of modern banking, Jews thus held a high proportion of peasant mortgages. This made them vulnerable to outbreaks of antisemitic violence and to accusations of parasitism.

These broad generalizations disguise a multitude of geographical and cultural variations. European Jews lived under different legal regimes, which evolved as European societies themselves evolved. Jewry was never completely culturally homogeneous. The Ashkenazi Jews of Central and Eastern Europe spoke Yiddish and had their own religious practices. Meanwhile the Sephardic Jews, who originated from Spain, Portugal and North Africa, had their own synagogues and liturgy, and spoke a different language, Ladino, although this was dying by the nineteenth century. The emancipation process was to lead to further social and cultural differentiation amongst European Jews. In particular, the non-emancipated Jews of Eastern Europe remained closest to traditional cultural practices, traditional dress, the dietary laws and religious observance. In the emancipated West, Jews were to become more secular and to adopt cultural behaviour common to all Western European society.

## The process of emancipation in Western Europe

Emancipation refers here to the liberation of Jews from all forms of discriminatory laws, prohibitions and taxes which restricted their social, economic and political opportunities as a group. It meant the acquisition of equal status, in social and political terms, with the rest of society. Emancipation was to produce enormous transformations in Jewish society and culture, but it emanated from arguments in Gentile society which Jews themselves were powerless to influence. Emancipation originated first in the Austrian Emperor Joseph II's Toleration Edict of 1782, which was a limited emancipation aimed at strengthening the power and resources of the rational absolutist state. Jews henceforth enjoyed greater geographical mobility. They were subjected to military service for the first time. The special taxes paid by Jews remained: the state could not afford to abolish them. This partial liberation was taken much further by the sweeping emancipation granted in the French Revolution, couched in a new language of abstract rights and individual freedoms. Both these measures were based on a very negative perception of Jewry and a desire to bring all sections of society within the authority of the state.

In 1791, the French National Constituent Assembly granted full citizenship to all French Jews. The Jews were accorded individual rights and at the same time they lost their autonomy as a separate community. The assimilationist agenda of the French Revolution was made explicit by the legislator Clermont-Tonnerre in 1789, when he declared: 'As a nation the Jews must be denied everything, as individuals they must be granted everything.'[3] The Jews were seen as backward and parasitical. They needed to be improved or, in the contemporary discourse of emancipation, 'regenerated'. They should be dragged away from money lending and petty trading into more useful activities like agriculture, skilled crafts and commerce. These assumptions were shared by both the supporters of emancipation and their critics. According to the critics, Jews should not be granted legal emancipation until they had 'improved' and could show they deserved liberation. For the supporters of emancipation, the introverted fanaticism of the Jews and their parasitical status were the result of centuries of persecution by European societies. Once the discriminatory legislation was removed, then Jews were confidently expected to assimilate and become full French citizens. This meant that they would gradually cease to be Jews altogether. For the Abbé Grégoire, one of the leading proponents of emancipation, this would merely be the prelude to the conversion of French Jews to Christianity.[4]

The French Revolution thus aimed to merge Jews completely into Christian society, as individuals enjoying full citizenship rights but no distinct community status. The revolutionary and Napoleonic armies spread these ideas to the rest of Europe. In Napoleonic Italy, the Jews were given civil rights, the ghetto gates were pulled down in Rome and Venice, and Jews were now permitted to live anywhere, buy land and seek employment in the public service. Not surprisingly, Italian Jews became strong supporters of the French administration. French legislation liberated Jews in the Netherlands, in Baden, in Westphalia, Frankfurt and Hamburg. In deference to local pressure, this legislation was not implemented in the Napoleonic Duchy of Warsaw. Nevertheless, a seismic shift had occurred in the situation of European Jewry and its relationship with the rest of society. The repercussions were to be felt throughout the following century.

Andrew Canepa has usefully distinguished three models of the emancipation process in Western Europe.[5] The first was the British model, in which there was no emancipation edict, but a gradual acquisition of the rights of citizenship by a series of legal rulings. By the nineteenth century, this amounted to almost complete legal equality for British Jews. In the second model, applicable most clearly to France, emancipation was achieved by a single, sweeping edict of liberation. In such a model, the legal details had to be subsequently worked out and they were not always worked out in a manner favourable to Jews. The fundamental issue of Jewish status, however, had been resolved and was no longer a matter for debate. In a third model, most clearly applicable in parts of German-speaking Europe, the Josephan legacy remained very important. In this model, emancipation was a slow and stuttering process in which the debate over Jewish liberation was continuous and the status of Jews remained in question. All three versions of emancipation and combinations of them were to be found in the main states of Western and Central Europe in the first half of the nineteenth century.

### The status of Jews in Western and Central Europe

How many Jews lived in Western and Central Europe? Estimates differ, but there were about 360,000 in Prussia, of whom 52,000 were in Posen.

Another quarter of a million lived in Galicia in the Habsburg Empire.[6] Vienna became a major Jewish centre only after restrictions on Jewish property ownership in the capital were lifted in 1848. In the 20 years following, the Jewish population of Vienna rose rapidly to 40,000.[7] There were 245,000 Jews in Hungary in 1830, and about 75,000 in Bohemia in 1850.[8] In Germany as a whole, there were an estimated 600,000 Jews in the middle of the century.[9] In France, the small Jewish population of about 40,000 at the time of the Revolution rose to about 86,000 by 1845.[10] There were about 40,000 British Jews, more than half of them in London, about the same number in the Netherlands with a similar concentration in Amsterdam, and a smaller Italian Jewish community which numbered about 30,000 in 1800, with the largest numbers in Rome and the port city of Livorno.[11]

In many Italian states, the discriminatory legislation of the Old Regime was restored after the end of Napoleonic rule. The Papal Inquisition was re-established. In Piedmont, Modena and the Papal States, Jews were forced back into the ghettos, once again prohibited from buying real estate, and excluded from jobs in government service. In Tuscany, on the other hand, including Livorno, the Jews' civil rights were confirmed, although they were still excluded from military service, and this can be seen as a benchmark of equal status everywhere. Similar regimes prevailed (as far as the Jews were concerned) in Parma and the Austrian provinces of Lombardy and Venetia. The Risorgimento liberals argued for Jewish emancipation. For Mazzini or D'Azeglio, a new Italy signified justice for all, even the Jews.[12] All the same, liberals envisaged emancipation as the first step towards total integration and the eventual conversion of Italian Jews to Catholicism. Piedmont was to take the lead in 1848, when King Carlo Alberto's Constitution (the *Statuto*) emancipated the Jews of Piedmont and even made them subject to conscription. This act resembled Canepa's second model of emancipation relying on an all-embracing government edict. Henceforth, the expansion of Piedmont in the Italian peninsula would bring Jewish emancipation in its wake. Italy's small and long-established Jewish population became one of the most assimilated in Western Europe.

In Germany, the Congress of Vienna left the issue of Jewish liberation to the decisions of individual German states. This meant that they were free to overthrow French legislation. The Jewish communities of Frankfurt and Hamburg were deprived of the rights accorded by French imperial rule. The cities of Bremen and Lübeck expelled the Jewish merchants who had settled there in the Napoleonic period. Throughout Germany, emancipation was slow and partial. In Prussia, legislation was introduced in 1812 to remove special taxes on Jews, to abolish rabbinical courts and to subject

Jews to military service. But employment in the public service was not yet open to them, and in 1818 the Prussian government excluded Jews from academic posts. In the Rhineland, Karl Marx's father Heinrich, descended from a family of rabbis, converted to Lutheranism after the French departed in order to keep practising law. Prussia had acquired the substantial Jewish population of Posen in the Polish Partitions of 1772, 1775 and 1795, and the Rhineland Jews became Prussian only after 1815, so that there was little uniformity of legislation in the various provinces of post-1815 Prussia. In Posen, where most Prussian Jews lived, licensing restrictions tried to limit Jewish involvement in innkeeping and the sale of alcohol. Jewish dealers were accused of corrupting the peasantry and competing unfairly with Christian traders. A special law of 1833 enabled Posen Jews to become naturalized, and by 1845, all Jews in Prussia were granted the 'privilege' of being drafted into the Prussian army.

Restrictions on civil rights and on Jewish mobility remained in force in southern Germany and in the Habsburg Empire. In Vienna itself, Jews could not buy property: Salomon Rothschild had to rent a town house there until 1842. In Bohemia, Czech Jews were allowed to own land in 1841, and residence restrictions were lifted in 1848. The Revolutions of 1848 produced contradictory results as far as Jews were concerned. German liberals accepted the need for Jewish emancipation, but they still hoped for Jewish assimilation into a new national polity. Anti-Jewish rhetoric of a very ancient kind was still heard even in progressive circles. The Young Hegelian Arnold Ruge, for example, called Jews 'maggots in the cheese of Christianity'.[13] What was new in 1848 was talk of equality, toleration and the rights and duties of the Jew as a citizen, reflecting the progress of liberal concepts over the previous half-century. The granting of full emancipation by the Frankfurt National Assembly was an important milestone, but its implementation was always dependent on individual states. Moreover, the economic depression produced anti-Jewish disturbances in Baden, Hesse and Silesia. The failures of the 1848 Revolutions effectively postponed full Jewish emancipation in Germany for another generation, while legal disabilities were not fully removed for all Austrian Jews until 1867. The Bohemian Jews, whose relationship with Czech nationalism had always been problematic, now retreated into the German cultural sphere. In the Habsburg Empire, Canepa's third model of emancipation seems most appropriate: Jews attended German-speaking state schools on the Josephan model, but their full emancipation was a very piecemeal affair.

The situation of British Jews was quite different, as Canepa stressed. By the beginning of the nineteenth century, Jews born in Britain became

British citizens, with civil and political rights and the right to own land. The discriminatory legislation encountered in Germany and parts of Italy no longer existed there. Unlike thousands of their counterparts on the continent, British Jews had become very urbanized and involved in skilled crafts as well as commercial life. The process of anglicization was gradual but effective, particularly amongst rich Sephardic families like that of future Prime Minister Benjamin Disraeli. Poorer Ashkenazi immigrants from Holland or Poland integrated much more slowly, but a wealthy Jewish bourgeois elite emerged.

There were still a few bastions of the English establishment which excluded Jews, like parliament and the universities of Oxford and Cambridge, but one by one they were conquered. In 1833, Francis Henry Goldsmid became the first Jew to be admitted to the Bar in Britain when he was exempted from the Christian oath of office. Further breakthroughs followed. In 1845, Jews were permitted to become London aldermen and, in 1846, Moses Montefiore was knighted and made a baronet. The most celebrated struggle of all, however, was that engaged by Lionel Rothschild for admission to the House of Commons. Rothschild was elected to parliament in 1847 as a Liberal member for the City of London, but was barred from sitting when he refused the Christian oath and insisted on affirming his allegiance on the Old Testament. He was only admitted to parliament in 1858, after being defiantly elected in his City constituency on four consecutive occasions. Only the opulent upper-crust of British Jewry could aspire to such achievements, but they stood as role models of social success for poor Jews everywhere.

In France, there were four quite separate Jewish communities. About 12 per cent of all French Jews in 1815 lived in and around Avignon. A long-standing Sephardic community lived in the southwest, principally in Bordeaux and Bayonne. A small but growing number were based in Paris. By far the largest group of French Jews, however, was the much poorer community of Alsace in eastern France, where three-quarters of French Jews lived in 1815.[14] This Yiddish-speaking community was the target of regular complaints about Jewish financial activities. Perhaps one-third of all mortgage loans in Alsace were in Jewish hands.[15]

Napoleon's so-called Infamous Decree (*Décret Infâme*) of 1808 imposed new restrictions on Jewish trade and money-lending for a period of ten years. This was a temporary setback in the emancipation process, but in 1818, when the Infamous Decree came up for renewal, the Bourbon regime let it lapse. In 1830, the French state also agreed to cover Jewish religious expenses. Jews entered politics and the professions, and were drawn increasingly to Paris. They became prominent financial entrepreneurs, like the Péreires. After the Revolution of February 1848, two Jews, Crémieux and Goudchaux, became members of the Provisional Government. Among conservatives, republicans and socialists, Jews played important roles in French society.

## Jews in Eastern Europe

The vast majority of European Jews, about 2 million of them, lived in western Russia and the Congress Kingdom of Poland. Here, in David Vital's phrase, lay the 'true centre of gravity of European Jewry'.[16] Until the great wave of transatlantic migration developed in the final decades of the nineteenth century, this region was the dynamic and traditional heart of world Jewry.

In Western Europe, Jewish emancipation was a sequel to the decline of feudal society and the access of the liberal bourgeoisie to social and political rights. In Eastern Europe, feudalism had not disappeared, the urban bourgeoisie was small and weak and the conditions which had produced emancipation in the West did not exist. The legal status of Polish Jews under Prussian or Habsburg rule slowly improved, but in Tsarist Russia no emancipation occurred. On the contrary, the Jews of Russia suffered a brutal and harrowing repression.

In Congress Poland, Tsar Alexander was prepared to grant the Jews certain rights, such as exemption from conscription, but only if they converted to Christianity. Any moves he might make were opposed by Czartoryski and the Polish aristocracy, who argued like their counterparts in the West that the Jews must reform themselves if they were ever to deserve freedom. Most Polish Jews were desperately poor and paid exorbitant special taxes. They could not own land which was an aristocratic monopoly. Yet a few urban Jews played a significant role in economic life. In Warsaw, they were vital to international commerce, acting as intermediaries in the grain export business. They handled mortgages and army supply contracts, and took leases on the collection of government duties on salt and tobacco. In the Polish capital this Jewish entrepreneurial elite was indispensable, and individual members of it were rewarded with special concessions to buy property outside the Jewish district. Prosperous Jews sent their sons to university in Warsaw or Cracow, joined Masonic Lodges and participated in Polish intellectual life. Many crafts and professions were still barred to them, and they did not enjoy full citizenship rights. This did not prevent Warsaw becoming as much of a magnet for Polish Jews as Paris was for French Jewry. By 1846, over a quarter of the population of Warsaw was Jewish.[17]

Beyond bourgeois society in Warsaw, any idea of Polish–Jewish solidarity was wishful thinking. In the Polish Revolution of 1830, most poor Jews did not support the Polish landowners and army officers who led the movement. Polish nationalism had as little to offer the majority of Jews as did the Russian Tsar. In fact Poles executed many Jews who were suspected of assisting the Russian enemy in 1830, and the revolutionary situation allowed the free expression of popular hostility towards Jews.[18] Only on the left-wing of socialism, in Marxist internationalist circles, would Poles and Jews eventually find some common ground.

In the East, the Partitions of Poland had greatly extended Russian territory, but left the Tsars with a new problem – about 400 000 Jews lived there, and this population had to be absorbed by a regime with an appalling reputation for brutality and intolerance. Furthermore, the Jewish population was expanding faster than the Christian population.[19] Catherine the Great had confined Jews to a band of territory in western Russia, stretching from the Baltic to the Black Sea. Even within this 'Pale of Settlement', Jews needed special permission to live in certain cities like Kiev. More than 4000 Jews lived in the port city of Odessa, where they managed the grain trade in conjunction with Greek merchants. In spite of enjoying government protection, the Odessa Jews suffered pogroms in 1821, 1849, 1859 and 1871.[20] Most Jews lived in small villages (*shtetl*), but they were periodically expelled and forced into the cities. In 1824, thousands of Jews were driven from their villages in Mogilev and Vitebsk provinces. In 1827, they were expelled from Grodno and even from Kiev itself, although this last expulsion was never completed.[21] The Jewish presence was seen as a corrupting influence and a threat to Russian peasant values. Jews were also excluded from merchant guilds and prohibited from employing Christian servants.

The paternalistic, religiously inspired dictatorship of Alexander I gave way to outright military coercion under his successor, Tsar Nicholas I. Nicholas used the army to pursue a policy of punitive assimilation. His edict of 1827 authorizing the conscription of Jewish boys of 12 years old and even younger was particularly barbarous. The quotas of young recruits were to be provided by the *kahal* (Jewish governing council) itself, and they were subject to 25 years of military service. If these recruits survived, they were unlikely to return to their villages and in effect were subjected to an ordeal of enforced de-Judaization. In barracks, they were beaten and starved until they submitted to Christian baptism.[22]

The policy of Russification dictated the assimilation of the Jews into the dominant Russian culture of the multi-ethnic Tsarist Empire. Between 1840 and 1855, a state campaign was launched to break down Jewish

*Map 9.1*   The Pale of Settlement

autonomy and cultural independence. In 1844, the *kahal* was abolished, and the taxes it collected were diverted to finance the government's educational schemes for Jews. While Jewish schools were brought under government control, secular schools were to be established to facilitate the process of integration. Tsar Nicholas's minister Uvarov tried to enlist enlightened Jews in his education project. Influenced by the Berlin Enlightenment, they welcomed the secular curriculum introduced in Odessa and Vilna, where Jews could be taught foreign languages, mathematics, science and other aspects of general European culture for the first time. This programme appealed to members of the Jewish intelligentsia who regarded the Yiddish-speakers of the *shtetl* as backward and narrow-minded. The power of traditional belief worked against Uvarov's experiment: in 1855, only 2500 students were attending his state schools for Jews.[23]

Eastern European Jews thus preserved their tradition and religious culture far longer than their counterparts in the West. Compared to Western Jews, they rarely converted to Christianity. Their rates of fertility and illiteracy were higher than in the West. At the same time, their poverty and relative isolation were also undiminished. Eastern European Jews generally knew as little of Christian society as it knew of them. They inhabited a highly segregated world. At the end of the nineteenth century, the Jewish migration from Tsarist Russia was a migration of traditionally orthodox Jews to a secularized West. A very different Jewish exodus was to occur after the fall of the Soviet Union, when Russian Jews emigrated from a secularized Communist society. Then, it might even be said, they left Russia to find out what being Jewish meant.

### Jewish assimilation and Jewish identity

How did Jews respond to the new opportunities for social mobility which opened up for them? In Western Europe, several choices were open. Some wholeheartedly embraced the goal of 'assimilation', defined here as abandoning Judaism and Jewish cultural roots, to achieve a complete merger with the rest of Western European society. This kind of assimilation, which implied a complete loss of Jewish identity, was what the original defenders of emancipation had hoped for. Other Jews achieved a level of 'acculturation' which fell short of full assimilation: in other words, they adopted the habits and tastes of European secular culture, without completely ceasing to identify themselves as Jews. This group perhaps experienced the most acute identity problems in the wake of emancipation. A third group of traditional Jews rejected assimilation, and attempted to preserve their cultural and above all religious distinctiveness. For them, merging with Christian society was tantamount to apostasy and betrayal.

The use of Hebrew, and the decline or persistence of the Yiddish language were important indicators of Jewish acculturation in Western Europe. Legislation in France, Prussia and the Habsburg Empire expressly prohibited the use of Hebrew in business transactions. The example of eastern France suggests that tradition died hard. Here acculturation was a very slow process, and the use of Alsatian Yiddish was common throughout this period. In the 1820s and 1830s, about one-half of Jewish brides in the villages of Alsace still signed their marriage certificates using Hebrew characters.[24] In the countryside, relatively few Jewish children were sent to public primary schools, and boys were still given distinctively Jewish names.

There were proposals in France and Germany to alter forms of worship in order to bring them more into line with dominant Christian practices. Some argued for the admission of women into the main part of the synagogue. Integrated Jews called for greater decorum and reverence during worship, instead of the common practice of conducting private conversations in the middle of religious ceremonies. There were proposals to imitate Christian worship by introducing an organ into synagogues, as well as recurrent suggestions to move the Jewish sabbath to Sunday. These reforms were condemned by the orthodox rabbis. The Bible and classic Jewish literature were subjected to critical modern scholarship by intellectuals like those in the *Wissenschaft des Judentums* (Jewish Learning) movement. A Jewish elite accepted the need to 'regenerate' the Jews, to modify the nature and religious practices of Judaism in order to fulfil their role as modern citizens. Social and cultural transformations worked fastest amongst the expanding Jewish urban bourgeoisie; the poorer Jews continued to use Hebrew and observe the dietary laws.

Bourgeois Jews joined the social world which their Christian counterparts frequented. Jewish entrepreneurs and bankers like Péreire were active in the Saint-Simonian movement. They became Freemasons, like Adolphe Crémieux, Sovereign Grand Master of the Scottish Rite in France in 1869, whose children converted to Catholicism. Such conversions were another indicator of the desire for acceptance and assimilation. Conversion was a path to social advancement for ambitious professionals. Karl Marx, born in 1818, was not circumcised and was baptized a Lutheran (in Germany converted Jews tended to become Protestants rather than Catholics).[25]

These processes posed dilemmas about the nature of Jewish identity. How far were attending state schools, adopting Christian names and vernacular languages compatible with true Judaism? Jews shared a traditional prayer for their return to Israel, but were they not now British,

French or Prussian citizens? What remained of a Jewish identity in the rapidly secularizing world of Western Europe? One aspect of Jewishness, at least, hardly changed: Jews everywhere largely practised endogamous marriage. In other words, Jews still tended to marry Jews. In the West, Jewish families became smaller, as Jews gradually adopted common bourgeois practices of family limitation, but their families generally remained foyers of Jewish solidarity. Even amongst the Jewish elite who converted to Christianity or became completely secularized, a sense of Jewish identity was rarely lost altogether. Jews had gained legal equality but not necessarily jettisoned all their communal traditions. Thus Adolphe Crémieux was an acculturated French lawyer and politician, a non-practising Jew who became a minister in the Provisional Government of 1848, and yet he championed Jewish causes all over Europe. As acculturated Jews became active in European society, they risked a double estrangement, both from their Jewish traditions, and ultimately from the bourgeois world to which they so much desired to belong. Secularized Jews could never go back to the old religion, but sometimes in spite of themselves, their Jewishness clung to them like a shadow. Benjamin Disraeli was a converted Jew who embraced these dilemmas with defiance and spectacular success. Always distrusted by the British upper classes as a Jew, a novelist and flamboyant dilettante, he became leader of the Conservative Party and the first British prime minister of Jewish origin. Disraeli celebrated British imperialism on one hand, and his Jewishness on the other, openly befriending the Rothschilds and basing some of his fictional characters on them. Even the most apparently assimilated Jews could take pride in some aspects of their Jewish identity.

British society was, as Todd Endelman argues, a paradigm of 'radical assimilation'.[26] Here the well-established Sephardic community, from which the Disraeli family came, were the first to acculturate to British life. In the course of the nineteenth century, however, all British Jews were subject to similar pressures for what French commentators called 'fusion sociale'. British Jewry, largely composed of immigrant Jews, had no strong communal structure to parallel Napoleon's system of Consistories in France, and had no dynamic intellectual leadership. Without the tradition of discriminating legislation which still existed in parts of continental Europe, conditions in Britain favoured Jewish assimilation.

## The case of the Rothschilds

The Rothschilds were an exceptional family by anyone's standards. Role models for socially mobile Jews, they were later targeted by both the Left and the Right as representative of all the evils of financial capitalism. Their massive wealth and success made them quite untypical of the mass of poor European Jews. Yet their story, superbly told by the financial historian Niall Ferguson, illustrates several of the themes of this chapter: they faced both the opportunities of emancipation and the problems of assimilation; and their fate was intertwined with the development of industrial and financial capitalism in the post-revolutionary era. 'Money is the god of our time, and Rothschild is his prophet', wrote the German (and Jewish) poet Heinrich Heine in 1841.[27]

Mayer Amschel Rothschild left the Frankfurt ghetto after 1811, when the French emancipated the Frankfurt Jews. He bought his first house nearby, and celebrated his escape from the claustrophobic world of the *Judengasse* by sleeping under the stars in his new garden. Mayer Amschel had been a 'court Jew' who had helped to manage the substantial investments of the Elector of Hesse-Cassel, accumulated from the profits of hiring mercenary soldiers to the European powers.

The peace of 1815 froze the emancipation process, but Mayer Amschel had already begun to make plans for his sons. His son Nathan had been sent to Manchester as a textile dealer, but Napoleon's exclusion of British exports from Europe turned him into a London banker. Nathan's experience in smuggling textile goods to the continent stood him in good stead – during the Peninsular War, he was able to supply the Duke of Wellington with the bullion he needed to finance his army, in shipments code-named 'Rabbi Mosche'. Using his family connections, Nathan organized the payment of British subsidies to her continental allies in the struggle against Napoleonic France, learning the skills of 'arbitrage', that is, profiting from fluctuations in the exchange rate as he dealt in different European currencies.

A multinational fraternity of Rothschilds was established after 1815 to make use of the fortune and the connections thus acquired from financing the Napoleonic Wars. Nathan's brothers James in Paris, Amschel in Frankfurt, Salomon in Vienna and eventually Carl in Naples formed a unique network, enabling the group to raise money for governments almost anywhere in Europe. If one branch suffered a loss, the other centres would absorb it, just as long as losses were not universal which was precisely what happened in the general crash of 1846–7. The Rothschilds were personal bankers for Wellington, Metternich and the British royal family. They raised loans for the Austrian government in 1820 and for Russia in 1822. They financed the French war in Spain in 1823. They raised sterling loans for the Prussian government: this was the first occasion when British investors bought foreign government bonds and it marks the genesis of the international bond market. In the first half of the nineteenth century, the combined capital of the Rothschilds vastly exceeded that of any other international bank. In the 1830s and 1840s, the bank diversified, as James Rothschild invested in railway building, taking a controlling interest in the new *Chemin de Fer du Nord*. Meanwhile Salomon invested in the new Austrian Lloyd steamship company, established in 1835. They had become not just bankers but industrial investors. Their only mistake, according to Ferguson, was not to establish a firm foothold in the United States.

The Rothschilds' support for Metternich and his Prussian allies led Heinrich Heine among others to see them as agents of reaction, the paymasters of post-revolutionary conservatism. There was nevertheless something subversive about their new role, which potentially undermined the old landed aristocracy who needed their resources and their credit. While serving, and sometimes aping the social elites of Europe, the Rothschilds represented a different ethos, the ethos of new money which did not respect the old. The Rothschilds often appalled aristocratic society by talking about money as if it mattered.[28]

The Rothschilds craved acceptance and social recognition, as the struggle of Lionel Rothschild, Nathan's son, to enter the House of Commons illustrated. They changed their names, Jakob becoming James and Kalman Carl. They bought suburban villas and town houses, the status symbols of the European aristocracy. Nathan acquired Gunnersbury Park, James his French chateaux and Carl the Villa Pignatelli near Naples. They acquired all the accoutrements of a French or English gentleman – the coat of arms, the racehorses, the hunting stable. They bought Rembrandts and Gainsboroughs, they hired Mendelssohn and Liszt to play at their *soirées*. In many ways they became part of the European social elite. They gradually abandoned sabbath observance, finding it impossible to neglect their business correspondence on a Saturday.

Yet in spite of this meteoric acculturation, the Rothschilds remained Jews. Unlike many contemporaries, they never converted to Christianity. As Carl said in 1814: 'I am a Jew in the depths of my heart, I prefer not to mix with the *meshumed* (converted) families.'[29] They often used their money to assist Jewish charities. In the early years of their rise to riches, the brothers corresponded with each other in Judendeutsch – a form of German written in Hebrew characters – which worked as a secret code. In Frankfurt, Amschel observed the sabbath and ate kosher; he even built a synagogue in his own house. Like so many other Jews, the Rothschilds married only Jews. In fact, they only married other Rothschild cousins, taking the same kind of genetic risk run by the inbred royalty of Europe. The exception only went to prove this rule of strict Jewish endogamy.

When, in 1839, Hannah Mayer Rothschild, Nathan's daughter, converted to marry Henry Fitzroy, younger son of Lord Southampton, she lost her right to an enormous dowry, but she also sparked off a huge family scandal. The Rothschilds, according to Ferguson, were 'incandescent' with rage and impotence.[30] The men, at least, were never allowed to 'marry out'.

The Rothschilds were mythical Jews, revered and demonized, imagined by admirers and critics alike to possess staggering riches and enormous clandestine power. Their story reveals the dazzling heights to which Jews could aspire in the era of emancipation. They acculturated, adopting the trappings of an aristocratic lifestyle. At the same time, their story shows the limits of assimilation, and the ambivalence of many Jews towards its attractions. The Rothschilds never denied their origins.

### Jew-hatred traditional and modern

There were other limits to Jewish assimilation, in the form of popular prejudices and hostility to Jews in general. To some extent, Jew-hatred in this period was fuelled by an emerging nationalism. In Bohemia, for example, Czech nationalists saw the Jews as vehicles of German culture and therefore the natural lackeys of the Austrian regime.[31] The youthful nationalists who formed the *Burschenschaften* (student guilds) in German universities like Jena excluded Jews and saw them as a group outside the national community, and a danger to its health and vigour. Herder, the eighteenth-century philosopher who inspired interest in a national popular culture, had written: 'The Jewish race is and remains in Europe an Asiatic people alien to our region.'[32] Hostility towards Jews remained an integral part of the nationalist aspirations of student youth in Germany.

This form of antagonism towards Jews should not, however, be exaggerated. Most often outbreaks of violence against Jews had more ancient origins. In times of hardship, peasants would react against the Jews who often held their mortgages and controlled interest rates. These fears lay behind the anti-Jewish riots in Alsace during the 1848 Revolution, and they were essentially a response to a medieval situation which had left the Jews as the main source of credit for local peasants. In the so-called 'Hep-Hep' riots which swept through many German cities in 1819, the underlying cause was not so much emerging German nationalism as the economic upheavals and shortages of the difficult postwar years. Jewish homes and stores were attacked and synagogues destroyed.

Hatred of Jews, as the Mortara Affair suggested, was not yet racially inspired. It most often had archaic and Christian roots. This was clear in cases of the 'blood libel' – the myth according to which Jews would murder Christian children to extract their blood to make Passover bread. Examples of the blood libel surfaced often in Eastern Europe, like the cases in Saratov (1851) and Velizh (1823–6). A child would die or disappear, a community would turn on the Jews, violence or imprisonment would follow, then the authorities would make more or less serious efforts to restore order and let justice run its course. In Velizh, the government closed all synagogues for nine years after a ritual murder accusation against Jews.[33]

There was certainly a literary Jew-hatred, too, exemplified by Dickens's manipulative and criminal Fagin in *Oliver Twist*, and the sinister financier Lucingen, who made several fictional appearances in Balzac's *Comédie Humaine*, ridiculed for his thick German accent and reminiscent of the Rothschilds. The conventional nineteenth-century view identified Jews as the epitome of commercial greed. They were the unacceptable face of emerging capitalism. In this role, they were attacked not only by Christian traditionalists, but also by elements on the socialist left. Toussenel made an impact in 1846 with his book *The Jews, Kings of the Epoch: A History of Financial Feudalism* which concluded that emancipation had been a mistake and cast the Jews as agents of capitalist oppression. This work resonated because its publication coincided with the bursting of the bubble in railway shares in which James Rothschild had been heavily involved. What is more, a horrible derailment on his northern railway in that same year caused 14 deaths and provoked vigorous denunciations in the press. Jew-hatred was thus many-sided: it had Christian roots, an economic context, and undertones both nationalist and socialist. The racial theories of modern antisemitism were later to build on these older prejudices.

## Conclusion

The process of Jewish emancipation was neither smooth nor uninterrupted nor uncontested. It nevertheless went hand in hand with the development of political liberalism and capitalism. An elite of well-integrated Jews appeared at the forefront of these modernizing forces. Yet the majority of their fellow Jews remained poor shopkeepers and dealers in second-hand goods.

Emancipation caused world Jewry to become more fragmented and heterogeneous both socially and culturally. As well as the differences between Sephardic and Ashkenazi Jews, there were now increasing gaps within Jewry between rich and poor, the acculturated and the traditionalist, the orthodox and the liberal (or 'reformed') and above all between East and West. The promise of full citizenship and assimilation seemed to bring about the unprecedented disintegration of the Jews.

This would however be a superficial conclusion. Predictions that Jews, once liberated, would lose their Jewishness and become indistinguishable from the rest of society were not fulfilled. Even the most acculturated Western Jews preserved a sense of their Jewish identity. Adolphe Crémieux, Nathan Rothschild and Benjamin Disraeli never ceased to be Jews, even when they or their children converted to Christianity. In any case, society would never let them forget their origins even if they had wanted to. Among these well-integrated elite circles, a modern and secular notion of Jewish identity developed.

The setbacks noted in this chapter certainly contributed to the formation of a renewed Jewish consciousness. For emancipated Jews who had achieved success and social promotion, incidents like the Mortara Affair, with which this chapter opened, sent out a wake-up call. Isidore Cahen sounded the alert for all Western Jews in these words: 'The Mortara Affair reveals, strips bare, the ultramontanist tendencies [i.e. tendencies to strengthen the power of the Pope]; it shows you the extent to which you may be afraid; let it be an alarm signal for you'.[34]

European Jewry needed to defend its collective interests, and it now had the platform and the resources to do so. In 1860, in the aftermath of the Mortara Affair, the first world organization of Jews, the Universal Jewish Alliance (*Alliance Israélite Universelle*), was established in Paris. It was a sign that a new sense of Jewish solidarity was developing. Paradoxically, this emerging pan-Jewish consciousness was articulated in Paris, the home of the French Revolution, where emancipation had been expected to erode Jewish separateness and lead to a new 'social fusion' of Jews and Christians. It seemed that at the very heart of liberated Western Jewry, a distinctive Jewish identity was alive and strong. The hopes of the emancipationists had not been fulfilled.

# 10    The City

## Introduction: what made Dostoevsky nervous

Eighteenth-century intellectuals saw the city as the snake-pit of debauchery and a trap for the unwary. It was a place where money ruled, where innocent peasant girls were seduced by worldly predators and so-called 'sophistication' had become an excuse for immoral behaviour. In the early nineteenth century, the material problems of urban life, such as the need for sewerage and a clean water supply, became more pressing than moral ones. The material and moral environments, however, were linked: a poor environment was unlikely to produce virtuous town-dwellers. As Charles Kingsley declared in a lecture in 1857: 'The moral state of a city depends – how far I know not, but frightfully, to an extent as yet uncalculated, and perhaps incalculable – on the physical state of that city; on the food, water, air, and lodging of its inhabitants.'[1] Rapid population growth made problems of poverty and sanitation more urgent. The pre-modern city was still made up of networks of dark, narrow alleys but it grew inexorably larger and the density of its teeming inhabitants more overpowering.

Today many would consider New York as the acme of metropolitan life in the West. Whether it excites or horrifies the visitor, it seems to represent the quintessence of urban civilization. In the late nineteenth century, Paris, with its new boulevards and department stores, seemed the ultimate in modernity. In the early nineteenth century, London played this role as the city which contained within itself the future of all other cities. The Russian novelist Dostoevsky visited London to see the Great Exhibition of 1851, and remarked: 'You feel nervous . . . a feeling of fear somehow creeps over you. Can this, you think, in fact be the final accomplishment of an ideal state of things? Is this the end, by any chance?'[2] This chapter must consider what it was about the city that alienated contemporaries and might have made Dostoevsky nervous. These factors include the sheer size of cities, their problems of poverty and unemployment, of crime and disease. In the 1830s and 1840s, well-to-do elites became increasingly afraid of the urban poor: their unhealthy tenements were the festering ground of lethal epidemics and of social unrest. And in 1848, European cities were hotbeds of revolution.

161

**Urban demography**

To begin with, the size of London was intimidating. In 1800, it was by far
the largest city in the Western world, and possibly anywhere, with the
exception of Peking. In 1850, it had more than 2.6 million inhabitants, but
its importance only becomes clear in comparison to other urban centres.
London was more than twice as large as its closest rival for size, namely
Paris, and twice as large as St Petersburg, Vienna and Berlin put together.
London's growth reflected urban expansion everywhere, as Table 10.1
shows. In 1800, the largest European cities were capital cities, centres of
law, culture and administration which sustained a royal or imperial court
and its innumerable suppliers and hangers-on. By mid-century, the new
industrial centres of Britain were joining this league of metropolitan giants.
In 1800, Europe had 22 cities with more than 100 000 inhabitants each; by
1851 there were 39 of them, and 11 of those were in the British Isles.[3] In a
mere decade between 1821 and 1831, the population of Bradford increased
by 66 per cent, that of Leeds by 47 per cent, those of Liverpool and
Manchester by 45 per cent.[4]

An expanding population, together with changes in the countryside,
including the enclosure of common land and the decline of cottage industry, drove people into the cities. Subsistence crises in 1816–17 and in
1846–7 brought starvation in country areas and accelerated the rural
exodus. Urban growth in the industrial north of England was rapid and
spectacular, but expansion was by no means confined to industrial towns.
Consider two very different cities which have been the subject of recent
studies. The Belgian city of Antwerp was a textile manufacturing centre in

*Table 10.1*   Population of Europe's ten largest cities[5]

|    | In 1800 | | In 1850–1 | |
| --- | --- | --- | --- | --- |
| 1  | London | 1,117,000 | London | 2,685,000 |
| 2  | Paris | 547,000 | Paris | 1,053,000 |
| 3  | Naples | 427,000 | St Petersburg | 485,000 |
| 4  | Moscow | 250,000 | Naples | 449,000 |
| 5  | Vienna | 247,000 | Vienna | 444,000 |
| 6  | St Petersburg | 220,000 | Berlin | 419,000 |
| 7  | Amsterdam | 200,000 | Liverpool | 376,000 |
| 8  | Lisbon | 180,000 | Moscow | 365,000 |
| 9  | Berlin | 172,000 | Glasgow | 357,000 |
| 10 | Dublin | 165,000 | Manchester | 303,000 |

decline, now searching for a new role as an international commercial port. Its population rose from about 55,000 in 1822 to 110,000 in 1860.[6] At the other end of Europe, the Ukrainian city of Kiev was developing from a frontier market town into an important regional capital and sugar-beet processing centre. It had a mere 20,000 inhabitants at the beginning of the century, but it had grown to 70,000 by 1870, when it was first linked by rail with Moscow and Odessa.[7]

Not only did cities grow in absolute terms, but so did the rate of urbanization: in other words, a greater proportion of the whole population now inhabited cities. The rate of urbanization is difficult to measure, since every state had its own definition of what qualified as a town. In 1846, for example, France defined a town as anywhere with a population over 2000, and by mid-century, about a half of France's population lived in towns thus defined.[8] This definition was appropriate, for France was predominantly a country of small market towns and semi-rural *bourgs*, with no equivalent as yet of the industrial concentrations which were developing in Lancashire or the Ruhr. The demographic historian Charles Pouthas found the greatest growth was in French medium-sized towns of between 20,000 and 50,000 inhabitants, and it occurred in the most prosperous years of the July Monarchy, before the economic and demographic catastrophe of 1846–7.[9] In post-Napoleonic Prussia, only about a quarter of the population lived in towns with over 2000 inhabitants, although there was an increasing movement of people towards the urbanized Rhineland.[10] Nowhere in Europe was as urbanized as Britain, where in 1801, one-fifth of the population already lived in cities with over 10,000 inhabitants, and this proportion rose to 38 per cent by the 1851 census.[11]

Urbanization in both industrial and pre-industrial areas was the result of a long-term trend towards population growth which had begun after 1750. It produced some distinct demographic features. High urban death rates were very common. In the Rhineland city of Köln, for example, the annual death rate was actually on the rise, reaching an average of 32.4 deaths per 1000 inhabitants by 1849, but there was nevertheless a surplus of births in the city.[12] Even cities with a surplus of births relied for their growth on migration from the countryside. Migrants did not usually come from very far afield: there was an enormous flow of people both in and out of Duisburg in the Ruhr, but most migrants had only travelled 60 or 70 kilometres, to find a new job in the city's factories, workshops and brickworks.[13] Sometimes migrants made regular seasonal journeys, like the French stone-mason Martin Nadaud, whose story we know from his autobiography.[14] Nadaud walked to Paris annually from his home in the Creuse to work on the building sites of the capital during the summer months, returning in winter when demand slackened. As with many of his compatriots, his seasonal migrations eventually culminated in permanent settlement in Paris.

In Britain, Irish immigrants fuelled urban expansion. The arrival of massive numbers of Irish predated the potato famine of 1846 with which it is often associated. By 1841, the Irish-born already made up 12 per cent of the population of Manchester and 17 per cent of the population of Liverpool. Further waves of Irish immigration occurred in the 1840s and 1850s, and by 1851 the Irish may have constituted as many as 30 per cent of Liverpool's population, if second-generation Irish are included.[15] The majority were poor, ill-educated and unskilled, and their arrival embarrassed a previous generation of Irish immigrants who were better-off and well-integrated into English society. The labour-force requirements of expanding cities were thus met by a flow of migrants, who were ready and likely to move on if demand for labour fluctuated. This created another source of anxiety for elites: not only were cities growing astronomically, but so at the same time were their floating populations, those masses of displaced and rootless people who were a potential threat to social stability.

Large-scale immigration could alter a city's population make-up. In pre-industrial cities, a considerable proportion of immigrants were women in their late 'teens or early twenties looking for work in domestic service, like the young North Brabant girls who flocked into early nineteenth-century Antwerp. This tended to distort the urban sex ratio, so that women greatly outnumbered men in the city's population. In industrial cities, this imbalance was reversed because most migrants seeking employment in factories or shipyards tended to be single young men. For example, mid-century Duisburg had a ratio of 107 men to every 100 women.[16] The migrant population was young and mobile and did not always seek to settle and marry. Partly as a result of this, and simply because of poverty, the urban rate of illegitimate births and abandoned children was high and rising. In early nineteenth-century Paris, between one-third and 40 per cent of all reported births were illegitimate. Single country girls who became pregnant had always found a refuge in large anonymous cities where no-one knew them and they could escape some of the stigma of an illegitimate birth. Many young single pregnant girls found their way to the free Maternité hospital. Immigrant women made up 82 per cent of single mothers in La Maternité during the nineteenth century, and their average age was 24.[17] These women presumably could not afford a midwife's fee, but they had found some means of assistance for themselves and their new-born child. But what of the thousands of other destitute immigrants whom the city swallowed up and then rejected when times were hard?

## Urban poverty

As cities grew, so did the problem of poverty. Of course, poverty was nothing new, and Malthus had argued that it was logically inevitable. Now, however, European cities experienced poverty on a mass scale, which far surpassed the ability of relief mechanisms to deal with it. And yet, the contours of poverty and responses to it had not substantially altered for centuries. Poverty was widespread but often temporary. Neither in agriculture nor in the urban environment was it normal to enjoy continuous employment. Many jobs were temporary or seasonal. Families eked out a precarious living from all kinds of petty street-trading, like the snail-sellers in Plate 12. As a result, many people might expect to face poverty at some

*Plate 12*   'Snail-Sellers in Naples'. This group of snail-sellers, probably photographed in the 1890s, was engaged in petty trading crucial for the survival of the urban poor in the pre-industrial city

*Source*:   Alinari Archives.

stage of their working life. A worker achieved his or her highest earning power as a young adult, when health and strength were good, but thereafter an individual could expect declining wages, intermittent employment and no formal provision for old age. To the natural vulnerability of the human life cycle we must add the effects of economic restructuring, including the process of industrialization itself which threw whole sectors of the economy on to the scrap heap.

How many people were poor? The answer naturally depends on how the historical poverty line is measured. The historian's yardstick is usually the number of individuals who were receiving some kind of charitable relief. Since relief organizations were very discriminating and refused help to many, this yardstick hides a proportion of the reality, but at least it is a criterion with some factual basis. In very broad terms, in ordinary years between 15 and 33 per cent of urban populations received charitable relief. But in crisis years, the poor of any city could number 40 to 50 per cent of the population. In a normal year in Köln, the municipality distributed bread to about 16 per cent of the population; but in the subsistence crisis of 1816, 39 per cent of Köln were on poor relief.[18] In Antwerp, the figures are comparable. In a normal year, 20–25 per cent of the city received some outdoor relief, but in 1849, 39 per cent of the city needed some aid.[19]

Various charitable organizations provided poor relief in the city, from the guilds and brotherhoods of penitents, to the foundling hospitals and municipal pawnshops (*monts de piété*), which were the credit banks of the poor, lending at anywhere between 25 per cent and 40 per cent interest. The hospitals provided 'indoor', or institutionalized poor relief, to be distinguished from 'outdoor' relief, like the handouts of bread and soup provided from time to time by individuals, or in doorways of churches and monasteries. As in the Old Regime, hospitals had very mixed functions. As well as tending the sick, disabled and dying, they confined the insane and they might also serve as houses of correction for beggars or prostitutes. As well as acting as institutions of poor relief, they simultaneously doubled as lunatic asylums and prisons. In Florence, the Pia Casa di Lavoro was both a refuge for the disabled poor and a jail for recidivist beggars.[20]

Institutions were highly selective about who qualified for poor relief. They tried to distinguish between the deserving and undeserving poor, attempting to separate the lazy and work-shy (undeserving) from those who had fallen on hard times through no particular fault of their own (deserving). They favoured the old over the young, and large families over single men and women. In Florence, the Congregation of San Giovanni Battista distributed bread, beds and blankets in an attempt to prevent the 'respectable poor' from lapsing into a state of permanent dependence on charity. The Congregation consistently identified families with female heads as especially vulnerable, but they tried to verify their deserving nature by making a visit to inspect their homes.[21]

Charitable institutions preferred to assist established town residents rather than recent arrivals, because they were afraid of encouraging an influx of beggars. In any case, resources could not provide for everyone. In Antwerp, the scale of the problem was indicated by the progressively stricter eligibility criteria for poor relief applied by the municipality. In the 1817 crisis, the municipal Charity Bureau had only been able to distribute a pittance to the needy. In 1818, therefore, the residence qualification for receipt of municipal poor relief was extended to four years. By 1845, it had doubled to eight years.[22] Good moral conduct and correct religious observance also distinguished the deserving poor from the rest. In a city of several religions like Amsterdam, this could be significant, since Calvinists, Lutherans, Catholics and Jews only gave poor relief to their co-religionists. Clearly the destitute needed to fall back on their own family networks of support, because municipal welfare only offered help for a select group. If they were migrants without such networks, they might resort to one of many age-old survival strategies, like begging, petty crime and prostitution.

Poor relief, however patchy and incoherent, fulfilled some of the functions of present-day old age pensions and social security provision. To call it a welfare system, however, would be going too far. For one thing, unless a charitable institution possessed substantial property assets, poor relief had a fragile financial basis. It might rely on private donations, the profits of the local municipal pawnshop and a fraction of the excise tax. Today welfare applicants may be means tested; in the early nineteenth century, they were subjected to tests of morality and religion. Moreover, recipients were expected to show gratitude and be suitably deferential. In Amsterdam, they were also obliged to have their children vaccinated against smallpox and to send them to school.[23]

This traditional Christian paternalism towards the poor existed side by side with a new, harsher mentality. The English Poor Law of 1834 (wherever it was implemented) abolished wage supplementation previously paid to the able-bodied poor out of parish funds. Instead, they could get help only in workhouses which were designed as deterrents to poverty and where sexual segregation was the rule even for married couples. Behind even traditional methods of poor relief, Marco van Leeuwen argues, lay a strategy for social control.[24] The poor, many of them immigrants as we have seen, constituted a reserve army of labour which the urban elites wanted to keep at their disposal. When employment was irregular, poor relief was a way of giving enough assistance during the winter months to dissuade the poor from leaving town. In return for the means of survival, it was hoped, the poor would desist from crime and begging, they would remain orderly and above all their labour would be available.

Everywhere the old systems of poor relief were inadequate. Contemporaries were shocked by the scale of human distress in the city, and by what we would today call the appearance of 'structural unemployment', inducing a poverty that seemed ineradicable rather than temporary. This was not necessarily the consequence of industrialization; rather it was the result of population expansion within a pre-industrial framework which could not contain the problem.

## Was the city sick?

High densities and inadequate infrastructure created severe social and material problems. In Louis Chevalier's classic analysis of Paris, these problems were the symptoms of a new urban pathology.[25] In other words, the city was sick. Historians today would not accept Chevalier's facile equation between the rootless and criminal elements on one hand, and the danger of revolution on the other. The revolutionaries of 1830 and 1848 were not marginalized people but well-established artisans and shopkeepers. Chevalier's analysis of Parisian social problems, however, still holds good as does his emphasis on the creeping paranoia of middle-class town-dwellers.

Chevalier's Paris, like London, was not a city of hideous smoking factories, but a centre of small-scale production based around the workshops of skilled craftsmen and the boutiques of *petits commerçants*. It was a crowded city full of immigrants, who rented furnished rooms in and near the historic centre. Of the 4000 inhabitants of the Place des Vosges, east of the town hall, only 40 per cent were born in Paris.[26] Immigrants from certain areas had traditional specializations. There were chimney-sweeps from Savoy, masons from the Limousin, water-carriers from the Auvergne, and market-gardeners from Normandy. Ninety per cent of domestic servants were usually of provincial origin. Life in the city of Hugo's *Les Misérables* revolved around the neighbourhood or *quartier*. The typical tenement building set around an inner courtyard with its intimate staircases formed a distinctive space for neighbourly sociability. The concierge's booth or the local wine merchant's shop were focal points for communal interaction. Paris still retained something of a Mediterranean quality in which much of life was carried out in public, including celebrations, private quarrels and domestic disputes. Life was lived visibly, open to collective scrutiny and judgment. In the 1850s, Haussmann's great boulevards were to sweep away many such *quartiers* and drive their working-class inhabitants to the outer suburbs. But Paris had become swollen. Its population reached the million mark in the late 1840s. In the central district of Arcis, north of the Chatelet, population density was 243 000 per square kilometre.[27] The bourgeoisie felt that the barbarians were at the gates.

Crime was one feature of the urban disease, and writers like Hugo and Balzac identified it as Paris's most serious problem. Criminality was no longer something exceptional or romanticized; it had become a banal feature of everyday life in the city. Suicide was another symptom of urban pathology and dislocation. In a normal year, there were about 350 reported suicides in Paris, but the figure rose to 900 in the depression year of 1847.[28] A high illegitimacy rate, abandoned children and conspicuous prostitution suggested an unprecedented accumulation of misery and inadequate social integration. As we shall see in the following section, cholera was the most spectacular symptom of nineteenth-century urban problems.

At the same time, an increasing segregation of classes into distinctive social spaces raised the level of anxiety further. In pre-industrial cities like Paris, all social classes intermingled with each other in the historic centre. In the city centre, social segregation was vertical rather than horizontal. In a Parisian apartment building, the bourgeois would occupy the first floor, known as the 'noble floor'. The inhabitant of this floor might also be the principal tenant, subletting the floors above to lodgers of more modest status. The higher you climbed the staircase, the lower down the social scale you went. At the very top of a five- or six-floor building was no luxurious modern penthouse, but the garrets of the starving poor. This social mixing persisted at least until the rebuilding of Paris after the 1850s, but in many cities there was an increasing separation of aristocratic or bourgeois and working-class residential districts.

City centres tended to be the location of both fine houses and traditional crafts, while new industrial areas grew up in the suburbs. Vienna was a classic example of a city formed in concentric social circles, with its aristocratic centre within the Ring, then the apartment residences of the bourgeoisie outside it, and the working-class suburbs on the periphery. In Amsterdam the merchant elite gathered around the central canals like the patrician Herengracht. In Kiev, there was a clear separation between the aristocratic core on the heights overlooking the river Dnieper, and the wooden houses of the commercial district down below on the river bank, extremely vulnerable to fire and flood.

Population expansion generated a slow trend towards further segregation of social space. Many bourgeois residents started to leave the historic centres and take up their residence in spacious villas on the outskirts. The

social dilution which characterized many inner cities was gradually transformed as neighbourhoods became more socially differentiated, with
densely populated working-class areas usually close to centres of work, and
bourgeois residential districts further away. This trend was very far from
uniform: some English cotton manufacturers still liked to live near their
mill, like Thornton in Mrs Gaskell's novel *North and South*. The presence of
domestic servants in the houses of the rich also ensured that daily contact
between different social classes was inevitable. Yet there was a perception
that the city was becoming more socially polarized. These distinctions
particularly impressed observers of Manchester, and they appeared alarming. Middle-class observers regarded the homogeneous working-class
districts of the industrial city as dangerous areas with low rates of religious
observance, where life was no longer framed by the paternal influence and
guidance of the bourgeoisie. Working-class suburbs were worlds unto themselves. In other words, they signified a loss of social control. Some employers attempted to counteract this development by constructing model
villages for their labour force, or simply by turning their workers into their
own tenants, as in the company towns of Krupp at Essen and Schneider at
Le Creusot in France.

Friedrich Engels was one of the few to put a positive spin on the
phenomenon of social polarization.[29] For him, the appearance of distinctive working-class areas in Manchester provided new conditions for working-class solidarity and mobilization. They offered the promise of
working-class independence and emancipation. Far from illustrating an
urban malaise, the workers' suburb opened up possibilities for developing
new forms of urban community. But a sense of local community could
develop amongst the industrial bourgeoisie, too, and Manchester once
again is a prime example of this solidarity. Its newspaper the *Manchester
Guardian* became a national institution, and in the 1840s, the city gave its
name to a whole school of liberal economics. As one of its protagonists,
John Bright, declared in the appropriately named Manchester Free Trade
Hall in 1851: 'We are called the Manchester party, and our policy is the
Manchester policy, and this building, I suppose, is the schoolroom of the
Manchester school.'[30] The civic pride of such elites was expressed in the
solid and austere architecture of northern English cities in the Victorian
age.

Engels offered a simplified vision of a complex society. Industrial cities
were exceptional, and among them Manchester itself was exceptional.
Overall, European observers perceived that large cities presented suitable
cases for investigation. In Britain and France, government reports and
parliamentary 'blue books' into prostitution, slum housing, public hygiene

and sanitation testified to the intense desire to diagnose the urban disease and to reduce it to objective statistical proportions. Urban sociology fascinated fiction writers, too. In *Hard Times*, Dickens caricatured the smoke and the monotony of the industrial city in his fictional Coketown. In *Oliver Twist*, he laid bare the networks of petty urban crime. In the 1840s, Eugène Sue's serialized novel *Les Mystères de Paris* was a bestseller, introducing middle-class readers to the exotic underworld of the Parisian poor. The city and its ills were subjected to a frenzy of documentation.

## Cholera

Epidemics of *cholera morbus* illustrated, as no other single symptom could, all that was dysfunctional about the early nineteenth-century European city. In the first epidemic wave between 1829 and 1832, the disease spread westward from India to afflict the entire European continent. There was another widespread epidemic in 1849, and many other local outbreaks throughout the century. In Italy, the worst cholera epidemic affected a quarter of a million people in 1854–5.[31] Between 1835 and 1885, Naples had eight cholera epidemics, as well as four typhoid outbreaks.[32] Between 1830 and 1872, Kiev suffered 12 cholera epidemics.[33] Cholera was a barometer of social inequalities and of the city's pathological state. Its recurrence in this period suggests that conditions we today associate with Third World cities were common in nineteenth-century Europe – namely overcrowding, chronic undernourishment and poor sanitation.

Cholera was a shocking way to die, and this rather than the death rate of its victims horrified contemporaries. Imbibed through faeces, the cholera bacillus lodges in the intestine. It rapidly produces severe vomiting, diarrhoea and loss of fluids. Victims suffer complete dehydration and die in their own excrement. In 'normal' outbreaks, fewer than 20 per cent of victims died, but they died quickly and in a sensational and pitiful fashion. Cholera was usually spread through infected water supplies, although before Koch isolated the cholera bacillus in 1884, contemporaries had a very limited understanding of its aetiology. It was spread by people on the move. Armies were notorious disease-carriers. Polish refugees fleeing the Russians in 1831 brought the disease with them, as did the Irish when they emigrated after the famine. In Italy, the starting-points for cholera outbreaks were the port cities with regular international traffic, like Genoa, Livorno, Venice and Naples.

Cholera thrived in insanitary and overcrowded conditions, and among individuals so undernourished that their physical resistance to disease was low. Such squalor was found in every European city. Take the French city of Limoges, where sewage ran in an open drain down the middle of streets. Private garbage was simply thrown out of windows. Corpses rotted unattended in graveyards. Animals were slaughtered in the street in the butchers' district and parts of the carcasses tossed away.[34] Alleyways were too narrow in the medieval core of some cities to allow disposal carts to penetrate. Housing, too, violated all modern norms of human dignity. In Brussels in 1846, 45 per cent of all families lived in a single room each, without taps or drains.[35] The worst European slums were to be found in Naples, where the popular districts had nowhere to expand, hemmed in by the sea on one side and the hills on the other. When Jesse White Mario visited the cellar-slums (*bassi*) of Naples in 1877, her Anglo-Saxon sensibilities were shocked to find two or three families to a room, and skeletal or rachitic children living in a damp atmosphere in which typhus was rampant. In lodging-houses near the port, three men shared the same dormitory bed, with an open cesspit in the middle of the floor.[36] In such an environment, disease spread like a bushfire in a hot summer wind.

The epidemic of 1832 killed about 18,000 in Paris.[37] It carried off the Prime Minister, Casimir Périer and, in Germany, its victims included the philosopher Hegel and military theorist Clausewitz. But these eminent examples are deceptive. Cholera was a discriminating disease. It struck the poor disproportionately. In the central areas of Paris, which as we have seen were intensely overcrowded, the mortality rate was four times higher than in the more salubrious area of the Champs Elysées.[38] The disease was particularly severe on the porters and labourers of Les Halles food markets. Cholera struck at all those who worked on or with water, the medium which carried the bacillus. Dockers, washerwomen and domestics were at risk. In Hamburg, stevedores and boatmen in contact with infected water from the river Elbe caught it.[39] In mid-century London, it killed six times more often in the dockland areas of Rotherhithe and Bermondsey than in the more gentrified districts of Kensington and Westminster.[40] The rich were insulated by better standards of hygiene, including private toilets rather than public latrines, and by servants who came between them and contaminated water. Cholera targeted poverty and squalor: it provided a map of social degradation and the inequalities of urban society.

Cholera induced the same sort of terror as the medieval plague, and it was treated at first in similar fashion – by isolating the victims. Medical theory was unsure whether cholera was 'contagious', that is, spread by personal contact from one individual to another, or 'miasmic', that is, a product of the foul atmosphere and the exhalations of the soil. The contagion theory justified isolation, quarantine measures, curfews and restrictions on public gatherings. The miasma theory justified providing more fresh air and paving the streets as part of a general improvement of the environment. In practice, both viewpoints called for political coercion and public investment. In 1830–1, different political cultures produced different prophylactic strategies. The authoritarian regimes of Eastern Europe reacted with a great show of force. An army of 60,000 troops formed a cordon along Prussia's eastern border with Poland and Russia, and travellers were only permitted to pass the frontier through designated fumigation stations (the mobilization of so many troops must have been a health hazard in itself).[41] The public resisted such interference with normal business. They saw corpses emerge from hospitals and imagined the doctors were poisoning people. In Russia cholera victims had to be forcibly removed to hospital, and occasionally a crowd would storm the hospitals to liberate the patients.[42] In 1832, Parisian ragpickers staged a riot because they were denied access to garbage dumps.[43]

Western governments had time to watch the disease draw closer in spite of quarantine measures, which seemed both ineffective and politically unenforceable. They leaned towards a policy of reforming public hygiene. In Britain the 1848 Public Health Act established a General Board of Health to oversee sewers, street-cleaning, drainage and the water supply. In 1855, the Nuisances Removal and Disease Protection Act allowed inspectors to enter private houses without notice and impose health regulations. The control of disease thus provoked new forms of state intervention and public regulation. At the same time, Catherine Kudlick argues, cholera victims were treated with more compassion. Like the victims of the AIDS epidemic, they were at first blamed and ostracized, as the upper classes wanted only to keep the poor at arm's length. By 1849, however, a more politically secure bourgeoisie reacted differently. The bureaucratic response was more constructive: the poor were less the cause of cholera, more its victims.[44]

## Conclusion: varieties of urban life

All towns were unique and this chapter has generalized about them mercilessly. There were administrative cities, industrial cities, trading centres and garrison towns. There were railway towns, spa towns and company towns. There were the sleepy timbered towns of southern Germany, the *heimat* or 'home towns', enjoying a tradition of independence (increasingly under threat). Their artisans produced for a local economy, while their guilds supported an entrenched ruling oligarchy and *bürgermeister* (mayor).[45] They contrasted with the energy and dynamism of Manchester, the business centre for a local constellation of textile towns like Stalybridge, Oldham and Rochdale and at the same time the hub of a world market. It is impossible to do justice to the complex variety of urban existences.

We may be a little clearer, however, about what it was in the largest cities that unnerved visitors like Dostoevsky. Observers were appalled by their utter size and density. They admired their prosperity, but noted the juxtaposition of opulent mansions and wretched slums. They were anxious about disease and crime and the apparent rootlessness of the urban poor. They were often afraid that society was increasingly dividing itself into 'two nations' of rich and poor, as Disraeli put it in his novel *Sybil*. The modern city, moreover, was a world of new and unsettling social relationships. Instead of familiar networks of friends, family and neighbourhood, the city was an arena which compelled many fleeting encounters with complete strangers. The city created new and disturbing forms of individual isolation. As Engels put it, this time describing the impersonalized masses of London: 'the brutal indifference, the unfeeling isolation of each . . . is nowhere so shamelessly bare-faced . . . as just here in the crowding of the great city.'[46]

# 11   The Peasant World

## Introduction: a gradual expansion

In the first half of the nineteenth century, industrialization outside Britain was extremely localized. Continental Europe was overwhelmingly agrarian, and the economies of Europe still depended to a greater or lesser extent on good weather, good grain harvests and rising agricultural production. There was indeed a gradual increase in agricultural productivity during this period, driven by the demands of an expanding urban population. Increased productivity, however, was not generated by any startling technical breakthrough or structural upheaval. Food supplies increased simply because more land went under the plough, while agricultural methods altered very little. In France, for example, the area devoted to arable farming grew by 20 per cent between 1815 and 1852, as more wasteland was appropriated for cultivation.[1] The expansion of the cultivated area inevitably had an effect on the environment: for example, deforestation accelerated. This period was characterized by slow change, in which some specialization and commercialization occurred.

European agriculture remained vulnerable to periodical subsistence crises, which had reverberations in the industrial economy. Serious food shortages were widespread in 1816–17, 1827–30 and in 1845–7, with high prices for necessities, starvation and famine conditions. In the post-revolutionary period, prices for agricultural produce fell, and price deflation was reinforced by competition from cheap Ukrainian wheat. Only in the second half of the century did European agriculture achieve prosperity, with greater commercialization, better transport facilities which helped to integrate national markets, and the development of savings banks to provide peasants with mortgages. Calmer waters lay ahead, but before reaching them, the peasant world had to navigate the desperate times which became known as the 'Hungry Forties'.

## A world of peasants

Nineteenth-century Europe was still a world of peasants. In mid-century France, almost two-thirds of the working population were employed in agriculture. In France and Italy, industrial and manufacturing workers did not form the majority of the labour force until the 1930s. In early nineteenth-century Austria, 80 per cent worked in agriculture, in Prussia the proportion was 70 per cent, and in southern Italy and Russia, 90 per cent of the population were peasants. European history is impossible to grasp without considering the millions who lived on the land. The rural masses, however, had yet to find a collective voice, and they lived under a variety of social and material conditions.

Peasants did not form a homogeneous class, and the label covers many different kinds of agricultural worker. The French Revolution had destroyed what remained of the seigneurial system in France, and the Napoleonic conquest of Europe overthrew the feudal system in the countryside in its wake. In Western Europe, peasants were landowners, but only a few owned enough land to support a family adequately. Millions of micro-landowners therefore needed to earn a supplementary income, perhaps in some branch of textile manufacture or by hiring out their labour to another landowner. In this way a small landowning peasant might double as an industrial worker and as a wage-labourer. The share-cropping system persisted in many less fertile areas of Europe. In this system, the owner provided his tenant with a farm lease and basic implements, in return for a share of the produce. The amount of the owner's share varied, but it notionally amounted to half of the crop. This system, known as *métayage* in southwestern France and *mezzadria* in central Italy, provided few incentives for investment in the future, especially where only short-term leases (nine years or less) were the norm. In areas where large commercial estates developed, a rural proletariat of landless peasants was at the mercy of agrarian entrepreneurs. This was the case in the open fields of Picardy, or in the highlands of Scotland, where at the beginning of this period hundreds of small crofters were driven from their meagre holdings in order to create vast commercial sheep-runs.

The ecclesiastical tithe (nominally one-tenth of the crop) had been abolished in the French Revolution, but it was still owed to the Church in Poland and the Austrian Empire, and in Hungary peasants paid an additional *nona* or ninth to the lord. The hatred of clerical tithes also fuelled endemic agrarian terrorism in pre-famine Ireland, laced in the 1820s with millenarian prophecies of the imminent annihilation of the heretical Protestant supremacy.

In Eastern Europe, which was the granary of the West, serfdom still prevailed. In the East, the serf owed the landlord and the Church dues and services which had long since become obsolete in Western Europe. In Russia, the peasant family remained the legal property of the landlord, who could buy or sell the serf like any other possession, bring him to justice in his own court and punish him, sometimes brutally, for minor offences. As for the Russian peasants' own land, the village commune, or *mir*, periodically made arrangements to equalize holdings. Wherever such a traditional peasant world was found, communal practices and collective rights were strongly defended against the demands of economic individualism. The European peasant, then, might be a serf, a landless labourer, a share-cropper, a part-time artisan or a micro-landowner, but one or two generalizations still apply. The world of the peasant, wherever he or she stood in the social hierarchy of the countryside, is associated with small-scale production, mainly for subsistence purposes rather than for sale on the market, and usually centred around the family (however defined) as the basic economic unit.

The material life of the peasant was constantly threatened by crises of high mortality and epidemic disease. Nevertheless, conditions were improving. The scourge of smallpox was being eliminated and, although local famines still occurred, widespread demographic catastrophes like that of 1846 were becoming rarer. Peasant families employed rational strategies to preserve their assets and protect their welfare. One of these was the strategic marriage. Peasant communities often had a high rate of geographical endogamy, in other words peasants married partners from nearby villages. Selecting a spouse was not an individual choice so much as a collective survival mechanism, and as such it would be managed by the families concerned and required the full consent of both of them. In parts of Europe where a dowry system operated, the dowry might be manipulated to concentrate the family's landholdings. None of these arrangements necessarily precluded love and affection within marriage.

Similarly, inheritance strategies would frequently be directed at keeping the small estate intact in the hands of a single heir, usually the eldest son. In France, the Revolution had introduced the principle of equal inheritance shares, but this was resisted in the patriarchal south, where the head of the household preferred to endow one of his sons. Younger children paid the price of such strategies – younger sons could be effectively disinherited, and less favoured daughters deprived of the dowry which would enhance their value in the marriage market, because their own marriages might threaten the unity of the family property. It was not uncommon in France's Massif Central for cousin to marry cousin – marrying a relative would help to keep the estate within the family.[2]

In the poorer mountain areas, seasonal migration was an important survival strategy. Sawing logs, digging potatoes and harvesting grapes, chestnuts, olives or cereals all demanded extra hands and provided supplementary wages for temporary migrant workers. Some itinerants sold rabbit- or moleskins, while in the French Alps they would hire themselves out as schoolteachers. Peasants from the Pyrenees specialized in peddling chapbooks and religious images. In Russia, peasant peddlers would stock up on pins and needles, knives and scissors at the annual fair in Nizhni Novgorod. As seasonal migrants they earned a little cash and their absence meant there was one fewer mouth to feed at home. They travelled hundreds of kilometres on foot, contradicting the cliché that the peasant world was closed and immobile.

Another strategy was the deliberate limitation of family size. Marrying at a relatively late age, waiting for long intervals between births and simply abstaining from sex were ways of reducing the number of mouths to feed where resources seemed finite. Family limitation was adopted particularly early in France, but in other parts of Western Europe, too, peasant families were getting smaller. Peter Laslett argued that the small nuclear family was very common in pre-modern England, and that the popular notion of the large extended peasant family was a myth.[3] His theory about the importance of the nuclear unit has since been confirmed by many studies on the European continent.[4] Extended families, however, certainly endured and many different kinds of family structure coexisted. The stem family united several generations under the same roof. In southwestern France, or in parts of the Balkans, many households had a more horizontal structure, consisting of alliances between cohabiting brothers and their wives from the same generation.

Diet was poor and monotonous and reflected the overwhelming predominance of grain cultivation. Peasants on a high cereal diet suffered from chronic malnutrition. The physical condition of southern French conscripts who came up for medical examination is a telling indicator of the debilitating consequences. In the department of the Bouches-du-Rhône, about a quarter of recruits were turned away between 1819 and 1826, because they were too small for the army (under 1.57 metres) while others had hernias, deformities or were generally too weak. Including those who did not show up for the call-up, about 40 per cent of conscripts in Provence never got past the medical.[5] In mountainous regions like the Alps, peasants had a diet rich in cabbages and turnips, but goitre (a swollen thyroid gland resulting from nutritional deficiency) was endemic: it was estimated that 30 000 suffered from it in the French Alps in 1851.[6] An endless diet of reheated soup was common, as was apparently the case for this peasant from the Paris region, whose diet was described by an administrator in 1833:

His breakfast consists of bread and cheese; his dinner is soup, sometimes with meat in it, and some cheese and fruit; his supper is the same soup he had at dinner, which was put in his bed and covered with the pillow to keep it warm, and also a salad with a lot of vinegar and a little bit of oil.[7]

This Frenchman seems relatively comfortable, and his equivalents elsewhere might have envied him. On the northern Italian plain, the habit of eating polenta (gruel made from maize) was already well-established. In fact two-thirds of peasants' sustenance here came from maize, and this dependency induced diseases like pellagra (a cracked skin condition).[8] Meat was rare except on feast days. Peasants rarely consumed white bread, eggs or poultry – this and all the best produce were too valuable to eat and were sold for cash. In Russia, black rye bread was the peasants' staple food. In Italy and the Balkans, goats provided a low-maintenance source of milk, cheese and meat. Peasants drank plenty of wine with a low alcohol content. If they lived in a rice-growing area, or near the coast where fresh fish was available, they were lucky.

Medical care was very rudimentary, if it was available at all. Outside the main urban centres, medical attention was often completely lacking. In the Paris region, for example, there was one medical officer for every 1750 inhabitants – a luxurious situation guaranteed by the proximity of the capital and the court at Versailles, – but in Brittany there was only one for every 5000 inhabitants.[9] Doctors were expensive, and a visit might cost the equivalent of a week's wages for an agricultural labourer. Even if a doctor was in reach, the quality of care left much to be desired by modern standards. They did provide quinine which is effective against malaria, and the French government funded smallpox vaccination campaigns in the 1820s; but bleeding the patient, purging, blistering and administering leeches were commonly though ineffectually prescribed. No wonder that peasants referred to alternative sources of medicine, the healers, 'cunning men' and white witches who provided cures and remedies all over rural Europe.

Village communities had a rich cultural life and distinct forms of socializing. In southern Europe, the street itself was the place for pulling up a chair in the evening and conversing with neighbours. On winter evenings, gatherings like the French *veillée* were a way of sharing warmth and light while working, talking and telling stories. Sunday Mass was another regular occasion where village society would converge. Social life was often sexually segregated: men would meet at the local bar or smithy, while women's social life revolved around the well, the local place where clothes were washed or the communal oven. Man and wife worked as a team.

Bourgeois folklorists saw peasant women bringing food to their men at table as servants might do, and drew superficial conclusions about male supremacy in peasant families. In practice, responsibilities and power were shared. The woman fetched water, washed linen, did the spinning and weaving, and ruled over the farmyard. The man was usually responsible for carrying wood, buying and selling livestock, planting and sowing. At harvest time, both men and women worked together, as they do in Millet's painting *Planting Potatoes*. Everyday tasks necessitated close co-operation between men and women.[10] The peasant calendar was punctuated with markets and fairs, saints' days and pilgrimages, which offered regular opportunities for drinking and sex. Village society tried to settle its disputes by family negotiation rather than by recourse to outside arbitration. Suspicion of strangers went hand in hand with a certain sense of solidarity: the entire community might be mobilized to fight a fire or search for missing livestock.

It is dangerous, however, to generalize about traditional societies across the entire continent, and it would be misleading to give the impression that they were completely static. The forces of change were affecting the agrarian economy, and the consequences of these processes must be considered.

### Economic change in the countryside

Agrarian life was changing, as the peasant world was subject to increasing pressures both from outside and from within itself. Four processes in particular were transforming the European countryside in the early nineteenth century.

The first of these was the process of serf emancipation, which proceeded in piecemeal fashion in Central and Eastern Europe. The long series of Prussian laws to emancipate the serfs began in 1807 and was not complete until 1850. Emancipation was introduced in Austria in 1848, in Hungary in 1853, in Russia in 1861 and in the Danubian Principalities in 1864. Emancipation signified an important change of status, in which the peasant was no longer legally bonded to and dependent on the landowner, but became a wage-earning worker. The terms of serf emancipation differed everywhere, depending on the influence which could be exerted by the landowning class. Emancipation did not necessarily make the peasant any better off in material terms, but this was not the primary object. The purpose was to increase productivity, by transforming the peasantry into wage labour and opening up new possibilities for peasant landownership. In Prussia, the East Prussian Junkers dictated the terms of the liberation of their serfs. Usually peasants had to 'redeem' their status by compensating the landlords for the obligations and services which they were abandoning. Sometimes they could only pay by surrendering some land to their former lord. Other German states followed Prussia's lead in liberating serfs with compensation for landlords. In areas of intensive cultivation, the landlords were always anxious to retain their labour force. In Habsburg Galicia, where the landowning class was mainly Polish, the Austrian Empire did not offer the gentry compensation. A similar situation prevailed in the Baltic provinces of Tsarist Russia. Here the landlords were of German origin, and the Tsarist government liberated the local peasants in 1816–19 in order to undermine the local nobility. But the Baltic peasants were liberated without land, which was a disaster for them. The special case of Russia will be discussed further below.

A second process of change resulted from population expansion, and this was universal. The growth of population had automatic consequences for Europe's agrarian systems. It put pressure on the land, forcing rents upwards and wages downwards. It led to a process of parcellization, in which landholdings shrank as they were progressively divided amongst many owners. In order to feed more mouths, more land went under the plough, commercial demand increased and there was more scope for specialization. On the other hand, small landowners found it hard to produce enough to survive, and low wages reduced their supplementary incomes. Many were forced to sell to larger proprietors, swelling the ranks of landless peasants. Germany in the decades before 1848 was showing symptoms of this crisis, such as the presence of more landless labourers, peasant migration, starvation and an increase in rural crimes like wood theft.[11] In France, this period was the apogee of rural civilization, in the sense that the countryside had never been so densely populated, and was never to be so again. The price to pay was an extraordinary fragmentation of peasant landholdings. In the small community of Bonnières on the River Seine, there were 364 independent landowners in 1829. But 73 per cent of them owned properties smaller than one hectare each.[12] In Russia, the village *mir* faced similar problems: it could not provide enough land for everybody without reducing the size of allotments. The average size of peasant holdings declined and peasants were increasingly forced into part-time work in rural industries.

Enclosure, or the privatization of common land, was a third important development in this period. Enclosures by parliamentary legislation had proceeded rapidly in Britain during the eighteenth century, but except in Denmark change elsewhere was more gradual. Peasants resisted the destruction of the collective basis of a fragile agrarian economy. In the

Kingdom of Naples, the partition of common land gave individual peasants only 1.5 hectares each at the most, and they often had to resell. As a result they were double losers – abandoning both some individual property and the benefit of common grazing land.[13] In France and parts of Germany, legislation ended common rights to grazing and gathering fuel in forests. The importance of this collective resource cannot be exaggerated. The sociologist Frédéric Leplay realized its value when he studied the Melouga family, a household of 15 people, living near Cauterets in the French Pyrenees.[14] The forest, he calculated, provided the family with 4450 kilograms of firewood annually, 880 kilograms of building wood, 936 kilograms of pine roots used for lighting, 6 kilograms of strawberries and raspberries, and 8 kilograms of salad herbs and leaves, and this list did not include material for clogs or the benefit of animal pasturage in the woods. The French Forest Code of 1827, the Prussian law of 1821 on wood theft, and subsequent legislation in Westphalia introduced a regime of severe policing to eliminate customary peasant rights and give free rein to ironmasters who used charcoal to fuel their furnaces.[15] In the name of agrarian individualism, a vital prop of the makeshift rural economy was thus removed.

Fourth, economic modernization brought new crops and greater specialization. Old ways of course persisted: for example, manure was still the main source of fertilizer and would remain so until the invention of chemical substitutes later in the century. But crops for feeding livestock, like turnips, alfalfa (lucerne) or clover, became more widespread, the cultivation of sugar-beet spread in northern Europe, and the potato was adopted in areas which had previously despised it as unfit for pigs. In Prussia, potato cultivation experienced a five-fold increase between 1816 and 1840.[16] The practice of leaving a certain proportion of land fallow for a year was gradually abandoned, except in poorer areas where it was needed to support some livestock and thus increase the supply of essential manure. The more efficient scythe replaced the sickle, and metal ploughs took the place of heavier traditional wooden ploughs. More land was brought under cultivation to feed expanding populations. Lüneberg heath was reclaimed, and in Tuscany an enormous project was launched to drain the malarial marshes of the Maremma. These innovations made much greater agricultural productivity possible.

There was more specialization, as subsistence agriculture adapted to the demands of growing urban markets. Increasingly, peasants turned from polyculture to a single crop with opportunities for profitable commercialization. The commercialization of agriculture developed fastest around the largest cities. Production in East Anglia, for instance, had long since become geared to the provision of the enormous London market. In the highly urbanized north of France, the expansion of manufacturing cities had an effect on local agriculture, and specialized market gardening developed. The Paris region created a similar demand for food produce, increasingly satisfied by asparagus-growing in Argenteuil, peaches from Montreuil or strawberries from Bagneux on the outskirts of the metropolis.[17] In Mediterranean Europe, wine, silk and olive production was increasingly commercialized. The plains of Lombardy produced 40 per cent of all Italian silk, and exported it chiefly to London, at least until the 1830s when imported silk from Bengal and China began to compete. The export of Lombard silk rose in value by 300 per cent between 1814 and 1841.[18] A combination of modernization, technical innovation and population growth all contributed to the slow transformation of agriculture in the first half of the nineteenth century. The result was greater productivity, but subsistence crises had not disappeared completely, and social tensions were exacerbated by economic changes.

## The consequences of agrarian change

The depressed state of the European economy after 1815 had dire effects on rural society. Price deflation reduced income from agricultural produce, and made it harder for German peasants to meet the redemption payments which followed serf emancipation. The return of Ukrainian wheat to European markets after the war also kept prices low for agricultural producers. This was the climate in which the English Corn Laws were enforced to protect domestic cereal production. In many areas of continental Europe, the indebtedness of both peasants and aristocratic landowners was aggravated. Peasant indebtedness could produce attacks on moneylenders, and this lay behind some antisemitic violence in the countryside in the prelude to the Revolutions of 1848.

In Hungary and Silesia, thousands died of starvation following the harvest failure of 1816. A catastrophic situation existed in Western Europe, too. In Normandy, harvesters would accept work in return for food alone, with no wages.[19] This desperate situation was repeated during the decade of the so-called 'Hungry Forties'. The potato blight struck all over Northern Europe, although the Irish population was particularly vulnerable because of its extraordinary dependence on this crop. In the Netherlands, as in Ireland, the potato was grown on small properties for subsistence purposes, and it had successfully sustained a rise in population since 1815. A high level of potato consumption, however, was a telling symptom of agrarian poverty. In 1845–6, the deadly fungus which proliferated in the warm humid weather destroyed three-quarters of the crop.[20] The nightmare of an old-style subsistence crisis recurred, but for the last time in Western Europe. In Ireland and the Netherlands, starvation, begging and an overall population decline resulted. Both British and Dutch governments were reluctant to intervene: the dogma of economic rationalism dictated that the market would resolve its own problems, even at the expense of hundreds of thousands of lives.

Clashes between peasants and authorities intensified in the 1830s and 1840s wherever there was a conflict over collective usage rights. In the Po valley in northern Italy, entrepreneurs who diverted water to irrigate their rice-fields might be targeted by collective violence: if the river flow was greatly diminished, it would not drive the mill which ground the peasants' grain.[21] Wood theft was a common form of protest in defence of customary practices. In the French Pyrenees, the *Guerre des Demoiselles* (see Chapter 6) expressed the resistance of local villages to the Forest Code, and such conflicts remained endemic. They were an important part of the 1848 Revolution, when peasants would vote for whichever regime seemed most likely to abolish the Forest Code. Desertion and draft-dodging, banditry, infringements of the Forest Code, and the incidence of carnival masquerades with a political content all led one historian to describe the peasants of this area as being in a state of chronic insubordination.[22] Elsewhere famine conditions turned insubordination into violent revolt. In 1846, the peasants of Galicia rose up against their Polish landlords in a bloody *jacquerie* which left over 1000 seigneurs and their agents dead. Here the peasants professed loyalty to the Emperor and their murderous rampage was apparently condoned by the Habsburg governor Stadion.

Clearly gradual economic modernization had not eliminated pauperization and extremes of social conflict in the countryside. Population pressure caused complete immiseration in backward parts of Europe. In 1859, one economist remarked that in many parts of the Kingdom of Naples it cost more to keep a donkey than a man.[23] In Italy in general employment for labourers was becoming scarcer. Employment depended on the seasonal demands of the agrarian cycle, and was in any case irregular. In the province of Salerno, a peasant might expect 200 days of paid employment in a year, and that was reckoning on a good year.[24] This was the background to peasant migration; from the 1840s onwards, the flight from the land gained momentum, as peasants moved to urban centres in search of wages. In France, as we have noted, the 1840s marked the high-point of peasant society, but the rural exodus which destroyed it was already under way.

## Russia

Russia, where serfs were not legally emancipated until Tsar Alexander I's edict of 1861, was a special case. It was special in the sense that the peasant question was posed far more acutely than anywhere else in post-revolutionary Europe. There were humanitarian and economic reasons to end serfdom, but a series of Tsars had not dared to make the leap of imagination necessary to achieve this. They feared social upheaval if peasants were no longer tied to the land, and political turmoil if the nobility was antagonized. As long as the rural masses remained impoverished, however, no real domestic consumer market could develop in Russia, and without such a market, economic growth was stunted. Serfdom was the central question with which Russian society wrestled in the era before emancipation.

In pre-emancipation Russia, there were 6.7 million privately owned male serfs, and a similar number of government-owned male serfs, although the number of the latter rose to over 8 million before the 1861 emancipation.[25] The serf owed the feudal lord a series of money dues and labour services. The majority of privately owned serfs owed up to three days' labour per week (*barshchina*) on the lord's estate, while others paid him dues (*obrok*). In northern Russia, money dues predominated, but in the more fertile 'black earth' regions, the serf's labour was more valuable to the landlord. Many peasants owed a combination of both *obrok* and *barshchina*. The lord's demands for labour would be more intense at harvest time, and he might call for peasants to help with transporting goods and building maintenance. The peasant paid a poll tax to the state as well as being liable for conscription. The best one can say about the Russian peasant's situation in the first half of the nineteenth century is that it was probably not getting any worse.[26]

State-owned serfs probably faced less burdensome obligations, but there was always a risk that a Tsar would donate them to a loyal aristocrat or requisition them for factory work. A relatively small number of serf-owners possessed the vast majority of serfs between them. In 1858, 3 per cent of serf-owners owned 44 per cent of all male serfs. Count Sheremetev personally owned 300,000 of them on his estates of 1.9 million acres, and their payments provided 75 per cent of his income.[27] He was of course exceptional in Eastern European terms: in Poland, Hungary and the Ukraine, thousands of petty nobles owned little more than their own peasants did. There were few limits to the legal power of the private serf-owner. He could sell his serfs, he could beat them or imprison them, and give or withhold permission for them to marry. The Russian nobility invested very little in improving their estates. They were content to draw the income to be spent on travel, indulging in Western fashions and the social season in St Petersburg or Moscow. The Russian aristocracy was chronically in debt, and by 1859, 66 per cent of all adult male serfs were mortgaged to state banks.[28] This was a major reason why the nobility eventually agreed to serf emancipation with compensation in 1861. The terms of emancipation were so burdensome to the peasants that a mass agrarian uprising occurred in 1905. These events, however, lie outside our period of study.

Peasant violence was endemic in the Russian countryside. It usually took the form of spontaneous outbursts of murderous fury, rather than adding up to any consistent political programme. According to Soviet historians, there were 1904 cases of serious disorder on private estates between 1826 and 1849 and their frequency was rising.[29] The manor-house would be looted and property burned down. Estate managers and often landlords themselves were murdered. The father of the novelist Dostoevsky was merely one of several hundred fatal victims of peasant violence. The fear of peasant revolt strengthened abolitionist sentiment. Liberal intellectuals had argued that the system was inhumane; liberal economists had argued that it was unproductive. What moved the Tsar more than either of these considerations, however, was the fear of a peasant uprising. The revolt in Galicia in 1846 had been a warning. As we shall see later in Chapter 15, rural agitation during the Crimean War threatened military recruitment and Russia's ability to fight a war efficiently. Serfdom, it seemed, had become a handicap to Russia's ability to act as a great European power.

## Conclusion

The world of the peasant often seems synonymous with tradition, prejudice and obstinate resistance to change. But were the peasants irremediably backward? In many cases, they had good economic reasons for rejecting innovations. In this period, labour was plentiful and it sometimes made more sense to use it more intensively rather than buy machinery. There was often little incentive to invest in the future, and refusal to do so was a rational choice rather than a symptom of backwardness. A share-cropper on a one-year lease had no reason to improve, and for thousands of micro-proprietors the size of their holding made mechanization irrelevant. In any case, investing in modern techniques is hardly an option when you have no capital and credit institutions do not exist.

It may therefore be superficial to identify the peasant with passivity and ignorance. The Russian *muzhik* did believe in a benevolent, paternalistic Tsar who would deliver him from oppression if only his eyes were opened to the suffering of his people. This naïve monarchism seems misguided and ridiculous, but it never ruled out subversive violence. On the contrary, the myth of the just Tsar legitimized an endless series of popular risings against nobles and officials. Rebels who expressed loyalty to the Tsar were always likely to receive lighter punishment. Were such peasant rebels stupid or cunning?

Traditional culture, and especially religious culture, was certainly important. In the Massif Central, Peter Jones found that Catholicism was the most powerful form of social cement integrating the rural community, entangled though it was in the peasant mind with pagan beliefs in magic.[30] Clan and kinship loyalties remained powerful, and they were obstacles to the development of wider national allegiances. Nevertheless, the peasant world was slowly being shaken out of its introversion. Some cultivators, such as wine or silk producers, were already market oriented and were touched by price fluctuations in distant markets. Railway development would eventually accelerate the slow integration of national economies. The rural violence which erupted in the European Revolutions of 1848 suggested that the apolitical peasantry was a myth. They lacked a common ideology, and a 'culture of deference' to social superiors persisted. Yet in 1848 rural agitation was widespread and, in parts of France, as we shall see in Chapter 14, pockets of rural society had even become republican.

# 12   The Crisis of the Artisans

Artisans, craft-workers, skilled tradesmen – however we label them – played a leading role in the urban economy of nineteenth-century Europe. Staples of consumption like bread, other food items and clothing, together with furniture and other luxury goods, were typically produced in their small workshops, where a master craftsman worked with a handful of journeymen and apprentices. They were threatened by industrialization and economic change helped to politicize them. They had not yet been displaced, however, for the mass manufacture of consumer goods lay in the future, at least outside industrialized Britain. In this chapter the role of the artisans must be considered, especially in the light of their participation in radical political movements. We have already noted the contribution of skilled artisans in the 1830 Revolutions, the 1834 Lyon uprising and the Chartist movement. The forces of economic change plunged many of them into difficulty in the 1840s, and the eruptions of 1848 had much of their social basis in the crisis of the artisans.

## Industry without factories

The beginnings of industrialization did not rely entirely on large factories and widespread mechanization, as is sometimes assumed. In its early stages, industrialization consisted of an intensification of small-scale production, centred on the artisan's workshop. In some cases, industrialization even caused a brief growth spurt in ancillary artisan trades. For example, the early mechanization of spinning temporarily created a greater demand for domestic weavers to supply the new cotton-mills. In any case, the industrialized areas of continental Europe were few and scattered in the first half of the century. They included Belgium, eastern France and the Rhineland – all regions of what became the dynamic economic hub of the European Union. They included other parts of Germany and the Habsburg Empire, too, like Saxony, Silesia and Bohemia. But apart from these localized areas of large-scale production, most of Europe depended on traditional forms of artisanal production.

Economic historians once used to characterize European economies as backward or retarded in the sense that they were all catching up with Britain's rapid industrializing spurt. This was a very Anglocentric view. French industry, for example, was not 'retarded' but had highly productive small workshops, and built on its existing strengths in luxury goods production. The silk workers of Lyon who rose in revolt in the 1830s (see Chapter 4) were not factory employees, but rather they represented an intense concentration of artisans' workshops. According to quantitative studies by Markovitch, small-scale household and craft production produced 60 per cent of France's industrial output in the mid-nineteenth century, and employed 70–75 per cent of all industrial workers.[1] About one-fifth of the population of the German states was still dependent on craft work in the middle of the nineteenth century.[2] Industrial Britain was significantly dubbed 'the workshop (rather than the factory) of the world', because much of British production was still conducted in small workshops, especially in the Midlands which specialized in nails and cutlery.[3]

In the 1970s, some economic historians coined the term 'proto-industrialization' to refer to concentrations of rural handicraft production. Proto-industrialization signified industrialization without factories, involving peasant and female labour, organized regionally and linked to the needs of the agricultural cycle. Such rural concentrations of industry thrived in times of population growth, allowing industrial activity to absorb surplus labour without reducing productive capacity in agriculture. In this period of proto-industrialization, a merchant capitalist exploited the poverty of peasant families who did not own enough land to guarantee their own survival. The merchant represented nascent capitalism, and drew one part of the peasant economy into wider market relationships.[4] The so-called 'proto-industrial' system persisted and indeed expanded in early nineteenth-century Europe. The concept, however, has not gone unchallenged. British historians in particular could see little that was new in a form of rural production which had existed since the fourteenth century.[5] Furthermore, proto-industrialization did not necessarily lead to the advent of industrial capitalism. In some cases, concentrations of rural industry fell into decline when faced with competition from cheaper factory goods. Proto-industrialization was often a regional dead-end rather than a prelude to full-scale industrialization.

Industrial production also depended on domestic or 'cottage' industry, in which a textile merchant 'put out' work to be completed at home, and later collected the finished product, paying piecework rates. The advantages of the 'putting-out' system for the merchant were his very low labour costs, and the fact that he did not have to pay for work space. On the other hand, he was obliged to travel to scattered households to distribute raw materials and collect finished products. He did not have a disciplined labour force at his command and he could never guarantee a uniform product with quality control. Only the surveillance of the labour process made possible by the factory would ensure this. The expansion of this 'putting-out' system could undercut the incomes of skilled urban craftsmen who resisted the uncontrollable growth of the workforce into outlying villages. In Britain, hundreds of thousands of outworkers formed an army of 'sweated' labour – in other words, they worked long, exhausting hours for low wages, and were vulnerable to periods of unemployment. So it would be a fallacy to imagine 'cottage industry' as a picturesque form of pre-industrial life: such miserable outworkers were spectacular casualties of the British Industrial Revolution.

Everywhere in Europe, the domestic textile industry was a major employer of women. In Italy during this period, there were probably more women than men engaged in industry. In early nineteenth-century Bologna, to take one example, 4000 women worked to make silk veils.[6] Domestic industry fitted in with the seasonal demands of subsistence agriculture. As long as it relied heavily on female labour, low wages were paid and it was often cheaper than factory labour. When industrial change started to concentrate domestic work in spinning and weaving mills, the consequences were drastic for the female industrial workforce. The home ceased to be a place of work, and a new separation between work and domesticity was created. Many women effectively lost their jobs, as traditional areas of production de-industrialized. Old linen and woollen industries disappeared from the west country of England and Languedoc in southwest France. The industrialization of one region could mean the pastoralization of another. Domestic industry had connected peasant labour with international markets, but mechanization put thousands of women out of work. Many entered the new spinning mills, but only if they were situated near their homes. The position of women in the mills was still secondary to that of male workers and their traditional skills were sometimes lost in the transition.

## Threats to artisan production

Artisan production had traditionally been organized by the medieval guilds, and this structure was everywhere breaking down. In every trade, the guild (of shoemakers or watchmakers or tapestry-weavers, for instance) had served some important functions. It maintained standards to guarantee the quality of production. It decided who should be admitted to its exclusive masterships. It regulated rates of pay and thus tried to control the labour market. It provided career prospects: a young apprentice could become a journeyman and, having learned the trade and produced a sample of work which passed the guild's rigorous quality test (his 'masterpiece'), the journeyman could then become a master in his turn. Guilds had their patron saints, and contributed to religious charities. They had their own processions on religious festivals, and elaborate rituals to mark initiation and other key moments in a member's career. Liberal economists, however, saw such practices as restrictions on trade. They preferred to deregulate industry, to encourage entrepreneurial initiatives outside the guild framework. They trusted in market forces to fix appropriate wage levels.

In 1791, the French Revolution had abolished the guilds, but in France, the *compagnonnages* remained. These fraternal associations of workers in a particular profession offered assistance and accommodation to journeymen on their traditional *tour de France*, when they travelled seeking work and learning their trade. They had a fierce loyalty to their profession, and they earned a bad reputation for violence against workers from rival organizations. When socialists considered the gang warfare which sometimes erupted between groups of artisans on the roads of France, they despaired of ever establishing a sense of working-class solidarity. Guilds survived in the Habsburg Empire, in Sweden and Denmark, and in several German states, even though their scope for controlling the market was limited by law. German master craftsmen supported the democratic movement in 1848, and pressed for a guild revival to protect their livelihoods.

Master artisans like those who dominated Lyon, Solingen or Sheffield were in a contradictory position. They were small producers and also employers. They resisted the development of large-scale capitalism, but at the same time they opposed new forms of workers' organization, preferring the traditional model of the guild which protected their craft from unskilled and unqualified labour. Tailors defended their traditional craft, resisting the spread of domestic work and the development of a ready-made clothes industry. In the 1830s, Parisian chair-makers downed tools when asked to unload timber – a demeaning task for a skilled wood-turner proud of his status. Such examples are a reminder that labour conflicts did often occur, although strikes (and of course trade unions) were strictly speaking illegal. As the example of the Parisian chair-makers also shows, such conflicts were not always about wage increases – issues of rank and privilege could be just as divisive.

Many workers were ultimately threatened by mechanization. The British handloom weavers are a well-known case of semi-skilled domestic outworkers reduced to starvation wages by new industrial processes. They numbered about a quarter of a million in Britain in the 1820s, with a high concentration in the villages of north Lancashire.[7] The adoption of power-looms drove down the piece-rates they earned, leaving them with little alternative employment except in one of the hated factories, possibly situated miles from home. The revolt of the Silesian weavers in 1844 is another example. Here linen-weaving had almost been driven into the ground by competition from British cotton. Silesian weavers reluctantly volunteered for employment in the cotton industry, and when wages contracted there too, they rose and attacked the mills.

The artisan trades were overcrowded, and their structures were too inelastic to respond to the over-supply of skilled labour. In Germany, a growing number of apprentices found access to masterships increasingly blocked. In Prussia between 1816 and 1849, it has been estimated that the number of masters rose by 65 per cent, while the number of aspiring journeymen and apprentices increased at double the rate by 124 per cent.[8] This situation inevitably drove wage levels down, and the traditional organizations of skilled trades could not prevent many of their members from facing impoverishment.

They were threatened, too, by the increasing mobility of labour. Immigration into the cities brought an influx of workers who were less skilled, less literate and less well organized than the traditional artisan. In Marseille, analysed by William Sewell, real wages were in decline, and younger workers arriving from the countryside added a new volatile stratum to the work-force.[9] The solidarity of the city's artisan community was breaking down, and the traditional culture of the Marseillais worker was being diluted. These processes aided the spread of socialism and radical anticlericalism. Ultimately, established communities of artisans could not prevent the expansion of outworking and the employment of less skilled immigrants for lower wages.

The artisan world was thus menaced from several directions. It faced cut-throat competition, skill dilution and falling real wages. Skilled workers under threat resisted the liberal dogma of unfettered industrial competition, and looked to some version of the guild to protect their jobs and wages. They backed new clubs and associations which tried to make governments and middle-class leaders more aware of 'la question sociale'.

### The social basis of popular politics

In both France and Germany, unrest among urban artisans played a major role in the Revolutions of 1848. In Paris, artisans and shopkeepers had always provided the revolutionary rank-and-file. They were the so-called *sans-culottes* of the first French Revolution, who had vigorously defended the rights of small property-owners against traitors and counter-revolutionaries in 1792–4. Such craft workers had a relatively high rate of literacy and long-standing organizational structures. This made them natural leaders of the labour movement in nineteenth-century Europe. They took pride in their craft and in the independence of their workshops. They, rather than factory workers, were the most articulate spokesmen for European socialism in this period, which meant that there was considerable continuity between the traditional guild or corporation of skilled masters, and the new trade unions or mutual aid societies. William Sewell has argued that modern working-class consciousness in France grew out of the artisan's view of the world, as it was transformed by the development of capitalism and shaped by the nineteenth-century revolutionary experience.[10]

In France, local skilled workers joined the Paris club movement to sponsor electoral programmes and promote Louis Blanc's idea of the 'organization of labour', urging the state to take responsibility for work and unemployment. In Germany, craftsmen and journeymen, as we have seen, joined the General German Workers' Fraternity and the fatherland associations in Saxony. They appealed for a single-chamber parliament, universal male suffrage, a progressive income tax and a constitution which would recognize the right to work.[11] They created their own newspapers and periodicals to defend their interests. The General German Workers' Fraternity had as its mouthpiece *Verbrüderung* (Brotherhood), edited in Berlin by the radical Stephen Born. In Paris, several attempts to establish a workers' press emerged. In 1839, the monthly *La Ruche populaire* (The People's Hive) was launched, followed by its rival *L'Atelier* (The Workshop), published from 1840 to 1850. Both were monthly periodicals, at least until the Revolution of February 1848 stimulated *L'Atelier* into a more rapid rhythm of publication. Both were produced and written by workers for workers. The group of Christian Socialists associated with *L'Atelier*, for example, included Corbon, a sculptor and Leneveux, a typographer. Other regular contributors included a locksmith and a margin-setter. They were skilled craft workers, many of them in the printing trade. Out of 75 contributors named by the journal, 26 were printers. They represented an artisan elite, interested in self-education and workers' co-operation.[12]

This elite of skilled workers included many autodidacts, or self-taught intellectuals. They had experienced only very intermittent schooling, and they struggled in grinding poverty to read, learn and educate themselves. They read by firelight or by candlelight when they could afford the price of a candle (there was very little gas-lighting in working-class houses anywhere before 1850). As yet, there were very few lending libraries available. Britain was the exception, where the libraries of the Mechanics' Institutes catered for self-improving artisans. British legislation of 1850 gave local municipal councils the right to levy one penny in local taxation to finance library services, and this was to be the foundation of Britain's distinctively decentralized and effective public library system.

The Chartist William Lovett described the three goals of the self-educated artisan as Bread, Knowledge and Freedom.[13] Some of his fellow militants pursued these objectives with a determination bordering on obsession. Thomas Cooper, also a Chartist militant, read as he worked at his shoemaker's bench, propping up his Latin grammar or his geometry textbook in front of him during meal breaks. He read the works of Shakespeare and Milton, learning long passages by heart, acquired with no tuition rudimentary Latin, French, Greek and Hebrew, not to mention the readings he undertook in history and literature, all in his young years. In 1828, at the age of 21, Cooper had a complete physical breakdown, and was confined to bed.[14] This thirst for book culture among artisan autodidacts, however, created a working-class intelligentsia, which would make its mark in journalism, public lecturing and in the organization of the early trade unions. It enabled a small elite to act as a vanguard for the rest. Thus in 1834, the French stonemason Martin Nadaud was being asked by fellow workers to read Etienne Cabet's journal aloud in his local wineshop. O'Connor's Chartist journal the *Northern Star* would be read aloud to eager groups in many workers' homes. Tailors would pay one of their co-workers to read aloud while they sat together working around a common table. In such ways, skilled workers improvised a culture even when they worked a 12- or a 14-hour day. Oral transmission allowed even the illiterate to 'read' the political press.

In times of economic depression, craft workers turned to a collective version of self-help. They formed producers' co-operatives and workers' associations, in self-defence against competition which continually undercut prices and made quality a low priority. Such small associations of tailors or carpenters were not exclusively, or even primarily, a form of defence against factory production. Rather they were a response to the increasing number of outworkers, who allowed the merchant capitalist to expand production without respecting wages or conditions determined by the guild.[15] Artisans implicitly defended what E. P. Thompson called a 'moral economy', in other words they were inspired by a belief in social justice, and the sense that unrestricted competition which took bread from workers' mouths was immoral and violated traditional standards of fair dealing.[16]

In the years before 1848, a series of conflicts testified to the depth of workers' unrest. Jonathan Sperber has documented the problems of small producers in the Rhineland, who faced intense competition and growing dependence on merchant middle-men to market their goods.[17] Winegrowers were being squeezed by higher taxes on their barrels. River workers were threatened by the expansion of rail transport. In the depression of 1846–7, menaced by famine and unemployment, popular action took violent forms. In Mainz, dockers tore up the railway lines. In Solingen, metal-workers destroyed the foundries. Workers and weavers attacked machines and the homes of manufacturers. Similar pressures existed in the Habsburg Empire. The cotton-printers of Prague demonstrated in 1844. There were outbreaks of machine-breaking in Bohemia. Jewish shops were also sometimes the targets of workers' protests.[18] Artisans faced many threats: they were losing control of the labour market, high quality goods were being challenged by cheaper manufactures and their trades were over-populated. In the critical conditions of 1846–7, these tensions broke out into violent protest.

Artisans, then, continued to dominate the labour movement. They sought means to insulate themselves against the dangers of individual competition. They formed mutual aid societies, which began as collective forms of insurance against funeral expenses, but which could also become strike funds. In this and other ways, modern forms of working-class organization developed out of a traditional mode of thought rooted in what Sewell called 'the corporate idiom'. Their great slogans of the 1840s were 'association', 'co-operation', and 'fraternity'. They believed that collective action could protect wages and conditions in a particular trade, and that associations of all trades could bring about a workers' brotherhood on a broader scale. They insisted on placing 'la question sociale' on the political agenda. In the Revolution of 1848, they thought for a moment that they had found new governments which would recognize these objectives.

## Conclusion

In the last two chapters, agriculture and industry have, purely for convenience, been discussed as though they were quite separate aspects of economic realities in early nineteenth-century Europe. They are, of course, closely connected. Traditional features of the European economies still persisted in the largely pre-industrial world of the early nineteenth century. A good grain harvest was crucial to growth and stability. A poor harvest, or more significantly a series of two or three poor harvests, spelt catastrophe. In times of shortage, food prices rose, and as they rose, more and more of the income of ordinary consumers was absorbed in buying bread for survival. As a result, there was nothing left to spend on other goods. This had a direct impact on the manufacturing sector: the consumer market evaporated, goods could not be sold and workers had to be dismissed. Widespread unemployment was the result in the crises and slumps of 1816–17, 1827–30 and 1846–7. In this way, the prosperity of agriculture was directly linked to the stability of industry.

The gradual process of industrialization, which followed a different rhythm in each state, involved a shift of resources from the countryside to the city. Only social and economic changes which increased agricultural productivity enabled society to support a large urban population. An 'agrarian revolution', based on commercialized agriculture and the replacement of bonded or serf labour by hired wage-workers, was one foundation for industrial progress. In our period, Western Europe had progressed much further towards this goal than had the East. The transformation of the pre-industrial agrarian system was far advanced in Britain; in Russia and on Europe's southern periphery it had barely begun.

Industrialization was a gradual process. New factories and cotton-spinning mills existed side by side with thousands of small enterprises, craft workshops, rural and domestic industrial activities. In a long period of transition, industrial workers continued to cultivate their plot of land when time and the season allowed. The industrial worker was often still a peasant. In Britain, for example, handloom weavers worked as casual farm labourers at harvest time. David Whitehead, a Lancashire fustian weaver, described his work as 'to milk morning and night and weave fustian the rest of the day'.[19] There was no great divide between industry and agriculture in the everyday lives of men like Whitehead.

Europe's population rise had repercussions on both urban and rural economies. The over-population of the countryside swelled the ranks of the landless and underemployed, and led to the fragmentation of landholdings. It created the conditions for the movement of people into the cities and industrial centres, which the French call the 'rural exodus' and which would gather momentum in the second half of the century. In the 1840s, the European countryside was as full of people as it would ever be again, and in 1846 it was overall as hungry as it would ever be. The tensions arising from economic change within the traditional economies would spill over into the Revolutions of 1848.

# 13 Bourgeois Culture and the Domestic Ideology

## In search of the bourgeoisie

Considering the time and energy historians have devoted to the bourgeoisie and the never-ending story of its rise through history, it is surprisingly hard to pin it down as a social category. Karl Marx concentrated on just one aspect of the nineteenth-century bourgeois – his role as a financial or industrial capitalist. The bourgeois, or burgher, however, had medieval and pre-capitalist origins, as member of a distinctive urban elite granted special privileges by royal charter. In spite of Marx, the bourgeoisie is a social stratum which can be envisaged as both pre-capitalist and capitalist. But this is only one of the problems inherent in defining the subject. The nineteenth century is sometimes labelled 'The Bourgeois Century', in which, following the French Revolution, the bourgeoisie at last consolidated its power in Europe. Yet, paradoxically, the bourgeoisie did not seem in a rush to command positions of political authority. In Britain, most Prime Ministers still came from the aristocracy: Lord Liverpool, Lord Palmerston and Lord Derby were examples in our period. Prussia, too, has often been characterized in terms of a paradox, as a developing industrial economy in which the East Prussian landed nobility (the Junkers) still retained control. The bourgeoisie remains elusive. Some historians have put it under the microscope only to find that it dissolved into different interest groups and professional organizations with no sense of common identity.[1] Sarah Maza perversely argued that the French bourgeoisie did not even exist before the 1820s, except in the social imagination.[2] Only then, she argues, did apologists elaborate ideologies which for the first time explicitly celebrated the values of the middling classes.

Several historians have tried to dispel the opaque mist which has enveloped the bourgeoisie. Lenore O'Boyle defined them as either businessmen, or members of the so-called 'liberal' professions like law and medicine, or government officials.[3] This classification defined a well-educated, but principally pre-industrial bourgeoisie. It did not specifically identify the *rentier*, the bourgeois who had no occupation but lived from

197

investment income from stocks and shares or, more commonly in this period, government bonds. Alfred Cobban insisted that the French bourgeoisie was a landowning class with very similar interests to those of the nobility.[4] In fact, the dominant notables of the July Monarchy in France, mentioned in Chapter 8, were an amalgamation of bourgeois and aristocratic property-owners. In yet another survey, Pamela Pilbeam included entrepreneurs, landowners, the professions and bureaucrats, in that order.[5]

Endeavouring to define the bourgeoisie, or to establish whether or not it existed at any particular moment, may be a futile exercise because its shape and functions were constantly shifting. As the English Marxist historian E. P. Thompson insisted, class is a process rather than a structure, and it is impossible to isolate a pure specimen of it. 'Like any other relationship', he wrote, '[class] is a fluency which evades analysis if we attempt to stop it dead at any given moment and anatomize its structure.'[6] The bourgeoisie, like any social formation, was in a state of permanent transition. Marx had a certain vision of its capitalist future, while others like Alfred Cobban had a certain vision of its Old Regime past. The European bourgeoisie was evolving, and that evolutionary process depended on broader economic changes like industrialization. It cannot be grasped except in relation to other groups like the aristocracies and the artisans. Its nature varied at different historical moments and in different national contexts. In our period, the British business elite had no continental equivalent in terms of influence and collective self-confidence. Outside Britain, law, the professions and government service had the strongest attraction for bourgeois ambitions.

All the above definitions draw a line between the bourgeoisie on one hand, and the lower middle-class or *petit bourgeois* artisans and shopkeepers on the other. This chapter also observes this porous but convenient barrier, and embraces the bourgeoisie as a group of lawyers and bureaucrats, shareholders and landowners, merchants and manufacturers. The terms 'bourgeois' and 'middle class' are virtually interchangeable here. If anything, 'bourgeois' is marginally preferable because it is easier to envisage the bourgeoisie as a ruling class than it is to attribute a dominant role to a group that is always defined in the middle of the hierarchy. The discussion focuses mainly on Western Europe, because in the less urbanized East, the bourgeoisie was less numerous, less prosperous and less articulate. In spite of national differences and conflicts within the ranks of the national bourgeoisies themselves, they shared some common values. Among them was a re-evaluation of family life which, although still patriarchal, idealized affectionate relationships between spouses and their children. This new domestic ideology was a specific characteristic of nineteenth-century bourgeois culture.

## Bourgeois wealth, bourgeois values, bourgeois leisure

Real estate remained an important source of wealth. Investment in land was secure and profitable. In France, where paying the land tax determined the right to vote, landownership was essential to citizenship. The bourgeoisie moved into the land market whenever it could at the expense of a struggling nobility. In East Prussia, for instance, 230 Junker estates went bankrupt between 1824 and 1834 in a period of declining prices for agricultural produce, and bourgeois purchasers took advantage. Land carried prestige and was a mark of social status, but social climbing went hand-in-hand with the need for a steady return on income. In Pilbeam's phrase, the bourgeois lust for land was motivated by 'snobbery plus five per cent'.[7] A rich Parisian bourgeois might use his wealth to buy several houses in the capital, together with blue-chip shares in the Banque de France. This passion for real estate is often seen as a sign of the lack of an entrepreneurial culture amongst the French bourgeoisie, but this was not necessarily the case. Land was the best security for raising a business loan, and property investment was quite compatible with investment in commerce.

Certain myths underpinned the acquisition of wealth. The myth of the self-made man idealized hard work, savings and individual effort as the keys to success. These were the nineteenth-century values which Prime Minister Margaret Thatcher wanted to revive in Britain in the 1980s. The implication of this myth was that poverty was the inevitable fate of those who did not subscribe to this demanding work ethic, and who improvidently squandered their earnings. Poverty, according to this harsh version, was what the poor deserved. The ideal of the self-made man was strongest in Protestant Britain, but very few British industrialists actually corresponded to the myth – they usually started out with some capital resources. The family often provided the backing needed, and the self-sufficient family firm was a persistent ideal, especially in countries where the banking system remained undeveloped.

The bourgeoisie optimistically believed in the transforming power of science and technology and the inevitability of progress. Their politics were elitist rather than democratic. They assumed that those without education and without a stake in the country (in the form of property) should be ineligible to vote. They believed that careers should be open to all, and that talent and merit rather than family connections should ensure promotion. The introduction of examinations for entry into the British civil service in the 1850s was an expression of this objective. Careers were becoming increasingly 'professionalized', as law, medicine, engineering and teaching gradually elaborated their own distinctive identities. Specialized areas were defined, training paths and institutions were identified, and professional standards were formulated and discussed in professional journals.

Was there such a thing as a bourgeois 'way of life'? Perhaps much of it was not specifically or exclusively bourgeois. Bourgeois frugality sometimes echoed peasant attitudes. The desire for land as a status symbol indicates emulation of an aristocratic lifestyle. Nevertheless, there was a *cuisine bourgeoise*, designed to achieve another kind of *juste milieu*: the bourgeois way of eating was refined but honest, shunning the rich ostentation of the aristocrat's table and at the same time avoiding the coarseness associated with peasant food. So influential did it become that it defined the world's conception of French cooking for a century and a half until *cuisine minceur* tried to dislodge the tradition. There was a bourgeois way of spending. The bourgeois spent his money discreetly, with one exception: his wife's clothes exhibited a colour and flair which contrasted with the male's traditional black suit and top hat. Through his wife's wardrobe, the bourgeois made a vicarious public statement of his wealth and status. There was a bourgeois taste in art, which tended towards realism tempered by sentimentality, favouring portraiture and genre scenes. There was also a bourgeois education, for the sons of bourgeois dominated schools at secondary level, and imbibed a curriculum usually inspired by classical literature and philosophy.

In France, the bourgeois household had its distinctive status symbols, as Adeline Daumard's thorough study showed. The wine-cellar, the mahogany furniture, the cashmere clothes and perhaps a silver dinner service were the desirable accoutrements of a bourgeois family.[8] The consumption of novels rose significantly in the 1830s and 1840s, and the educated bourgeoisie, including wives and daughters, formed an important part of the fiction-reading public. In the immediate post-revolutionary years, the entire European public devoured the novels of Walter Scott, whose heroes like Ivanhoe and Rob Roy behaved in anything but a bourgeois fashion. At the end of our period, they were likely to be enjoying Dumas's equally un-bourgeois *Three Musketeers* or his *Count of Monte Cristo*, featuring a nineteenth-century superman bent on revenge against the corrupt bourgeoisie of the July Monarchy. Romantic novelists and the literary bohemia in general despised the bourgeoisie as tasteless philistines, but their readers were the bourgeois public whom they caricatured.

In spite of the insults of writers and artists, bourgeois culture was not a contradiction in terms. In Paris, over 13 per cent of businessmen owned a musical instrument, and music was an essential part of middle-class socializing.[9] In Vienna, musical soirées (*Hauskonzerte*) in the homes of wealthy bankers and civil servants reflected a changing musical public, which included the well-off bourgeoisie and not just aristocratic patrons. They brought both amateur and professional musicians together for impromptu performances of Schubert songs, dancing and parlour games. Schubert and other composers wrote pieces specifically for this domestic milieu. Public concerts were booming in this period, with the support of the middle-class public, according to Weber's study of concert-going in several capital cities.[10] Concert programmes were changing to cater for less demanding tastes. Whereas Beethoven's last public concert, given at the Kärntnerthor in Vienna in 1824 and including the Ninth Symphony, was unprofitable and appreciated by a dwindling number of connoisseurs, a much larger public was being swept away first by Rossini's flamboyant music and then by the virtuoso violinist Paganini. At the height of the Paganini craze in 1828, people queued for hours in Vienna for tickets to see the dazzling performer.[11]

This period is associated with the Biedermeier style in art and interior decoration. Just as 'bourgeois' was a term with negative connotations, so Biedermeier too was a name coined retrospectively and condescendingly to refer to bourgeois culture in Germany and Austria. It derived originally from a series of satirical newspaper articles in 1855, which created a fictional character called Gottlieb Biedermeier, who was taken to personify bourgeois narrowness and complacency.[12] The Biedermeier style was a domestic style, which valued plain, homely virtues. It celebrated the warmth and comfort of the family and revelled in a cosiness bordering on schmalz. The pot-plants, polished wooden furniture and family portraits of the Biedermeier drawing-room were essential to a bourgeois family life that was provincial in spirit and nostalgic for peace and order (see Plate 13). It was a life which increasingly turned in on itself and which valued the quality of its own domestic space.

**The domestic ideology**

The new emphasis on domestic values corresponded to an increasingly rigid division of gender roles or the 'separation of spheres'. The middle-class male was considered intellectually and emotionally suited to act in the public sphere, the harshly competitive world of business and politics, while acting in the private or domestic sphere was the specific destiny of women. The separation of spheres was a model or an ideal rather than an exact description of what actually happened in a bourgeois home. It did not mean that men played no domestic or parenting role; nor did it necessarily mean that wives had no public role. Following the Californian sociologist Lyn

*Plate 13*   A Biedermeier interior. Children are at the centre of the Begas family in
this otherwise very posed scene. The portrait suggests some gendered
activities, Cologne cathedral is visible through the window and the artist
himself is sketching on the extreme right of the group

*Source*:   Karl Begas, *The Begas Family*, 1821, Rheinisches Bildarchiv, Stadt Köln.

Lofland, we might envisage a third sphere, a 'parochial realm', comprising
networks of friends, neighbours and peers, acting in a community which
transcended the individual household without becoming completely
public.[13] Nevertheless, the idea of the public/private dichotomy greatly
influenced the development of gender roles. The separation of spheres
reflected a new respect for domestic life. It was based on the ideal of
marriage as a relationship of affection, companionship and mutual respect,
and not simply a business contract or an expedient family merger. It also
reflected a new attempt to provide a loving environment for children.

For the bourgeois male, the ideal home was a refuge from a stressful
world. The notion of the home as a haven of tranquillity and repose lay

behind the move of many middle-class families out of city centres into suburban villas. The home was woman's destiny in the nineteenth century for four main reasons. First, it was considered to correspond with her natural instincts. A woman was thought to be naturally fulfilled by motherhood and home-making. Second, it was a woman's social responsibility to provide a good education for her children and stand as a moral guardian for the whole family. Third, the notion of separate spheres and the different capacities of men and women was underpinned by contemporary medical discourse, in which the woman had certain weaknesses which were biologically determined. For example, she was considered genetically unfit for sustained intellectual work. The menstrual cycle and the nature of the uterus supposedly made her emotionally vulnerable, and liable to the specifically female condition of 'hysteria'. Fourth, the educational system reinforced the notion of separate spheres. If women were educated at all in early nineteenth-century Europe, they were taught the skills of home-making in preparation for marriage. Some parts of the curriculum, like mathematics, were considered unfeminine, fostering a calculating reason which was a male characteristic and not one which women were fitted to learn. The separation of spheres was reflected in the arrangement of space within the bourgeois household. The men had a study, and perhaps a smoking-room or billiard-room, where they retired after dinner. The women read and did needlework in the drawing-room. Later in the century, this conception of separate gender roles would produce a reaction: the psychoanalyst Carl Jung was to emphasize the achievement of an integrated personality, combining the 'male' and 'female' characteristics in every individual, and this seems a particularly relevant response to the domestic ideology of the nineteenth-century bourgeoisie.

Women had their own territory. The mistress of the house, sometimes known abusively as the 'Minister of the Interior', kept order in the house and planned the day for her team of maids and servants, over whom she had the power of hiring and firing. She was responsible for the economical management of the household budget, she kept inventories of linen, and recorded tradesmen's deliveries and accounts. A growing literature advised her how to succeed at these tasks, including Mrs Beaton's celebrated *Household Management* (1859). In Germany, a whole genre of *Hausfrau* literature and magazines instructed the woman on the organization of the domestic sphere and the need for cleanliness and keeping a tidy linen closet. They needed to keep the family in good health, and maintain moral standards. The woman's moral superiority was recognized and idealized by the Catholic Church. Indeed, religion was often at the heart of the woman's private life, as she attended Church and confession and made charitable visits to the poor and the sick. Bonnie Smith found that up to the 1840s, the bourgeois women of northern France played an active business role in their textile firms, as accountants, personnel managers and quality controllers.[14] At first there was a close relationship between the private home and the company premises. Increasingly, however, they withdrew from these organizing roles, concentrating more on the home and child care. A widening gap opened up between home and the cotton mill.

Domestic servants, the majority of them female, were a familiar and indispensable part of the bourgeois household. Domestic service was by far the largest employer of women, both before and after industrialization. In 1851, 40 per cent of all working women in Britain were domestics, whereas only 22 per cent were factory workers.[15] In Munich in 1828, 14 per cent of the population were domestic servants.[16] In France, there were over 900 000 servants in 1851, 68 per cent of them women, and demand was rising.[17] More and more lower-middle-class families wanted at least one maid, for this signified middle-class status. But if they could only afford one servant, she had to do everything.

A day's work might begin at 6 a.m., when the fire had to be lit, and finish at 10 p.m. Meals had to be prepared, the washing-up done, children needed looking after, the house cleaned, the steps scrubbed, the beds made, the shopping and laundry done, the silver polished. All this was accomplished without running water; it was the maid's job to fill the water-buckets at the pump and bring them upstairs to the apartment. In Paris apartment buildings, they lodged in tiny rooms on the sixth floor. They had little time or space to eat, and no legal day off until 1906. Most servant girls came from rural backgrounds. In Versailles, between 1825 and 1853, 60 per cent of them came from the country.[18] Their 'pay' might consist in part of food and board, and hand-me-down clothes from the employer's family. Sometimes they never saw any wages: their pay would be sent directly home to their father. At the exhibition on tuberculosis held in Geneva in 1906, visitors were shown a reconstruction of a maid's room on the Champs-Elysées, alongside a model of a cell from the women's prison at Fresnes: the point was that the prison cell was lighter, cleaner, more airy and it had running water.[19] Female servants had little scope for getting married or starting a family, unless they sent their infant out to a wet-nurse. If they did marry, it meant that they would quit their job. In London in 1851, only 2 per cent of domestic servants were married. Their worst fate was to fall pregnant (possibly to the employer or his son) and thus get dismissed.

For the bourgeois employer, the ideal maid was Christian and remained eternally single. She would be devoted to the interests of the family above all else. The bourgeois nightmare was to hire someone who remained a stranger within the household, spreading discord, seducing the husband or son (but it was usually the other way round) or corrupting the virginal daughter of the house.

Although women enjoyed considerable power and responsibility within their allotted sphere, male authority dominated the decision-making process within the household. The marital relationship was ideally an affectionate bond between equals, but ultimately patriarchy ruled. A married woman had no independent legal status. Her body, any property she owned and any money she earned were legally at her husband's disposal. The father had exclusive legal control over their children, and could remove them from the home without his wife's permission if he saw fit. He could punish and discipline her and in some countries put her in prison. According to Lawrence Stone's general assessment of the wife's legal status in England: 'under the patriarchal system of values, as expressed in the enacted law as it endured until the nineteenth century, a married woman was the nearest approximation in a free society to a slave'.[20] This of course was the legal situation: it did not necessarily mean that women were normally treated this way, especially by the 1840s. In practice, the legal subordination of the wife was regarded as quite compatible with a loving marriage.

In Catholic countries, and possibly everywhere, the separation of spheres produced a growing gender dichotomy in religious observance. The daily lives of bourgeois women revolved around charitable visits, attending confession and observing religious holidays. The Catholic Church glorified their reproductive role and, through the cult of the Blessed Virgin, idealized female purity and submission. For men, however, Church-going was a declining practice. Their attitudes tended to be more secular, and the Church's teachings seemed more and more irrelevant to the world of money-making which they inhabited. Although they tolerated their wives' pious observance, they were suspicious of the clergy's influence over women and saw it as proof of women's innate irrationality.[21] The Catholic Church's attitude towards feminine devotion was always ambiguous. In southern Germany, reformers inside and outside the Catholic Church waged a campaign against priestly celibacy in the early 1830s. In defending the celibacy of priests, the Catholic establishment revealed its underlying misogyny, condemning the corrupting influence of women, and invoking the ancient stereotype of the woman as sexual temptress.[22]

Family values were supported in Protestant countries by the religious context of Evangelicalism, the movement for moral reform which saw the family as a starting-point for religious revival. Evangelical Protestantism promoted a middle-class work ethic which distinguished the bourgeois from the spendthrift and irrational working classes. Evangelicals stressed the need for family stability and the woman's duty to obey her spouse. They valued family prayers and Bible readings, often led by the male head of the household. The Cadburys, a Quaker family who started as drapers and shopkeepers in Birmingham, illustrate the British milieu of Protestant Dissent. Elizabeth Cadbury worked in the family shop and ran the household. At the same time, she gave birth to ten children in the 15 years of her married life to Richard Tapper Cadbury. Gradually, however, according to Davidoff and Hall, the Cadbury women became less and less involved in business life, leaving the decisions and responsibility increasingly to the men. At the same time, they became more involved in philanthropic duties, supporting temperance and antislavery causes. The business expanded, and the family home shifted from central Birmingham to suburban Edgbaston, creating a wider physical gap between work and domesticity. The layout of the family home reflected bourgeois domestic priorities. It had a playroom and a nursery for the children, a dining-room, a drawing-room and a garden.[23] Here was a happy, sheltered refuge for the husband after his daily buffeting in the rough and amoral world of business, where children were cared for and the woman maintained tranquillity and moral virtue.

Children were taught to read and write within the family. Families produced a great body of correspondence which sustained an extended kinship network and informed it of notable family events. The Duméril-Metzdorff family of Alsace produced a family archive of over 3000 surviving letters, spanning a continuous period from 1795 to 1933.[24] As they show, personal correspondence often implied a wide family audience. Some letters had several different authors, each writing their own message to the recipients. Others related family news designed to be read aloud, or passed between various members of the family. Family correspondence was directed to a wide group of readers. There was often very little about private correspondence that was actually private.

Many rituals, some old some new, defined the bourgeois family. Births were home births, with males excluded, in an age when only the poor and dying went to a hospital. It was paradoxical that in a culture which idealized motherhood, giving birth was a highly dangerous activity. Deaths from post-natal infections were not uncommon. In the French city of Rouen in mid-century, the maternal death rate was 11 per cent (in hospitals childbirth was twice as dangerous).[25] The family met for dinner on Sunday, and in the week mealtimes gradually changed to synchronize with office hours. From the 1840s, Christmas became more of a family festival, and the Christmas tree became more generally accepted, especially in Northern

Europe. On high religious festivals, the family went to Mass together. They gave each other gifts at New Year (*étrennes* in France). The English invented the idea of the honeymoon in the country, which became more popular from the 1830s. This reflected a new conception of the privacy of the couple, who were permitted to consummate the marriage free from the usual family surveillance over the event. It became normal for couples to sleep together in double beds and to talk to each other in more familiar tones. French spouses called each other intimately 'tu' instead of 'vous'.[26] If the man went away on a business trip, the couple would expect each other to write daily. In these detailed ways, the ideal bourgeois family became a more closely bonded relationship.

The pre-industrial family had been an economic unit, and this remained true for the European peasantry. But the separation of private and public spheres transformed the bourgeois home into a place of consumption rather than production. Women had an important economic role as consumers. The first department stores opened in the mid-nineteenth century, like the Bon Marché in Paris. The department store was a new and attractive phenomenon, beckoning the bourgeois women who were its main customers. The store was a symbol of the new commodity capitalism, a machine for the circulation of goods and symbols, and it was itself a sign of urban modernity. Shopping increasingly drew women into the public space of the city, the stores and cafés of London and Paris. They were there to see and also to be seen. For the bourgeois couple, women's clothing was a major indicator of status. The new department store was an alluring dream factory, whose goods were all objects of female desire.

## Divorce

The study of divorce and marital breakdown often reveals underlying assumptions about the proper or improper behaviour of spouses. Although only the most extreme cases ever came to court, they often give historians clues about what held less dramatic marriages together. In the early nineteenth century, the Christian definition of marriage as a holy sacrament was still a powerful deterrent against separation. But the hold of religious teachings about the indissolubility of the marriage bond was weakening. In 1792, the French Revolution had instituted the most liberal divorce law yet known, and although Napoleon's Civil Code severely moderated its impact, traditional conceptions of marriage had been dealt a serious blow. The story of legal separations in the post-revolutionary era illustrates three of the main themes already touched on in this chapter. First, patriarchal values remained strong, and the gender hierarchy, we may speculate, was accepted by the vast majority of husbands and wives. On the other hand, the rise in divorces and separations reflected new conceptions of companionate marriage and domesticity. It signified a greater recognition that individual happiness was important, and not always achieved by a rigid observance of theological injunctions. For an increasing number of unhappy spouses, loveless marriages were no longer tolerable. The best remedy for a dysfunctional relationship was to end it. The third theme is the gradual secularization of marriage and divorce, which, with important exceptions, were becoming matters exclusively for the civil administration.

In the early nineteenth century, divorce was not permitted in Catholic or Orthodox countries. It was illegal in Spain, Portugal and Italy after 1815 and in Russia only a tiny number was allowed. In France, divorce had been made illegal by the Bourbon regime in 1816, and it was not legalized there until 1884. In Protestant countries, the situation was different. Divorce was legal in Switzerland, the Netherlands and in Presbyterian Scotland (which had a different legal system to that of England). In Prussia, divorce had been made legal in 1794, but in the post-revolutionary climate of conservatism, both Protestant and Catholic Churches increasingly refused to remarry divorcees.[27] The possibility of remarriage was a major consideration for divorce petitioners everywhere. England was the odd country out amongst Protestant societies. Divorce was not legal in England until 1857. Even after the Divorce Act, it remained a solution chiefly available to the aristocracy and the wealthy middle classes. Only they could afford the legal costs, and as property-owners, they were the main social groups concerned about the transmission of property to legitimate heirs. Almost everywhere, divorce was an urban phenomenon: peasants rarely resorted to litigation.

In France, divorce was not permitted until the Naquet Law of 1884. When the legalization of divorce reappeared briefly on the political agenda in 1848, it provoked the anger of Catholics. Frédéric Ozanam, founder of the St Vincent de Paul Society, taught that marriage was a mutual sacrifice, in which the woman surrendered her beauty and virginity and the man his independence. Such sacrifices had to be supported not undermined.[28] A legal separation was possible but rare, and it did not give either party the possibility of remarriage. Legal separation, like divorce in other countries, could be granted on grounds of physical violence or adultery. According to the Napoleonic Code, however, a double standard operated in cases of infidelity. A wife could only obtain a separation if her husband's adultery was especially flagrant, that is to say if it occurred under the marital roof, perhaps with a maidservant. On the other hand, infidelity of any kind committed by the wife would justify a husband's request for a legal separation. Both the courts and the ruling classes were keen to defend the lineage: in a patrilineal society, it was imperative that possessions were handed down to genetically-sound heirs. This was why the wife's fidelity was more highly prized than that of her partner. A little male 'profligacy', as the phrase went, could be pardoned, but the wife's infidelity threatened the purity of the blood line. As for separation on the grounds of cruelty, a certain level of physical violence and verbal abuse between spouses was socially acceptable, as long as the wife's life was not put at risk. A husband was permitted to chastise his wife and French courts were rarely convinced that evidence of routine beatings justified a break-up.[29]

The legalization of divorce was a progressive step for women. In Prussia, by the mid-1840s women were three times as likely to initiate divorce proceedings as men, and in England after the Divorce Act of 1857, over 40 per cent of petitioners were women.[30] Before the English Divorce Law, the rich could resort to various legal remedies. The landed gentry sued the ecclesiastical courts for a legal separation on the grounds of cruelty or adultery. Alternatively, a husband could bring a civil action against his wife's lover to repair his wounded honour. Divorce was only possible, however, through an individual act of parliament, and between 30 and 50 of them only were granted per decade from 1820 to 1850.[31] The 1857 law removed the jurisdiction of the ecclesiastical courts and of parliament and put the matter in the hands of a new and purely secular divorce court. It attempted, with moderate success, to make divorce more accessible to women. Contrary to many predictions, the trickle of divorces did not become a flood. The poor were still effectively excluded which is probably what the law's main protagonist Lord Palmerston intended. Those with little or no property could sign a private separation agreement or just walk out of the marriage. In southern England, wife-sales still persisted, in which the woman, haltered like livestock, was publicly auctioned and handed over to the highest bidder. Thomas Hardy famously dramatized such a wife-sale in his novel *The Mayor of Casterbridge*. By the time he was writing (the 1890s), the practice had been stamped out. Wife-sales were grossly offensive to bourgeois values, and were seen as deplorable examples of lower-class degradation. They had been eradicated in England by the 1840s.[32]

Divorce was gradually becoming more accessible to women, at least middle-class women, and there was a growing realization that the double sexual standard was unjust. Nevertheless, male authority was not about to legislate itself away. The issue of the custody of children of a broken marriage also reflected prevailing views of gender roles and child care. It was taken for granted by the law that custody was the automatic right of the father. Gradually the new cult of domesticity and the popularizing of breast-feeding achieved some recognition of the mother's role as a potential custodian. In England, the Child Custody Bill of 1839 allowed the courts for the first time to award the custody of children under 7 to the mother. This clearly indicated a new consideration for the nurturing role of mothers. Wives who had been unfaithful, however, and who were therefore stigmatized as the 'guilty party', were by definition considered unfit for custody. So when Lady Rosebery was caught in bed with her lover in 1815, she became terribly distraught and her first instinct was to gather her children together. But she was prevented by force and, as the transgressor, she would never see them again without her husband's permission.[33]

Patriarchy and conservatism ruled in Russia. Whereas in England marriage at a public registry office was recognized in 1836, in Russia, the Orthodox Church took full responsibility for adjudicating the indissolubility of marriage. The Church only approved a small number of divorces: 58 per year were granted on average between 1836 and 1860 for the entire Russian Empire. Most of these were justified by desertion or the exile of a spouse to Siberia. Neither violence not adultery were normally considered sufficient grounds for divorce, as far as the Russian Orthodox Church was concerned. If one spouse was Jewish, however, and refused to convert, then divorce could be contemplated. The same was true where the husband joined the *skoptsy*, a heretical sect which practised self-castration – a severe handicap, one imagines, in the pursuit of conjugal bliss. The Russian case throws into relief the progress of secular ideas and the widening availability of divorce in Western Europe, especially in Protestant countries. In Prussia there were about 3000 divorces per year, and in Belgium the divorce rate was 900 times higher per size of population than in Russia.[34] In the West, the bourgeois ideal of the marriage as a site of love, desire and affection was gaining ground, even though it remained in tension with conceptions of patriarchy.

## Challenges to conventional gender expectations

Bourgeois norms of domesticity and the proper role of women were challenged by a small number of feminists, socialists, and political activists. Charles Fourier and some of the Saint-Simonians, for instance, urged sexual liberation and gender equality. The legalization of divorce was supported by Saint-Simonians like Suzanne Voilquin, who publicly 'divorced' her husband in 1833. It was also supported by the international socialist Flora Tristan, who was constantly dogged by her own estranged husband, who shot and injured her in 1838. For Tristan, who travelled, published and lectured to French workers, there was no need for women to play a subservient or purely domestic role in the world.

Feminists like Flora Tristan believed that women were capable of superior levels of emotional intelligence, moral virtue and compassion, and that social reform needed to be guided by these essentially feminine qualities. Like other socialist women, however, she fundamentally accepted the gender dichotomy on which conventional notions were also based: men and women possessed inherently different characteristics. They were opposites but complementary to each other. The male and female principles were sometimes envisaged as locked in a cosmic polarity. For Tristan, God had two genders, combining both male and female essences.

Socialist women usually accepted the ideal of a monogamous but equal marriage, and they realized more clearly than male Saint-Simonians that without women's economic independence, gender equality would be illusory. They took motherhood seriously. Suzanne Voilquin, who caught venereal disease from her husband, subsequently had many miscarriages. She worked as a midwife and her frustrated maternal longings were the tragedy of her life. Saint-Simonian women like Voilquin were frustrated by their subordinate position within the movement. For a sect so open to female membership, Saint-Simonianism allowed surprisingly few women in leadership roles. Their charismatic leader Prosper Enfantin persuaded many of them to decamp to Egypt in search of the female Messiah – a development which should be recognized as the insanity it really was. In many respects, feminist ideas developed as a critique of Enfantin, rather than as the fruit of his inspiration.

Groups of women were particularly active in the 1848 Revolutions. In Paris, they founded a new newspaper, *La Voix des Femmes*, which brought together activists from different social classes to present a women's agenda to the Provisional Government. To take another example, middle-class women in Stuttgart organized a milk boycott in 1849 to protest against price rises. Here women's action was typically limited to an area of domestic consumption, and it was attacked by working-class women – namely the milk delivery girls who struggled to make ends meet. The milk boycott illustrated another problem of women's political action: in attending meetings and rallies, they were accused of neglecting home duties. But on this occasion they succeeded.[35] In the German revolutions of 1848, women formed their own associations for mutual assistance and education. In Berlin, a University for the Female Sex opened in 1850. One of the leading German feminists, Louise Otto, whose journal *Frauen-Zeitung* was published in 1849, argued that women should enter commerce and teaching and should not be dependent on a man's income.[36] Otto lived with her sisters in a household without men. She married when she was 39 and was soon widowed. Even she did not fundamentally attack contemporary notions of sexual difference which underpinned the sexual division of labour. She denounced George Sand as a hermaphrodite, who had abandoned her family responsibilities.[37] If women demanded greater access to higher education, it was to make them better mothers with a broad knowledge of the world.

## Conclusions

The European bourgeoisie of lawyers, officials, *rentiers* and businessmen was in the process of becoming a more self-conscious and dominant class, and this process had advanced much further in urbanized Northern and Western Europe than in Southern and Eastern Europe. Sometimes bourgeois values were not purely 'bourgeois' – they bore the enduring stamp of peasant reflexes or artisan traditions, backgrounds from which some business families had once emerged. At the same time, the bourgeoisie confronted and made compromises with the powerful holders of older landed wealth.

In the family values they adopted, the Western bourgeois were pioneers. Marriages were still part of a general strategy of family advancement, as they were for other social groups. The middle class, however, believed more and more strongly that love, affection and companionship should also be part of marriage. At the same time, they gave a higher priority to providing love and support for their children. The fact that they were having fewer of them strengthened this new investment in their welfare. The bourgeois family pioneered a new sense of privacy. The family made its own entertainment, provided its own emotional sustenance, retreated to the suburbs and created a haven of domestic peace. In the architecture of middle-class homes the public space of reception areas was separated from the private inner sanctum of the couple, and this was distinguished in turn from rooms upstairs devoted to the children. At the same time, the legal framework which underpinned the institution of marriage gave ultimate authority to the male head of the household. The division between public and private lives reflected the underlying assumption that men and women had different talents and capacities. When it came to important decisions, this philosophy of sexual difference did not make men and women equal.

These new values were part of Victorianism, a term still identified today in the British context with prudish and hypocritical attitudes towards sex. Bourgeois values, however, were much more than this cliché suggests, signifying a faith in science, technology and progress, in rational government and limited representative institutions, and in moderation as a rule of life. Was Victorianism a European or just a purely British phenomenon? As far as it refers to the influence of Protestant Dissent and evangelical Christianity in fostering a work ethic and a drive for self-improvement, it had few parallels outside Britain and northern Germany. As far as other things are concerned, including the politics of gender and the family, the European bourgeoisies did share common ground.

# 14   The Revolutions of 1848

## Introduction: romantic failure or apprenticeship in democracy?

In 1848 a wave of revolutions swept regimes from power all over the continent of Europe, except for its peripheries – Britain, Russia and Spain. In Paris, the monarchy of Louis-Philippe was overthrown, and a republic proclaimed. In Berlin, the Prussian monarchy acceded to liberal demands for a constitution, and a makeshift parliament of lawyers, academics and professional men assembled in Frankfurt to plan the unification of Germany. In Prague, a congress met to discuss revolutionary moves towards self-government for Slav peoples. In Budapest, a national revolution led by the Magyar gentry threatened Austrian rule and was soon to declare Hungarian independence. Another revolution of students and workers erupted at the very heart of the Habsburg Empire in Vienna itself. Milan and Venice, then under Austrian rule, were in revolution, and in Rome, the Pope fled as the Holy City became a revolutionary republic.

The 1848 revolutions enjoyed rapid initial success, as liberals (some middle class, some aristocrats) had the support of lower-class artisans in bringing down authoritarian monarchies. But their victory was almost too good to be true. Before long, the democratic hopes of February 1848 vanished, as conservatism reasserted its authority. In France itself, the headquarters of European revolutions, Louis-Napoleon (the nephew of the great Napoleon) became president of the republic and in 1851 seized dictatorial power as the Emperor Napoleon III. In Germany, Frederick William of Prussia found he had little to fear from the impotent Frankfurt Parliament. Habsburg forces pulverized revolutionary movements one by one, in Vienna, Prague and northern Italy. Only in Hungary did the struggle smoulder on until Austrians and Russians combined to snuff it out in 1849.

What united all these revolutions? The Revolutions of 1848 seemed to have common origins and to end in a common failure. The root cause of all the 1848 Revolutions was a general economic crisis affecting the entire continent, which stemmed from poor grain and potato harvests in 1846 and 1847. The resulting hardship was worsened by a financial crash, as the bubble of investment in railway development burst. In 1848 and 1849,

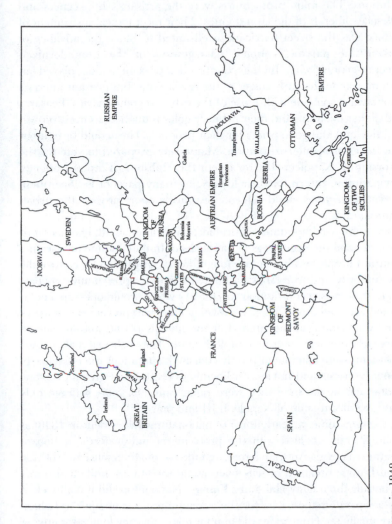

*Map 14.1*  Europe in 1848

*Source:*  Jonathan Sperber, *The European Revolutions, 1848–51*, Cambridge University Press, 1984.

however, the economic situation gradually improved, which helped the conservative cause. Dictatorship and the force of arms put an end to the revolutionary threat.

Another common feature was the essentially urban nature of the 1848 Revolutions. The main protagonists were the artisans, shopkeepers and middle-class liberals of the largest cities. Their most typical instrument of resistance was the street barricade, well-suited to block the advance of troops in the narrow, cobbled passageways of the unmodernized nineteenth-century city. In the countryside, peasant action played an important role in the early stages of the revolutions, but peasant interests did not always coincide with those of the urban revolutionaries. Peasants feared higher taxation, and their primary goals remained, as ever, possession of the land and good prices for their produce. They could be enlisted by the forces of counter-revolution. Many were prepared to vote for the dictatorship of Napoleon III, or accept the Habsburg Empire's offer of emancipation in return for their loyalty. In many parts of Europe, then, conservative regimes could rely on peasant support against the urban revolutionaries.

There were two important political ideas at work in 1848: liberal constitutionalism, and the beginnings of nationalism. In the absolute monarchies of Central Europe, revolutionaries fought for a constitution, to control the king's authority and to establish a limited form of representative government. In their eyes, a constitution was the key which would open up a political role for the educated, property owning elite, and prevent the abuse of power by a tyrannical monarch. But the liberals of the mid-nineteenth century were not democrats in a modern sense. They believed that workers and peasants were illiterate or poorly educated, and under the influence of reactionary priests and nobles. So liberals were afraid of giving everyone the vote, and at the time they were right: universal male suffrage only brought the dictatorship of Napoleon III into power.

At the same time, an early form of nationalism was evident in 1848, as German liberals wrestled with the problems of unity, northern Italians fought the occupying Austrian forces, and the nationalist intellectuals of East Central Europe dreamed of self-government, sometimes inside and sometimes outside the mighty Habsburg Empire. Nationalists did not all seek to create a separate nation state for their community – although the Italians and eventually the Hungarians did aim for this – but they fought for greater political autonomy, more access to government jobs and more recognition of national languages, cultures and economic interests. Before 1848, the liberal constitutionalists and nationalists fought together – they were often in fact the same people. With the collapse of the Revolutions of 1848, however, this bond was broken. The defeat of liberal constitutionalism in 1848 gave conservative regimes the chance to capture the nationalists' programme and use it to their own advantage, as happened in Prussia. In the next half-century, nationalism was to acquire a mass following, and it grew in strength at the expense of liberalism.

The example of France was always a little out of step with the rest of Europe. In 1848, France already had a representative system and a constitutional monarchy. Revolutionaries in Italy and Germany found themselves fighting for exactly the kind of regime which was overthrown in Paris in 1848. In France there was another political force emerging, and this was socialism. French socialism, as discussed in Chapter 4, owed nothing to Marxism, and it had its roots in artisan and peasant politics rather than in an industrial work-force. It looked beyond liberal political solutions to a republic which would guarantee social justice for all.

These events have been interpreted in many different ways. For some historians, the Revolutions represented romantic folly, the impossible dreams of the poets and writers who often played a leading role in 1848. Hence Lewis Namier contemptuously dubbed 1848 the 'Revolution of the Intellectuals'.[1] Others focus on the revolutionary failure to bring about lasting political change (although some things *did* change, like the abolition of slavery in the French colonies, the introduction of universal male suffrage in France and the abolition of serfdom in the Austrian lands). A third perspective is the social analysis of the forces at work in 1848. Commentators on both the left and the right have dissected the class struggles in which the middle-class revolutionaries found themselves in armed opposition against the urban workers, who had been their former allies when the issue was to challenge the monarchy. This social view owes much to Karl Marx and Friedrich Engels, who were acute observers of the 1848 revolutions in Paris and Germany.

A fourth view is possible, which finds the significance of 1848 in the extraordinary mass mobilization and political participation of the period. The revolutions of 1848 were, in Maurice Agulhon's view, an 'apprenticeship in democracy'.[2] In the outpourings of the press, the debates of political clubs, in direct action at the barricades, and above all through the ballot box, new forms of participatory democracy were taking shape. In April 1848, universal (male) suffrage meant that the French people voted as a whole for the first time for half a century. The extraordinarily high turn-out of voters revealed the power of republican democracy. Workers, peasants and women were politically involved as never before. In future, governments could not afford to ignore this new level of popular politicization.

## The Revolution of 1848 in France (1848–1852)

In strictly chronological terms, the 1848 Revolutions began not in Paris, but in Switzerland, where in 1847 the Protestant cantons defeated attempts by Catholic cantons to secede from the federation. A federal and democratic Swiss state was created, and the European powers were too distracted by their own problems to take preventive action. In early 1848, revolutions also broke out in Palermo and Naples. Nevertheless, even if Paris did not provide the initial spark, events there were bound to have great significance and to alarm all European rulers.

The February Revolution in Paris was brought about, like most revolutionary outbreaks, by a combination of an economic and a political crisis. The economic crisis was of two kinds: in one sense, it was a traditional crisis, perhaps the last of its kind, provoked by bad harvests in 1846 and 1847, which brought food shortages, followed by a downturn in manufacturing industry and subsequent unemployment. This was the familiar but deadly chain reaction which followed in the wake of an old-style subsistence crisis. At the same time, the stock market, recently booming as a result of railway investment, crashed. This was a new sort of crisis, resulting in a shortage of credit and liquidity, the calling-in of loans and business bankruptcies. It was significant that the depth of the crisis was reached in 1846–7, and that when the revolution broke out in February 1848, the economy was starting to recover. Perhaps this gradual easing of the economic crisis had an effect on the course of the revolution. For 1848 did not follow the pattern of 1789, when revolutionary regimes had become increasingly more radical. In this Revolution, conservative politics were on the rise in 1848 and 1849.

The political crisis had its roots in the campaign to extend the franchise, limited under the July Monarchy by a property qualification. Prime Minister Guizot consistently refused to endorse a broadening of the electorate. His catchphrase 'Enrichissez-vous!' (Make yourself rich!) summed up the materialism of French society in the 1840s, but it was also a recommendation for gradual political change. As individuals grew rich, Guizot was saying, so more of them would naturally qualify for the vote without any need for legislative reform. Guizot wanted the electorate to expand by incremental creep, but the democratic movement was impatient for change. Fighting started on the Paris boulevards when a demonstration in favour of franchise reform was banned. The regime very quickly lost its nerve. Guizot resigned, Louis-Philippe fled to Britain and the Second Republic was proclaimed (it was the successor to the First Republic of 1792–1804).

The new Provisional Government was headed by the poet-historian

Alphonse de Lamartine, who hastily assured European governments that this French republic, unlike its predecessor, had no aggressive intentions. The government abolished the death penalty and swept away slavery in the colonies. A special Commission was established at the Luxembourg Palace (the Luxembourg Commission) to take measures to deal with the unemployment crisis, and did so by providing waged work in state-sponsored 'National Workshops'. A 10-hour day was introduced. This resembled what socialists like Louis Blanc had been demanding, although they regarded the right to work as a state responsibility at all times, not just in a temporary emergency. The Provisional Government was careful to distance itself from the Luxembourg Commission, so that if it came to grief the radicals would be discredited. In order to finance the scheme, the Republic raised taxes, levying a 45-centimes surcharge on France's four main taxes, which was very unpopular in the countryside.

The February Revolution sparked off an unprecedented outburst of political activity. The club movement became active and there was an explosion of pamphlets and newspapers. According to Peter Amann, 203 popular societies were operating in the Paris area by mid-April 1848, with a total membership of at least 50,000.[3] Most of them had their basis in the local neighbourhood, but they were powerful agents of politicization. It was here, at the grass-roots, that many working-class Parisians experienced and participated in the democratic process for the first time. The clubs could organize electoral programmes and their combined strength was capable of mobilizing hundreds of thousands of demonstrators in the streets of the capital.

The first elections under universal male suffrage were held in April, and 84 per cent of adult males voted. The massive turnout made this a major development in the history of democratic participation in Europe. The results, however, revealed a trend to more moderate policies. In May, several political clubs were closed and Blanqui was arrested. In June 1848, the republican government closed down the National Workshops, which had tried in vain to accommodate over 100,000 unemployed in Paris. The sight of workers idle on Parisian street corners made the respectable middle classes uneasy. The workshops were expensive and smacked of socialism. The decision to disband them, however, provoked a major popular uprising in the streets of Paris, known as the 'June Days' of 1848. For Karl Marx, this conflict, brutally suppressed by General Cavaignac, represented the shape of things to come: workers and bourgeois had been united in 1830, and again in February 1848, but at the June barricades, the bourgeoisie and the urban proletariat were in direct confrontation for the first time, with bloody consequences. About 3000 rebels were killed, and over 11,000 arrested. June 1848 seemed like a class war, which exposed the shallowness of the class fraternization of February.

Was Marx correct in characterizing the June Days as an armed clash between bourgeoisie and proletariat? The answer is no, if we translate 'proletariat' as wage-earning factory hands, the modern industrial proletariat to which Marxists looked as the vanguard of the future socialist revolution. The Parisian working class was not yet a factory proletariat in this sense, for the industrial production of the city was still largely in the hands of small craft workshops. With the exception of a few railway workers, the June insurgents were from the older established trades in the building, clothing, metalwork and service industries.[4] The rank-and-file of the 1848 Revolution were skilled artisans and small shopkeepers, the nineteenth-century descendants of the *sans-culottes* of 1793, as discussed in Chapter 12. The industrialized areas of northern and eastern France remained quiet. Marx's analysis, therefore, only carries some weight if it refers to the very mixed working classes of Paris as a whole. Even then, it is important to realize that workers fought on *both* sides of the barricades in June. Rootless and unemployed workers were promised a small daily wage to enlist in the Mobile Guard, and many fought against the June uprising.[5] Marx rather too conveniently dismissed these class renegades as the *lumpenproletariat*.

Having disposed of revolutionary threats in the capital, the Second Republic became increasingly conservative. Its main task was to devise a new Constitution. The 10-hour day was abolished, and the right to work forgotten. The nature of the presidency posed the most difficult problem. Would the new president be elected by a direct popular vote based on universal male suffrage, or would he be voted in by a majority in the Chamber of Deputies? The verdict favoured a popular election, which made likely the emergence of a strong executive, boosted by a mandate from the people. To make a Bonapartist dictatorship less likely, the Republic decreed that the president's term of office would be limited to four years. This nevertheless ensured the election as president of Louis-Napoleon, nephew of the great Napoleon, who crushed his nearest rival Cavaignac by 5.5 million votes to 1.45 million. Louis-Napoleon secured 74 per cent of the votes cast, and Cavaignac only 19.5 per cent. The leading radical candidate, Ledru-Rollin, came further behind with 370,000 votes. Once again, as in 1800–4, a massive popular vote legitimized a Bonapartist presidency of the Republic, at least until 1852.

His name itself was a legend, and enough to ensure electoral victory in the countryside. The dynasty was identified with the glorious achievements of his uncle, although there was absolutely no intention to provoke a war in Europe. His appeal lay in the fact that he alone amongst the presidential candidates had a name which all Frenchmen knew. In the countryside, a vote for Louis-Napoleon was often a vote against the 45-centimes tax surcharge, and a vote against the domination of the bourgeois notables. Louis-Napoleon also received some working-class support. He was not associated with the repression of the June Days, and some socialists including Louis Blanc saw in him the promise of social reform. Louis-Napoleon was, after all, the author of a book on the problem of poverty, and his personal interest in social progress seemed to differentiate him from his illustrious ancestor. In his youth, he had been associated with the *Carbonari* in Italy, and seemed sympathetic to liberal-nationalist causes. Louis-Napoleon, however, meant different things to different people. For the bourgeoisie, he was a man of order, and a protection against any repeat of the June Days. Like all Bonapartes, he had the army behind him – an additional guarantee against social upheaval. His candidature succeeded because all groups could read something into it: his intentions were so opaque that he could pose simultaneously as a liberal and a defender of law and order. Meanwhile, the clique of Orleanist politicians like Adolphe Thiers mistakenly believed they could manipulate him. Louis-Napoleon allowed them to cherish this illusion until it was time to establish his own personal dictatorship.

Between 1849 and 1851, the period of the bourgeois republic, a power struggle ensued between President Louis-Napoleon, fortified by his popular mandate, and the deputies in the National Assembly, moderate republicans who defended parliamentary liberalism. In 1850, they reimposed a property qualification to limit the electorate – this was an important reversal of the universal suffrage declared in 1848, and it disenfranchised about 30 per cent of voters.[6] Louis-Napoleon cultivated the Catholic electorate. In 1849 a French army defeated the revolution in Rome (discussed later in this chapter) and restored the authority of the Pope. France became the chief protector of the Papacy. The Falloux Law of 1850 gave the clergy more control over secondary education. In the country as a whole, radical activity was suppressed. Left-leaning mayors were sacked, anti-government newspapers were prosecuted and political clubs were either closed or forced underground.[7] In the backlash following the June Days, the slightest manifestation of socialist allegiance was silenced. In the Vaucluse department, for instance, there were arrests at 29 funerals where mourners wore red ties.[8]

Louis-Napoleon's biggest problem was to avoid the expiry of his presidential term in 1852. A hostile majority in the Chamber of Deputies blocked constitutional revision. Louis-Napoleon, therefore, had only one means of perpetuating his power: an illegal *coup d'état*. In December 1851, on the anniversary of the Battle of Austerlitz, Louis-Napoleon dissolved the Assembly, arrested opposition deputies, and proclaimed the return of universal suffrage, the instrument of his authority. Republican deputies appealed for popular support against this constitutional violation, but to no avail in the capital. There was little reason why the people of Paris would defend the parliamentary majority which had closed the National Workshops in 1848 and suppressed the June insurrection. But there was resistance in the countryside, particularly in the southeast. In the uprising of 1851, peasants and rural artisans defended the legality of the republican constitution against the illegal seizure of power. They were the 'dem-socs', who had looked forward to the elections of 1852 as an opportunity to elect a new republican regime, devoted to democracy and social justice. Their action illustrates the radicalization of the countryside and the fruits of France's democratic apprenticeship. About 100,000 rebels were involved, of whom about 27,000 were tried and 9500 deported to Algeria.[9] The peasant emperor, Magraw reminds us, came to power by suppressing the largest rural rising in Western Europe.[10]

The rising, however, failed. A plebiscite on the proclamation of the Second Empire produced 7.4 million votes for the new Emperor Napoleon III. For Karl Marx, this plebiscite represented a peasant counter-revolution, manipulated by Louis-Napoleon against all that was progressive in 1848. Marx's celebrated pamphlet, *The 18th Brumaire of Louis-Napoleon*, compared the seizure of power unfavourably with Napoleon I's *coup* in 1799. 'Hegel remarks', he wrote, 'that all facts and personages of great importance in world history occur, as it were, twice. He forgot to add: the first time as tragedy, the second as farce'.[11] For Victor Hugo, too, writing in exile, Louis-Napoleon would always be 'Le petit Napoléon', a dwarf cavorting on the shoulders of a giant. The French Left would think twice before flirting again with popular Bonapartism.

## The Revolutions of 1848 in Germany

Revolution broke out in 1848 against a background of economic unrest in several German capitals, including Munich and Dresden, but the struggle in Prussia would be decisive. The revolutionaries envisaged German unity under a constitutional monarchy with a parliamentary system, but these aims posed a direct challenge to the ruling Hohenzollern dynasty. The events of 1848 were a landmark in the history of parliamentary liberalism in Germany, but ultimately they signalled the defeat of liberal forces, as well as exposing the contradictions of the nationalist cause.

When in March barricades went up in Berlin, 230 were killed in the street-fighting, 90 per cent of them being the journeymen and craftworkers who made up the rank-and-file of the urban revolutions everywhere.[12] The number of industrial workers involved was relatively small. Frederick William IV acquiesced to demands for a constitution, and historians have since wondered why the king did not immediately authorize the army to crush the Revolution. His reluctance to use force seems uncharacteristic for a Prussian ruler. One possible explanation is that he was unsure of the loyalty of the military, but again, historical examples of disobedience in the Prussian army are few and far between.[13] Perhaps the king believed a compromise could be engineered, and briefly imagined that he could neutralize the revolution by putting himself at its head. But he had a low tolerance of democracy and soon withdrew to Potsdam. The army remained in reserve, and it was the strongest force in Germany. As long as it remained at the monarchy's disposal, it would decide the fate of the Revolution.

New governments led by moderate constitutionalists were appointed, like the Camphausen ministry in Prussia, and von Gagern's government in Rhine-Hesse. The German states now elected representatives, according to their different voting systems, who convened at the Paulskirche in Frankfurt to discuss the unity of Germany. In Prussia, universal suffrage operated for males over 24, which signified an unprecedented advance in political democracy. In Württemberg and the independent cities, the franchise was relatively democratic, but property qualifications made it more socially exclusive in Saxony and Baden. Overall, 75 per cent of adult German males now had the vote.[14] The very existence of an elected and all-German institution inspired great hope. The Diet of the German Confederation gave its authority to the decisions of the preliminary parliament (*Vorparliament*). The Frankfurt Parliament, however, is often saddled with the failure of German liberalism in 1848. It has been described as little more than a talking-shop, where lawyers and Heidelberg professors indulged in utopian discussions but actually achieved very little. Frederick Engels was particularly frustrated by the academic-style debates in Frankfurt which he dubbed 'parliamentary cretinism'.[15] In fact, out of 812 representatives in Frankfurt enumerated by Siemann, 53.7 per cent were public servants, judges or local government officials, and another 18.3 per cent were lawyers, doctors or writers.[16] This was certainly a learned gathering, as the election of Professor Moritz Arndt and the former *Burschenschaftler* von Gagern as its first two presidents demonstrated. The lower classes were represented by just four craftsmen. The parliament elaborated the *Grundrechte* – a declaration of the Fundamental Rights of the

German People. In the new Germany, liberal freedoms and the protection of private property would be guaranteed. There would be an independent judiciary, the equality of all religions and Jewish emancipation. This abortive but well-intentioned document offered guidelines for constitutions in all German states.

This was the outcome of fervent debates generated by the Revolution, about universal suffrage, republicanism, the right to work and the need for a progressive income tax (but the *Grundrechte* did not recognize the last three of these). Like France, revolutionary Germany experienced a media explosion. There were over 400 newspapers in Prussia alone in 1847, and 622 in 1849.[17] Marx's *Neue Rheinische Zeitung* appeared six times per week with a print-run of 5000 copies. The political press was read aloud and discussed in taverns and coffee-houses. Political clubs mushroomed: there were nearly 400 of them in the Rhineland.[18] There was a flood of petitioning activity: the Frankfurt Parliament received 17,000 of them.[19] In April, a revolutionary uprising was suppressed in Baden. In this atmosphere of feverish activity, all classes of German society were learning to be a democratic society.

Much of the criticism of liberal inertia in Frankfurt is unfair. The Frankfurt Parliament had very few realistic options. Essentially, it had little executive power. It could not create a unified Germany by force, because it had very little at its disposal. The Central Power commanded only the former forces of the German Confederation, which were used mainly to repress the democratic movement in Saxony and Frankfurt itself. It relied on the goodwill of existing German governments, who were not prepared to abdicate a part of their sovereignty. Nevertheless, the Frankfurt Parliament tried to co-opt them. In March 1849, it eventually offered the imperial crown of Germany to Frederick William of Prussia, but the king believed his authority was God-given and he had no intention of accepting such a title at the hands of a mere parliamentary assembly. Privately he called the Frankfurt Parliament a *Sauparlament* (a parliament of pigs).[20] The Frankfurt Assembly hoped for a 'Velvet Revolution', but the German princes would not give it to them. Frankfurt, wrote Engels, was always the parliament of an imaginary country.[21]

The notion of a united Germany posed insuperable problems. If the new national state was to be based on the territory of the German Confederation, difficult questions would have to be answered about the German population of Poland and the Czech lands. The Polish population of Poznan posed another problem in the definition of a culturally homogeneous Germany. Neither the Poles nor the Czechs wished fully to endorse the Germanizing projects of the Frankfurt Parliament. This is not to forget the issue of German-speaking Austria: culturally there was a certain logic in

including Austria (the *Grossdeutsch* or Greater German alternative), but politically it was not a practical proposition. The Frankfurt Parliament invited
Archduke John of Austria to act as 'Reich administrator', but a German
state including Austria was an impossible dream as long as Austria was the
heartland of the enormous Habsburg Empire, and 80 per cent of Habsburg
subjects were non-Germans. The more pragmatic *Kleindeutsch* or Little
German solution eventually prevailed, when the King of Prussia was
elected Emperor in 1849.

The historian Brian Vick has clearly summarized what was at stake in
the arguments between a Little and a Greater Germany.[22] The *Kleindeutsch*
solution would produce a Germany dominated by Prussia and the Prussian
model of a centralized state under Protestant leadership. The Catholic
states of southern Germany were reluctant to endorse this vision. The
*Grossdeutsch* alternative would produce a much less homogeneous state in
cultural and religious terms. It promised a loose federal structure with some
recognition of its Catholic population. This version embodied a more flexible interpretation of German citizenship, but it was hardly acceptable to
Prussia.

Relations between the middle-class liberals in Frankfurt, and the lower
classes, both urban artisans and peasants, were also problematic. The
liberal nationalists of 1848 were generally members of the propertied and
professional middle classes and were afraid of a social revolution. They
could hardly ignore, however, the level of political agitation which 1848
had engendered. According to Sperber, over one million Germans joined a
political club in the 1848 revolution, and 25,000 workers converged on the
Frankfurt Parliament in spring 1848 to protest their grievances.[23] Yet the
Assembly failed to harness the anger of peasant violence or of starving
unemployed artisans, and offered no programme of social reform. Artisans
demanded shorter hours, a minimum wage and a stronger defence of the
guild system, but these aims seemed in conflict with economic liberalism.
When pushed by popular insurrections in May 1849 to make concessions
to the lower classes, the liberals turned to the established authorities to
restore order and protect property. As a consequence, the revolution failed.
Aristocrats like Otto von Bismarck could mobilize the peasants on their
own estates against the liberals, and Karl Marx accused the German bourgeoisie of being gutless revolutionaries. In his view, only an appeal to the
people could have overthrown existing rulers and implemented the
Frankfurt programme, but this was a step which the liberals were not
prepared to contemplate.

Karl Marx's analysis of the inherent timidity of the German bourgeoisie
has come under heavy fire recently, even from historians with left-wing

sympathies. Pogge von Strandmann has argued on the basis of his study of Mecklenberg that the German revolutions of 1848 were far more varied than Marx's one-dimensional view might suggest.[24] He indicates that changing local coalitions between landowners, peasants and artisans make a generalized class analysis unworkable. David Blackbourn and Geoff Eley take a long-term perspective to argue that German history should not be judged on the basis of what *ought* to have happened in 1848.[25] They challenge the tendency to measure German liberalism against the yardstick of the British or the French liberal bourgeoisie. It is illogical to consider the British or French transitions to bourgeois society as normal and orthodox, while regarding German liberalism as in contrast stunted, flawed and aberrant. In the later nineteenth century, there was a 'silent bourgeois revolution' in Germany, which was not, however, accompanied by a bourgeois takeover of the state. These two radical British historians are not merely presenting a critique of Marx; they are also refuting A. J. P. Taylor's notion that Germany took the wrong path in 1848, – 'a turning-point which German history failed to turn'.[26] Taylor's now-discredited interpretation was formulated in the immediate aftermath of Hitler's Third Reich, and it misleadingly implies there is a 'correct' route for every nation to take.

The Frankfurt Parliament, for all its hesitancy, was very belligerent towards its neighbours, feeling that a war of liberation would help to unite Germany. Some envisaged a conflict between Germanic and Slav cultures as something inevitable and possibly deadly. Wilhelm Jordan's dismissal of the Poles as no more than 'charming mazurka dancers' was relatively benign; but others spoke of a possible war of extermination in Central Europe between progressive Germany and the menacing Slavic millions.[27] The main enemy for liberals was reactionary Russia, but their war against the Tsar was merely rhetorical. A real war began against a rather different opponent – Denmark – over the Danish annexation of Schleswig. The Schleswig war was conducted in the name of Germany as a whole, but inevitably it was effectively fought by the army of Prussia. Once the Prussians, pressed by Britain to withdraw, decided that little more was to be gained from the conflict, they unilaterally signed an armistice with the Danes at Malmö in September 1848. The Frankfurt Parliament was absolutely powerless to do anything about this. It voted to reject the armistice but, bowing to Prussian power and international diplomatic pressure, it changed its mind. Radical protests shook the city, but the Left was defeated.

The autumn of 1848 was a turning-point in the Revolution. Everywhere in Europe the fires of revolution seemed to be going out, although they still burned on in Hungary, Rome and Venice. The defeat of the Viennese

Revolution of October 1848 further assisted the recovery of monarchical counter-revolution. In December, the king dissolved the Prussian National Assembly and introduced his own constitution. In Germany, however, another phase of radicalization emerged. In 1849, there were attempts to win acceptance for the Frankfurt constitution, which Jonathan Sperber and others have seen as a 'second revolution'. There were insurrections in Dusseldorf and the Palatinate, but Prussian troops crushed them. In the southwest, the democratic left enjoyed popular support, but it lacked the organization and the means to challenge the armies of the conservative powers.

The Frankfurt Parliament presided over an unprecedented political experience, which mobilized sections of society embarking on their democratic apprenticeship for the first time. Yet its national project was defeated by Prussian power and the inherent contradictions within its own ambitions. Subsequent events were to show that the liberal nationalists of 1848 were quite prepared to abandon their liberalism for the sake of national unity. The idea of a liberal-parliamentary Germany was defeated, but democracy would be sacrificed to unify Germany. Bismarck was to take over their nationalist programme, and achieved it by other means – not by democracy, but by force.

## The Revolutions of 1848 in the Habsburg Empire

In 1989, another wave of Central European revolutions aspired to German unity and self-determination for national groups. Unlike the communist regimes of the 1980s, however, the Habsburg Empire was not on the verge of dissolution. The Habsburg monarchy was a vast ethnic patchwork, a multi-racial state which was especially vulnerable to the explosion of nationalism which occurred in 1848. It was held together by its dynasty, by its army, and by the fear in the minds of many smaller national groups that without the Empire, they would be crushed by Germans or Hungarians. In 1848, national movements erupted, then competed with each other, and were finally picked off one by one by the Habsburg forces.

The crisis and harvest failures of 1847 created widespread suffering. Near Salzburg, people were reduced to making bread with clover. One-third of the population of Linz was destitute, and in Bohemia factories were going bankrupt.[28] In March 1848, a liberal revolution broke out in Vienna itself and Metternich, now 73 and going deaf, immediately fled, perhaps sensing the arrival of the catastrophe he had struggled to avoid. As one story has it, he later crossed paths with ex-French leader Guizot on the steps of

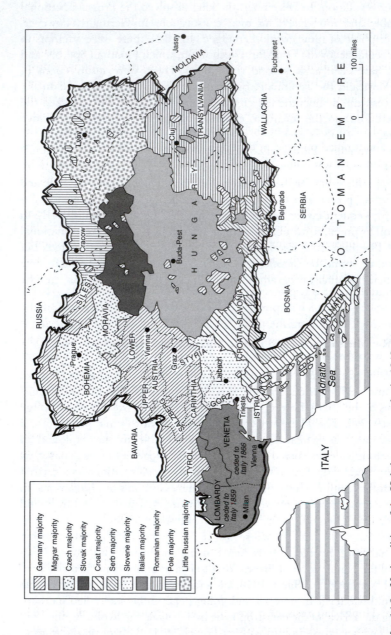

*Map 14.2* Nationalities of the Habsburg monarchy in 1848

*Source:* Random House, reprinted from Robin Okey, *Eastern Europe, 1740–1980: Feudalism to Communism*, London (Hutchinson), 1982.

the British Museum: the arch-conservative and the bourgeois parliamentarian were very different victims of the 1848 Revolutions.[29] Vienna had the most articulate and substantial bourgeoisie of any imperial city, together with thousands of handicraft workers who faced unemployment. Censorship was abolished and a middle-class National Guard was formed, including an 'Academic Legion' of students, to prevent the looting of property. As in Paris, a 10-hour day and schemes for unemployment relief were introduced in Vienna, but then withdrawn, which alienated the working class. In May, universal male suffrage was proclaimed. The Emperor retreated to Innsbruck, but the monarchy never lost the support of the army, and it relied on peasant backing, too. With these powerful resources at its command, it was able to crush the Viennese radicals in October 1848. The 18-year-old Franz Josef then replaced the feeble Ferdinand as Emperor.

In Prague, a movement for Czech independence demanded a free press, religious freedom and equality for the Czech and German languages. The Czech revolutionaries generally saw the autonomy they desired as something achievable within the framework of the Habsburg Empire. The Czechs feared being swallowed up within a greater Germany, and they preferred the relatively protective umbrella of Austria. This was the basis of Austro-Slavism, which expressed the common interest of Slavs and the Empire itself in limiting the power of the dominant races – the Germans and the Magyars. Unfortunately for the Czechs, the Habsburg monarchy was slow to recognize this concept, because it was reluctant to antagonize its German elite. The Czech nationalist Palacký boycotted the Frankfurt Parliament, and instead summoned a vast Slav Congress which assembled in Prague. The Congress divided itself into a Czech and Slovak section, a southern Slav section and a Polish-Ukrainian section. The majority of participants were intellectuals and professionals, and several had held positions in the Habsburg bureaucracy. Unfortunately the Poles and Ukrainians wrangled for so long with each other over protocol that they never actually got as far as the agenda.[30] Palacký did succeed in drafting his *Manifesto to the Nations of Europe*, which asserted the claims of Slav nationality, and proposed a federation of equal nationalities within the Habsburg Empire. Radicalism and respect for the Empire sat together very uneasily here, as was pointed out by the Russian anarchist Bakunin, who attended the Congress. When in June 1848 the Austrian general Windischgrätz started to bombard the city, the Czech Revolution collapsed and the Slav Congress evaporated.

The Hungarian resistance was the most threatening of all the 1848 Revolutions. The Hungarian revolutionaries and nationalists were quite unlike the bourgeois republicans of the Parisian Revolution. Their strength lay amongst the petty landowning Magyar nobility, who ruled over a subordinate Slav peasantry. Whereas 60 per cent of the members of the parliament in Vienna were bourgeois, 74 per cent of the Budapest parliament were noblemen.[31] Unlike the Czechs who saw their future within the Habsburg Empire, the Hungarians, under their leader Lajos Kossuth, demanded political independence from the predominantly German administration in Vienna. They wanted their own autonomous parliament, their own army and their own system of taxation. They indeed obtained their own Diet, with suffrage based on a property qualification and the ability to speak Magyar. About one in four adult males were entitled to vote, but over 70 per cent of those elected to it were Magyar landlords.[32] Croatians, Serbs and Slovaks enjoyed second-class status in an independent Hungary. Their demands for national autonomy were regarded as treasonous in Budapest.

In 1849, the Hungarian Revolution declared independence from Viennese rule, strengthened by Kossuth's decision to grant peasant emancipation with compensation for landlords. In fact the majority of peasants in Hungary would be freed without land, but such a concession to the rural masses was rare for the nationalist and constitutionalist revolutionaries of 1848. The Habsburg monarchy, however, rallied. The Emperor, too, had granted peasant emancipation in the Austrian lands, and in so doing he ensured peasant loyalty to the regime. Peasants voted too, and made up a quarter of the membership of the Viennese parliament. They won much more generous terms from the Habsburgs than did the Prussian peasants after 1807 or the Russians in 1861.

As one by one the Czech, Viennese and Italian Revolutions were defeated by force, the Empire could commit more of its troops to the struggle against Hungary. The Habsburgs had another card up their sleeve: they called on the subject races to resist Magyar domination. The Croatian nationalist movement saw Hungary as its oppressor and for them loyalty to Austria was likely to pay dividends. The Governor of Croatia, Josip Jelačić, an aristocrat and supporter of the Illyrian cause, led an army against the Magyars. He did so without authorization and, according to the historian Alan Sked, ruined the chance of a negotiated compromise between Hungarians and Croatians.[33] Nevertheless, the Hungarians held out against Romanians and Croatians until 1849, when they faced Russian military intervention against them. The Hungarian revolution was isolated. The alliance of the conservative powers (Russia and Austria) against continental revolutions which had been forged in 1815 was clearly still operational, in spite of the overthrow of its architect Metternich. In reality the Russian army contributed little to the defeat of Kossuth. The brutal repression conducted by the Austrians under

Haynau was more effective. The Russian army had cholera and moved slowly across the countryside, like 'a witless but benevolent giant'.[34] About 50,000 Hungarians were killed in the war, and Austria suffered similar losses. The Russians lost a few hundred in combat and 11,000 to cholera. Kossuth had a haircut, took a false passport under the name of James Bloomfield and fled to Turkey.[35]

There were two main secrets of Habsburg survival in 1848. First, the clash of different nationalist movements could be exploited by the imperial government. For example, Vienna could play off the competing interests of Hungarians and Croatians against each other. Hungarians, Czechs and Italians never acted together against Vienna, although the fate of each movement depended on what happened elsewhere in the Empire. On the contrary, Austrian liberals congratulated Radetsky on the defeat of the Italians, and thanked Windischgrätz for eliminating the threat of Slav nationalism, apparently blind to the reality that these generals were sealing the fate of the Viennese Revolution too. Several groups, including Czechs, Slovaks and Croatians (though not Italians or Hungarians), relied on imperial protection against the more powerful local forces of German or Magyar domination. Second, the Empire granted peasant emancipation from labour services (*robot*) and seigneurial obligations in September 1848. This made it easier for the government to crush the Viennese and Prague revolutions. Peasant emancipation in Austria was only indirectly an achievement of 1848, rather it was used as an instrument to perpetuate dynastic rule.

## The Revolutions of 1848 in Italy

The 1848 Revolutions actually began in Sicily, where Palermo rose in January to demand home rule from Naples. Then a liberal revolution in Naples forced King Ferdinand to grant a constitution. The Neapolitan liberals made it their priority to re-integrate Sicily into a unified kingdom, and an army was sent to achieve this. The struggle against Sicily, however, allowed King Ferdinand to re-establish his authority in the capital.

Political life in Italy, as we saw in Chapter 8, had been effervescent since the election of Pius IX in 1846. The Austrian military occupation of Ferrara in the Papal States in 1847 aroused a new wave of sympathy for the Pope. The events of 1848, however, fully exposed the shallowness of Pius's so-called 'liberalism'. The 1848 Revolutions brought a torrent of constitutional concessions from Italian rulers. In Piedmont, Carlo Alberto issued his *Statuto*, which resembled the French 1830 Constitution, and inaugurated a two-chamber parliament elected on a limited franchise. At the first parliamentary elections, 74 per cent of the small electorate turned out to vote.[36] Ferdinand of Naples issued a constitution, and even the Pope granted one, but he fled Rome soon afterwards and insisted that it had been extracted from him under duress.

A Roman Republic was established under the leadership of Mazzini, who donated his salary to the hospitals and made plans to take over Church property and lease it to peasants. Censorship was abolished, and a lay judicial system was set up. But the fate of the Papacy was a matter of international and not just local concern. In 1849, Louis-Napoleon despatched a French military expedition under General Oudinot, which met spirited but hopeless resistance from a patriotic force assembled to defend Rome by Giuseppe Garibaldi, a guerrilla leader who had fought in various South American campaigns and had once been a member of Mazzini's Young Italy. His legion of young bourgeois, students and South Americans numbered over 1200. For the first time they adopted the distinctive red shirts of Garibaldi's 'Thousand'. Their bohemian appearance and general indiscipline frightened no-one. They defeated the Neapolitans but were no match for the French.

Revolutions broke out in Milan and Venice. They showed that, since 1815, the Habsburg regime had wasted its opportunity to gain the co-operation of northern Italian elites as Napoleon had done. More than that, it had made enemies of them by 1848. In Lombardy, radicals had organized a tobacco boycott to protest against the Austrian tobacco monopoly, and cigar smokers were challenged in the streets of Milan. Militants drew a direct parallel with the American boycott of English tea before the war of American Independence.[37] Indirect taxation and conscription were resented. Austrian police measures escalated, regulating the Milan carnival, clamping down on anything that resembled a street demonstration, banning subversive songs and arresting suspects. About 700 prisoners were locked up in the Castello of Milan by March 1848. Metternich continued to blame 'that bastard race of a decadent aristocracy . . . lawyers without briefs . . . literati without knowledge'.[38] In spite of the presence of Radetsky's garrison, mainly composed of Czechs, Moravian and Tyrolean troops, revolution broke out, and a popular uprising took control of the city. The insurrection of March 1848 is known as the 'Five Days' (*Cinque Giornate*) of Milan, and is one of the rare instances of direct popular involvement in defence of the national cause. More than 1600 barricades spontaneously appeared, and the Milanese grabbed any weapons that came to hand, including lances and swords which were props at La Scala opera house.[39] The rising expressed the Milanese hatred of Austrian rule, their opposition to Habsburg bureaucracy, censorship, conscription and indirect taxation. Radetsky evacuated the city. About 10,000 of the Italian troops in his army had deserted, and he did not trust the loyalty of those who remained under Austrian colours. Radetsky hoped for a 'Galician solution' – in other words he pinned his faith in a peasant uprising against Italian liberals, But he hoped in vain.[40] For a moment, the *Cinque Giornate* seemed to justify Mazzini's faith in popular insurrection.

In Venice the revolution was initially virtually bloodless. The ancient republic was revived under the leadership of Daniele Manin, an eminent lawyer and a descendant of the last Doge. Manin earned his popularity by abolishing the Austrian personal tax, and by reducing the salt tax by one-third. But there were limits to his moderate policies. He was wary of the peasant militias which formed in the hinterland, often backed by rural priests. Manin's revolution was led by wealthy landowners, who were unlikely to sympathize with peasant demands for agrarian reform. In Paul Ginsborg's interpretation, Manin failed because of the fear of arming the people common to many revolutionaries in 1848.[41] The Venetian leadership was paralysed by the danger of social revolt, and did not arm the peasants of the Veneto who might have saved their revolution.

Manin's Venice was a socially-conservative republic enjoying universal male suffrage. By insisting on the republican form of government, however, Venice took a double risk: it cut itself off from the Piedmontese monarchy's struggle against Austria, and it laid itself open to radical Mazzinian influences. Manin crushed the Mazzinian opposition, and eventually bowed to the majority's preference for a merger with the kingdom of Piedmont. This about-turn came too late to save Venice from defeat. Manin's republic faced a long siege until Venice, racked by famine and cholera, capitulated. The republican idea now seemed dead.

Any uprising for national unity implied a military confrontation with Austria. The Italian democrats were not strong enough to embark on this struggle, and the Pope could not contemplate a war against the most important Catholic power in Europe. The overthrow of Austrian domination would rely on the most powerful Italian state and the only one that was independent, namely Piedmont-Sardinia. Carlo Alberto was prepared to put himself at the head of the struggle, and invaded Lombardy. His aim was not to unite Italy, but to weaken Austria and enlarge his kingdom. At the same time, he was determined to distance himself from the republicanism which prevailed in Paris and Milan, and to prevent the democratic movement from seizing the initiative. Italy, he said, will go it alone (*Italia farà da sé*), and he personally assumed supreme command. Unfortunately the response from the rest of Italy was poor. Contingents were sent from

Tuscany and the Papal States, but not all were prepared to cross the River Po, and most were untrained volunteers. At Custozza (July 1848) and subsequently at Novara in Piedmont, Marshal Radetsky defeated the Piedmontese forces. Even after the defeat at Custozza, Carlo Alberto wanted to continue the struggle. He realized that, whatever the outcome, to do so would give Piedmont enormous prestige in nationalist circles. At Novara he threw himself into the thick of the fighting. Narciso Nada describes him as a Shakespearean figure, seeking death in battle rather than face the defeat of his projects.[42] His companions were blown to pieces, but Carlo Alberto survived. He abdicated, but left one important legacy – his *Statuto* which would eventually provide the institutional framework for a united Italy. It was clear, however, that Carlo Alberto's slogan represented a bankrupt policy. The lesson for Italian patriots was that Italy could do very little on its own: next time it needed help from outside, and this would come from Austria's rivals, the French.

The Italian revolutions of 1848 had created an opportunity for unity against Austrian domination. Lombardy, Venetia, Parma and Modena all voted for a merger with Piedmont, but this new enlarged state barely lasted a month. The sad reality was that Italians were deeply disunited. The Palermo uprising had no national vision. Neapolitan liberals had fought against Sicilian separatism. Revolutionary leaders like Cattaneo in Milan and Manin in Venice were very reluctant to throw in their hand with Piedmont. At the same time, Carlo Alberto would not be dictated to by Mazzinian radicals or the republicans of Milan. Neither the Milanese nor the Piedmontese came to the assistance of Venice under siege. There was perhaps an even more fundamental rift between the bourgeois leadership and their allies amongst the urban artisans on one hand, and the peasantry on the other. Rural upheavals took the form of anti-fiscal agitation, arson, the occupation of the estates of the wealthy, and the traditional defence of peasants' collective rights. Either in spite of agrarian violence, or because of it, democratic forces never made meaningful contact with this restless peasant world.

Italians could take heart only from the March rising in Milan, and the contribution of Garibaldi to the national cause. Garibaldi was idolized because of his exotic and adventurous past, and his evident lack of interest in accumulating personal wealth or power. His defence of Uruguay in its war against Argentina had made him the 'invincible gringo'.[43] The defence of Rome made Mazzini and Garibaldi international heroes.[44] The myth of Garibaldi was already becoming more important than his actual achievements. Indeed, Garibaldi's retreat from Rome was just as much a part of his personal myth as the defence of Rome itself. Dodging Austrian surveillance, refused entry to towns which saw him as too dangerous to shelter, Garibaldi nevertheless escaped across the Romagna and Tuscany. *En route* near Ravenna he lost his most loyal companion and supporter, his pregnant Brazilian wife Anita Ribiero da Silva, the unsung heroine of the Italian Risorgimento.

## Conclusion and interpretations

At first, the conservative regimes had appeared to lose their nerve in the face of widespread uprisings. In any revolution, however, the role of the army is crucial, and everywhere in Europe armed force defeated the Revolutions. In contrast to the revolutions of 1989, this time soldiers did what they were told. The Prussian army ultimately held the fate of the German Revolutions in its grasp. A French army overthrew the Roman Republic, and Russian troops assisted in liquidating the Hungarian movement. The multinational Austrian armies stayed united to defeat the Italian and Czech Revolutions. In fact Radetsky's army, with its Bohemian infantry, Hungarian cavalry, Austrian artillery and Italian light horse was a microcosm of the unity which the Habsburg Empire had been trying to achieve for a century. None of the established monarchies were dislodged. The Habsburg Empire survived the threat of German nationalism in 1848, and it was to survive the defeat of 1866 at the hands of Prussia. Radetsky's victories had preserved it and so made the *Grossdeutsch* solution for a united Germany unthinkable. Romantic hopes did not endure the onslaught of cold steel and cannon-fire. The intellectual fascination for the virtues of 'le peuple' gave way to the hard-headed *Realpolitik* of Napoleon III in France, Bismarck in Prussia and Cavour in Piedmont.

What then did the 1848 Revolutions achieve? They were not utter failures as some accounts suggest. In Central Europe the disappearance of serfdom was completed. Slavery had been abolished in the French Empire. France experienced universal male suffrage for the first time since a brief moment in 1793. Switzerland, Piedmont and even Prussia gained some form of constitution. Europe had begun to discuss the issue of national self-determination.

On the whole, however, the 1848 Revolutions had shown that nationalism was still weak. As we saw in Chapter 5, it was essentially a doctrine of the liberal intelligentsia and some members of the commercial classes. In Poland and Hungary, the 'nation' referred only to the nobility. The rural masses remained indifferent to it, and nationalist ideologies had no mass appeal. The forces of constitutionalism had also proved hesitant and limited. Liberalism meant extracting a constitution from an authoritarian monarchy; it did not, except for a few radicals, imply a broad-based representative democracy. Nineteenth-century liberals assumed that political rights should be limited to men with property, for only they had a real stake in the country. In their view, the vote should be confined to those with enough education and leisure to think intelligently about political issues. In practice, this excluded peasants and workers. The result was that an individual with popular appeal, like Louis-Napoleon, could manipulate universal suffrage in order to defeat moderate parliamentary liberalism. In France in 1848, giving the vote to the masses produced a dictatorship, plunging liberal intellectuals into despair and disillusionment.

Between 1815 and 1848 the forces of liberal constitutionalism and nationalism had gone hand-in-hand. The outcome of 1848 suggested that revolutionaries were prepared to sacrifice their liberal ideals if they could achieve progress towards national unity. This was especially true in Germany, where liberals came round to supporting Bismarck in his pursuit of a greater Prussia.

The most significant element of the 1848 Revolutions was that they created a deeper level of politicization. All over Europe, there was an explosion of the newspaper press, of electioneering, of protest demonstrations of many kinds, of mass meetings and petitions, and of political clubs. This unprecedented political activity extended the growing public sphere outlined in Chapter 7. As Jonathan Sperber reminds us, the vote would not be as democratic as this, nor would political life be so vigorous until the early twentieth century. The 1848 Revolutions were 'an apprenticeship in democracy' with long-term consequences. In many ways they built on the democratic activism of the Revolution of 1789, but they brought this experience to almost the entire European continent.[45]

What of the peripheries which were apparently immune from the revolutionary outbreak of 1848? 'What remains standing in Europe?', Tsar Nicholas complacently asked Queen Victoria, and answered his own question – 'Britain and Russia'.[46] Why was there no revolution in Britain or Russia? In Britain, political liberalism was far from weak. It had already achieved the Parliamentary Reform Act of 1832 and the Repeal of the Corn Laws in 1846. Britain already was an established constitutional monarchy and in spite of the crisis of 1831, a revolution was not needed to secure the influential position of the liberal bourgeoisie. Furthermore, London probably had a more efficient police force in place by 1848 than did Paris or Milan. Miles Taylor argues that the Empire acted as a safety-valve for British social tensions which enabled it to survive 1848.[47] He further suggests that Britain had exported constitutional issues to the colonies, and thus *did* face a series of rebellions in 1848–50, for example in Ceylon and the Cape Colony. In Australia and New Zealand, campaigns for representative government had many echoes of 1848. Henry Parkes, radical supporter of the extension of voting rights in New South Wales, was a great admirer of Lamartine. In Russia, the situation was the opposite – the liberal bourgeoisie was far too weak to pose a threat to Tsarism. Britain, it could be argued, had already had its equivalent of 1848 in the Chartist movement. Russia would eventually have its own 1848 Revolution – but in 1905.

In terms of economic progress, the two countries were at opposite poles. Britain had passed through an industrial revolution which was and would remain unique. Russia, in contrast to Western Europe, was an overwhelmingly peasant society which did not try to industrialize until the 1890s. The 1848 Revolutions occurred in those societies gathered towards the middle of such a spectrum, in countries which were beginning to experience the consequences of economic change, the commercialization of agriculture and the advent of the railways. The resulting economic unrest was intensified in periodic crises like that of 1846–8, and it assisted the general mobilization which made the Revolutions possible.

# 15  The Crimean War and Beyond

## Politics after 1848

The failures of 1848 wrecked the hopes of many liberals and reformers, who were thrown into despair by the collapse of democracy and the popular election of Louis-Napoleon. The Russian exile Alexander Herzen, for example, felt bitter anguish as he witnessed the triumph of reactionary forces all over Europe. 'With profound sorrow', he wrote in 1856, 'I watched and recorded the success of the forces of dissolution and the decline of the Republic, of France, of Europe. From Russia came no gleam of light in the distance . . . Russia lay speechless, as though dead, covered with bruises, like an unfortunate peasant-woman at the feet of her master, beaten by his heavy fists.'[1] Tsar Nicholas I enforced a rigid quarantine to protect Holy Russia from contamination by Western liberal ideas. In Austria, the Kremsier Constitution of 1849 was never put into effect, and reaction returned to power under the government of Prince Schwarzenburg. In 1850 at Olmütz, Prussia and Austria agreed to revive the German Confederation and with it Metternich's repressive laws. It seemed to some observers with a historical memory that Europe was entering yet another phase of post-revolutionary restoration. For one German liberal, 1850 looked like 'a second edition of the Metternichian system, on cheaper paper and on worse type'.[2]

Yet the struggles for constitutionalism had not been totally in vain. Piedmont retained its constitution, and so did Prussia, where in 1849 the three-class voting system was established, based solely on propertied wealth. About 15 per cent of the richest voters elected two-thirds of the deputies, while the other 85 per cent of voters in Class 3 voted for the remaining third. The revolutionary impulse was exhausted, and in its wake the attention of the Great Powers turned again to international affairs.

## The Eastern Question and the Crimean War, 1853–1856

In 1815, the European statesmen who designed the peace of Vienna had found no long-term solution to the Eastern Question. They had been too focused on the Rhine, the Baltic and northern Italy to pay serious attention to their rivalries in the East. As a result, the chronic vulnerability of the Ottoman Empire posed security problems in the Balkans and eastern Mediterranean, and provided an opportunity for Russia to extend her influence. Instability in the Ottoman Empire plagued international relations during the 1830s and 1840s, and growing Russian hegemony in the region haunted governments in Western and Central Europe. In 1853, a prolonged and inconclusive diplomatic crisis eventually drifted into the Crimean War, which threw long-standing tensions into stark relief. Apart from minor confrontations in the Baltic and Kamchatka, most of the fighting was confined to the tiny Crimean peninsula on the northern coast of the Black Sea (see Map 15.1). This was the most serious international conflict since 1815. It had important consequences for the pattern of international relations which had emerged in post-revolutionary Europe: Russia and Austria became estranged, while Britain and France became allies. In this sense, what appeared to be a minor war over trivial issues marked the end of Europe's post-revolutionary era.

The Great Powers could not ignore the Eastern Question in the 1830s and 1840s, because the Ottoman Empire was regularly shaken by revolts like the War of Greek Independence, and by power struggles between the Sultan in Constantinople and local pashas in the far-flung regions of his Empire. Local rulers owed the Sultan allegiance, but were able to pursue their own military ambitions within a very loose imperial framework. The most threatening local ruler from the Sultan's point of view was the Pasha of Egypt, Mohammed Ali, also known as Mehmet Ali, and his son Ibrahim. A new force was rising in the region: a professional army had been created in Egypt, supported by schools, cannon foundries and the arsenal of Alexandria. Mehmet, encouraged by the French, introduced modernizing reforms including the establishment of a printing house, although he himself was illiterate. Choosing his name is significant for how we interpret his importance. Egyptian nationalists know him as Mohammed Ali, claiming him as one of the founders of modern Egypt, who only failed to set up an independent state because of British opposition. But this view is anachronistic. Mehmet, to use his Turkish name, was not a modern nationalist but rather a chieftain with essentially dynastic aims which he pursued within a traditional Ottoman framework. The Egyptian peasantry themselves paid the price of his extravagant ambitions.

In 1831, Mehmet's son Ibrahim seized Syria, and defeated the Sultan's army at Konya in central Turkey. At Unkiar-Skelessi in 1833, the Sultan signed an eight-year defensive alliance with Russia, which agreed to shore up the failing Empire in return for a Turkish agreement to close the 'Straits'

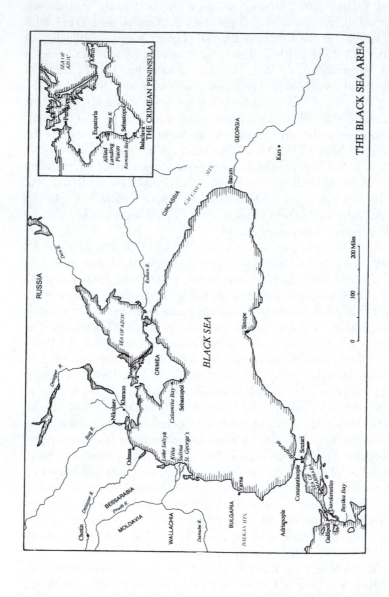

*Map 15.1* The Black Sea area in the Crimean War

*Source:* University Press of New England, reprinted from Norman Rich, *Why the Crimean War? A Cautionary Tale*, London (New England UP), 1985.

(the entrance to the Black Sea) to all foreign warships. Russian troops appeared in Constantinople – an alarming development for the Western powers. But Egypt remained a threat. In 1838 Mehmet Ali defied Sultan Mahmud by declaring Egypt and Syria independent. In 1839, Ibrahim again defeated the Turkish army, the Sultan died and the Ottoman fleet defected to the Egyptians. At the Straits Convention of 1841, not only Russia, but all the Great Powers imposed peace, giving Mehmet Ali hereditary rule in Egypt, and allowing Ibrahim to govern southern Syria for his own lifetime. After a revolt in Lebanon against Mehmet was crushed by British, Turkish and Austrian forces, Mehmet and Ibrahim lost their Syrian conquests.

The Straits Convention was a humiliating defeat for the French, who had commercial interests in Egypt and had supported Mehmet Ali but ultimately were not prepared to go to war for him. Britain and Russia had implicitly agreed that, at least for the time being, preserving the Ottoman Empire was a lesser evil than allowing it to crumble. So the Western powers remained divided, to the benefit of Russia which won international acceptance for the closure of the Straits. Although the Ottoman Empire had been rescued, the problem of Turkish weakness was unresolved and fears of Russian encroachment persisted.

The Crimean War began with trivial quarrels between French Catholics and Russian Orthodox clergy over the custody of Christian sanctuaries in Palestine. Napoleon III, eager to consolidate the Catholic vote in France, demanded protection for the Christian sites of Jerusalem and posed as the protector of Catholic monks there. The Great Powers had always used such transparent pretexts to justify their political interference in the Ottoman Empire. At the same time, Russia claimed to protect the interests of 12 million Orthodox Christian subjects of the Sultan. Behind this posturing lay more substantial national interests. For Napoleon III, France's interests lay in breaking up the alliance of conservative powers which had organized the peace of 1815. For Russia, there were both economic and strategic interests at stake. The Straits were an important outlet for Ukrainian grain exports, and it was vital that control of this channel did not pass into hostile hands. Maintaining Turkey in a dependent relationship seemed the best means of extending Russian hegemony in the region.

Britain, like Russia, had interests beyond Europe itself. Britain and Russia were likely to collide in many different theatres, from the Baltic and the Mediterranean to Afghanistan and Central Asia. British commercial interests favoured the preservation of the Ottoman Empire: the value of British exports to Turkey rose from £1 million in 1825 to about £8.5 million on the eve of war, while the Danubian Principalities had overtaken

Russia itself as Britain's most prolific source of imported grain.[3] Russia, however, controlled the mouth of the Danube, and so could obstruct grain exports from the principalities, giving Russian Black Sea ports a commercial advantage.[4] An independent Turkey would improve Britain's security in the eastern Mediterranean, and a stable Near East would guarantee Britain's precious land route to India, although Russia never seriously threatened it. The British feared that Tsar Nicholas planned to dismember the Ottoman Empire, and they sought to counter Russian influence by any means. In the Crimea, the means were, by British standards, unorthodox. They included defending a barbaric and declining Moslem Empire, and forming an alliance with a descendant of their ancestral foe, Napoleon Bonaparte. But the violent Russophobia of the English public overcame all national inhibitions, and fuelled Palmerston's confrontational style of diplomacy. According to Paul Schroeder's assessment, the global balance of power at this historical moment rested on a bipolar confrontation between Britain and Russia.[5] The Turks' only hope of influencing events lay in playing Russia off against the Western powers. In Constantinople, British ambassador Redcliffe urged the Turks to reject Russia's demands for privileges and immunities for Christians. Turkish religious leaders denounced all concessions to the Christians and called for a Holy War.

Russia was thus isolated, but the key would be the attitude of Austria. Austria did not want any conflict to spill over into the Balkans, as happened when a revolt against the Turks erupted in Montenegro in 1852. Any Balkan war might endanger the integrity of the Habsburg Empire, as it was to do in the years before 1914. Austria had collaborated closely with Russia since the Napoleonic wars, but now declared its neutrality. Fear of Russian expansion, which had always made Metternich anxious, got the better of all other reflexes. Schroeder argued that Austria pursued a sensible peace policy, which was frustrated by the belligerence of Britain and France. But Austria's 'neutrality' antagonized both Russia and the Western powers.[6]

When the Turks rejected Russia's demands in 1853, the Tsar occupied the Danubian Principalities, assuming Austrian support which was not forthcoming. Nicholas envisaged that Christian uprisings against Turkey would follow, but a series of Balkan revolutions was exactly what Austria wanted to avoid.[7] Eventually, in 1854, Austria secured a Russian withdrawal from the Principalities, and the Austrians themselves marched into Bucharest. By this time, the Western powers were already at war with Russia. When, in 1853, the Russian fleet destroyed a Turkish squadron at Sinope, the British and French entered the Black Sea. Their attack centred on the Russian naval base of Sebastopol in the Crimea.

The Allies fought inconclusive engagements at the Alma, Balaclava and

Inkerman, which were celebrated as victories in street names all over the British Empire. Ironclad warships made their first appearance. On land, the struggle became the first trench war in modern history. Sebastopol fell only after a year-long siege. Guns with rifled barrels gave the Western powers greater shooting range than the Russians' smooth-bore weapons, allowing them to force victory against two million mobilized Russians. In fact most of the Russian army was elsewhere, guarding against possible uprisings in Poland or Finland which never eventuated. In the Crimea, the battlefield was not always the most dangerous place to be. Men dropped like flies without ever engaging the enemy. Baumgart estimates that about 640,000 soldiers and sailors died in the war, about 80 per cent of them from disease or infected wounds.[8] Florence Nightingale's contribution to improved conditions in British military hospitals was remarkable, but it only took effect in 1855. The war exposed the incompetence of all European armies, staffed by aristocrats whose main qualifications for high rank were family connections or the ability to buy their position. About three-quarters of the entire British officer corps had attained their position by purchasing their rank, a system not fully abolished until 1871.[9] While the British navy successfully controlled the Black Sea, the army was led by bickering aristocrats, who had plenty of courage but showed a bewildering lack of professional expertise and good sense. They included the quarrelsome Lord Cardigan, who turned up for the war in his private yacht, to which he withdrew after becoming a national hero in the suicidal Charge of the Light Brigade. Lord Raglan had lost an arm at Waterloo, but he had not fought for 40 years and had never commanded an army in the field. The media attacked him mercilessly; this was the first modern war to be reported and photographed by war correspondents (see Plates 14 and 15). Raglan died of cholera in 1855.

In the Peace of Paris in 1856, the Turkish Sultan agreed to recognize the civil rights of non-Moslems, while the Black Sea was demilitarized and became freely accessible. Russia lost her control over the Danubian Principalities, and was forced to give up some territory in Bessarabia to Moldavia (which she regained in 1878). Russia thus lost control over the mouth of the Danube. Russia's credibility as a first-rank military power was thrown into question. Without a railway line to the Crimea, her supplies were very slow to reach the front. There were local peasant revolts against the call-up, often inspired by rumours of imminent serf liberation.[10] Tsar Alexander II succeeded Nicholas I in 1855, and presided over a period of introspection and domestic reform, which led to the serf emancipation edict of 1861. 'Russia is not sulking', said Russian diplomat Prince Gorchakov in 1856, 'she is gathering her strength (*elle se recueille*).'

*Plate 14*   Fenton, 'La Cantinière' at the Crimea. The French army's canteen-
women were reportedly very popular with troops of all nationalities in the
Crimean War

*Source*:   Photo by Roger Fenton, 1855, Gernsheim Collection, Harry Ransom Humanities
Research Center, University of Texas at Austin.

*Plate 15* Crimean war wounded inspected by Queen Victoria at Chatham, 1855. Of these two British soldiers, one had a head wound, the other lost a leg in the Crimea. The photo, with a description of their wounds, went into the queen's private Crimean War photo album

*Source*: Photo of Thomas Walker and Joseph Conolly, by Howlett and Cundall, 1855, from Royal Archives, Windsor, in the Imperial War Museum, London.

The Russian retreat from European affairs had important consequences. The alliance of conservative powers which had emerged from the coalition against Napoleon after 1813 was now in ruins. Austria's pro-Western 'neutrality' in the Crimean War had transformed the Russo–Austrian alliance which only a few years previously had brought Tsarist troops into

Hungary to suppress the 1848 Revolution. Austria's only firm ally was now Prussia, which had not been involved in the Crimean War. With the demise of the Concert of Europe and in particular of the Holy Alliance, the international climate grew much more favourable to nationalist movements. An independent Romania became conceivable after 1859 when the Danubian Principalities elected a single ruler, and Italy was unified in 1861. The Crimea created a new European constellation in which some nationalist movements found the international support which allowed them to succeed. As David Goldfrank suggests, the Crimean War, rather than the 1848 Revolutions, was the real 'springtime of the peoples'.[11] The post-revolutionary system which had organized Europe since 1815 had collapsed.

## Conclusion: 1856 as a turning-point

It is much harder to identify the end of post-revolutionary Europe than its beginning. The period surveyed by this book began very clearly in 1814–15 with the defeat of Napoleon, the Restoration of the Bourbons and the Peace of Vienna. In contrast, many logical closing dates are possible. In France, the seizure of power by Louis-Napoleon in 1851, followed by the inauguration of the Second Empire, form a natural break. In Russia, the serf emancipation of 1861 broke with centuries of feudalism and turned Tsarism into a reforming monarchy. In Italy, the crisis of 1860–1 brought about unification. All these are turning-points in the history of individual nations, but the Crimean War was an influential moment for Europe as a whole. It brought to an end the system of international relations set up at Vienna in 1815. That system had attempted to prevent future French aggression, but in 1859 nothing stopped Napoleon III from going to war with Piedmont against Austria. The so-called Concert of Europe had, under Metternich's supervision, tried to suppress liberal and nationalist revolutionary outbreaks all over Europe. Although 1848 had shown the bankruptcy of this policy, the alliance of the conservative powers (Austria, Prussia and Russia) emerged intact. After the Crimean War, this was no longer the case. Within 15 years, new nation-states had been created in both Italy and Germany. The Crimea had also underlined one great omission of the Treaty of Vienna in 1815 – its failure to resolve the 'Eastern Question'. Instability in the Balkans would continue to worry European statesmen in the second half of the century, and here lay the seeds of the First World War.

Four principal themes run through the history of post-revolutionary Europe. First, I have suggested some parallels and contrasts between the rupture of 1815 and the Revolutions of 1989–91. The fall of the French Empire, like the fall of Soviet hegemony, ushered in a period of turbulence and transition, although in each case the process of transition was contested and it was not immediately clear where the transition was actually leading. 1815 and 1989 both produced a world dominated by a single super-power – the United States of America in 1989, and Great Britain in 1815 which now found new markets opening up for her manufactured goods. Neither of these great changes could wipe the slate entirely clean. They left behind them memories and nostalgias which reverberated through the following decades. In France in particular, every regime faced the problem of remembering and forgetting the revolutionary past.

Second, this period was not simply a Restoration of old regimes and old elites. Like other contemporary historians, I have underlined continuities with the revolutionary and Napoleonic decades.[12] In France, the returning Bourbons adopted many of the Napoleonic reforms which had enormously strengthened the French state. Elsewhere in Europe, rulers selectively retained many innovations of French imperial rule. This is one reason why the 'Restoration' is an inadequate label for Europe after 1815, and why I have preferred to describe it as 'Post-revolutionary Europe'.

The title 'Restoration and reaction' gives a very negative view of the decades after 1815. A third recurrent theme of this book has been a more positive development: the appearance of new forms of democratic politics. The expansion of the newspaper press was fundamental to this, but voting, petitioning, demonstrating, joining clubs and supporting causes like the abolition of slavery all indicated a broad process of politicization. Without the rise of the public sphere in which political ideas could be debated, the revolutionary outbreak of 1848 would be inconceivable.

On the other hand, modern nationalism was in a very embryonic stage. Avoiding the anachronistic tendency to read strong national movements back into the past from a vantage-point in the 1890s, my fourth concern has been to demonstrate the fragility of nationalism. In the early nineteenth century, nationalism involved small intellectual groups with little influence, and had nothing to offer the masses. In the light of this, Metternich's refusal to accommodate national aspirations becomes more understandable. Nationalist ideas did not threaten the stability of Europe until they became mass movements, and this was a development of the 1890s rather than of 1848.

In the 1850s, the post-revolutionary era was over. The European economy enjoyed a boom. After the hardships of the 1840s, prosperity returned, and so did a relatively stable political and social climate. Even rebellious Britain entered a period of mid-Victorian calm and 'equipoise'.

Everywhere in Europe, the old monarchies seemed resurgent in the second half of the century. Buoyed by economic recovery, they now tried to make emerging forms of mass politics work in their favour. An age of nationalism and industrialization would follow, in which dynasties and traditional landed elites mobilized mass support to perpetuate their domination.

## Afterword – Europe overseas

Europe was rapidly extending its powerful presence in other parts of the globe. The British Empire in Africa, the Cape Colony, India, Canada, Australia and New Zealand is the most spectacular example of Europe's growing world domination. In 1819, Stamford Raffles founded Singapore. In 1858, the British government formally took over the administration of India from the East India Company. Between 1815 and the 1860s, more than seven million emigrants left the British Isles, mainly for North America and Australia where the discovery of gold attracted tens of thousands of hopefuls.[13] In Canada, Australia, New Zealand and the Cape, the imperial relationship was transformed to incorporate new forms of representative government. Investors, migrants and missionaries were reshaping the world beyond Europe.

In the Napoleonic Wars and the 1820s, Britain's informal empire expanded further into South America. This was the age of the great liberators, as Simon Bolivar established greater Colombia (comprising modern Colombia, Venezuela and Equador), San Martin founded the Argentine Republic and Bernardo O'Higgins created independent Chile. Peru and Mexico also became independent of Spanish rule. In 1808, the Portuguese monarchy, transplanted to Rio de Janeiro, opened up Brazilian ports to international trade, so that all of South America was available to British commerce. 'Spanish America is free', pronounced British Prime Minister George Canning in 1824, 'and if we do not mismanage our matters sadly, she is English.' Canning gave official British recognition to the new republics of Mexico, Argentina and Colombia and to independent Brazil. By 1827, British trade with Latin America was worth four times as much as US trade with the region.[14]

Brazil came under constant pressure from Britain in the post-Napoleonic era to abolish the slave trade. Brazil was the major destination for the African slave traffic: between 1811 and 1870, it absorbed over 60 per cent of all African slaves sent to the Americas.[15] Local traders and landowners, however, as well as the Brazilian government, argued that imported slave labour was essential for the agricultural development of

Brazil's vast interior. Indeed, British demand itself helped to stimulate the production of coffee, cotton and sugar by slave labour. At the Congress of Vienna, Britain and Portugal had agreed to end the slave trade north of the Equator, and in 1830, legislation suspended the entry of slaves into Brazil. None of this managed to interrupt the illegal entry of slaves. Just as the United States, today's super-power, attempts to stifle the international drug traffic, so in the early nineteenth century, Britain assumed the role of stamping out slavery. Brazil did abolish the slave trade in 1850, and slavery itself in 1888. But in the first half of the century, about 1.6 million African slaves arrived in Brazil.[16]

Europe imposed its power in the Far East, where British and Indian forces compelled the Chinese Empire to accept the sale of opium in exchange for tea and other produce. Opium sales were a mere detail in the effort to extend European trade and imperialism into China. In 1842, Britain acquired the lease to Hong Kong, and Shanghai was also opened to foreign commerce. The result of the so-called first 'Opium War' of 1839–42 was to open China up to economic exploitation by all the European powers.

In 1830, the French invaded Algeria, following a petty diplomatic quarrel and a long naval blockade, ostensibly designed to protect European shipping from North African piracy on the high seas (the 'Barbary pirates'). The government of Charles X, however, was looking for a military success which would boost its electoral fortunes. It failed to achieve this, and after the 1830 Revolution, the July Monarchy was left facing the consequences. After a period of hesitancy and incoherence, France decided in 1834 to perpetuate its tenuous colonial presence and appointed a Governor-General. It began a slow and difficult period of settlement. By 1846, the European population of Algeria had risen to over 100,000, the majority of them not French but mainly Spanish, Maltese or Neapolitan settlers.[17] Communal systems of land tenure were dismantled, while native farmers were expropriated and forced to work as day-labourers for the struggling colonists.

European settlement was largely confined to the coast and the Sahel (west of Algiers). In the interior, it was a different story. In the Oran region, the charismatic Emir Abd el-Kader led a classic armed struggle against the Christian invader, which developed into a full-scale war in 1839. French expropriations of peasant land, the thoughtless destruction of Moslem cemeteries, and the conversion of mosques into barracks or Catholic churches strengthened local resistance. Abd el-Kader tried, unsuccessfully in the end, to unite Arab and Berber forces in a common cause. In areas he controlled, he governed according to the principles of the Koran. He banned wine, tobacco and prostitution. He imposed a boycott of imported European goods. He lived frugally: when harvests were poor, he took nothing but milk for days on end. By 1846, over 100,000 troops had been mobilized to defeat him – over one-third of the entire French army.[18] Marshal Bugeaud's scorched-earth tactics, involving the destruction of crops, olive groves and orchards and the slaughtering of entire villages, eventually forced Abd el-Kader's surrender in 1847. After living through the 1848 Revolution in French prisons, he was permitted to live in exile in Damascus.

Hand-in-hand with armed conquest went scientific investigation. Missions of cartographers, anthropologists, botanists and architects followed in the wake of the military, just as they had accompanied Bonaparte's expedition to Egypt in 1798. A French expedition 'discovered' the Peloponnese in the aftermath of the Greek War of Independence, and another scientific mission went to North Africa in 1839. Intellectuals helped to disseminate knowledge and construct an image of the Mediterranean world. They were inspired by the rediscovery of Antiquity. In unearthing the remains of the Roman Empire in North Africa, they invited parallels between Roman and French imperialism, and suggested that the Maghreb could be integrated into Europe's cultural heritage. For better or for worse, the European powers were dominating and mapping the entire globe.

# Notes

## Introduction: rethinking post-revolutionary Europe

1. London (Collins/Fontana), 1967, translated from *De la Restauration à Révolution*.
2. André Jardin and André-Jean Tudesq, *Restoration and Reaction, 1815–1848*, translated from *La France des Notables*, Cambridge and Paris (CUP/MSH), 1983.
3. Georges Weill, *L'Eveil des nationalités et le mouvement libéral, 1815–1848*, Paris (PUF), 1960.
4. Jonathan Sperber, *The European Revolutions, 1848–51*, Cambridge (CUP), 1984, p. 54.

## Chapter 1    Endings and beginnings: Europe in 1815

1. Michael Broers, *Europe Under Napoleon, 1799–1815*, London (Arnold), 1996.
2. Marco Meriggi, 'State and Society in Post-Napoleonic Italy', in David Laven and Lucy Riall, eds, *Napoleon's Legacy: Problems of Government in Restoration Europe*, Oxford and New York (Berg), 2000, p. 50.
3. Michael Broers, *Europe After Napoleon: Revolution, Reaction and Romanticism, 1814–1848*, Manchester (Manchester UP), 1996; André Jardin and André-Jean Tudesq, *Restoration and Reaction, 1815–1848*, Cambridge and Paris (CUP and MSH), 1983. Laven and Riall, *Napoleon's Legacy* is closer to my own viewpoint.
4. Alan B. Spitzer, 'La République souterraine', in François Furet and Mona Ozouf, *Le Siècle de l'Avènement républicain*, Paris (Gallimard), 1993, pp. 345–69.
5. Karl Marx, *The 18th Brumaire of Louis Bonaparte*, Moscow (Progress), 1954, p. 10. My version.
6. Janet M. Hartley, *Alexander I*, London (Longman), 1994, pp. 116–17 and 127–8.
7. Pierre Ayçoberry, *Cologne entre Napoléon et Bismarck: la croissance d'une ville rhénane*, Paris (Aubier), 1981, pp. 67–8.

251

8. Michael John, 'The Napoleonic Legacy and the Problem of Restoration in Central Europe: The German Confederation', in Laven and Riall, *Napoleon's Legacy*, p. 85.

9. Norman Davies, *God's Playground: A History of Poland, vol. 2, 1795 to the Present*, Oxford (Clarendon Press), 1981, *passim*.

10. Hartley, *Alexander*, pp. 151–3.

11. Roy Bridge, 'Allied Diplomacy in Peacetime: The Failure of the Congress "System", 1815–23', in Alan Sked, ed., *Europe's Balance of Power, 1815–1848*, Basingstoke UK (Macmillan), 1979, pp. 48 and 52.

12. Paul W. Schroeder, *The Transformation of European Politics, 1763–1848*, Oxford (Clarendon Press), 1994, p. 577.

13. H. G. Schenk, *The Aftermath of the Napoleonic Wars: The Concert of Europe – An Experiment*, New York (OUP), 1947, p. 70.

## Chapter 2   Re-inventing the monarchy: France, 1814–1830

1. Kirsten Schultz, *Tropical Versailles: Empire, Monarchy, and the Portuguese Royal Court in Rio de Janeiro, 1808–1821*, New York (Routledge), 2001.

2. Annie Duprat, 'Une Guerre des Images: Louis XVIII, Napoléon et la France, en 1815', *Revue d'histoire moderne et contemporaine*, 47:3, 2000, pp. 490–2.

3. Philip G. Dwyer, *Talleyrand*, London (Longman), 2002, pp. 1–5.

4. Avner Ben-Amos, *Funerals, Politics and Memory in Modern France, 1789–1996*, Oxford (OUP), 2000, p. 59.

5. Edgar Leon Newman, 'Lost Illusions: The Regicides in France During the Bourbon Restoration', *Nineteenth-Century French Studies*, 19, 1981, pp. 45–74.

6. Gwynne Lewis, *The Second Vendée: The Continuity of Counter-Revolution in the Department of the Gard, 1789–1815*, Oxford (Clarendon Press), 1978.

7. Daniel Resnick, *The White Terror and the Political Reaction after Waterloo*, Cambridge, MA (HUP), 1966, p. 118.

8. Nicholas Richardson, *The French Prefectoral Corps, 1814–1830*, Cambridge (CUP), 1966, pp. 9–11 and 127.

9. David Higgs, *UltraRoyalism in Toulouse: From its Origins to the Revolution of 1830*, Baltimore (Johns Hopkins UP), 1973, pp. 1–9 and 177.

10. Jean-Clément Martin, *La Vendée de la Mémoire, 1800–1980*, Paris (Seuil), 1989, pp. 23–78.

11. Jean Fourcassié, *Villèle*, Paris (Fayard), 1954, p. 446.

12. Pascal Simonetti, 'Mourir comme un Bourbon: Louis XVIII, 1824', *Revue d'histoire moderne et contemporaine*, 42:1, 1995, pp. 91–106.

13. Richard Holroyd, 'The Bourbon Army', *Historical Journal*, 14:3, 1971, pp. 529–52.
14. Sheryl T. Kroen, *Politics and Theater: The Crisis of Legitimacy in Restoration France, 1815–1830*, Berkeley (UCP), 2000, pp. 48–54.
15. Michel Vovelle, 'La Marseillaise: la guerre ou la paix', in Pierre Nora, ed., *Les Lieux de Mémoire, vol. 1: La République*, Paris (nrf/Gallimard), 1984, pp. 105–7.
16. Guillaume de Bertier de Sauvigny, *The Bourbon Restoration*, Philadelphia (Philadephia UP), 1966, p. 308.
17. Mary S. Hartman, 'The Sacrilege Law of 1825 in France: A Study in Anticlericalism and Mythmaking', *JMH*, 44:1, 1972, pp. 21–37.
18. Martyn Lyons, 'Fires of Expiation: Book-Burnings and Catholic Missions in Restoration France', *French History*, 10:2, 1996, pp. 240–66.
19. Kroen, *Politics and Theater*, ch. 2.
20. Ibid., ch. 6.
21. Françoise Waquet, *Les Fêtes Royales sous la Restauration ou l'Ancien Régime retrouvé*, Paris (Arts et Métiers graphiques), 1981, pp. 43 and 109–30.
22. Richard A. Jackson, *Vive le Roi! A History of the French Coronation from Charles V to Charles X*, Chapel Hill (North Carolina UP), 1984, p. 198.
23. Geoffrey Cubitt, *The Jesuit Myth: Conspiracy Theory and Politics in Nineteenth-Century France*, Oxford (Clarendon Press), 1993.
24. Jo Burr Margadant, 'The Duchesse de Berry and Royalist Political Culture in Postrevolutionary France', *History Workshop Journal*, 43, 1997, pp. 23–52.
25. Sauvigny, *Bourbon Restoration*, p. 269.
26. Pierre Rosanvallon, *La Monarchie impossible: les Chartes de 1814 et de 1830*, Paris (Fayard), 1994.
27. Kroen, *Politics and Theater*, p. 201.

## Chapter 3  Conservatism and political repression, 1815–1830

1. Michael Broers, 'Sexual Politics and Political Ideology under the Savoyard Monarchy, 1814–21', *English Historical Review*, 114:457, 1999, pp. 607–35.
2. Massimo d'Azeglio, *I Miei Ricordi*, Milan (Feltrinelli), 1963, p. 119 (first published 1867).
3. Roy Bridge, 'Allied Diplomacy in Peacetime: The Failure of the Congress "System", 1815–23', in Alan Sked, ed., *Europe's Balance of Power, 1815–1848*, Basingstoke UK (Macmillan), 1979, pp. 44–5.

4. H. G. Schenk, *The Aftermath of the Napoleonic Wars: The Concert of Europe – An Experiment*, New York (OUP), 1947, p. 121.

5. Henry Kissinger, *A World Restored*, London (Gollancz), 1973, p. 249.

6. Alan Sked, 'The Metternich System, 1815–1848', in Sked, *Europe's Balance of Power*, pp. 100–7.

7. Simonetta Soldani, 'Il 1830 in Europa: Dinamica e articolazioni di una crisi generale', *Studi Storici*, 13:2, April–June 1972, p. 371 (the second of two articles in the same volume).

8. David Blackbourn, *The Long Nineteenth Century: A History of Germany, 1780–1918*, New York and Oxford (OUP), 1998, p. 123.

9. H. Hardtwig and H. Hinze, eds, *Vom Deutschen Bund zum Kaiserreich, 1815–1871, Deutsche Geschichte in Quellen und Darstellung*, bd 7, Stuttgart (Philipp Reclam), 1997, p. 69.

10. James J. Sheehan, *German History 1770–1866*, Oxford (Clarendon), 1989, p. 446.

11. Hardtwig and Hinze, *Vom Deutschen Bund zum Kaiserreich*, p. 71.

12. David Laven, *Venice and Venetia under the Habsburgs, 1815–1835*, Oxford (OUP), 2000, pp. 25–6.

13. Narciso Nada, 'Il Piemonte Sabaudo dal 1814 al 1861', in Giuseppe Galasso, ed., *Storia d'Italia*, vol. 8, pt 2, Turin (UTET), 1993, pp. 103–125.

14. Giorgio Candeloro, *Storia dell'Italia moderna, vol. 2: Dalla Restaurazione alle Rivoluzione Nazionale*, Milan (Feltrinelli), 1994, p. 42 (first published 1958).

15. Romano Paolo Coppini, 'Il Granducato di Toscana dagli "anni francesi" all'Unità', in Galasso, *Storia d'Italia*, vol. 13, pt 3, pp. 172–220.

16. Marcella Pincherle Ara, 'L'Austria di fronte alla crisi d'un ducato italiano: Parma tra Maria Luigi e Carlo II', *Rivista Storica Italiana*, 108:1, 1996, pp. 88–9.

17. Bianca Montale, *Parma nel Risorgimento: istituzioni e società (1814–1859)*, Milan (Franco Angeli), 1993, pp. 13–14.

18. Marino Berengo, *Intellettuali e librai nella Milano della Restaurazione*, Turin (Einaudi), 1980.

19. John A. Davis, 'Cultures of Interdiction: The Politics of Censorship in Italy from Napoleon to the Restoration', in David Laven and Lucy Riall, eds, *Napoleon's Legacy: Problems of Government in Restoration Europe*, Oxford (Berg, 2000), pp. 237–56.

20. Candeloro, *Storia dell'Italia moderna, vol. 2*, pp. 76–97.

21. Nada, 'Il Piemonte sabaudo', pp. 154–61.

22. Schenk, *Aftermath of the Napoleonic Wars*, pp. 140–1.

23. Josep Fontana Lazaro, *La Quiebra de la monarquía absoluta, 1814–20*, Barcelona (Editorial Ariel), 2nd edn, 1974, pp. 56–68.
24. Raymond Carr, *Spain, 1808–1975*, 2nd edn, Oxford (Clarendon Press), 1982, pp. 184–8.
25. E. P. Thompson, *The Making of the English Working Class*, Harmondsworth UK (Penguin), 1968, p. 752.
26. W. H. Zawadski, *A Man of Honour: Adam Czartoryski as a Statesman of Russia and Poland, 1795–1831*, Oxford (Clarendon Press), 1993, pp. 246–86.
27. Marc Raeff, *The Decembrist Movement*, Englewood Cliffs NJ (Prentice-Hall), 1966, p. 101.
28. Marc Raeff, *The Origins of the Russian Intelligentsia: The 18th Century Nobility*, New York (Harcourt, Brace & World), 1966.
29. Leo Tolstoy, *War and Peace*, Book 12, chs 49–50.
30. Raeff, *Decembrist Movement*, p. 3.
31. John McManners, 'Autocracy and Serfdom: Russia to 1850', in his *Lectures on European History, 1789–1914*, Oxford (Blackwell), 1966, p. 172.
32. P. S. Squire, *The Third Department*, Cambridge (CUP), 1968, pp. 95 and 161.

**Chapter 4   The underground republic: opposition movements, 1815–1848**

1. Alan B. Spitzer, 'La république souterraine' in François Furet and Mona Ozouf, *Le Siècle de l'Avènement républicain*, Paris (Gallimard), 1993, pp. 345–69.
2. Alan B. Spitzer, *The French Generation of 1820*, Princeton NJ (PUP), 1987.
3. Lenore O'Boyle, 'The Problem of an Excess of Educated Men in Western Europe, 1800–1850', *JMH*, 42, 1970, pp. 472–95.
4. H. G. Schenk, *The Aftermath of the Napoleonic Wars: The Concert of Europe – An Experiment*, New York (OUP), 1947, p. 179.
5. Jean-Claude Caron, *Générations Romantiques: les étudiants de Paris et le Quartier Latin, 1814–1851*, Paris (Armand Colin), 1991, p. 197.
6. Rainer Elkar, 'Young Germans and Young Germany', in *Generations in Conflict: Youth Revolt and Generation Formation in Germany, 1770–1968*, ed. M. Roseman, Cambridge (CUP), 1995, p. 77.
7. R. John Rath, 'The *Carbonari*: Their Origins, Initiation Rites, and Aims', *AmHistRev*, 69, 1963, pp. 353–70.

8. Ibid., p. 370; Alan B.Spitzer, *Old Hatreds and Young Hopes: The French Carbonari against the Bourbon Restoration*, Cambridge MA (HUP), 1971, p. 241.

9. Peter Savigear, 'Carbonarism and the French Army, 1815–24', *History*, 54, 1969, p. 202.

10. Filippo Buonarroti, *La Conspiration pour l'Egalité, dite de Babeuf*, Brussels (Librairie romantique), 1828.

11. Maurice Dommanget, *Les Idées politiques et sociales d'Auguste Blanqui*, Paris (Rivière), 1957.

12. J. L. Talmon, *The Origins of Totalitarian Democracy*, London (Mercury), 1961.

13. Alexis De Tocqueville, *Recollections*, ed. J. P. Mayer, New York (Meridian), 1959, p. 130.

14. R. S. Alexander, *Bonapartism and Revolutionary Tradition in France: The Fédérés of 1815*, Cambridge (CUP), 1991.

15. R. S. Alexander, 'Restoration Republicanism Reconsidered', *French History*, 8:4, 1994, pp. 442–69.

16. Bernard Ménager, *Les Napoléon du peuple*, Paris (Aubier), 1988, pp. 20–3.

17. Ibid., p. 58.

18. Barbara Day-Hickman, *Napoleonic Art: Nationalism and the Spirit of Rebellion in France, 1815–1848*, Newark (Delaware UP), 1999.

19. Jean Tulard, 'Le Retour des Cendres', in Pierre Nora, ed., *Les Lieux de Mémoire, vol. 2*, Paris (Quarto-Gallimard), 1997, pp. 1729–53.

20. Robert J. Bezucha, *The Lyon Uprising of 1834: Social and Political Conflict in the Early July Monarchy*, Cambridge MA (HUP), 1974, p. 25.

21. Ibid., pp. 8, 42 and 54.

22. Iorwerth Prothero, *Radical Artisans in England and France, 1830–1870*, Cambridge (CUP), 1997, p. 51.

23. Ronald Aminzade, *Ballots and Barricades: Class Formation and Republican Politics in France, 1830–1871*, Princeton NJ (PUP), 1993, p. 112.

24. Bezucha, *Lyon Uprising*, p. 75.

25. Maurice Agulhon, *The Republic in the Village: The People of the Var from the French Revolution to the Second Republic*, Cambridge (CUP/MSH), 1982.

26. Peter McPhee, 'The Seed-Time of the Republic: Society and Politics in the Pyrénées-Orientales, 1848–51', *Australian Journal of Politics and History*, 22:2, 1976, pp. 196–213.

27. Franco della Peruta, *Milano nel Risorgimento dall'età napoleonica alle Cinque Giornate*, Milan (Edizioni Comune de Milano), 1998, p. 202.

28. Alain Corbin and Jean-Marie Mayeur, eds, *La Barricade (Actes du colloque de 1995)*, Paris (Publications de la Sorbonne), 1997, p. 15; Peruta, *Milano nel Risorgimento*, p. 179.

29. T. J. Clark, *The Absolute Bourgeois, Artists and Politics in France, 1848–1851*, London (Thames & Hudson), 1973, p. 27.

30. Pamela Pilbeam, *French Socialists Before Marx: Workers, Women and the Social Question in France*, London (Acumen), 2000, p. 146.

31. Michèle Riot-Sarcey, *Le Réel de l'Utopie: essai sur le politique au XIXe siècle*, Paris (Albin Michel), 1998, pp. 76–7.

32. Jonathan Beecher, *Charles Fourier, the Visionary and his World*, Berkeley (UCP), 1986, Introduction and p. 313.

33. Ibid., pp. 277–91.

34. Ibid., pp. 303–11.

35. Pilbeam, *French Socialists Before Marx*, pp. 1–2.

36. Christopher H. Johnson, *Utopian Communism in France: Cabet and the Icarians, 1839–1851*, Ithaca NY (Cornell UP), 1974, p. 57.

37. Ibid., pp. 82 and 147.

38. Pamela Pilbeam, 'Dream Worlds? Religion and the Early Socialists in France', *Historical Journal*, 43:2, 2000, pp. 499–515.

39. Beecher, *Charles Fourier*, p. 500.

## Chapter 5 The fragility of nationalism

1. Miroslav Hroch, *Social Preconditions of National Revival in Europe*, Cambridge (CUP), 1985, pp. 23–5.

2. Simonetta Soldani, 'Approaching Europe in the Name of the Nation: The Italian Revolution, 1846–49', in Dieter Dowe et al., eds, *Europe in 1848: Revolution and Reform*, New York and Oxford (Berghahn), 2000, p. 61.

3. E. J. Hobsbawm and Terence Ranger, eds, *The Invention of Tradition*, Cambridge (CUP), 1983; Benedict Anderson, *Imagined Communities: Reflections on the Origins and Spread of Nationalism*, London (Verso), 1983; Ernest Gellner, *Nations and Nationalism*, Oxford (Blackwell), 1983.

4. Anne-Marie Thiesse, *La Création des identités nationales: Europe, 18e–19e siècle*, Paris (Seuil), 1999, p. 14.

5. Anthony D. Smith, *National Identity*, Harmondsworth UK (Penguin), 1991, ch. 2.

6. Hroch, *Social Preconditions*, p. 97.

7. F. Barnard, *Herder's Social and Political Thought – from Enlightenment to Nationalism*, Oxford (Clarendon), 1965, p. 71.

8. V. Spencer, 'Herder and Nationalism: reclaiming the principle of cultural respect', *Australian Journal of Politics and History*, 43:1, 1997, pp. 6–7.

9. Brian E. Vick, *Defining Germany: The 1848 Frankfurt Parliamentarians and National Identity*, Cambridge MA (HUP), 2002, pp. 27–8.

10. Roland Sussex, 'Lingua Nostra: The 19th-century Slavonic Language Revivals', in R. Sussex and J. C. Eade, eds, *Culture and Nationalism in 19th-Century Eastern Europe*, Columbus OH (Slavica), 1985, p. 113.

11. Ivan T. Berend, *History Derailed: Central and Eastern Europe in the Long Nineteenth Century*, Berkeley (UCP), 2003, pp. 51–3.

12. Hroch, *Social Preconditions*, p. 72.

13. Ibid., pp. 34–5.

14. Ibid., pp. 117–23.

15. Uffe Østergård, 'Language and National Identity in the Danish Nation-State in the 19th Century', *History of European Ideas*, 16:1–3, 1993, pp. 213–18.

16. Xosé-Manoel Núñez, 'The Region as *Essence* of the Fatherland: Regionalist Variants of Spanish Nationalism (1840–1936)', *EHQ*, 31:4, 2001, pp. 483–518.

17. Hillel J. Kieval, *Languages of Community: The Jewish Experience in the Czech lands*, Berkeley (UCP), 2000, pp. 121–2.

18. Thiesse, *Création des identités*, pp. 106–7.

19. Istvan Deak, *The Lawful Revolution: Louis Kossuth and the Hungarians, 1848–1849*, New York (Columbia UP), 1979, pp. 25–7.

20. Brendan Simms, *The Struggle for Mastery in Germany, 1779–1850*, New York (St Martin's Press – now Palgrave Macmillan), 1998, p. 192.

21. Robin Okey, *The Habsburg Monarchy from Enlightenment to Eclipse*, New York (St Martin's Press – now Palgrave Macmillan), 2001, p. 108.

22. Stanley Z. Pech, 'The Nationalist Movements of the Austrian Slavs in 1848: A Comparative Sociological Profile', *Histoire Sociale/Social History*, 9, 1976, pp. 344–50.

23. Thiesse, *Création des identités*, pp. 83–5.

24. Denis Mack Smith, *Mazzini*, London and New Haven CT (YUP), 1994, p. 6.

25. G. D. Stark, 'The Ideology of the German *Burschenschaft* Generation', *European Studies Review*, 8, 1978, p. 339.

26. George S. Williamson, 'What killed August von Kotzebue? The Temptations of Virtue and the Political Theology of German Nationalism, 1789–1819', *JMH*, 72:4, 2000, pp. 890–943.

27. R. R. Lutz, 'The German Revolutionary Student Movement, 1819–1833', *Central European History*, 4:3, 1971, pp. 239–41.

28. Robert Lee, ' "Relative Backwardness" and Long-Run Development: Economic, Demographic and Social Changes', in Mary Fulbrook, ed.,

*German History since 1800*, London (Arnold), 1997, p. 81; H. Hahn, *Geschichte des Deutschen Zollvereins*, Göttingen (Vandenhoeck & Ruprecht), 1984, p. 20.

29. Hahn, *Geschichte*, pp. 25–7.
30. Lee, ' "Relative Backwardness" ', p. 67.
31. W. R. Lee, 'Economic Development and the State in Nineteenth-Century Germany', *Economic History Review*, 41:3, 1988, pp. 346–67.
32. A. J. P. Taylor, *The Course of German History*, New York (Coward-McCann), 1946, p. 62.
33. Alan Sked, *The Decline and Fall of the Habsburg Empire, 1815–1918*, London (Longman), 1989, p. 13.
34. Charles and Barbara Jelavich, *The Establishment of the Balkan National States, 1804–1920*, Seattle (Washington UP), 1986, p. 46.
35. G. D. Frangos, 'The *Philike Etaireia*, 1814–1821: A Social and Historical Analysis', unpublished PhD dissertation, Columbia University, New York, 1971.
36. William St Clair, *That Greece Might Still Be Free: The Philhellenes in the War of Independence*, London (OUP), 1972.
37. C. M. Woodhouse, *Capodistria: The Founder of Greek Independence, 1821–9*, London (OUP), 1973, ch. 12.
38. C. W. Crawley, *The Question of Greek Independence: A Study of British Policy in the Near East, 1821–33*, Cambridge (CUP), 1930, pp. 134–5.
39. Soldani, 'Approaching Europe', p. 67.

## Chapter 6    The Revolutions of 1830

1. Clive Church, *Europe in 1830: Revolution and Political Change*, London (Allen & Unwin), 1983.
2. Ibid., p. 5.
3. Pamela M. Pilbeam, *The 1830 Revolution in France*, Basingstoke UK (Macmillan), 1991, p. 63.
4. David Pinkney, *The French Revolution of 1830*, Princeton NJ (PUP), 1972, p. 64.
5. Edgar Leon Newman, 'The Blouse and the Frock Coat: The alliance of the common people of Paris with the liberal leadership and the middle class during the last years of the Bourbon Restoration', *JMH*, 46, 1974, pp. 26–59.
6. Pinkney, *French Revolution of 1830*, p. 257.
7. Karl Marx, *The 18th Brumaire of Louis-Napoleon*, Peking (Foreign Language Press), 1978, p. 42.

8. J. P. T. Bury and Robert Tombs, *Thiers, 1797–1877: A Political Life*, London (Allen & Unwin), 1986, pp. 37–8.

9. Pinkney, *French Revolution of 1830*, p. 295.

10. Ibid., pp. 289–95.

11. Martyn Lyons, *Le Triomphe du Livre: une histoire sociologique de la lecture dans la France du XIXe siècle*, Paris (Promodis), 1987, p. 86.

12. Pamela Pilbeam, 'Popular violence in provincial France after the 1830 Revolution', *English Historical Review*, 91, 1976, pp. 278–97.

13. Peter Sahlins, *Forest Rites: The War of the Demoiselles in Nineteenth-Century France*, Cambridge MA (HUP), 1994.

14. Elie Halévy, *A History of the English People in the Nineteenth Century, vol. 3: The Triumph of Reform, 1830–41*, London (Benn), 1950, first French edn 1932.

15. Michael Brock, *The Great Reform Act*, London (Hutchinson), 1973, p. 336.

16. Ibid., pp. 312–13.

17. Asa Briggs, *The Age of Improvement, 1783–1867*, London (Longmans), 1959, p. 261.

18. Gwyn A. Williams, *The Merthyr Rising*, London (Croom Helm), 1978, p. 18.

19. E. J. Hobsbawm and George Rudé, *Captain Swing*, London (Lawrence & Wishart), 1969, p. 17.

20. Ibid., p. 262.

21. Jonathan Steinberg, *Why Switzerland?*, Cambridge (CUP), 1996, p. 42.

22. Church, *Europe in 1830*, p. 65.

23. Gérald Arlettaz, *Libéralisme et Société dans le canton de Vaud, 1814–45*, Lausanne (Bibliothèque historique vaudoise), 1980, pp. 95 and 112.

24. Giorgio Candeloro, *Storia dell'Italia moderna, vol. 2: Dalla Restaurazione alle Rivoluzione Nazionale*, Milan (Feltrinelli), 1994, pp. 192–5.

25. E. H. Kossmann, *The Low Countries, 1780–1940*, Oxford (Clarendon Press), 1978.

26. Simonetta Soldani, 'Il 1830 in Europa: Dinamica e articolazioni di una crisi generale', *Studi Storici*, 13:2, April–June 1972, pp. 344–8.

27. Kossmann, *Low Countries*, pp. 170–1.

28. W. H. Zawadzki, *A Man of Honour: Adam Czartoryski as a Statesman of Russia and Poland, 1795–1831*, Oxford (Clarendon Press), p. 302.

29. R. F. Leslie, *Polish Politics and the Revolution of November 1830*, Westport CT (Greenwood), 1969, p. 178.

30. Norman Davies, *God's Playground: A History of Poland, vol. 2: 1795 to the Present*, Oxford (Clarendon), 1981, p. 322.

31. Zawadzki, *Man of Honour*, p. 313.

32. Church, *Europe in 1830*, p. 182.

## Chapter 7   The rise of public opinion

1. Jürgen Habermas, *The Structural Transformation of the Public Sphere: An Inquiry into a Category of Bourgeois Society*, Cambridge (Polity), 1992, ch. 3.
2. Massimo d'Azeglio, *Degli Ultimi Casi di Romagna*, Lugano (Tipografia della Svizzera Italiana), 1946, p. 117.
3. Richard D. Altick, *The English Common Reader: A Social History of the Mass Reading Public, 1800–1900*, Chicago (Chicago UP), 1957, pp. 324–6.
4. Jean-Pierre Aguet, 'Le Tirage des quotidiens de Paris sous la monarchie de Juillet', *Revue suisse d'histoire*, 10, 1960, p. 237.
5. Claude Bellanger, Jacques Godechot et al., *Histoire générale de la presse française*, 5 vols, Paris (PUF), 1969–76, vol. 2, pp. 108–9.
6. Nelly Furman, *La Revue des deux mondes et le romantisme, 1831–48*, Geneva (Droz), 1975, pp. 17 and 73.
7. Romano Paolo Coppini, 'Il Granducato di Toscana dagli "anni francesi" all'Unità', in Giuseppe Galasso, ed., *Storia d'Italia*, vol. 13, pt 3, Torino (UTET), pp. 233–43.
8. David S. Kerr, *Caricature and French Political Culture, 1830–1848: Charles Philipon and the Illustrated Press*, Oxford (Clarendon), 2000, pp. 52 and 133.
9. J. P. T. Bury and Robert Tombs, *Thiers, 1797–1877: A Political Life*, London (Allen & Unwin), 1986, p. 146.
10. Emmanuel Fureix, 'Un Rituel d'opposition sous la Restauration: les funérailles libérales à Paris, 1820–1830', *Genèses*, 46, 2002, p. 78.
11. Maurice Agulhon, *The Republic in the Village: The People of the Var from the French Revolution to the Second Republic*, Cambridge (CUP/MSH), 1982, pp. 124–50.
12. Robin Okey, *Habsburg Monarchy from Enlightenment to Eclipse*, New York (St Martin's – now Palgrave Macmillan), 2001, p. 103.
13. James J. Sheehan, *German History, 1770–1866*, Oxford (Clarendon), 1989, p. 631.
14. Marta Petrusewicz, *Come il Meridionale divenne una questione: rappresentazioni del Sud prima e dopo il Quarantotto*, Catanzaro (Rubbettino), 1998, ch. 2.
15. P. Siebert, *Der Literarische Salon – Literatur und Geselligkeit zwischen Aufklärung und Vormärz*, Stuttgart (Metzler), 1993, 102.
16. P. Wilhelmy, *Der Berliner Salon im 19. Jahrhundert, 1780–1914*, Berlin (De Gruyter), 1989, pp. 133–40.
17. Dagmar Herzog, *Intimacy and Exclusion: Religious Politics in Pre-Revolutionary Baden*, Princeton NJ (PUP), 1996.
18. Wolfram Siemann, *The German Revolution of 1848–49*, Basingstoke UK (Macmilllan – now Palgrave Macmillan), 1998, pp. 90–1 and 98–9.

19. M. Wettengel, *Die Revolution von 1848–49 im Rhein-Main-Raum. Politische Vereine und Revolutionsalltag in Großherzogtum Hesse, Herzogtum Nassau und der Freien Stadt Frankfurt*, Wiesbaden (Historische Kommision für Nassau), 1989, pp. 36–44.
20. Jonathan Sperber, *Rhineland Radicals: The Democratic Movement and the Revolution of 1848–1849*, Princeton NJ (PUP), 1991, p. 112.
21. Jonathan Sperber, *Revolutionary Europe, 1780–1850*, Harlow UK (Longman), 2000, p. 285.
22. David Turley, *The Culture of English Anti-Slavery, 1780–1860*, London (Routledge), 1991, p. 48.
23. Ibid., pp. 78–9.
24. Clare Midgley, *Women Against Slavery: The British Campaigns, 1780–1870*, London (Routledge), 1992, p. 159.
25. Paul M. Kielstra, *The Politics of Slave Trade Suppression in Britain and France, 1814–48*, London (Macmillan), 2000, p. 114.
26. Lawrence C. Jennings, *French Anti-Slavery: The Movement for the Abolition of Slavery in France, 1802–1848*, Cambridge (CUP), 2000, p. 49.
27. Ibid., p. 198.

## Chapter 8    The 'juste milieu' and gathering unrest, 1830–1848

1. Jo Burr Margadant, 'Gender, vice, and the political imaginary in postrevolutionary France: Reinterpreting the failure of the July Monarchy, 1830–1848', *AmHistRev*, 104:5, 1999, pp. 1461–96.
2. Michael Marrinan, *Painting Politics for Louis-Philippe: Art and Ideology in Orleanist France, 1830–48*, New Haven CT (YUP), 1988, pp. 17–18.
3. André-Jean Tudesq, *Les Grands Notables en France, 1840–49: étude historique d'une psychologie sociale*, 2 vols, Paris (PUF), 1964, II, p. 857.
4. Douglas Johnson, *Guizot*, London (RKP), 1963, p. 70.
5. Narciso Nada, 'Il Piemonte Sabaudo dal 1814 al 1861', in Giuseppe Galasso, ed., *Storia d'Italia*, vol. 8, pt 2, Turin (UTET), 1993, p. 197.
6. Denis Mack Smith, *Victor Emanuel, Cavour and the Risorgimento*, London (OUP), 1971, pp. 49–50.
7. Rosario Romeo, *Vita di Cavour*, Rome and Bari (Laterza), 1984, pp. 239–45.
8. Luciano Cafagna, *Cavour*, Bologna (Il Mulino), 1999, p. 185.
9. José Alvarez Junco and Adrian Shubert, eds, *Spanish History since 1808*, London (Arnold), 2000, p. 27.

10. E. P. Thompson, *The Making of the English Working Class*, Harmondsworth UK (Penguin), 1968, pp. 913–5.

11. Gareth Stedman Jones, *Languages of Class: Studies in English Working-Class History, 1832–1982*, Cambridge (CUP), 1983, pp. 168–74.

12. Dorothy Thompson, *The Chartists*, London (Temple Smith), 1984, pp. 51–2.

13. John K. Walton, *Chartism*, London (Routledge), 1999, p. 27.

14. David Goodway, *London Chartism, 1838–48*, Cambridge (CUP), 1982.

15. R. K. Webb, *Modern England from the 18th Century to the Present*, London (George Allen & Unwin), 1980, p. 250.

16. Gérard Cholvy and Yves-Marie Hilaire, *Histoire religieuse de la France contemporaine, 1, 1800–1880*, Toulouse (Privat), 1985, p. 39.

17. Robin Lenman, 'Germany', in Robert J. Goldstein, ed., *The War for the Public Mind: Political Censorship in Nineteenth-Century Europe*, Westport CT (Praeger), 2000, p. 47.

## Chapter 9    The Jews: the dilemmas of emancipation

1. David I. Kertzer, *The Kidnapping of Edgardo Mortara*, New York (Knopf), 1997.

2. David Vital, *A People Apart: The Jews in Europe, 1789–1939*, Oxford (OUP), 1999, pp. 19–22.

3. Ibid., p. 44.

4. Paula E. Hyman, *The Jews of Modern France*, Berkeley (UCP), 1998, pp. 20–1.

5. Andrew M. Canepa, 'Emancipation and Jewish response in mid-19th century Italy', *EHQ*, 16, 1986, p. 430.

6. Artur Eisenbach, *The Emancipation of the Jews in Poland, 1780–1870*, ed. A. Polonsky, Oxford (Blackwell), 1991, pp. 198 and 203.

7. Karina Sonnenberg-Stern, *Emancipation and Poverty: The Ashkenazi Jews of Amsterdam, 1796–1850*, Basingstoke (Macmillan), 2000, p. 8.

8. Ivan T. Berend, *History Derailed: Central and Eastern Europe in the Long Nineteenth Century*, Berkeley (UCP), 2003, p. 203; Hillel J. Kieval, *Languages of Community: The Jewish Experience in the Czech Lands*, Berkeley (UCP), 2000, p. 23.

9. Michael Graetz, *The Jews in Nineteenth-Century France: From the French Revolution to the Alliance Israélite Universelle*, Stanford (Stanford UP), 1996, p. 2.

10. Phyllis Cohen Albert, *The Modernization of French Jewry: Consistory and Community in the Nineteenth Century*, Hanover NH (Brandeis UP), 1977, p. 3.

11. Vital, *A People Apart*, p. 40; Sonnenberg-Stern, *Emancipation and Poverty*, pp. 14 and 21; Franco della Peruta, 'Gli ebrei nel Risorgimento fra interdizioni ed emancipazione', in *Storia d'Italia, Annali XI,2: Gli Ebrei in Italia*, ed. C. Vivanti, Turin (Einaudi), 1997, pp. 1135–6.

12. Della Peruta, 'Gli ebrei', pp. 1155–62.

13. Brian Vick, *Defining Germany: The Frankfurt Parliamentarians and National Identity*, Cambridge MA (HUP), 2002, p. 88.

14. Albert, *Modernization of French Jewry*, p. 15.

15. Paula E. Hyman, *The Emancipation of the Jews of Alsace: Acculturation and Tradition in the Nineteenth Century*, New Haven CT (YUP), 1991, p. 13.

16. Vital, *A People Apart*, p. 69.

17. Ibid., p. 134.

18. Shmuel Almog, *Nationalism and Anti-Semitism in Modern Europe, 1815–1945*, Oxford (Pergamon), 1990, pp. 17–32.

19. Norman Davies, *God's Playground: A History of Poland, vol. 2: 1795 to the Present*, Oxford (Clarendon), 1981, p. 244.

20. Maria Vassilikou, 'Greeks and Jews in Salonika and Odessa: Inter-ethnic relations in cosmopolitan port cities', in David Cesarani, ed., *Port Jews: Jewish Communities in Cosmopolitan Maritime Trading Centres, 1550–1950*, London (Frank Cass), 2002, pp. 155–72.

21. S. M. Dubnow, *History of the Jews in Russia and Poland from the Earliest Times until the Present Day*, Philadelphia (Jewish Publication Society of America), 2 vols, 1916–18, vol. 1, pp. 406–7 and vol. 2, 30–1.

22. Ibid., vol. 2, pp. 18–27.

23. Vital, *A People Apart*, p. 154–5.

24. Hyman, *Emancipation of the Jews of Alsace*, p. 66.

25. Vital, *A People Apart*, pp. 124–6.

26. Todd Endelman, *Radical Assimilation in English Jewry History, 1656–1945*, Bloomington IN (Indiana UP), 1990.

27. Niall Ferguson, *The House of Rothschild*, 2 vols, Harmondsworth UK (Penguin), 2000, vol. 1, p. 17.

28. Ibid., vol. 1, pp. 197–9.

29. Ibid., vol. 1, p. 167.

30. Ibid., vol. 1, p. 321.

31. Almog, *Nationalism and Anti-Semitism*, pp. 17–32.

32. Vital, *A People Apart*, p. 249.

33. Dubnow, *History of the Jews*, vol. 2, p. 83.

34. Graetz, *Jews in Nineteenth-Century France*, p. 246.

## Chapter 10    The city

1. Asa Briggs, 'The Human Aggregate', in *The Victorian City: Images and Realities*, vol. 1, ed. H. J. Dyos and Michael Wolff, London (RKP), 1977, pp. 84–5.

2. Peter Ackroyd, *London, the Biography*, London (Vintage), 2001, p. 202.

3. B. R. Mitchell, *European Historical Statistics, 1750–1975*, London (Macmillan), 1981, pp. 86–9.

4. Asa Briggs, *Victorian Cities*, Harmondsworth UK (Penguin), 1968, p. 86.

5. Mitchell, *European Historical Statistics*, pp. 86–9.

6. Catharina Lis, *Social Change and the Labouring Poor: Antwerp, 1770–1860*, New Haven CT (YUP), 1986, p. 41.

7. Michael F. Hamm, *Kiev: A Portrait, 1800–1917*, Princeton NJ (PUP), 1993, p.xi.

8. John M. Merriman, 'Introduction', in *French Cities in the Nineteenth Century*, ed. John M. Merriman, London (Hutchinson), 1982, pp. 18–21.

9. Charles A. Pouthas, *La population française pendant la première moitié du 19e siècle*, Paris (PUF), 1956.

10. James J. Sheehan, *German History, 1770–1866*, Oxford (Clarendon), 1989, p. 485.

11. Eric E. Lampard, 'The urbanising world', in Dyos and Wolff, *Victorian City*, vol. 1, p. 4.

12. Pierre Ayçoberry, *Cologne entre Napoléon et Bismarck: la croissance d'une ville rhénane*, Paris (Aubier), 1981, pp. 18 and 155.

13. James H. Jackson jr, *Migration and Urbanization in the Ruhr Valley, 1821–1914*, Boston MA (Humanities Press), 1997, p. 72.

14. Martin Nadaud, *Mémoires de Léonard, ancien garçon maçon*, intro. by Maurice Agulhon, Paris (Hachette), 1976, first published 1895.

15. Richard Dennis, *English Industrial Cities of the Nineteenth Century: A Social Geography*, Cambridge (CUP), 1984, p. 35.

16. Jackson, *Ruhr Valley*, p. 65.

17. Rachel Fuchs and Leslie Page Moch, 'Pregnant, single and far from home: Migrant women in nineteenth-century Paris', *AmHistRev*, 95:4, 1990, pp. 1007–31.

18. Ayçoberry, *Cologne*, p. 98.

19. Lis, *Antwerp*, pp. 110–11.

20. Giovanni Gozzini, 'The poor and the life cycle in nineteenth-century Florence, 1813–59', *Social History*, 18:3, 1993, pp. 299–317.

21. Stuart Woolf, *The Poor in Western Europe in the Eighteenth and Nineteenth Centuries*, London (Methuen), 1986, pp. 171 and 209.

22. Lis, *Antwerp*, p. 43.
23. Marco H. D. van Leeuwen, *The Logic of Charity: Amsterdam, 1800–1850*, Basingstoke UK (Palgrave Macmillan), 2000, pp. 68–73.
24. Ibid., pp. 5–6, 149–50, 185.
25. Louis Chevalier, *Classes laborieuses et classes dangereuses à Paris pendant la première moitié du XIXe siècle*, Paris (Plon), 1958.
26. Jean Ibanès, 'La population de la place des Vosges et de ses environs en 1791', in *Contributions à l'histoire demographique de la Révolution française*, Paris, 1962.
27. Chevalier, *Classes laborieuses*, p. 226.
28. Ibid., p. 345.
29. Friedrich Engels, *The Condition of the Working Class in England*, Oxford (Blackwell), 1971.
30. Briggs, *Victorian Cities*, p. 126.
31. Anna Lucia Forti Messina, 'L'Italia dell'Ottocento di fronte al colera', in *Storia d'Italia, vol. 7: Malattia e Medicina*, ed. Franco della Peruta, Turin (Einaudi), 1984, p. 456.
32. Frank M. Snowden, *Naples in the Time of Cholera, 1884–1911*, Cambridge (CUP), 1995, pp. 15–16.
33. Hamm, *Kiev*, p. 46.
34. John M. Merriman, *The Red City: Limoges and the French Nineteenth Century*, New York (OUP), 1982, p. 6
35. Lis, *Antwerp*, p. 78.
36. Jesse White Mario, *La Miseria in Napoli*, Naples (Quarto Potere), 1978, pp. 34–8 (first published 1877).
37. Catherine Kudlick, *Cholera in Post-revolutionary Paris: A Cultural History*, Berkeley (UCP), 1996, p. 1.
38. Ibid., pp. 16 and 54.
39. Richard J. Evans, *Death in Hamburg: Society and Politics in the Cholera Years, 1830–1910*, Oxford (Clarendon Press), 1987, p. 435.
40. Richard J. Evans, 'Epidemics and revolutions: Cholera in nineteenth-century Europe', *Past and Present*, 120, 1988, p. 130.
41. Peter Baldwin, *Contagion and the State in Europe, 1830–1930*, Cambridge (CUP), 1999, pp. 40–5.
42. Ibid., pp. 47 and 63.
43. Kudlick, *Cholera*, pp. 178–9.
44. Ibid., pp. 207–9.
45. Mack Walker, *German Home Towns: Community, State and General Estate, 1648–1871*, Ithaca NY (Cornell UP), 1971.
46. Ackroyd, *London*, p. 393.

**Chapter 11 The peasant world**

1. Annie Moulin, *Peasantry and Society in France since 1789*, Cambridge and Paris (CUP/MSH), 1991, p. 49.

2. P. M. Jones, *Politics and Rural Society: The Southern Massif Central, c.1750–1880*, Cambridge (CUP), 1985, pp. 114–18.

3. Peter Laslett, *Household and Family in Past Time*, Cambridge (CUP), 1972.

4. Jean-François Soulet, *Les Pyrénées au 19e siècle*, 2 vols., Toulouse (Eché), 1987, vol. 1, p. 301–11.

5. Jean-Paul Aron, Paul Dumont and Emmanuel le Roy, *Anthropologie du conscrit français, 1819–26*, Paris (Mouton), 1972, pp. 86 and 172.

6. Philippe Vigier, *La Seconde République dans la région alpine: étude politique et sociale*, 2 vols, Paris (PUF), 1963, vol. 1, pp. 128–9.

7. Evelyn B. Ackerman, *Village on the Seine: Tradition and Change in Bonnières, 1815–1914*, Ithaca NY (Cornell UP), 1978, p. 31.

8. Franco della Peruta, 'L'Alimentazione dei contadini nella Lombardia dell'ottocento', *Il Risorgimento*, 44:2, 1992, pp. 187–200.

9. Evelyn B. Ackerman, *Health Care in the Parisian Countryside, 1800–1914*, New Brunswick NJ (Rutgers UP), 1990, pp. 45–6.

10. Martine Segalen, *Love and Power in the Peasant Family: Rural France in the 19th Century*, Oxford (Blackwell), 1983.

11. David Blackbourn, *The Long Nineteenth Century: A History of Germany, 1780–1918*, Oxford (OUP), 1998, pp. 112–3.

12. Ackerman, *Village on the Seine*, p. 73.

13. Giorgio Candeloro, *Storia dell'Italia moderna, vol. 2: Dalla Restaurazione alle Rivoluzione Nazionale*, Milan (Feltrinelli), 1994, p. 318.

14. Soulet, *Pyrénées*, vol. 1, pp. 299–300.

15. Josef Mooser, 'Property and wood theft: Agrarian capitalism and social conflict in rural society, 1800–1850: A Westphalian case study', in Robert G. Moeller, ed., *Peasants and Lords in Modern Germany: Recent Studies in Agricultural History*, Boston MA (Allen and Unwin), 1986, pp. 52–80.

16. James J. Sheehan, *German History, 1770–1866*, Oxford (Clarendon), 1989, p. 479.

17. Jean Vidalenc, *Le Peuple des Campagnes: la société française, 1815–1848*, Paris (Rivière), 1970, p. 79.

18. Candeloro, *Storia dell'Italia moderna, vol. 2*, pp. 255–7.

19. Vidalenc, *Peuple des Campagnes*, p. 351.

20. M. Bergman, 'The potato blight in the Netherlands and its social consequences, 1845–47', *International Review of Social History*, 12, 1967, pp. 390–431.

21. Dora M. Dumont, 'Strange and exorbitant demands: Rural labour in 19th-century Bologna', *EHQ*, 30:4, 2000, p. 471.

22. Christian Thibon, *Pays de Sault; les pyrénées audoises au XIXe siècle; les villages et l'Etat*, Paris (CNRS), 1988, pp. 50–6.

23. John Davis, *Società e Imprenditori nel Regno borbonico, 1815–1860*, Rome and Bari (Laterza), 1979, p. 20.

24. Ibid., p. 60.

25. David Moon, *The Russian Peasantry, 1600–1930: The World the Peasants Made*, London (Longman), 1999, p. 99.

26. Jerome Blum, *Lord and Peasant in Russia from the 9th to the 19th Century*, Princeton NJ (PUP), 1961.

27. Jerome Blum, *The End of the Old Order in Rural Europe*, Princeton NJ (PUP), 1978, pp. 25 and 157.

28. Ibid., p. 169.

29. Ibid., p. 333.

30. Jones, *Politics and Rural Society*, pp. 128–34.

## Chapter 12  The crisis of the artisans

1. Ronald Aminzade, *Ballots and Barricades: Class Formation and Republican Politics in France, 1830–1871*, Princeton NJ (PUP), 1993, p. 64.

2. David Blackbourn, *The Long Nineteenth Century: A History of Germany, 1780–1918*, Oxford (OUP), 1998, p. 113.

3. Ralph Samuel, 'The Workshop of the World: Steam power and hand technology in mid-Victorian Britain', *History Workshop Journal*, no. 3, 1977, pp. 6–72.

4. Peter Kriedte, Hans Medick and Jürgen Schlumbohm, *Industrialization before Industrialization*, Cambridge (CUP/MSH), 1981, pp. 12–37.

5. D. C. Coleman, 'Proto-industrialisation: A concept too many', *Economic History Review*, 36:3, 1983, pp. 435–48.

6. Simonetta O. Cammarosano, 'Labouring women in northern and central Italy in the 19th century', in John A. Davis and Paul Ginsborg, eds, *Society and Politics in the Age of the Risorgimento: Essays in Honour of Denis Mack Smith*, Cambridge (CUP), 1991, pp. 156 and 173.

7. Duncan Bythell, *The Handloom Weavers*, Cambridge (CUP), 1969, p. 57.

8. James J. Sheehan, *German History, 1770–1866*, Oxford (Clarendon), 1989, p. 492.

9. William H. Sewell, 'Social change and the rise of working-class politics in 19th-century Marseille', *Past and Present*, 65, 1974, pp. 96–7.

10. William H. Sewell, *Work and Revolution in France: The Language of Labour from the Old Régime to 1848*, Cambridge (CUP), 1980.

11. Wolfram Siemann, *The German Revolution of 1848–49*, New York (St Martin's – now Palgrave Macmillan), 1998, pp. 94–9.

12. Martyn Lyons, *Readers and Society in 19th-Century France*, Basingstoke UK (Palgrave Macmillan), 2002, pp. 25–6.

13. David Vincent, *Bread, Knowledge and Freedom: A Study of 19th-Century Working-Class Autobiography*, London (Europa), 1981.

14. Thomas Cooper, *The Life of Thomas Cooper, Written by Himself*, London (Hodder & Stoughton), 1872, p. 57; Martyn Lyons, 'New readers in the nineteenth century: Women, children, workers', in Guglielmo Cavallo and Roger Chartier, eds, *A History of Reading in the West*, Cambridge (Polity), 1999, pp. 331–42.

15. Dick Geary, 'Artisans, protest and labour organization in Germany, 1815–1870', *EHQ*, 16, 1986, pp. 374–5.

16. E. P. Thompson, 'The moral economy of the English crowd in the 18th century', in his *Customs in Common*, Harmondsworth UK (Penguin), 1993, ch. 4.

17. Jonathan Sperber, *Rhineland Radicals: The Democratic Movement and the Revolution of 1848–49*, Princeton NJ (PUP), 1991, pp. 33 and 74 and 162–5.

18. Robin Okey, *The Habsburg Monarchy from Enlightenment to Eclipse*, New York (St Martin's – now Palgrave Macmillan), 2001, pp. 84–8.

19. Cit. Bythell, *Handloom Weavers*, pp. 58–9.

## Chapter 13   Bourgeois culture and the domestic ideology

1. Theodore Zeldin, *France, 1848–1945*, 2 vols, Oxford (Clarendon), 1973–7, vol. 1, pt 1.

2. Sarah Maza, *The Myth of the French Bourgeoisie: An Essay on the Social Imaginary, 1750–1850*, Cambridge MA (HUP), 2003.

3. Lenore O'Boyle, 'The middle classes in Western Europe, 1815–48', *AmHistRev*, 71:3, 1966, pp. 826–45.

4. Alfred Cobban, 'The middle class in France, 1815–48, in his *France since the Revolution*, London (Cape), 1970, pp. 7–21.

5. Pamela M. Pilbeam, *The Middle Classes in Europe, 1789–1914: France, Germany, Italy, and Russia*, Basingstoke UK (Macmillan), 1990.

6. E. P. Thompson, *The Making of the English Working Class*, Harmondsworth UK (Penguin), 1968, p. 9.

7. Pilbeam, *Middle Classes*, p. 71.

8. Adeline Daumard, *Les Bourgeois de Paris au 19e siècle*, Paris (Flammarion), 1970, pp. 73–4.

9. Ibid., p. 75.

10. William Weber, *Music and the Middle Class: The Social Structure of Concert Life in London, Paris and Vienna*, London (Croom Helm), 1975.

11. Alice M. Hanson, *Musical Life in Biedermeier Vienna*, Cambridge (CUP), 1985, pp. 104–7.

12. Ibid., p. 1.

13. Lyn H. Lofland, *The Public Realm: Exploring the City's Quintessential Social Territory*, New York (Aldine de Gruyter), 1998, pp. 10–11.

14. Bonnie G. Smith, *The Ladies of the Leisure Class: The Bourgeoises of Northern France in the 19th Century*, Princeton NJ (PUP), 1981, ch. 3.

15. Joan W. Scott, 'The woman worker', in Geneviève Fraisse and Michelle Perrot, eds, *A History of Women in the West, vol. IV: Emerging Feminism from Revolution to World War*, Cambridge MA (Belknap), 1993, p. 404.

16. Deborah Simonton, *A History of European Women's Work, 1700 to the Present*, London (Routledge), 1998, pp. 87–111.

17. Theresa McBride, *The Domestic Revolution: The Modernisation of Household Service in England and France, 1820–1920*, London (Croom Helm), 1976, pp. 36 and 45.

18. Simonton, *European Women's Work*, pp. 87–111.

19. Anne Martin-Fugier, 'La bonne', in Jean-Paul Aron, ed., *Misérable et Glorieuse: la femme du XIXe siècle*, Brussels (Complexe), 1984, p. 32.

20. Lawrence Stone, *Road to Divorce, England, 1530–1987*, Oxford (OUP), 1990, p. 13.

21. Smith, *Ladies of the Leisure Class*, pp. 94–5.

22. Dagmar Herzog, *Intimacy and Exclusion: Religious Politics in Pre-Revolutionary Baden*, Princeton NJ (PUP), 1996, pp. 32–4.

23. Leonore Davidoff and Catherine Hall, *Family Fortunes: Men and Women of the English Middle Class, 1780–1850*, London (Hutchinson), 1987, pp. 29–73.

24. Cécile Dauphin, Pierrette Lebrun-Pézerat and Danièle Poublan, eds, *Ces Bonnes Lettres: une correspondance familiale au XIXe siècle*, Paris (Albin Michel), 1995.

25. Yvonne Knibiehler, 'Bodies and hearts', in Fraisse and Perrot, *History of Women*, 4, p. 333.

26. Anne Martin-Fugier, 'Bourgeois Rituals', in Michelle Perrot, ed., *A History of Private Life, vol. 4: From the Fires of Revolution to The Great War*, Cambridge MA (Belknap), 1990, pp. 261–337.

27. Ute Frevert, *Women in German History: From Bourgeois Emancipation to Sexual Liberation*, Oxford (Berg), 1989, pp. 63–72.

28. William Fortescue, 'Divorce debated and deferred: The French debate on divorce and the Crémieux Divorce Bill of 1848', *French History*, 7:2, 1993, p. 152.

29. William M. Reddy, 'Marriage, honour and the public sphere in post-revolutionary France: *séparations de corps*, 1815–48', *JMH*, 65:3, 1993, p. 449.

30. D. Blasius, 'Bürgerliche Rechtsgleichheit und die Ungleichheit der Geschlechter. Das Scheidungsrecht im historischen Vergleich', in Ute Frevert, ed., *Bürgerinnen und Bürger*, Göttingen (Vandenhoeck & Ruprecht), 1988, p. 77; Stone, *Road to Divorce*, p. 385.

31. Stone, *Road to Divorce*, p. 325.

32. Ibid., p. 144.

33. Ibid., p. 341.

34. Gregory L. Freeze, 'Bringing order to the Russian family: Marriage and divorce in imperial Russia, 1760–1860', *JMH*, 62:4, 1990, pp. 709–46.

35. B. Binder, ' "Die Farbe der Milch hat sich … ins Himmelblaue verstiegen". Der Milchboykott 1849 in Stuttgart', in C. Lipp, ed., *Schimpfende Weiber und patriotische Jungfrauen – Frauen im Vormärz und in der Revolution*, Baden-Baden (Elster), 1986, pp. 161–4.

36. Frevert, *Women in German History*, ch. 7.

37. Gabrielle Hauch, 'Women's spaces in the men's Revolution of 1848', in Dieter Dowe et al., eds, *Europe in 1848: Revolution and Reform*, New York and Oxford (Berghahn), 2000, p. 672.

## Chapter 14   The Revolutions of 1848

1. Lewis Namier, *1848: The Revolution of the Intellectuals*, London (OUP), 1946.

2. Maurice Agulhon, *The Republican Experiment, 1848–52*, New York (CUP), 1983, translated from *1848 ou l'apprentissage de la République*, Paris (Seuil), 1973.

3. Peter Amann, *Revolution and Mass Democracy: The Paris Club Movement of 1848*, Princeton NJ (PUP), 1975, pp. 33–5.

4. Roger Price, *The French Second Republic: A Social History*, London (Batsford), 1972, p. 164.

5. Charles Tilly and L. Lees, 'Le peuple de juin 1848, *Annales ESC*, 29, 1974, pp. 1061–91; P. Caspard, 'Aspects de la lutte des classes en 1848: le recrutement de la garde nationale mobile', *Revue historique*, no. 511, 1974, pp. 81–106.

6. Roger Magraw, *France, 1815–1914: The Bourgeois Century*, London (Fontana), 1983, p. 141.
7. John M. Merriman, *The Agony of the Republic: The Repression of the Left in Revolutionary France, 1848–51*, New Haven CT (YUP), 1978.
8. Magraw, *France, 1815–1914*, p. 151.
9. Agulhon, *Republican Experiment*, appendix.
10. Magraw, *France 1815–1914*, p. 155.
11. Marx, *Eighteenth Brumaire*, many editions, opening paragraph.
12. Reinhard Rürup, *Deutschland im 19. Jahrhundert, 1815–1871*, Göttingen (Vandenhoeck & Ruprecht), 1984, pp. 178–9.
13. Jonathan Sperber, *The European Revolutions, 1848–1851*, Cambridge (CUP), 1984, p. 115.
14. Wolfram Siemann, *The German Revolution of 1848–49*, New York (St Martin's – now Palgrave Macmillan), 1998, p. 81.
15. Frederick Engels, *Revolution and Counter-Revolution in Germany*, Peking (Foreign Languages Press), 1977, p. 117.
16. Siemann, *German Revolution*, pp. 121–3.
17. Ibid., p. 113.
18. Jonathan Sperber, *Rhineland Radicals: The Democratic Movement and the Revolution of 1848–49*, Princeton NJ (PUP), 1991, pp. 196 and 212.
19. Siemann, *German Revolution*, p. 177.
20. K. Breitenborn, 'Aus dem Breifwechsel zwischen Friedrich Wilhelm IV von Preussen und Graf Anton zu Stolberg-Wernigerode im Jahre 1848', *Zeitschrift fürGeschichtswissenschaft*, 30:3, 1982, p. 230.
21. Engels, *Revolution and Counter-Revolution*, pp. 57–61.
22. Brian Vick, *Defining Germany: The Frankfurt Parliamentarians and National Identity*, Cambridge MA (HUP), 2002, pp. 162–72.
23. Sperber, *European Revolutions*, pp. 150 and 162–3.
24. Hartmut Pogge von Strandmann, 'The German Revolutions of 1848 and the *Sonderweg* of Mecklenberg', in R. J. W. Evans and H. Pogge von Strandmann, eds, *The Revolutions in Europe, 1848–1849: From Reform to Reaction*, Oxford (OUP), 2000, ch. 6.
25. David Blackbourn and Geoff Eley, *The Peculiarities of German History: Bourgeois Society and Politics in Nineteenth-Century Germany*, Oxford (OUP), 1984, pp. 159–75.
26. A. J. P. Taylor, *The Course of German History*, London (Hamish Hamilton), 1945, p. 68.
27. Vick, *Defining Germany*, pp. 155 and 192–202.
28. C. A. Macartney, *The Habsburg Empire, 1790–1918*, London (Weidenfeld & Nicolson), 1971, p. 313.

29. Paul Ginsborg, *Daniele Manin and the Venetian Revolution of 1848–49*, Cambridge (CUP), 1979, p. 364.
30. Lawrence D. Orton, *The Prague Slav Congress of 1848*, Boulder CO and New York (East European Quarterly and Columbia UP), 1978, pp. 6–7, 63, 72.
31. Robin Okey, *The Habsburg Monarchy from Enlightenment to Eclipse*, New York (St Martin's – now Palgrave Macmillan), 2001, p. 135.
32. Macartney, *Habsburg Empire*, p. 378.
33. Alan Sked, *The Decline and Fall of the Habsburg Empire, 1815–1918*, New York (Longman), 1989, pp. 96–7.
34. Istvan Deak, *The Lawful Revolution: Louis Kossuth and the Hungarians, 1848–1849*, New York (Columbia UP), 1979, p. 305.
35. Ibid., p. 329.
36. Narciso Nada, 'Il Piemonte sabaudo dal 1814 al 1861', in Giuseppe Galasso, ed., *Storia d'Italia*, vol. 8, pt 2, Turin (UTET), 1993, p. 300.
37. Franco della Peruta, *Milano nel Risorgimento dall'età napoleonica alle Cinque Giornate*, Milan (Edizioni Comune de Milan), 1992, p. 132.
38. Ibid., p. 149.
39. Ibid., p. 178.
40. Alan Sked, *The Survival of the Habsburg Empire: Radetsky, the Imperial Army and the Class War, 1848*, London (Longman), 1979, p. 56.
41. Ginsborg, *Daniele Manin*, pp. 157, 165 and 369.
42. Nada, 'Il Piemonte sabaudo', pp. 338–9.
43. Alfonso Scirocco, *Garibaldi: battaglie, amori, ideali di un cittadino del mondo*, Rome-Bari (Laterza), 2001, p. 116.
44. Denis Mack Smith, *Mazzini*, New Haven CT (YUP), 1994, p. 75.
45. Sperber, *European Revolutions*, pp. 255–8.
46. Namier, *Revolution of the Intellectuals*, p. 3.
47. Miles Taylor, 'The 1848 Revolutions and the British Empire', *Past & Present*, 166, 2000, pp. 146–80.

## Chapter 15   The Crimean War and beyond

1. Alexander Herzen, *My Past and Thoughts*, London (Chatto & Windus), 1974, p. 347.
2. James J. Sheehan, *German History, 1770–1866*, Oxford (Clarendon), 1989, p. 723.
3. John Shelton Curtiss, *Russia's Crimean War*, Durham NC (Duke UP), 1979, p. 23.

4. Barbara Jelavich, *Russia's Balkan Entanglements, 1806–1914*, Cambridge (CUP), 1991, p. 100.

5. Paul Schroeder, 'Did the Vienna settlement rest on a balance of power?', *AmHistRev*, 97:3, 1992, pp. 683–706, subsequent discussion and rejoinder.

6. Paul Schroeder, *Austria, Great Britain and the Crimean War: The Destruction of the European Concert*, Ithaca NY (Cornell UP), 1972.

7. Winfried Baumgart, *The Crimean War, 1853–1856*, London (Arnold), 1999, pp. 26–7.

8. Ibid., pp. 143 and 216.

9. Geoffrey Best, *War and Society in Revolutionary Europe, 1770–1870*, London (Collins/Fontana), 1982, p. 238.

10. Curtiss, *Russia's Crimean War*, pp. 536–47.

11. David M. Goldfrank, *The Origins of the Crimean War*, London (Longman), 1994, p. 293.

12. David Laven and Lucy Riall, *Napoleon's Legacy: Problems of Government in Restoration Europe*, Oxford (Berg), 2000.

13. Asa Briggs, *The Age of Improvement, 1783–1867*, London (Longman), 1959, p. 388.

14. H. G. Schenk, *The Aftermath of the Napoleonic Wars: The Concert of Europe – An Experiment*, New York (OUP), 1947, p. 189.

15. Paulo Roberto de Almeida, 'O Brasil e a diplomacia do tráfico, 1810–1850', *Locus*, 4:2, 1998, p. 12.

16. Ibid., p. 12.

17. Charles-André Julien, *Histoire de l'Algérie contemporaine*, 2 vols, Paris (PUF), 1964, vol. 1, p. 250.

18. Ibid., vol. 1, p. 178.

# Recommended Further Reading

This select bibliography offers suggestions for further reading designed for the English-reading student and teacher. Works in other languages, and more specialized works, are detailed in the endnotes.

## General works

It is hard to imagine that over 40 years have passed since the publication of E. J. Hobsbawm's marvellous *The Age of Revolution: Europe, 1789–1848* (London: Weidenfeld & Nicolson, 1962 and Sphere Books, 1973 and 1977). Hobsbawm focused on the dual revolution emanating from Britain and France, although he was very sensitive to Europe's links with the non-European world. His book dealt with broad themes, without clearly accessible chronological reference points. Amongst other general works, Robert Gildea, *Barricades and Borders: Europe, 1800–1914* (Oxford: OUP, 1987) offers many insights. Jonathan Sperber, *Revolutionary Europe, 1780–1850* (Harlow UK: Longman, 2000), takes a semi-thematic approach, dealing well with the transformation of the agrarian economy and the conflict over political participation.

## Economic and demographic history

For the economic and demographic history of the continent, refer to the *Fontana Economic History of Europe*, vols 3 and 4 (London, 1973), and Alan S. Milward and S. B. Saul, *The Economic Development of Continental Europe, 1780–1870* (London: Allen & Unwin, 1973). B. R. Mitchell, *European Historical Statistics, 1750–1975* (London: Macmillan, 1981) is useful for reference purposes. *History Derailed: Central and Eastern Europe in the Long Nineteenth Century* (Berkeley: UCP, 2003), by the Hungarian-American historian Ivan T. Berend, contains much more than economic history, and is part of a trilogy which uses the centre–periphery model of development.

275

## International relations

The history of international relations in the post-revolutionary age has been renewed by Paul W. Schroeder's *The Transformation of European Politics, 1763–1848* (Oxford: Clarendon, 1994), which treats the topic in unrivalled and magisterial fashion. See also Paul Schroeder, 'Did the Vienna Settlement Rest on a Balance of Power?', *AmHistRev*, 97:3, 1992, 683–706, with subsequent discussion and rejoinder. Students may also consult Alan Sked, ed., *Europe's Balance of Power, 1815–1848* (Basingstoke UK: Macmillan, 1979), and Matthew S. Anderson, *The Eastern Question, 1774–1923: A Study in International Relations* (London: Macmillan, 1966).

## Post-1815 regimes

On post-1815 regimes, David Laven and Lucy Riall, *Napoleon's Legacy: Problems of Government in Restoration Europe* (Oxford: Berg, 2000) argues convincingly that 'Restoration' is a misnomer. On the themes of revolution and repression in Europe as a whole, see R. John Rath, 'The *Carbonari*: Their Origins, Initiation Rites, and Aims', *AmHistRev*, 69, 1963, 353–70, and Lenore O'Boyle, 'The Problem of an Excess of Educated Men in Western Europe, 1800–1850', *JMH*, 42, 1970, 472–95. Robert J. Goldstein has covered the workings of censorship Europe-wide in *Political Repression in 19th Century Europe* (London: Croom Helm, 1983), followed by Robert J. Goldstein, ed., *The War for the Public Mind: Political Censorship in Nineteenth-Century Europe* (Westport CT: Praeger, 2000).

## Early socialist thinkers

A good general survey of early socialist thinkers is provided by Pamela Pilbeam, *French Socialists Before Marx: Workers, Women and the Social Question in France* (London: Acumen, 2000). The best works on individual figures are Jonathan Beecher, *Charles Fourier, the Visionary and his World* (Berkeley: UCP, 1986), a definitive work which has 500 pages of text and an excellent bibliography; and Christopher H. Johnson, *Utopian Communism in France: Cabet and the Icarians, 1839–1851* (Ithaca NY: Cornell UP, 1974). On the 'woman question', see for preference Susan Grogan, *French Socialism and Sexual Difference* (Basingstoke UK: Macmillan, 1992) and the same author's *Flora Tristan: Life Stories* (London: Routledge, 1998).

## Nationalism

Amongst a number of highly stimulating works on nationalism, see Benedict Anderson, *Imagined Communities: Reflections on the Origins and Spread of Nationalism* (London: Verso, 1983), and Ernest Gellner, *Nations and Nationalism* (Oxford: Blackwell, 1983). These can be supplemented by interesting viewpoints in E. J. Hobsbawm and Terence Ranger, eds, *The Invention of Tradition* (Cambridge: CUP, 1983) and E.J. Hobsbawm, *Nations and Nationalism since 1780: Programme, Myth, Reality* (Cambridge: CUP, 1990). Also indispensable for thinking about this topic are Miroslav Hroch, *Social Preconditions of National Revival in Europe* (Cambridge: CUP, 1985), and Anthony D. Smith, *National Identity* (Harmondsworth UK: Penguin, 1991). These can be read in conjunction with Stanley Z. Pech, 'The nationalist movements of the Austrian Slavs in 1848: A comparative sociological profile', *Histoire Sociale/Social History*, 9, 1976, pp. 336–56.

## 1830 Revolutions

The 1830 Revolutions are well covered by Clive Church, *Europe in 1830: Revolution and Political Change* (London: Allen & Unwin, 1983), which, incidentally, has good maps. The best works on 1830 in France are Pamela M. Pilbeam, *The 1830 Revolution in France* (Basingstoke UK: Macmillan, 1991), which is fresher than the very reliable David Pinkney, *The French Revolution of 1830* (Princeton NJ: PUP, 1972). Essential reading includes Edgar Leon Newman, 'The blouse and the frock coat: the alliance of the common people of Paris with the liberal leadership and the middle class during the last years of the Bourbon Restoration', *JMH*, 46, 1974, 26–59. On Poland, consult R. F. Leslie, *Polish Politics and the Revolution of November 1830* (Westport CT: Greenwood, 1969). On Britain, Michael Brock, *The Great Reform Act* (London: Hutchinson, 1973) is full and reliable, while J. R. Dinwiddy, *From Luddism to the First Reform Bill: Reform in England, 1810–1832* (Oxford: Blackwell, 1986) is very useful. A little more inspiring, however, are Gwyn A. Williams, *The Merthyr Rising* (London: Croom Helm, 1978), and E. J. Hobsbawm and George Rudé, *Captain Swing* (London: Lawrence & Wishart, 1969).

## Political biographies

Useful political biographies worth noting are by Philip G. Dwyer, *Talleyrand* (London: Longman, 2002), J. P. T. Bury and Robert Tombs, *Thiers,*

*1797–1877: A Political Life* (London: Allen & Unwin, 1986), and the mother of them all, Douglas Johnson, *Guizot* (London: RKP, 1963). W. H. Zawadski, *A Man of Honour: Adam Czartoryski as a Statesman of Russia and Poland, 1795–1831* (Oxford: Clarendon, 1993) makes a contribution to the history of both countries. For the personalities of the Italian Risorgimento, see Denis Mack Smith, *Mazzini* (New Haven CT: YUP, 1994) and his *Cavour* (New York: Knopf, 1985).

**France**

Turning to single-country histories, for general histories of France use Roger Magraw, *France, 1815–1914: The Bourgeois Century* (London: Fontana, 1983), and Peter McPhee, *A Social History of France, 1780–1880* (London: Routledge, 1992). André Jardin and André-Jean Tudesq, *Restoration and Reaction, 1815–1848* (Cambridge: CUP/MSH, 1983) covers a shorter time-span but remains in the traditional mould. Guillaume de Bertier de Sauvigny, *The Bourbon Restoration* (Philadelphia: Philadelphia UP, 1966), is still serviceable in spite of its royalist biases. On royalism, see Daniel Resnick, *The White Terror and the Political Reaction after Waterloo* (Cambridge MA: HUP, 1966), and David Higgs, *UltraRoyalism in Toulouse: From its Origins to the Revolution of 1830* (Baltimore MD: Johns Hopkins UP, 1973). The historiography of the Bourbon Restoration has been regenerated by the new cultural history, whose main exemplar here is Sheryl T. Kroen, *Politics and Theater: The Crisis of Legitimacy in Restoration France, 1815–1830* (Berkeley: UCP, 2000). See also in this vein Jo Burr Margadant, 'The Duchesse de Berry and Royalist Political Culture in Postrevolutionary France', *History Workshop Journal*, 43, 1997, 23–52, which I find more convincing than her similar work on the July Monarchy.

Geoffrey Cubitt deals thoroughly with an important theme in *The Jesuit Myth: Conspiracy Theory and Politics in Nineteenth-Century France* (Oxford: Clarendon, 1993). Alan B. Spitzer chronicles a sad tale of futility in *Old Hatreds and Young Hopes: The French Carbonari against the Bourbon Restoration* (Cambridge MA: HUP, 1971). Michael Marrinan, *Painting Politics for Louis-Philippe: Art and Ideology in Orleanist France, 1830–48* (New Haven CT: YUP, 1988) is an excellent art-historical essay on history and memory. Amongst a huge literature on workers and peasants, I have learned most from Robert J. Bezucha, *The Lyon Uprising of 1834: Social and Political Conflict in the Early July Monarchy* (Cambridge MA: HUP, 1974), Roger Magraw, *History of the French Working Class*, 2 vols (Oxford: Blackwell, 1992), and the classic regional study by Maurice Agulhon, *The Republic in the Village: The People of the Var from the French Revolution to the Second Republic* (Cambridge: CUP/MSH, 1982).

## Germany

Students of Germany are now well served by essays in Mary Fulbrook, ed., *German History since 1800* (London: Arnold, 1997), as well as the highly recommended James J. Sheehan, *German History, 1770–1866* (Oxford: Clarendon, 1989). Sheehan's *German Liberalism in the 19th Century* (Chicago: University of Chicago Press, 1978) is also very valuable. The work of Thomas Nipperdey is translated into English as *Germany from Napoleon to Bismarck, 1800–66* (Dublin: Gill & Macmillan, 1996), and David Blackbourn, *The Long Nineteenth Century: A History of Germany, 1780–1918* (Oxford: OUP, 1998) has plenty to offer. Works with a narrower focus include Brendan Simms, *The Struggle for Mastery in Germany, 1779–1850* (New York: St Martin's – now Palgrave Macmillan, 1998), and John Breuilly, *Austria, Prussia and Germany, 1806–1871* (London: Longman, 2002), which includes useful documents translated into English. On revolutionary movements after 1815, see G. D. Stark, 'The Ideology of the German Burschenschaft Generation', *European Studies Review*, 8, 1978, and George S. Williamson, 'What killed August von Kotzebue? The Temptations of Virtue and the Political Theology of German Nationalism, 1789–1819', *JMH*, 72:4, 2000, 890–943. On the economy, consult W.R. Lee, 'Economic Development and the State in Nineteenth-Century Germany', *Economic History Review*, 41:3, 1988, 346–67. Dagmar Herzog discusses attitudes to women and Jews in *Intimacy and Exclusion: Religious Politics in Pre-Revolutionary Baden* (Princeton NJ: PUP, 1996).

## Habsburg Empire

There are several good general histories of the Habsburg Empire. C. A. Macartney, *The Habsburg Empire, 1780–1918* (London: Weidenfeld & Nicolson, 1971) is extremely detailed, and beginning students will prefer the excellent Robin Okey, *Eastern Europe, 1740–1980: Feudalism to Communism* (London: Hutchinson, 1982), and his subsequent *The Habsburg Monarchy from Enlightenment to Eclipse* (New York: St Martin's – now Palgrave Macmillan, 2001). A. J. P. Taylor's *The Habsburg Monarchy, 1809–1918* (Harmondsworth UK: Peregrine, 1964) is dated but lively, while Alan Sked's *The Decline and Fall of the Habsburg Empire, 1815–1918* (New York: Longman, 1989) is less so.

## Britain

On Britain, the list is potentially endless, but I still use Asa Briggs, *The Age of Improvement, 1783–1867* (London: Longman, 1959), and R. K. Webb, *Modern England from the 18th Century to the Present* (London: George Allen & Unwin, 1980). In addition, Harold Perkin, *Origins of Modern English Society* (London: Routledge, 1991), and E. P. Thompson, *The Making of the English Working Class* (Harmondsworth UK: Penguin, 1968) should be well-known to students of British history. On radicalism use M. I. Thomis and P. Holt, *Threats of Revolution in Britain, 1789–1848* (London: Macmillan, 1977). There are now many summaries of Chartism which are accessible to students, such as J. T. Ward, *Chartism* (London: Batsford, 1973), John K. Walton, *Chartism* (London: Routledge, 1999), and Edward Royle, *Chartism* (London: Longman, 1986). Dorothy Thompson, *The Chartists* (London: Temple Smith, 1984) is more detailed, and the title of Gareth Stedman Jones, *Languages of Class: Studies in English Working-Class History, 1832–1982* (Cambridge: CUP, 1983) reflects the new emphasis on discourse analysis.

## Russia

For Russia, see Paul Dukes, *A History of Russia: Medieval, Modern, Contemporary* (Durham NC: Duke UP, 3rd edn, 1998), and Nicholas Riasonovsky, *A History of Russia* (New York: OUP, 4th edn, 1984). Consult Janet M. Hartley, *Alexander I* (London: Longman, 1994) in Longman's 'Profiles in Power' series. Marc Raeff, *The Decembrist Movement* (Englewood Cliffs NJ: Prentice-Hall, 1966) is the classic treatment of its subject. The political police are discussed in P. S. Squire, *The Third Department* (Cambridge: CUP, 1968). Nicholas Riasanovsky, *Nicholas I and Official Nationality in Russia, 1825–55* (Berkeley: UCP, 1967) is also useful.

## Poland, The Netherlands and Scandinavia

On Poland, Norman Davies, *God's Playground: A History of Poland, vol. 2: 1795 to the Present* (Oxford: Clarendon, 1981) is a sparkling read. For the Netherlands, consult E. H. Kossmann, *The Low Countries, 1780–1940* (Oxford: Clarendon, 1978). For Scandinavia, T. K. Derry, *A History of Scandinavia* (Minneapolis: Minnesota UP, 1979) is brief but helpful on this period.

## Italy

For Italy, consult John A. Davis, ed., *Italy in the Nineteenth Century, 1796–1900* (Oxford: OUP, 2000), and Stuart Woolf, *A History of Italy, 1700–1860: The Social Constraints of Political Change* (London: Methuen, 1979), rather than Harry Hearder, *Italy in the Age of the Risorgimento 1790–1870* (New York: Longman, 1983). The works of Denis Mack Smith are indispensable, particularly *Italy: A Modern History* (Ann Arbor: Michigan UP, 1969). On individual Italian states, David Laven questions some traditionally negative views of Habsburg rule in his *Venice and Venetia under the Habsburgs, 1815–35* (Oxford: OUP, 2002). Rome is covered by Frank J. Coppa, *The Modern Papacy since 1789* (London: Longman, 1998), and E. E. Y. Hales, *Pio Nono* (London: Eyre & Spottiswoode, 1956). G. M. Trevelyan's once-celebrated Garibaldi trilogy is now an unfashionable but very enjoyable example of the defunct heroic interpretation of the Risorgimento. Students may refer to the European University Institute's website on Italian history at http://vlib.iue.it/hist-italy/index.html.

## Spain, Portugal and Greece

Students of Spanish history need to select chapters from Raymond Carr, *Spain, 1808–1975* (Oxford: Clarendon, 2nd edn, 1982), and José Alvarez Junco and Adrian Shubert, eds, *Spanish History since 1808* (London: Arnold, 2000), before referring to Charles Esdaile, *Spain in the Liberal Age: From Constitution to Civil War, 1808–1939* (Malden MA: Blackwell, 2000). For Portugal, David Birmingham, *A Concise History of Portugal* (Cambridge: CUP, 1993) is more interesting than H. V. Livermore, *A New History of Portugal* (Cambridge: CUP, 2nd edn, 1976).

A short accessible summary of the Greek struggle for independence is currently lacking. Refer instead to the general works listed above, and to Charles and Barbara Jelavich, *The Establishment of the Balkan National States, 1804–1920* (Seattle: Washington UP, 1986).

## Peasants

On the peasant world, the best studies in English have been produced about France and Russia. See Jerome Blum, *The End of the Old Order in Rural Europe* (Princeton NJ: PUP, 1978), and the same author's *Lord and Peasant in Russia from the 9th to the 19th Century* (Princeton NJ: PUP, 1961). David Moon,

*The Russian Peasantry, 1600–1930: The World the Peasants Made* (London: Longman, 1999) is an excellent more recent work. On France, see Annie Moulin, *Peasantry and Society in France since 1789* (Cambridge: CUP/MSH, 1991). Martine Segalen, *Love and Power in the Peasant Family: Rural France in the 19th Century* (Oxford: Blackwell, 1983) takes the approach of a cultural anthropologist, and so in a way does Peter Sahlins, *Forest Rites: The War of the Demoiselles in Nineteenth-Century France* (Cambridge, MA: HUP, 1994). The politicization of the countryside is treated in Peter McPhee, *The Politics of Rural Life: Political Mobilization in the French Countryside, 1846–52* (Oxford: Clarendon, 1992), and Ted Margadant, *French Peasants in Revolt: The Insurrection of 1851* (Princeton NJ: PUP, 1979).

**Artisans and craftworkers**

For works on artisans and craftworkers, I strongly recommend Geoffrey Crossick and H.-G. Haupt, eds, *The Petite Bourgeoisie in Europe, 1780–1914: Enterprise, Family and Independence* (London: Routledge, 1998). For Germany, see also Dick Geary, 'Artisans, protest and labour organisation in Germany, 1815–1870', *EHQ*, 16, 1986, 369–77. For France, W. H. Sewell, *Work and Revolution in France: The Language of Labor from the Old Regime to 1848* (Cambridge: CUP, 1980), is an important work. Add Iorwerth Prothero, *Radical Artisans in England and France, 1830–1870* (Cambridge: CUP, 1997), and works on Chartism listed above. David Vincent's *Bread, Knowledge and Freedom: A Study of 19th-Century Working-Class Autobiography* (London: Europa, 1981) is full of insights into British artisan culture.

**1848 Revolutions**

The best and most up-to-date overview of the 1848 Revolutions is Jonathan Sperber, *The European Revolutions, 1848–1851* (Cambridge: CUP, 1984), which puts the action in its social and economic context. A less demanding summary for beginners is provided by Peter N. Stearns in *1848: The Revolutionary Tide in Europe* (New York: Norton, 1974), or by Jean Sigmann, *1848: The Romantic and Democratic Revolutions in Europe* (London: Allen & Unwin, 1973). For 1848 in Eastern Europe, students with a grasp of the main events should consult Lewis Namier's *1848: The Revolution of the Intellectuals* (London: OUP, 1946), which remains a classic. A series of useful essays is available in R. J. W. Evans and Hartmut Pogge von Strandmann, eds, *The Revolutions in Europe, 1848–1849: From Reform to Reaction* (Oxford: OUP, 2000). Then pick the eyes out of Dieter Dowe et al., eds, *Europe in 1848: Revolution and Reform* (New York and Oxford: Berghahn, 2000), which is over 1000 pages long, has a slight German bias and is full of 'typos'. For reference purposes use the Encyclopaedia of 1848 Revolutions at http://www.cats.ohiou.edu/~Chastain/index.htm. Ohio State University is responsible for this anthology, as it is for the Thomson Learning series *Exploring the European Past* at http://etep.thomsonlearning.com. This includes, for those who have purchased access, a teaching module on the 1848 Revolutions.

For the 1848 Revolution in France, I strongly recommend Sharif Gemie, *French Revolutions, 1815–1914: An Introduction* (Edinburgh: Edinburgh UP, 1999) for beginning students. See also Maurice Agulhon, *The Republican Experiment, 1848–52* (Cambridge: CUP, 1983), and the useful Roger Price, *The French Second Republic: A Social History* (London: Batsford, 1972). Two additional texts have acquired a lasting reputation: Karl Marx, *The 18th Brumaire of Louis Bonaparte* (many editions), and Ernest Labrousse, '1789, 1830, 1848: How Revolutions are Born', in F. Crouzet, W. H Chaloner and W. M. Stern, eds, *Essays in European Economic History, 1789–1914* (London: Arnold, 1969). More specialist works are T. J. Clark, *The Absolute Bourgeois, Artists and Politics in France 1848–1851* (London: Thames & Hudson, 1973), and John M. Merriman, *The Agony of the Republic: The Repression of the Left in Revolutionary France, 1848–51* (New Haven CT: YUP, 1978).

On Germany, apart from the general works listed above, see the indispensable Wolfram Siemann, *The German Revolution of 1848–49* (New York: St Martin's – now Palgrave Macmillan, 1998), and Jonathan Sperber, *Rhineland Radicals: The Democratic Movement and the Revolution of 1848–49* (Princeton NJ: PUP, 1991). Brian Vick's *Defining Germany: The 1848 Frankfurt Parliamentarians and National Identity* (Cambridge MA: HUP, 2002) is a helpful analysis of nationalist discourse. On Italy, add Paul Ginsborg, *Daniele Manin and the Venetian Revolution of 1848–49* (Cambridge: CUP, 1979). Alan Sked's *The Survival of the Habsburg Empire: Radetsky, the Imperial Army and the Class War, 1848* (London: Longman, 1979) began life as a doctoral thesis supervised by A. J. P. Taylor, and argues that Radetsky saved the Empire. For the rest of the Habsburg Empire, see R. J. Rath, *The Viennese Revolution of 1848* (Austin: Texas UP, 1957), Lawrence D. Orton, *The Prague Slav Congress of 1848* (Boulder CO and New York: East European Quarterly and Columbia UP, 1978), and Istvan Deak, *The Lawful Revolution: Louis Kossuth and the Hungarians, 1848–1849* (New York: Columbia UP, 1979).

## Antislavery

The recent literature on the antislavery movements includes David Turley, *The Culture of English Anti-Slavery, 1780–1860* (London: Routledge, 1991), and Clare Midgley, *Women Against Slavery: The British Campaigns, 1780–1870* (London: Routledge, 1992). For French material, see Paul M. Kielstra, *The Politics of Slave Trade Suppression in Britain and France, 1814–48* (Basingstoke: Palgrave Macmillan, 2000), and Lawrence C. Jennings, *French Anti-Slavery: The Movement for the Abolition of Slavery in France, 1802–1848* (Cambridge: CUP, 2000).

## Cities

For the history of cities in the early nineteenth century, I have referred to Asa Briggs, *Victorian Cities* (Harmondsworth UK: Penguin, 1968), and Richard Dennis, *English Industrial Cities of the Nineteenth Century: A Social Geography* (Cambridge: CUP, 1984) for the British context. Other useful cases for study are provided by the following: Catharina Lis, *Social Change and the Labouring Poor: Antwerp, 1770–1860* (New Haven CT: YUP, 1986); Michael F. Hamm, *Kiev: A Portrait, 1800–1917* (Princeton NJ: PUP, 1993); John M. Merriman, ed., *French Cities in the Nineteenth Century* (London: Hutchinson, 1982); Marco H. D. van Leeuwen, *The Logic of Charity: Amsterdam, 1800–1850* (Basingstoke UK: Palgrave Macmillan, 2000); and Mack Walker, *German Home Towns: Community, State and General Estate, 1648–1871* (Ithaca NY: Cornell UP, 1971).

## Cholera

Students of cholera should begin with the general survey in Richard J. Evans, 'Epidemics and revolutions: Cholera in nineteenth-century Europe', *Past & Present*, 120, 1988, 123–46, taken with Asa Briggs, 'Cholera and Society', in his *Collected Essays*, vol. 2 (Urbana: Illinois UP, 1985). Louis Chevalier, *Labouring Classes and Dangerous Classes in Paris during the First Half of the 19th Century* (London: RKP, 1973) is a classic on this topic, but should be followed with Catherine Kudlick, *Cholera in Post-revolutionary Paris: A Cultural History* (Berkeley: UCP, 1996). I also recommend Peter Baldwin, *Contagion and the State in Europe, 1830–1930* (Cambridge: CUP, 1999) on government responses.

# Jews

The historiography of European Jewry includes some works of exceptional scholarship. For example, David Vital, *A People Apart: The Jews in Europe, 1789–1939* (Oxford: OUP, 1999) is brilliant and stimulating. Antisemitic 'affairs' are well chronicled by David I. Kertzer, *The Kidnapping of Edgardo Mortara* (New York: Knop), 1997), and Jonathan Frankel, *The Damascus Affair: 'Ritual Murder', Politics and the Jews in 1840* (Cambridge: CUP, 1997). Amongst a surfeit of books on French Jews, I prefer Paula E. Hyman, *The Jews of Modern France* (Berkeley: UCP, 1998), and the same author's *The Emancipation of the Jews of Alsace: Acculturation and Tradition in the Nineteenth Century* (New Haven CT: YUP, 1991), together with Michael Graetz, *The Jews in Nineteenth-Century France: From the French Revolution to the Alliance Israélite Universelle* (Stanford CA: Stanford UP, 1996). Andrew M. Canepa, 'Emancipation and Jewish response in mid-19th century Italy', *EHQ*, 16, 1986, 403–39 is useful on Italy, while Artur Eisenbach, *The Emancipation of the Jews in Poland, 1780–1870* (Oxford: Blackwell, 1991) concentrates on legal aspects. Other studies include Karina Sonnenberg-Stern, *Emancipation and Poverty: The Ashkenazi Jews of Amsterdam, 1796–1850* (London: Macmillan, 2000), and Todd M. Endelman, *Radical Assimilation in English Jewry History, 1656–1945* (Bloomington IN: Indiana UP, 1990). Hillel J. Kieval, *Languages of Community: The Jewish Experience in the Czech Lands* (Berkeley: UCP, 2000) makes an essential contribution. I am full of admiration for the outstanding Niall Ferguson, *The House of Rothschild*, 2 vols (Harmondsworth UK: Penguin, 2000), by a non-Jewish financial historian.

# The bourgeoisie

For attempts to define the bourgeoisie, see Lenore O'Boyle, 'The middle classes in Western Europe, 1815–48', *AmHistRev*, 71:3, 1966, 826–45, and Alfred Cobban, 'The middle class in France, 1815–48', in his *France since the Revolution* (London: Cape, 1970). A more substantial and general account is to be found in Pamela M. Pilbeam, *The Middle Classes in Europe, 1789–1914: France, Germany, Italy, and Russia* (Basingstoke UK: Macmillan, 1990). Sarah Maza, *The Myth of the French Bourgeoisie: An Essay on the Social Imaginary, 1750–1850* (Cambridge MA: HUP, 2003) is provocative but doesn't disturb the furniture too much as far as the 1830s and 1840s are concerned. On the bourgeois family and culture, see Bonnie G. Smith, *The Ladies of the Leisure Class: The Bourgeoises of Northern France in the 19th Century* (Princeton NJ: PUP, 1981), and Michelle Perrot, ed., *A History of Private Life, vol. 4: From the Fires of Revolution to the Great War* (Cambridge MA: Belknap, 1990). The best work on bourgeois family history in Britain includes Lawrence Stone, *Road to Divorce, England, 1530–1987* (Oxford: OUP, 1990), and Leonore Davidoff and Catherine Hall, *Family Fortunes: Men and Women of the English Middle Class, 1780–1850* (London: Hutchinson, 1987).

## Gender

The best general introduction on gender history in my opinion is Glenda Sluga and Barbara Caine, *Gendering European History, 1780–1920* (London: Leicester UP, 2000). Very useful contributions are made by Geneviève Fraisse and Michelle Perrot, eds, *A History of Women in the West, IV: Emerging Feminism from Revolution to World War* (Cambridge MA: Belknap, 1993), which draws heavily on French material, and Ute Frevert, *Women in German History: From Bourgeois Emancipation to Sexual Liberation* (Oxford: Berg, 1989). From a number of studies on women's work, I prefer the fundamental Joan Scott and Louise Tilly, 'Women's Work and the Family in 19th-Century Europe', *Comparative Studies in Society and History*, 17:1, 1975, 36–64, as well as Deborah Simonton, *A History of European Women's Work, 1700 to the Present* (London: Routledge, 1998), and the more narrowly focused Sally Alexander, *Women's Work in 19th Century London: A Study of the Years 1820–1850* (London: Journeyman, 1983). On particular professions, see Jill Harsin, *Policing Prostitution in 19th Century Paris* (Princeton NJ: PUP, 1985), Judith R. Walkowitz, *Prostitution and Victorian Society: Women, Class and the State* (Cambridge: CUP, 1980), and Theresa McBride, *The Domestic Revolution: The Modernisation of Household Service in England and France, 1820–1920* (London: Croom Helm, 1976).

## Crimean War

On the Crimean War, the best general introduction is by Winfried Baumgart, *The Crimean War, 1853–1856* (London: Arnold, 1999). If you wish to sidestep very specialized works in diplomatic history, try David M. Goldfrank, *The Origins of the Crimean War* (London: Longman, 1994), Barbara Jelavich, *Russia's Balkan Entanglements, 1806–1914* (Cambridge: CUP, 1991), and Norman Rich, *Why the Crimean War? A Cautionary Tale* (Hanover NH: New England UP, 1985).

# Index

287